Situational Crime Prevention

Situational Crime Prevention

Successful Case Studies

Second Edition

edited by
Ronald V. Clarke

LYNNE
RIENNER
PUBLISHERS

BOULDER
LONDON

Published in the United States of America in 2010 by
Lynne Rienner Publishers, Inc.
1800 30th Street, Boulder, Colorado 80301
www.rienner.com

and in the United Kingdom by
Lynne Rienner Publishers, Inc.
3 Henrietta Street, Covent Garden, London WC2E 8LU

ISBN: 978-0-911577-38-9 (pb : alk. paper)

First published in 1997 by Criminal Justice Press.
Reprinted here from the original edition.

Printed and bound in the United States of America

The paper used in this publication meets the requirements
of the American National Standard for Permanence of
Paper for Printed Library Materials Z39.48-1992.

10   9   8   7

Contents

Continued...

Contents (cont.)

Continued...

Contents (cont.)

vii

Preface

Only five years ago the first edition of this book was published, yet a number of important developments during these years have made necessary this second, extensively revised volume. Most striking is the large increase in the successful applications of situational prevention reported in the literature. For the first edition it was difficult to collect sufficient case studies to reproduce. For this second edition, the twenty-three studies included are merely a sample of the three or four times that number considered. Indeed, the difficulty on this occasion was not in finding enough studies, but in deciding which to exclude. Ten of the case studies in the first edition which had proved particularly informative in classroom discussions were retained and, of the thirteen new ones, three were specially written or adapted for this volume.

These twenty-three case studies encompass a broader range of settings and offenses, including "everyday" crimes committed by ordinary people. Indeed, the wider application of situational measures, together with developments in preventive technology, has led to an expanded classification of opportunity-reducing techniques described in the Introduction. To the twelve techniques included in the first edition that increase the effort or risks of crime and reduce its rewards, four techniques that "remove excuses" for crime have now been added.

Some new concepts that are expanding the reach and appeal of situational prevention are also discussed in the Introduction. As anticipated in the first edition, the concept of "diffusion of benefits" (the idea that focused crime prevention efforts can sometimes bring benefits beyond the targeted settings) has served as a useful counterpoint to hypothesized displacement effects, which, in several recent reviews, have not been found to be as extensive or pervasive as some critics had argued. Another important new concept is that of repeat victimization, which is proving to be as valuable as that of "hot spots" in helping to focus crime prevention effort. Both concepts are also helping to focus experiments in problem-oriented policing, which shares many common features with situational prevention, and which has been embraced in recent years by many of the Nation's most progressive police forces.

The focus on crime prevention successes has been retained in this second edition, though the Introduction includes discussion of some failures of situational prevention as well as of ethical and other problems of implementation. As evidence accumulates that situational prevention is effective in a wide variety of contexts, evaluations might increasingly probe the limits of the approach and make comparisons between different ways of reducing opportunities. This will require a broader methodological approach, including detailed analyses of the implementation process. As discussed in the Introduction, however, the main purpose of evaluation should be to refine the principles of opportunity reduction rather than attempt to produce concrete data about the effectiveness of situational measures in all settings.

As situational prevention becomes better known, scholars from a wider range of disciplines may be drawn into discussions of the theoretical, political and ethical implications of an approach to crime prevention focused not upon changing offenders, but on modifying the settings in which crimes occur. The implications are indeed profound. They involve questions about the determinants of behavior as well as about criminal justice policy. They raise moral questions about society's attitudes to crime and criminals, and philosophical and political questions about the kind of society in which we wish to live. On the other hand, choice may be an illusion since irreversible social change has already occurred and it is our attitudes that may be lagging. Indeed, it may be that concepts of the State, the family and the community — the mainstays of current criminal policy — have less relevance today in a world that is shaped principally by economic forces, but in which individuals place a premium on autonomy in their daily lives. To adjust to these social changes, new concepts, including situational crime prevention, must be accommodated within the academic and political discourses on crime control.

Ronald V. Clarke
Rutgers

Acknowledgment

Much of the new material in the revised Introduction to this book comes from Clarke (1995) and from recent papers written jointly with Marcus Felson, Ross Homel and David Weisburd. I am grateful to Graeme Newman of Harrow and Heston for guiding me through the process of producing this new edition (as well as for advice on matters of substance) and to students in my graduate classes on crime prevention for helping me focus my thoughts.

ix

Acknowledgments

The original citations for each of the case studies reprinted are given in the *Editor's Notes* preceding each study. Thanks are due to the authors and publishers concerned.

Case Study #1, #12 and #17 are © British Crown Copyright (respectively 1994, 1997 and 1991) and are reprinted with the permission of the Controller of Her Majesty's Stationery Office. The views expressed are those of the authors and do not necessarily reflect the views or policy of the Home Office or any other government department.

Case Study #2, #6, #10, #21 and #22 are reproduced by permission of Criminal Justice Press.

Case Study #3, #4, #5, #8, #11, #13, #19 and #20 are reproduced by permission of Elsevier Science Ireland, Ltd.

Case Study #7 and *#18* are reprinted with permission of the National Swedish Council for Crime Prevention.

Case Study #9 is reprinted by permission of Oxford University Press.

Case Study #23 is reprinted with the permission of Canada Law Book, Inc., 240 Edward Street, Aurora, Ontario L4G 3S9.

About the Editor

Ronald Clarke is Professor and Dean at the School of Criminal Justice, Rutgers, The State University of New Jersey. Trained as a psychologist, he holds a master's degree (1965) and a Ph.D. (1968) from the University of London. He was formerly Director of the British government's criminological research department (The Home Office Research and Planning Unit), where he had a significant role in the development of situational crime prevention. He also helped to establish the Home Office Crime Prevention Unit and the now regularly repeated British Crime Survey. He has held faculty appointments in criminal justice at The University at Albany and Temple University. He is the editor of *Crime Prevention Studies* and his books include *Designing out Crime* (1980, with Pat Mayhew), *The Reasoning Criminal* (1986, with Derek Cornish) and *Routine Activity and Rational Choice* (1993, with Marcus Felson).

PART ONE

Introduction
by
Ronald V. Clarke

S ITUATIONAL CRIME PREVENTION departs radically from most criminology in its orientation (Clarke, 1980; Clarke and Mayhew, 1980). Proceeding from an analysis of the circumstances giving rise to specific kinds of crime, it introduces discrete managerial and environmental change to reduce the opportunity for those crimes to occur. Thus it is focused on the settings for crime, rather than upon those committing criminal acts. It seeks to forestall the occurrence of crime, rather than to detect and sanction offenders. It seeks not to eliminate criminal or delinquent tendencies through improvement of society or its institutions, but merely to make criminal action less attractive to offenders. Central to this enterprise is not the criminal justice system, but a host of public and private organizations and agencies — schools, hospitals, transit systems, shops and malls, manufacturing businesses and phone companies, local parks and entertainment facilities, pubs and parking lots — whose products, services and operations spawn opportunities for a vast range of different crimes.

As illustrated by the case studies in this volume, dozens of documented examples now exist of successful situational prevention involving such measures as surveillance cameras for subway systems and parking facilities, defensible space architecture in public housing, target hardening of apartment blocks and individual residences, electronic access for cars and for telephone systems, street closures and traffic schemes for residential neighborhoods, alcohol controls at festivals and sporting fixtures, training in conflict management for publicans and bouncers, and improved stocktaking and record keeping procedures in warehouse and retail outlets (cf. Clarke, 1995).

Many of these successes were obtained by hard-pressed managers seeking practical ways to solve troublesome crime problems confronting their businesses or agencies. Only rarely were they assisted by criminologists, who, excepting a small handful of government researchers overseas, have generally shown little interest in situational prevention. In addition, situational prevention has rarely been accorded attention in policy debates about crime control, especially those in the United States.

This neglect stems from two mistakes of modern criminology. First, the problem of explaining crime has been confused with the problem of explaining the criminal (Gottfredson and Hirschi, 1990). Most criminological theories have been concerned with explaining why certain individuals or groups, exposed to particular psychological or social influences, or with particular inherited traits, are more likely to become involved in delinquency or crime. But this is not the same as explaining why crime occurs. The commission of a crime requires not merely the existence of a motivated offender, but, as every detective story reader knows, it also requires the opportunity for crime. In Cohen and Felson's (1979) terminology, it also requires the availability of a suitable target and the absence of a capable guardian. Thus, crime cannot be explained simply by explaining criminal dispositions. It also has to be shown how such dispositions interact with situational factors favoring crime to produce a criminal act (Ekblom, 1994).

The second related mistake of modern criminology has been to confuse the problem of controlling crime with that of dealing with the criminal (Wilkins, 1990) The surest route to reducing crime, it has been assumed, is to focus on the offender or potential offender. Most textbook discussions of crime control have therefore distinguished only between two broad kinds of measures, formal and informal social control. Formal control refers to society's formally constituted legal institutions of the Law and the criminal justice system designed to sanction offenders, to confine or rehabilitate them, and to deter crime among the population at large. Informal social control refers to society's attempts to induce conformity through the socialization of young people into the norms of society, and through people's supervision of each other's behavior, reinforced by rule making, admonition and censure. Whether formal or informal, these controls are exclusively focused upon offenders, actual or potential.

It has been argued that one important consequence of failing to separate the problems of dealing with offenders and controlling crime has been to divert the criminal justice system from its essential purpose of dispensing justice (von Hirsch, 1976). More germane to the present discussion, however, is that this failure has also resulted in the criminological and policy neglect of a third important group of crime control measures, additional to formal and informal social controls, but intertwined with and dependent on them. These are the extensive "routine precautions" taken by individuals and organizations (Felson and Clarke, 1995). Every day, we all do such things as lock our doors, secure our valuables, counsel our children, and guard our purses to reduce the risk of crime. To this end, we also buy houses in safe neighborhoods, we invest in burglar alarms and we avoid dangerous places and people. Similarly, schools, factories, offices, shops and many other organizations and agencies routinely take a host of precautions to safeguard themselves, their employees and their clients from crime. It is into this group of crime control measures that situational crime prevention fits. Indeed, it can be regarded as the scientific arm of routine precautions, designed to make them more efficient and beneficial to society as a whole.

Criminologists and policy analysts have assumed that the principal value of these precautions is not in reducing overall crime rates, but in protecting individual people and agencies from victimization. This is partly because situational measures focused on particular places or highly specific categories of crime cannot make much impression on the overall crime statistics. It has also been assumed, however, that faced with impediments offenders will merely displace their attention elsewhere, with no net reduction in crime.

This assumption flows directly from the dispositional error of modern criminology and, as shown below, is not supported by empirical research which has generally found rather little displacement. Reducing opportunities for crime can indeed bring substantial net reductions in crime. As this evidence becomes more widely known, and situational prevention is taken more seriously by policy makers, the debate will move on to the ethical and ideological implications of situational measures. This is already apparent in countries such as Britain and the Netherlands where situational prevention is becoming an integral, though still small, component of government crime policy. As Garland (1996) has argued, these countries have seen a shift in the discourse of crime control, which is no longer seen to be the exclusive province of the government, but something that must be shared with all sectors of society. Consequently, a multitude of public and private actors are now finding that their routine precautions are becoming a matter of public duty. More significantly, governments now seem to be promoting a range of precautionary measures that many people find objectionable. When video surveillance of public places and street closures in residential areas become part of official policy, fears of Orwellian methods of social control are unleashed. These concerns are reinforced by developments in technology that make people believe government control is becoming too pervasive, intrusive and powerful.

These worries about the application of situational controls are widespread, and have become entangled with diverse ideological objections from across the political spectrum. The Right, especially in America (cf. Bright, 1992), sees situational prevention as an irrelevant response to crime because it neglects issues of moral culpability and punishment. Moreover, it "punishes" the law-abiding by infringing freedom and privacy. The Left characterizes it as politically and socially naive in its neglect of the role of social and economic inequities in causation and of political muscle in the definition of crime (Young, 1988). Liberals assert that by "tinkering" with symptoms it diverts attention from the need to tackle the "root causes" of crime such as unemployment, racial discrimination, substandard housing, inadequate schooling and inconsistent parenting (Bottoms, 1990). Before exploring these points in more depth, however, a more detailed account of situational crime prevention and its theoretical background is needed.

Definition of Situational Prevention

Situational prevention comprises opportunity-reducing measures that (1) are directed at highly specific forms of crime, (2) involve the management, design or manipulation of the immediate environment in as systematic and permanent way as possible, (3) make crime more difficult and risky, or less rewarding and excusable as judged by a wide range of offenders.

Several features of the definition relevant to the more extended discussion of situational crime prevention below should be noted. First, it makes clear that situational measures must be tailored to highly specific categories of crime, which means that distinctions must be made, not between broad categories such as burglary and robbery, but rather between the different kinds of offenses falling under each of these categories. Thus, Poyner and Webb (1991) have recently argued that preventing domestic burglaries targeted on electronic goods may require different measures from those needed to prevent domestic burglaries targeted on cash or jewelry. This is because of the many differences that existed between the two kinds of burglary in the British city they studied. When the targets were cash or jewelry, burglaries occurred mostly in older homes near to the city center and apparently were committed by offenders operating on foot. When the targets were electronic goods such as TVs and VCRs, the burglaries generally took place in newer, more distant suburbs and were committed by offenders with cars. The cars were needed to transport the stolen goods and had to be parked near to the house but not so close as to attract attention. The lay-out of housing in the newer suburbs allowed these conditions to be met and Poyner and Webb's preventive suggestions consisted principally of means to counter the lack of natural surveillance of parking places and roadways in new housing developments. These suggestions were quite different from those they made to prevent burglary in the inner city, which focused more on improving security and surveillance at the burglar's point of entry.

The need to tailor measures to particular offenses should not be taken to imply that offenders are specialists (cf. Cornish and Clarke, 1988) — only that the commission of specific kinds of crime depends crucially on a constellation of particular environmental opportunities and that these opportunities may need to be blocked in highly specific ways. Indeed, the second important feature of the definition of situational prevention is the implicit recognition that a wide range of offenders, attempting to satisfy a variety of motives and employing a variety of methods, may be involved in even highly specific offenses. It is further recognized that all people have some probability of committing crime depending on the circumstances in which they find themselves. Thus situational prevention does not draw hard distinctions between criminals and others.

The third point deriving from the definition is that changing the environment is designed to affect assessments made by potential offenders about the costs and benefits associated with committing particular crimes. These judgments are dependent on specific features of the objective situation and determine the likelihood of the offense occurring. This implies some rationality and a considerable degree of adaptability on the part of offenders.

The definition recognizes, fourth, that the judgments made by potential offenders include some evaluation of the moral costs of offending. We may all be prepared to steal small items from our employers, but few of us would be willing to mug old ladies in the street. Not all offenses are equally reprehensible, even in the eyes of the most hardened offenders. This means that making it harder to find excuses for criminal action may be sometimes be an effective opportunity-reduction technique. It also means that differences in the moral acceptability of various offenses will impose limits on the scope of displacement.

Finally, the definition of situational prevention is deliberately general in that it makes no mention of any particular category of crime. Rather, situational prevention is assumed to be applicable to every kind of crime, not just to "opportunistic" or acquisitive property offenses, but also to more calculated or deeply-motivated offenses. Whether offenses are carefully planned or fueled by hate and rage, they are all heavily affected by situational contingencies (Tedeschi and Felson, 1994). Thus, rates of homicide are importantly influenced by the availability of handguns. All offenders, however emotionally aroused or determined, take some account of the risks and difficulties of particular situations.

With respect to crimes thought to be the province of "hardened" offenders, evidence is now accumulating of successes achieved by situational measures, including the virtual elimination of aircraft hijackings by baggage screening (Wilkinson, 1986) and substantial reductions in robbery achieved by target hardening measures in post offices (Ekblom, 1988b), convenience stores (*Case Study #14*) and banks (Gabor, 1990; Grandjean, 1990; Clarke *et al.*, 1991).

Crimes of sex and violence have been regarded as less amenable to situational controls because they are less common and less likely to cluster in time and space (Heal and Laycock, 1986; Gabor, 1990). However, some examples will be provided below of the successful control of violence through deflecting offenders (for example, by preventing the congregation of large groups of drunken youths at pub-closing time) or through situational controls on alcohol and weapons. One particularly instructive example of controls on a "crime facilitator" is provided by the introduction of Caller-ID in New Jersey, which, by threatening the anonymity of callers, seems to have produced a substantial reduction in obscene phone calling (*Case Study #5*). Without this evidence, many people might have argued that obscene phone calling, a sexual crime that seems to strike at random, is precisely the kind of offense that would be unamenable to situational controls. A similar argument might have been made about domestic violence, but encouraging evidence is beginning to emerge from an experimental program in England that providing personal alarms to repeat victims may inhibit the aggressor (Farrell and Pease, 1993).

The lesson is that the limits of situational prevention should be established by closely analyzing the circumstances of highly specific kinds of offense, rather than by theoretical arguments about the presumed nature of motives for broad categories of crime such as sexual or violent offenses.

The Four Components of Situational Crime Prevention

As mentioned, much existing activity falling under the definition of situational crime prevention represents problem-solving undertaken by managers in a variety of public and private agencies. In some instances, mistakes might have been avoided and less time taken to develop solutions had those involved been familiar with the elements of situational prevention. One purpose of this book, therefore, is to consolidate the knowledge obtained through these independent efforts and to show how the criminological framework provided by situational prevention enables the lessons learned from dealing with specific crimes in specialized contexts to be more broadly generalized. This framework has four components:

1. A theoretical foundation drawing principally upon routine activity and rational choice approaches,

2. A standard methodology based on the action research paradigm,

3. A set of opportunity-reducing techniques, and

4. A body of evaluated practice including studies of displacement.

Theoretical Origins—The Role of Situational Factors in Crime

The development of situational prevention was stimulated by the results of work on correctional treatments undertaken in the 1960s and 1970s by the Home Office Research Unit, the British government's criminological research department (Clarke and Cornish, 1983). This work contributed to the demise of the rehabilitative ideal (Martinson, 1974; Brody, 1976) and forced researchers in the Unit, charged with making a practical contribution to criminal policy, to review the scope and effectiveness of other forms of crime control. The review concluded that there was little scope for reducing crime through the essentially marginal adjustments that were practically and ethically feasible in relation to policies of incapacitation, deterrent sentencing, preventive policing or "social" prevention (Tilley, 1993c). But it did identify opportunity-reduction as a worthwhile topic for further research, largely on the basis of some findings about misbehavior in institutions. It had been discovered in the course of the work on rehabilitation that the probability of a youth's absconding or re-offending while resident in a probation hostel or training school seemed to depend more upon the nature of the institutional regime to which he was exposed than on his personality or background (Tizard *et al.*, 1975). Particularly important appeared to be the opportunities for misbehavior provided by the institutional regime — opportunities that could be "designed out."

If institutional misconduct could in theory be controlled by manipulating situational factors, it was reasoned that the same might be true of other, everyday forms of crime. Though not consistent with most current theory, support for the Home Office position was found in criminological research that had found immediate situational influences to be playing an important role in crime, including: Burt's (1925) studies of delinquency in London, showing that higher rates of property offending in the winter were promoted by longer hours of darkness; Hartshorne and May's (1928) experimental studies of deceit, showing that the likelihood of dishonest behavior by children was dependent on the level of supervision afforded; geographical studies showing that the distribution of particular crimes is related to the presence of particular targets and locations such as business premises, drinking clubs, and parking lots (Engstad, 1975); and demonstrations that fluctuations in auto theft reflect the number of opportunities as measured by the numbers of registered vehicles (e.g. Wilkins, 1964).

The Home Office position was also consistent with psychological research on personality traits and behavior that was finding a greater than expected role for situational influences (Mischel, 1968), and with an emerging body of work on the sociology of deviance, including studies by: Matza (1964) who argued against deep motivational commitment to deviance in favor of a "drift" into misconduct; Briar and Piliavin (1965) who stressed situational inducements and lack of commitment to conformity; and Yablonsky (1962) and Short and Strodtbeck (1965) who evidenced the pressures to deviance conferred by working class gang membership.

Taken together, this body of work suggested that criminal conduct was much more susceptible to variations in opportunity and to transitory pressures and inducements than conventional "dispositional" theories allowed. It was also becoming clear from interviews with residential burglars (Scarr, 1973; Reppetto, 1974; Brantingham and Brantingham, 1975; and Waller and Okihiro, 1979) that the avoidance of risk and effort plays a large part in target selection decisions. This dynamic view of crime provided a more satisfactory basis for situational prevention and led to the formulation of a simple "choice" model (Clarke, 1977; 1980). This required information not only about the offender's background and current circumstances, but also about the offender's (i) immediate motives and intentions, (ii) moods and feelings, (iii) moral judgments regarding the act in question, (iv) perception of criminal opportunities and ability to take advantage of them or create them, and (v) assessment of the risks of being caught as well as of the likely consequences.

This model, dubbed "situational control theory" by Downes and Rock (1982), was subsequently developed into the rational choice perspective on crime (see below), but it served initially to deflect criminological criticism of the atheoretical nature of situational prevention and, more importantly, to guide thinking about practical ways of reducing opportunities for crime.

Defensible Space, CPTED and Problem-Oriented Policing

While the concept of situational prevention was British in origin, its development was soon influenced by two independent (Jeffery, 1977), but nonetheless related, strands of policy research in the United States. These involved the concepts of "defensible space" (Newman, 1972) and "crime prevention through environmental design" or CPTED (Jeffery, 1971), both of which had preceded situational prevention, but, because of the trans-Atlantic delay in the dissemination of ideas, had not been the stimulus to its development.

Oscar Newman's "defensible space" ideas represented a brilliant attempt to use architectural form to rescue public housing in the United States from the depredations of crime. Newman, an architect, believed that the design of public housing developments discouraged residents from taking responsibility for public areas and from exercising their normal "territorial" instincts to exclude predatory offenders. In particular, he criticized the large scale of the buildings which made it impossible for residents to recognize strangers, the multitude of unsupervised access points that made it easy for offenders to enter projects and to escape after committing crime, the location of projects in high crime areas, and their stark appearance which contributed to the stigma attaching to them. Newman supported these criticisms with statistical analyses of crime in public housing. He also provided a wealth of detailed design suggestions for creating "defensible space" through reducing anonymity, increasing surveillance and reducing escape routes for offenders.

"Defensible space" has sometimes been described as merely an extension of Jane Jacobs' (1961) ideas about the relationship between crime and the layout of streets and land use in American cities. As noted by Coleman (1985), however, this fails to do justice to Newman's unique contribution. He was focused upon buildings and architecture rather than urban planning, he moved beyond description to undertake quantitative analyses of the relation between specific design features and crime, and he was deeply involved in implementing change through the introduction of design modifications in housing developments. Despite the theoretical and methodological criticisms made of his work (see Mayhew, 1979, for a review), Newman's ideas have greatly influenced the design of public housing all over the world (Coleman, 1985). In particular, they have helped to rid many cities of high rise public housing blocks. With regard to the present discussion, they also stimulated efforts by the Home Office researchers engaged on situational prevention to undertake some early tests of "defensible space" notions in a British context (Wilson, 1978; Mayhew *et al.* 1979).[1]

In addition to Jane Jacobs, other influences on Newman included architectural ideas about the relation between environment and behavior and ethological writings on "territoriality" by authors such as Ardrey (1966). This mix of ideas was rather different from that giving rise to C. Ray Jeffery's (1971) concept of "crime prevention through environmental design." Jeffery claimed that the failures of the criminal justice system (in terms of limited reformative capacity, cruelty and inequity) stemmed from a flawed model of crime, in which "... the genetic basis of behavior is denied and... the environments in which crimes occur are ignored" (Jeffery, 1977: 10). Drawing upon a "biosocial theory of learning," he argued that punishment and treatment philosophies had to be abandoned in favor of a preventive approach which took due account of both genetic predisposition and the physical environment.

American criminology has been unreceptive to genetic explanations of behavior and Jeffery's general theory of criminal behavior has enjoyed less success than his concept of CPTED. Encompassing a broader set of techniques than "defensible space" and extending beyond the residential context, CPTED was adopted by the Westinghouse Corporation as the more suitable designation for its ambitious program of research to extend the defensible space concept to school and commercial sites. Unfortunately, this research produced disappointingly meager results — perhaps because "territorial" behavior is less natural outside residential settings (Jeffery, 1977: 45) — and government and research interest in CPTED has lagged in America in the 1980s and 1990s. Nevertheless, CPTED has enjoyed much success at a practical training level among police, due largely to the work of Tim Crowe and his associates (Crowe, 1991, Crowe and Zahm, 1994). Jeffrey's ideas also provided encouragement to the Home Office team and have been developed in empirical projects undertaken by some of his former students, including Patricia and Paul Brantingham and Ronald Hunter whose work is represented among the case studies included in this book.

"Problem-oriented policing" (Goldstein, 1979) constituted a somewhat later influence on the development of situational prevention. Goldstein argued that the route to greater operational effectiveness for the police was not through improvements in organization and management, but through the detailed analysis of the everyday problems they handle and the devising of tailor-made solutions. This process requires "identifying these problems in more precise terms, researching each problem, documenting the nature of the current police response, assessing its adequacy and the adequacy of existing authority and resources, engaging in a broad exploration of alternatives to present responses, weighing the merits of these alternatives, and choosing from among them" (Goldstein, 1979: 236).

This formulation of problem-oriented policing — captured in the four-stage SARA model, Scanning, Analysis, Response and Assessment — reflects the same action research paradigm underpinning situational prevention (cf. Goldstein, 1990:103; Hope, 1994; Clarke, 1997). Nevertheless, some important differences exist between the concepts. In particular, problem-oriented policing is not exclusively focused on crime and is primarily a police management approach; situational prevention, on the other hand, is a crime control approach that can be utilized within any organizational or management structure and is open, not just to the police, but to whoever can muster the resources to tackle the problem in hand.

With respect to crime control, therefore, situational prevention represents a broader approach than problem-oriented policing. Because it encompasses the entire range of environments (and objects) involved in crime and because it encompasses legal and management as well as design solutions, situational prevention is also broader than CPTED (which tends to be focused on design of the built environment). For example, server intervention programs to control drunken driving and the provision of "call trace" facilities to private telephone subscribers as a deterrent to obscene phone calling would more readily fall under the definition of situational, than CPTED measures.

The Rational Choice Perspective

The earlier "choice" model formulated to guide situational prevention efforts has more recently been developed into a "rational choice" perspective on crime (Clarke and Cornish, 1985; Cornish and Clarke, 1986). This borrows concepts from economic theories of crime (e.g. Becker, 1968), but seeks to avoid some of the criticisms made of these theories, including that: (i) economic models mostly ignore rewards of crime that cannot easily be translated into cash equivalents; (ii) economic theories have not been sensitive to the great variety of behaviors falling under the general label of crime, with their variety of costs and benefits, and instead have tended to lump them together as a single variable in their equations; (iii) the formal mathematical modeling of criminal choices in economic theories often demands data that are unavailable or can only be pressed into service by making unrealistic assumptions about what they represent; and, finally, (iv) the image in economic theory of the self-maximizing decision maker, carefully calculating his or her advantage, does not fit the opportunistic and reckless nature of much crime (Clarke and Felson, 1993).

Under the new formulation, relationships between concepts were expressed, not in mathematical terms as was the case in Becker's normative model, but in the form of "decision" diagrams (Clarke and Cornish, 1985; Cornish and Clarke, 1986). Concepts were adapted from the other disciplines involved in the analysis of criminal decision making, as well as economics, to give greater weight to non-instrumental motives for crime and the "limited" or "bounded" nature of the rational processes involved. It was assumed, in other words, that crime is purposive behavior designed to meet the offender's commonplace needs for such things as money, status, sex and excitement, and that meeting these needs involves the making of (sometimes quite rudimentary) decisions and choices, constrained as these are by limits of time and ability and the availability of relevant information.

A second important new premise was that a decision-making approach to crime requires that a fundamental distinction be made between criminal involvement and criminal events (a distinction paralleling that between criminality and crime). Criminal involvement refers to the processes through which individuals choose (i) to become initially involved in particular forms of crime, (ii) to continue, and (iii) to desist. The decision process at each of these stages is influenced by a different set of factors and needs to be separately modeled. In the same way, the decision processes involved in the commission of a particular crime (i.e. the criminal event) are dependent upon their own special categories of information. Involvement decisions are characteristically multistage and extend over substantial periods of time. Event decisions, on the other hand, are frequently shorter processes, utilizing more circumscribed information largely relating to immediate circumstances and situations.

Finally, and this is of special importance for situational prevention, it was recognized that the decision processes and information utilized could vary greatly among offenses. To ignore these differences, and the situational contingencies associated with them, may be to reduce significantly the scope for intervention.

Cornish and Clarke's formulation of the rational choice perspective has been characterized by Opp (1997) as a "wide" model compared with the "narrow" economic formulation. This wide model was primarily developed to assist thinking about situational prevention, but it was not intended to be limited to this role. Indeed, Cornish (1993) has argued that many features of the rational choice perspective make it particularly suitable to serve as a criminological "metatheory" with a broad role in the explanation of a variety of criminological phenomena.

Environmental Criminology, Routine Activities and Lifestyles

Rational choice premises have generally been supported by recent studies in which offenders have been interviewed about motives, methods and target choices (Cromwell, 1996). The offenders concerned have included burglars (e.g. Walsh, 1980; Maguire, 1982; Bennett and Wright, 1984; Nee and Taylor 1988; Cromwell *et al.*, 1991; Biron and Ladouceur, 1991; Wright and Decker, 1994; Wiersma, 1996), shoplifters (Walsh, 1978; Carroll and Weaver, 1986), car thieves (Light *et al.*, 1993; McCullough *et al.*, 1990; Spencer, 1992), muggers (Lejeune, 1977; Feeney, 1986) bank and commercial robbers (New South Wales Bureau of Crime Statistics and Research, 1987; Normandeau and Gabor, 1987; Kube, 1988; Nugent *et al.*, 1989) and offenders using violence (Indermaur, 1996; Morrison and O'Donnell, 1996).

These studies of offender decision making constitute one of two major analytic paths followed in the past decade by "environmental criminology" (Brantingham and Brantingham, 1991). The other path has involved "objective analysis of the spatial and temporal variation in crime patterns in order to discover aggregate factors influencing the patterns" (Brantingham and Brantingham, 1991: 239). When such analyses involve aggregate crime rates or "macro" level data for countries or states, they rarely produce findings with preventive implications. "Micro" level analyses, on the other hand, of specific categories of crime occurring in specific kinds of buildings or sites are generally the most productive in preventive terms (Kennedy, 1990).

Analyses at an intermediary "meso" level can also lead to useful preventive suggestions as shown by Poyner and Webb's (1991) study mentioned above of domestic burglary in two British communities. This study is also illustrative of research on the criminal's "journey to work" undertaken, among others, by Brantingham and Brantingham (1975), Maguire (1982) and Rengert and Wasilchick (1985). Among the findings of these studies are that the risks of commercial robbery may be increased by being located close to a main road and those of domestic burglary by being located on the outskirts of an affluent area. In both cases, the explanation is that the offender's target search time is thereby reduced.

Research on the criminal's journey to work is conceptually related to another body of criminological work — routine activity theory — which has also contributed to the theoretical base of situational prevention. The routine activity approach stated three minimal elements for direct-contact predatory crime: a likely offender, a suitable target, and the absence of a capable guardian against crime (Cohen and Felson, 1979). It avoids speculation about the source of the offender's motivation, which distinguishes it immediately from most other criminological theories. Instead, it focuses upon the convergence in space and time of the three elements of crime, that is to say upon the conditions favoring the occurrence of a criminal event, rather than the development of a criminal disposition. This reflects its intellectual roots in the human ecology of Amos Hawley (1950), who recognized that the timing of different activities by hour of day and day of week are important for the understanding of human society. These points are also central to the routine activity approach, which is focused upon changes from moment to moment and hour to hour in where people are, what they are doing, and what happens to them as a result (Clarke and Felson, 1993; Felson, 1994a). In support of their approach, Cohen and Felson (1979) sought to demonstrate that increases in residential burglary in the United States between 1960 and 1970 could largely be explained by changes in "routine activities" such as the increasing proportion of empty homes in the day (due to more single person households and greater female participation in the labor force) and the increased portability of televisions and other electrical goods.

Cohen and Felson's analysis also illustrates the relationship between routine activity theory and the victimological work on "lifestyles," stimulated by the flood of National Crime Survey data first released in the 1970s (Hindelang *et al.*, 1978). One of the tenets of "lifestyle" theory is that the differential risks of victimization are partly a function of differential exposure to offenders (Fattah, 1993). This exposure varies not only with the sociodemographic characteristics of the victim (age, race, place of residence, etc.), but also with the victim's lifestyle. A person's work and leisure activities that increase exposure to potential offenders (such as alcohol consumption in public places or late-night use of public transport) increase the risks of victimization. The implication of this is that risks might be reduced by modifying patterns of activity. A further important finding of victimological research, the implications of which are being explored in a series of recent studies by Ken Pease and colleagues (for a review, see Farrell and Pease, 1993), is that some people and targets are repeatedly subject to victimization and might therefore be prime candidates for preventive attention (see *Case Study #15*). A similar point has been made by Sherman *et al.* (1989) in relation to the "hot spots" of crime, places that are the source of repeated calls for assistance to the police.

Lifestyle and routine activity theories have both made opportunity a respectable topic of research in criminology and have helped attract serious scholarly interest to situational prevention. Both theories are still evolving and Felson himself has made some attempts to expand the scope of routine activity theory. He has defined minimal elements for some categories of crime other than direct-contact predatory offenses (Felson, 1992) and, in order to accommodate social control theory (Hirschi, 1969), has proposed a fourth minimal element for predatory crimes, "the intimate handler", or someone who knows the likely offender well-enough to afford a substantial brake on the latter's activities (Felson, 1986). Clarke (1992) has argued that the contribution of routine activity theory to crime prevention could be enhanced by adding a fifth element which he refers to as "crime facilitators," These are such things as automobiles, credit cards and weapons that comprise the essential tools for particular forms of crime.

The Opportunity Structure for Crime

Environmental criminology, the rational choice perspective and routine activity and lifestyle theories have all helped to strengthen situational prevention in different ways, reflecting their different origins and the purposes for which they were developed. By interviews with offenders and analysis of crime patterns, environmental criminology has provided rich information about the motives and methods of offenders, which has been valuable in thinking about counter measures. The rational choice perspective has provided a framework under which to organize such information so that individual studies produce more general benefits. As will be seen below, it has also assisted analysis of displacement. Lifestyle theory has focused attention on what victims might do to reduce their risks of crime. And routine activity theory has served to extend preventive options by directing attention to features of the three essential elements of crime and their convergence. For example, the idea of convergence has led to the suggestion that "deflecting offenders" be recognized as a distinct technique of situational prevention (Clarke, 1992).

Cusson (1986) has argued that the differences among the various theoretical approaches may turn out to be mainly of historical interest and that a synthesis is inevitable and desirable. The model of the opportunity structure for crime presented in Figure 1 represents one such attempt at integration.

Under this model, which includes the dispositional variables of traditional criminology as well as the situational ones of the newer theories, there are three components of the *criminal opportunity structure*. These are *targets* (cars, convenience stores, ATM machines, etc.), *victims* (e.g. women alone, drunks, strangers) and crime *facilitators*. These latter include tools, such as guns and cars, as well as disinhibitors such as alcohol or other drugs.[2]

The supply of targets and their nature is a function of (i) the *physical environment*, including the layout of cities, the kinds of housing, technology and communications, transportation and retailing systems, the numbers of vehicles and the supply of drugs and alcohol, and (ii) the *lifestyles and routine activities* of the population, including patterns of leisure, work, residence and shopping; these patterns either hinder or facilitate guardianship. The physical environment also determines the supply of facilitators, while lifestyles and routine activities play a large part in supplying the victims of personal and sexual attacks. Physical environment and lifestyles and routine activities are themselves determined by the broader *socio-economic structure* of society, including demography, geography, urbanization and industrialization, health and educational policy, and legal and

FIGURE 1
THE OPPORTUNITY STRUCTURE FOR CRIME

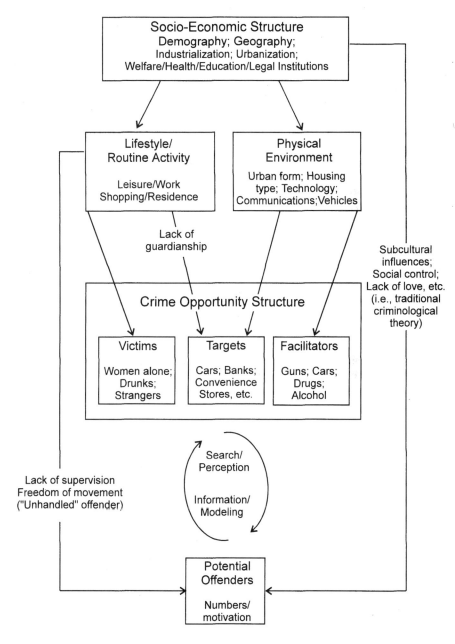

Source: Clarke (1995)

political institutions. The numbers of *potential offenders* and their motives is also partly determined by the socio-economic structure of society through many of the mechanisms (alienation, subcultural influence, neglect and lack of love, etc.) identified by traditional criminology, and partly by lifestyle and routine activities which impact upon the nature of social control afforded by "intimate handlers" and in other ways.

The opportunity structure is not simply a physical entity, defined at any one point in time by the nature of the physical environment and the routine activities of the population. Rather, a complex interplay between potential offenders and the supply of victims, targets and facilitators determines the scale and nature of opportunities for crime. Potential offenders learn about criminal opportunities from their peers, the media and their own observation, but they are differentially sensitized to this information as well as being differentially motivated to seek out and create opportunities. Thus, offender perceptions and judgments about risks, effort and rewards play an important part in defining the opportunity structure. These judgments also play a determining role at the subsequent stage of crime commission, where Figure 1 stops short.

Before moving from the theoretical background of situational crime prevention to its other components, some questions about the scope and reach of situational prevention arising from the model of the opportunity structure should be addressed. The first is that, if everything seems to flow from the socio-economic structure, should not preventive effort be focused at that level? Could not large scale reductions in a wide range of crimes be achieved by tackling the disposition to offend through improved welfare and educational programs? Would this not be more efficient than undertaking the vast number of small-scale efforts to address highly specific crime problems implied by the situational focus?

One answer to these questions is that "social" crime prevention is already focused at the socio-economic level and that the opportunity structure requires attention in its own right. However, Morris and Hawkins (1970) and Wilson (1975) have noted that we do not know how to bring about some of the needed social changes, such as making parents love their children more. As for better welfare and education, these may be seen as desirable but often as demanding resources that society cannot afford. Finally, when Sweden and some other European countries enhanced welfare and achieved more equitable income distribution, this was followed not by reductions in crime but by increases (Smith, 1995).

A second question concerns deterrence and is as follows: Rather than attempting to manipulate the opportunity structure (with the attendant costs and inconvenience of this strategy), might it not be more efficient simply to raise the stakes of offending through heavier punishments? In fact, interviews with offenders have shown that they pay much closer attention to the immediate chances of getting caught than to the nature of the punishment they might receive later. Rather than increasing punishment, it is therefore more efficient to make the offender more fearful of being caught, and one component of situational prevention does indeed consist of increasing the risks of being caught through a process that Cusson (1993) refers to as "situational deterrence."

A final set of questions concerns the interplay between the objective reality of the opportunity structure and the way this is perceived by potential offenders. How do offenders learn about criminal opportunities and what factors come into play when they make decisions about which ones to pursue? What proportion of crimes are the result of opportunities seized, and what proportion of ones that are sought or created (Maguire, 1980; Bennett and Wright, 1984). At issue here is the question of whether opportunities for crime really are in infinite supply as some have argued. If so, this has serious implications for a strategy advocating their reduction. What matter the few reductions that can be achieved in criminal opportunities if these are infinite?

Consideration of the realities of crime helps provide an answer. While it may be true in theory that every dwelling and automobile provides not just one opportunity for crime, but, if considered over time, a set of almost endless opportunities, this ignores the fact that households and automobiles are afforded substantial guardianship for much of the time (Clarke, 1984). Even when unguarded, they may in actuality provide few rewards for crime. The average household contains only a few portable goods that can be converted into cash and there are limits to the number of stolen VCRs and television sets that the offender can store. It is also unclear how many such "hot" items can be off-loaded onto the market without provoking a determined response from law enforcement. Clarification of these issues needs to be sought in more research of the kind recently published by Cromwell *et al.* (1991), in which they undertook detailed interviews with residential burglars about their working methods.

The Action Research Methodology

The standard methodology for a situational project, situational prevention's second component, is a version of the action research model in which researchers and practitioners work together to analyze and define the problem, to identify and try out possible solutions, to evaluate the results and, if necessary, to repeat the cycle until success is achieved (Lewin, 1947). The influence of the action research paradigm can be seen in the following specification of the five stages of a situational prevention project (Gladstone, 1980):

1. collection of data about the nature and dimensions of the specific crime problem;
2. analysis of the situational conditions that permit or facilitate the commission of the crimes in question;
3. systematic study of possible means of blocking opportunities for these particular crimes, including analysis of costs;
4. implementation of the most promising, feasible and economic measures;
5. monitoring of results and dissemination of experience.

As mentioned, this is essentially the same problem-solving methodology used in problem-oriented policing as well as in many other forms of social intervention, and because of its extensive pedigree has required little modification for use in situational crime prevention. However, it represents an ideal not always followed in practice.

Sixteen Opportunity-Reducing Techniques

Unlike the action research methodology which has seen little modification, the classification of opportunity-reducing techniques, the third component of situational prevention, is constantly undergoing change. This is made necessary by developments (i) in theory which suggest new ways of reducing opportunities, (ii) in practice as new forms of crime are addressed by situational prevention, and (iii) in technology which opens up new vistas for prevention, just as it does for crime. The fact that the classification of techniques is constantly being refined is evidence of the vitality of the situational approach and, indeed, these re-classifications help further to stimulate its development by calling attention to new forms of opportunity-reduction.

In the first edition of this book a classification of twelve opportunity-reducing techniques was introduced, itself a modification of an earlier classification proposed by Hough *et al.*(1980). In introducing the new classification, it was noted that the techniques served three purposes, implicit in the rational choice assumptions of situational prevention, of increasing the risks, increasing the difficulties, and reducing the rewards of crime.

This classification has recently been modified by Clarke and Homel (1997) to encompass a fourth purpose of situational prevention implicit in rational choice theory, which is to increase shame and guilt or, more particularly, to "remove excuses" for crime.[3] This reflects the fact that situational measures, having first been used to prevent a variety of "street" and predatory crimes, have more recently also been applied against income tax evasion, traffic offenses (including drunk driving), sexual harassment and theft of employers' property, which are as much the province of "ordinary citizens" as of "hardened offenders" (see Gabor's, 1994, book *Everybody Does It!* for a review of these crimes, and the earlier seminal paper by Ross, 1960, on traffic offenses as "folk crimes"). Opportunities for these offenses arise in the course of everyday life for most people and do not have to be sought in the same way as opportunities for autotheft or burglary. The very frequency of these opportunities, together with the generally higher social status of offenders, may contribute to the relative lack of moral opprobrium attached to taking advantage of them. This lack of condemnation and the relative ease of commission suggest that, rather than by increasing the risks of detection, these offenses might more effectively be prevented by increasing the incentives or pressures to comply with the law (Sparrow, 1994).

The addition of this fourth rational choice category represents more explicit recognition of the fact that offenders make judgments about the morality of their own behavior and that they frequently rationalize their conduct to "neutralize" what would otherwise be incapacitating feelings of guilt or shame thorough such excuses as, "He deserved it," "I was just borrowing it" and "I only slapped her." These rationalizations may be especially important for ordinary people responding to everyday temptations to break the law. Though overlooked in the classification of situational techniques in the first edition of this book, the role of rationalizations was clearly identified in the original formulation of the rational choice perspective on which it was based (Clarke and Cornish, 1985; Cornish and Clarke, 1986).

Rationalizations are also given a central role by two other criminological theories, Sykes and Matza's (1957) social deviance theory of "techniques of neutralization" and Bandura's (1976) social learning theory of violence, which makes use of the concept of "self-exoneration" (Wortley, 1986). The parallels between these concepts are remarkable (though Bandura appears to have been unaware of Sykes and Matza's earlier work) and this degree of congruence gives further reason to think that removing excuses or rationalizations may be an important preventive strategy.

Clarke and Homel's (1997) modification of the classification in the first edition of this book, left eight of the original categories untouched, modified the remaining four and added four new ones for a total of sixteen techniques (see Table 1).

In proposing the new classification, Clarke and Homel recognized a specific danger of including the manipulation of shame and guilt as a purpose of situational prevention. This is the danger of entangling situational prevention in attempts to bring about long-term changes in dispositions to offend — a fundamentally different approach to crime prevention (Newman, 1997). They justified their course by pointing out that a choice has to be made between maintaining the clarity of the situational approach but limiting its application, or extending its reach and complicating its definition. So long as the measures to induce guilt or shame are focused on highly specific categories of offending and are delivered at the point when criminal decisions are being made, they believe that the danger can be avoided of confusing the nature of situational prevention. For example, the message "Shoplifting is stealing" is much more likely to affect the situational calculus, and would thus qualify as a situational measure, when displayed in high risk stores than when displayed on school notice boards where it is intended to reduce the disposition to theft.

Before describing the sixteen techniques, and presenting examples of each, it should be noted that there is some unavoidable overlap among categories. For example, measures that increase the effort demanded for crime and delay the offender will also increase the risks of apprehension. This means that there is sometimes difficulty in deciding where a particular measure best fits into the classification in Table 1, and indeed some measures can serve more than one purpose.

1. Target hardening. An obvious, often highly effective way of reducing criminal opportunities is to obstruct the vandal or the thief by physical barriers through the use of locks, safes, screens or reinforced materials. Changes in design, including a slug rejecter device substantially reduced the use of slugs in New York parking meters (Decker, 1972)[4] and, more recently, in the ticket machines of the London Underground (Clarke *et al.*, 1994). Transparent screens to shield the bus driver significantly reduced assaults on one transit system (Poyner *et al.*, 1988); anti-bandit screens on post office counters in London in the 1980s was conservatively estimated by Ekblom (1988b) to have cut robberies by 40 percent; and the installation of fixed and "pop-up" screens is believed to have been an important element in reducing over-the-counter robberies in Australian banks (Clarke *et al.*, 1991). A strengthened coin box has been identified in several studies as a significant factor in reducing incidents of theft and damage to public telephones in Britain and Australia (Wilson, 1990; Challinger, 1991; Bridgeman, 1997). *Case Study #1* in this volume shows that the introduction of steering locks on both new and old cars in Germany in 1963 produced a substantial decline in the rate of car theft for the country that has persisted to this day and that these locks have conferred similar benefits in Britain and America (Webb, 1994).

2. Access control. Access control refers to measures intended to exclude potential offenders from places such as offices, factories and apartment blocks. The portcullises, moats and drawbridges of medieval castles suggest its preventive pedigree may be as lengthy as that of target hardening. It is also a central component of defensible space, arguably the start of scientific interest in situational prevention. A sophisticated form of access control lies in the use of electronic personal identification numbers (PINs) that are needed to gain access to computer systems and bank accounts. Poyner and Webb (1987b) found that a combination of access controls introduced on a South London public housing estate, including entry phones, fencing around apartment blocks and electronic access to the parking garage, achieved a significant reduction in vandalism and theft. They also found that the introduction of a reception desk on the ground floor of a tower block led to a marked reduction in vandalism, graffiti and other incivilities. *Case Study #2* shows that the installation of entryphones, and the demolition of walkways linking buildings, significantly reduced robberies and purse-snatchings at Lisson Green, another London public housing estate.

TABLE 1
SIXTEEN OPPORTUNITY-REDUCING TECHNIQUES

Increasing Perceived Effort	Increasing Perceived Risks	Reducing Anticipated Rewards	Removing Excuses
1. Target hardening Slug rejecter device Steering locks Bandit screens	*5. Entry/exit screening* Automatic ticket gates Baggage screening Merchandise tags	*9. Target removal* Removable car radio Women's refuges Phonecard	*13. Rule setting* Customs declaration Harassment codes Hotel registration
2. Access control Parking lot barriers Fenced yards Entry phones	*6. Formal surveillance* Red light cameras Burglar alarms Security guards	*10. Identifying property* Property marking Vehicle licensing Cattle branding	*14. Stimulating conscience* Roadside speedometers "Shoplifting is stealing" "Idiots drink and drive"
3. Deflecting offenders Bus stop placement Tavern location Street closures	*7. Surveillance by employees* Pay phone location Park attendants CCTV systems	*11. Reducing temptation* Gender-neutral listings Off-street parking Rapid repair	*15. Controlling disinhibitors* Drinking-age laws Ignition interlock V-chip
4. Controlling facilitators Credit card photo Gun controls Caller-ID	*8. Natural surveillance* Defensible space Street lighting Cab driver I.D.	*12. Denying benefits* Ink merchandise tags PIN for car radios Graffiti cleaning	*16. Facilitating compliance* Easy library checkout Public lavatories Trash bins

Source: Adapted from Clarke and Homel (1997)

3. Deflecting offenders. At soccer matches in Britain, rival groups of fans have been segregated in the stadium to reduce fighting and their arrival and departure has been scheduled to avoid the periods of waiting around that promote trouble (Clarke, 1983). Scheduling the last bus to leave immediately after pub closing time, is intended to interfere with another of Britain's less admirable traditions, the closing time brawl. Hope (1985) has suggested that crowds of drunken young people on the streets at closing time could also be reduced by avoiding the concentration of licensed premises in particular parts of the city. Bell and Burke (1989) show that the leasing of a downtown parking lot in Arlington, Texas, relieved severe congestion on weekend nights in nearby streets, and associated crime problems, by providing a venue for teenage cruising. These are all examples of "deflecting offenders" away from crime targets, a situational technique suggested by routine activity theory. Further examples are provided by case studies in this volume. Thus, in *Case Study #4*, Poyner and Webb (1987a) show that thefts from shopping bags at markets in Birmingham, England, were substantially reduced by reducing congestion around the stalls, which increased the difficulty of pickpocketing and other "stealth" thefts. Matthews (1990) shows that a road closure scheme to deflect cruising "johns" contributed to the rehabilitation of a red light district in a North London suburb (*Case Study #3*).

4. *Controlling facilitators.* Saloons in the Wild West routinely required customers to surrender their weapons on entry because of the risk of drunken gun fights. In more recent times, the manufacture of "less lethal weapons" in the form of guns that shoot wax bullets, electricity or tranquilizers has been advocated (Hemenway and Weil, 1990). The Scottish Council on Crime (1975) suggested that in some pubs beer should be served in plastic mugs to prevent their use as weapons, and recent studies in Britain of the injury potential of different kinds of broken glass have led to the recommendation that toughened glass be used for beer glasses (Shepherd and Brickley, 1992). Controls on a range of other crime facilitators have been proposed including checks and credit cards (which facilitate fraud) and telephones (which may facilitate drug dealing, frauds and sexual harassment). To reduce drug dealing, pay phones have been removed from places where drug dealers congregate or have been altered to make them more difficult to use for dealing (Natarajan *et al.*, 1996). A new computerized phone system in Rikers Island jails substantially reduced illicit phone calls by inmates and also had the unexpected benefit of reducing fights over access to the phones (La Vigne, 1994). Two case studies included in this volume illustrate the value of other controls on telephones. In *Case Study #5*, Clarke (1990) showed that the introduction in New Jersey of Caller-ID, a service which allows the person answering the phone to read the number calling, resulted in a reduction of about 25 percent in obscene and annoying telephone calls. Bichler and Clarke (1996) showed that re-programming pay phones at the Port Authority Bus Terminal in Manhattan prevented illicit access to toll lines and wiped out a multi-million dollar scam perpetrated by hustlers drawn to the building by the opportunities for fraud (*Case Study #6*). Finally, Knutsson and Kuhlhorn (1981) have shown that the introduction of identification procedures in Sweden produced a dramatic decline in the number of reported check frauds (*Case Study #7*).

5. *Entry/exit screening.* Entry screening differs from access control in that the purpose is less to exclude potential offenders than to increase the likelihood of detecting those not in conformity with entry requirements. These requirements may relate to prohibited goods and objects or, alternatively, to possession of tickets and documents. Exit screens, on the other hand, serve primarily to deter theft by detecting objects that should not be removed from the protected area, such as items not paid for at a shop. Developments in electronics have resulted in the increasing use of these situational techniques in retailing, as evidenced by the spread of merchandise tagging, bar-coding and "electronic point of sales" systems (Hope, 1991). In *Case Study #8*, DiLonardo (1996) shows that electronic merchandise tags on clothing can achieve significant reductions in shoplifting of the order of 35-75 percent in American stores. Similar, though not as strong, effects were reported in Britain (Bamfield, 1994). Scherdin (1986) reports that the installation of book detection screens, as found in thousands of libraries, reduced thefts of both books and audiovisual materials at one University of Wisconsin library by more than 80 percent. The installation of

automatic ticket gates on the 63 central zone stations of the London Underground resulted in a two-thirds reduction of fare evasion throughout the system (Clarke, 1993). In a "low tech" example of entry screening, the redesign of tickets to facilitate their inspection on Vancouver ferries produced a two-thirds reduction in fare evasion (DesChamps *et al.*, 1991). Finally, the most famous example of this technique concerns the introduction of baggage and passenger screening at most major airports in the world during the early 1970s. This contributed to a precipitate reduction in the number of airline hijackings from about 70 per year to about 15 (Wilkinson, 1977, 1986; Landes, 1978).

   6. Formal surveillance. Formal surveillance is provided by police, security guards and store detectives, whose main function is to furnish a deterrent threat to potential offenders. One example of the successful useful use of security personnel is provided by *Case Study #10* which describes a bike patrol used to curb auto thefts from a commuter parking lot in Vancouver. The surveillance afforded by security personnel may be enhanced by electronic hardware, for example by burglar alarms and closed circuit television (CCTV). In their study of an affluent suburban community close to Philadelphia, Hakim *et al.* (1995) concluded that widespread ownership of burglar alarms reduced police costs by lowering burglary rates for the community at large. One element of "Biting Back," the preventive program focused on repeat victims of burglary in a English town, included the temporary installation of silent alarms in victims' homes (*Case Study #15*). In Australia, Homel (1993) reported that the introduction in 1982 of random breath testing (RBT) in New South Wales cut alcohol-related fatal crashes by more than a third relative to the previous three years, declines that persisted as a result of a continued high level of RBT enforcement. Also in Australia, Bourne and Cooke (1993) show that the widespread deployment of photo radar in the State of Victoria was the major factor in substantially reduced levels of speeding in 1991/2, contributing to an overall decline of 45% in traffic fatalities. An experiment with "red light" cameras in Scotland was also found to be successful in preventing motorists "running the red" (Scottish Office Central Research Unit, 1995)[5]. Several studies in Britain, two reproduced in this volume, have found CCTV cameras to be effective in reducing crime. When CCTV cameras were installed for the use of security personnel at a university's parking lots, Poyner (1991) found a substantial reduction in thefts (*Case Study #11*). Appreciable reductions in a variety of crimes have been reported by Brown (1996) following installation of CCTV for police use in the centers of three British cities (*Case Study #12*). Not all the successful examples of formal surveillance involve the use of technology. For example, rates of vandalism, assault and fare dodging on subways and trams in three Dutch cities were substantially reduced when 1,200 "VICs" were employed to serve as safety, information and control inspectors (*Case Study #9*). Masuda (1992) showed that systematic, daily counting by security personnel of items of high risk merchandise, such as VCRs and camcorders, resulted in declines of between 80-100% in thefts by employees at a large electronics merchandiser in New Jersey (*Case Study #13*). Lastly, ways of enhancing police surveillance by enlisting the help of the public are continually being expanded, including informant hotlines, "crime stopper" programs and "curfew decals" on automobiles, which indicate to patrolling police that the vehicle is not normally in use late at night (Clarke and Harris, 1992a).

   7. Surveillance by employees. In addition to their primary function, some employees, particularly those dealing with the public, also perform a surveillance role by virtue of their position. These include a variety of "place managers" (Eck, 1995; Felson, 1995) such as shop assistants, hotel doormen, park keepers, parking lot attendants and train conductors. All these employees assume some responsibility for monitoring conduct in their workplaces. Canadian research has shown that apartment blocks with doormen are less vulnerable to burglary (Waller and Okihiro, 1979). In Britain, less vandalism has been found on buses with conductors (Mayhew *et al.*, 1976) and on public housing estates with resident caretakers (Department of Environment, 1977). Public telephones in Britain which get some surveillance by employees, such as those in pubs or railway stations, also suffer fewer attacks (Markus, 1984). A two-thirds reduction in offenses at a parking lot in England followed the employment of attendants to cover high risks periods of the day (Laycock and Austin, 1992). Rewarding cashiers for detection of forged or stolen credit cards helped to reduce annual losses from credit card frauds by nearly $1 million dollars at an electronics retailer in New Jersey (Masuda, 1993). Once again, CCTV surveillance has been found effective when these cameras are provided for employee use. Cameras installed for use of station staff produced substantial reductions in muggings and thefts at four high risk stations on the London Underground (Mayhew *et al.*, 1979). Vandalism of seats on a fleet of 80 double-deck buses in England was substantially reduced through the provision of CCTV for drivers, though only a few buses were equipped with the cameras (Poyner, 1988). Finally, in *Case Study #14*, Hunter and Jeffery (1992) report that ten out of fourteen studies they reviewed found that having two clerks on duty, especially at night, was an effective robbery prevention measure (see also Bellamy, 1996).

8. *Natural surveillance.* Householders may trim bushes at the front of their homes and banks may light the interior of their premises at night in attempting to capitalize upon the "natural" surveillance provided by people going about their everyday business. Enhancing natural surveillance is a prime objective of improved street lighting (Tien *et al.*, 1979; Ramsay, 1991a), of defensible space (Mayhew, 1979; Coleman, 1985), and of "neighborhood watch" (Bennett, 1990; Rosenbaum, 1988). Though results have not been uniformly positive, some successes in the use of all three measures have been reported. An "apartment watch" program combined with target hardening achieved an 82% reduction in reported burglaries in four apartment blocks in Ottawa (Meredith and Paquette, 1992). Cocoon neighborhood watch, whereby immediately surrounding homes were alerted after a burglary, was an element of the successful "Biting Back" scheme to reduce repeat burglaries described in *Case Study #15*. In his most recent publication, Oscar Newman (1996) reports some successes in reducing crime in public housing developments in the United States through application of defensible space principles. One component of a program that significantly reduced burglary on a commercial strip in Portland, Oregon, was improved lighting of the exterior of the stores (Griswold, 1984). Enhanced lighting in a public housing estate in Dudley, England, produced crime reductions with little evidence of displacement (*Case Study #16*). In one "low-tech" example, components of successful robbery prevention in convenience stores in Florida included an unobstructed view of the store's interior from outside and location of stores near evening commercial activity (Hunter and Jeffery, 1992). Finally, "How's my driving?" decals with 1-800 telephone numbers displayed on the backs of trucks, and cab driver I.D.'s displayed for passengers, facilitate natural surveillance of the behavior of both groups of drivers.

9. *Target removal.* A church in Northern Spain has recently installed a machine at its entrance that allows people to use their bank or credit cards to make donations. (In reporting this development, a local Spanish newspaper could not resist the headline "Through Visa

Toward God," *New York Times,* February 1, 1997, p.F2). The person making the donation has a receipt for tax purposes and the church may receive larger gifts. Since money is not being deposited, the church has also reduced its theft risk through "target removal." An earlier application of this same situational technique, quoted by Pease (1997), comes from the days of the Californian Gold Rush. Plagued by robberies of stage coaches, one mine started casting its silver into 400-pound cubes, about one foot on each side. These were simply too heavy for a robber, or even a gang of them, to carry off on horseback (Lingenfelter, 1986). Other examples of target removal come from attempts to deal with attacks on public telephones in Great Britain and Australia (Bridgeman, 1997). Because the kiosk itself (specially the glass) is more frequently vandalized than the phone, kiosks in high risk locations have been replaced by booths. In addition, the smaller, highly vulnerable, glass panes in earlier kiosks have been replaced by larger panes in more recent designs. A third pay phone example is provided by the introduction of the Phonecard, which by dispensing with the need for pay phones to store large sums of cash, has removed an important target for theft. A variety of cash reduction measures, including the use of safes with time locks, substantially reduced robberies of betting shops in Australia (Clarke and McGrath, 1990). Pease (1991) has shown that a package of measures to prevent repeat victimization of houses on a public housing estate in Britain, including the removal of gas and electric coin meters which were frequent targets for theft (Hill, 1986; Cooper, 1989), reduced burglaries on the estate from 526 in the year before intervention to 132 three years later. *Case Study #14,* shows that cash reduction has consistently been found to reduce the risks of convenience store robbery. Perhaps the best known example of cash reduction, however, concerns the introduction of exact fare systems and safes on buses, which dramatically reduced bus robberies in New York (Chaiken *et al.,* 1974) and in 18 other cities in the late 1960s (Stanford Research Institute, 1970). Finally, a successful "low tech" application of target removal that consisted of persuading in-patients to surrender their valuables for safekeeping, or not to bring them to the hospital, has been described by Moore (1987).

   10. Identifying property. Writing one's name in a book is a simple form of property marking — a space is provided in this book for that purpose. The most developed programs of identifying property relate to vehicles. Registration of motor vehicles was required in some U.S. states from almost the beginning of the century and, subsequently, all vehicles sold in the United States were required to carry a unique Vehicle Identification Number (or VIN). More recently, the Motor Vehicle Theft Law Enforcement Act 1984 has mandated the marking of all major body parts of "high risk" automobiles with the VINs. One of the last U.S. states to require vehicle registration was Illinois in 1934, whereupon vehicle thefts declined from 28,000 in the previous year to about 13,000 (Hall, 1952). Although "operation identification" programs have had a checkered history in the United States (Zaharchuk and Lynch, 1977; Heller *et al.,* 1975), Laycock (1991) shows in *Case Study #17* that property marking undertaken in three small communities in Wales, combined with extensive media publicity, nearly halved the number of reported domestic burglaries.

   11. Reducing temptation. In certain city streets it is unwise to wear gold chains or leave cars parked which are attractive to joyriders. (Throughout the 1980s, the Chevrolet Camaro constituted an American example of the latter, Clarke and Harris, 1992b). Some temptations are less obvious. For example, phone directories which are not gender-neutral might promote obscene phone-calls to women. It has also been found in extensive experimental research that the mere presence of a weapon, such as a gun, can induce aggressive responses in some people. Known as the "weapons effect" (Berkowitz and LePage, 1967), this gives further support to gun control. The weapons effect barely enters the subjective world of potential offenders and James Wise (1982) has argued that this is also true of many inducements to vandalism, for example when the surface characteristics of a wall almost invite graffiti. Many of his suggestions for a "gentle deterrent" to vandalism consist of reducing such temptations. For example, he has suggested that the glass covering fire alarm handles should be mirrored because bad luck would follow its breaking. Another example of reducing temptation is "rapid repair" on the grounds that leaving damaged items unrepaired invites further attacks. Samdahl and Christensen (1985) provided support for this policy by demonstrating that picnic tables that had been scratched and carved were more than twice as likely to be damaged further than other tables. Zimbardo (1973) showed that a car left parked in poor condition in an inner city area rapidly attracted further depredation. Smith (1996) found that school boys in England who admitted recent similar vandalism acts, reported they would be more likely to damage fences or write on them when these already showed signs of vandalism and graffiti. Substantially reduced rates of crime and vandalism on the metropolitan railways of Victoria, Australia, were reported by Carr and Spring (1993) following the introduction of "Travel Safe," a program consisting of rapid repair of vandalism and graffiti as well as of more generally enhanced security. This advocacy of rapid repair and good maintenance has been taken a step further by Wilson and Kelling (1982) who have argued in their famous "broken windows" article that the failure to deal promptly with minor signs of decay in a community, such as panhandling or soliciting by prostitutes, can result in a quickly deteriorating situation as hardened offenders move into the area to exploit the break-down in control. Finally, in *Case Study # 18*, Kuhlhorn shows how removing the temptation to understate income, by permitting income statements to be cross-checked by computer, reduced welfare frauds in Sweden.

12. Denying benefits. Related to reducing temptation, but conceptually distinct, is denying the benefits of crime to offenders. The recent development of security-coded car radios that require a thief to know the radio's PIN before it can be used in another vehicle constitutes an excellent example of this principle. Cars fitted with these radios have been found to have lower theft rates in studies in Australia (NRMA Insurance Ltd. 1990) and in Germany and the United States (Braga and Clarke, 1994). These successes suggest that this principle might usefully be extended to VCR's and TV's so as to reduce the rewards of burglary. A further example of the principle in action is provided by "ink tags," which are designed to deny shoplifters the benefits of stealing. If tampered with, these tags release ink and indelibly stain garments to which they are attached, and these tags may be even more effective than the familiar electronic merchandise tags (DiLonardo and Clarke, 1996). Finally, in *Case Study #19*, Sloan-Howitt and Kelling (1990) document the remarkable success achieved within five years by the New York Transit Authority in ridding its subway cars of graffiti, an important component of which was a policy of immediate cleansing. This denied offenders the gratification of seeing their work on public display.

13. Rule setting. All organizations find it necessary to have rules about conduct in their fields of governance. For example, most businesses regulate employees' telephone use and all retail establishments require their employees to follow strict cash handling and stock control procedures. Organizations such as hospitals, schools, parks, transportation systems, hotels and restaurants must, in addition, regulate the conduct of the clienteles they serve. Any ambiguity in these regulations will be exploited where it is to the advantage of the individual. (Most attempts to avoid income tax relate to those sections of the IRS tax return that are more difficult to investigate Klepper and Nagin, 1987). One important strand of situational prevention, therefore, is rule setting — the introduction of new rules or procedures (and the clarification of those in place), which are intended to remove any ambiguity concerning the acceptability of conduct. For example, in attempting to reduce "no-shows," many restaurants will only accept reservations if callers leave a telephone number where they can be contacted if they do not appear. Some popular restaurants are now also requiring that reservations be accompanied by a credit card number against which a charge can be made for no-shows. A Manhattan restaurant reports that the scheme reduced no-shows at Thanksgiving from a total of 65 in the year before the scheme was introduced to zero in the two subsequent years (*New York Times*, January 31, 1996, p. C3). The same edition of the *New York Times* (p. B3) reports that taxicab fares from Kennedy airport to Manhattan have been fixed at a standard $30 to prevent visitors being cheated. Fisherman in California have also recently been required to wear their fishing licenses, rather than merely to carry them, in a successful effort to get more anglers to comply with license purchase requirements (*New York Times*, November 10, 1993, p.C5). Not all such rules require the backing of the law. In an attempt to produce consensual crowd management at the Australian Motorcycle Grand Prix in 1991, riders were permitted to operate camp sites for their fellow motorcyclists and were encouraged to develop rules and procedures for use of the facilities. This helped to eliminate the brawls between the police and motorcyclists which had marred the event in previous years (Veno and Veno, 1993). Finally, in *Case Study # 20*, Challinger demonstrates a marked reduction in "refund frauds" when new rules were introduced by stores in Australia requiring "proof of purchase" receipts.

14. Stimulating conscience. This situational technique can be distinguished from society's more general informal social control by its focus on specific forms of crime occurring in discrete, highly limited settings (Clarke and Homel, 1997). Rather than attempting to bring about lasting changes in generalized attitudes to law breaking, these measures serve simply to stimulate feelings of conscience at the point of contemplating the commission of a specific kind of offense. For example, signs at store entrances announce that "shoplifting is stealing" and in the Port Authority Bus Terminal in Manhattan they proclaim that "Smoking here is illegal, selfish and rude." Mobile roadside speed monitors have been used to give immediate feedback (without issuing fines) to individual cars traveling above the speed limit (Casey and Lund, 1993). An example of a more intensive and coordinated attempt to increase such informal sanctions is provided by recent advertising campaigns mounted in Australia to reinforce the powerful deterrent impact of random breath testing (Cavallo and Drummond, 1994). These made use of the slogan, "Good mates don't let mates drink and drive." Finally, in Britain, government television campaigns that accompany crackdowns on those who evade purchasing licenses required to own a television (the license fees help to finance the British Broadcasting Corporation) show those detected being treated by the police and courts as "common criminals." The British government has been repeating its advertising campaigns for more than two decades and claims (though without producing evidence) that applications for television licenses sharply increase whenever the campaigns are mounted.

15. Controlling disinhibitors. Crime is not only facilitated by tools such as weapons, but also by psychological disinhibitors, which include: (i) alcohol and drugs, which undermine the usual social or moral inhibitions, or impair perception and cognition so that offenders are less aware of breaking the law (White and Humeniuk, 1994); (ii) propaganda, which can be directed at the dehumanization of target groups (such as Jews — see Bauer, 1990) and can provide the moral certainties and justifications that ordinary people need to commit atrocities and war crimes (Ellul, 1965); and (iii) television violence, which like propaganda, might "reduce or break down those inhibitions against being violent that parents and other socializing agencies have been building up in boys" (Belson, 1978: 17). The "V-chip," which under the Telecommunications Act of 1996 will become a feature of every new television set sold in America (Makris, 1996), allows parents to block reception of violent television programs. This is a situational response to the problem and constitutes an example of "controlling disinhibitors," though most examples of this technique relate to controls on drinking. Access to cars by intoxicated drivers can be restricted by breathalyzers built into the ignition, a measure that is sometimes mandated for recidivist drunk drivers (Jones and Wood, 1989; Morse and Elliott, 1990). A faculty-student committee at Rutgers University decided that beer should be served from kegs rather than cases at dormitory parties on grounds that (1) cases are easier to conceal and (2) in the words of a student: "If you have one keg and a line of 20 people behind it, people will get less alcohol than if you had a refrigerator and people were throwing out beer" (*New York Times*, September 13, 1991). The value of controls on drinking have been demonstrated in a variety of studies. Bjor *et al.* (1992) argue that "rationing" the amount of alcohol that individuals could bring into a Swedish resort town on Midsummer Eve helped to reduce drunkenness and disorderly conduct. Olsson and Wikstrom (1982, 1984) concluded that permanent closing of liquor stores on Saturdays in Sweden had reduced crimes of public drunkenness, assault and vandalism, and domestic disturbances in the summer months, and perhaps also for the remainder of the year. Introduction of a widely supported local ordinance banning the consumption of alcohol in public in central Coventry in England was followed by large reductions in complaints of insulting behavior and in numbers of people who regarded public drinking as a problem in the city (Ramsay, 1991b). *Case Study #21*, shows how the promotion of responsible drinking practices and other attempts to control intoxication led to a marked reduction in alcohol-related crime in the nightlife district in Surfers Paradise, a large resort in Queensland, Australia (Homel *et al.*, 1997).

  16. Facilitating compliance. When Lombroso suggested in the 19th century that people should be locked up for publicly urinating in the streets, his pupil Ferri suggested an alternative more in keeping with the spirit of this book — the provision of public urinals (Hackler, 1978:12). Ferri's suggestion constitutes an example of facilitating compliance, the sixteenth opportunity-reducing technique. This has wide application and includes subsidized taxi rides home for those who have been drinking, litter bins and "graffiti boards" (the latter of which are supplied for people's public messages), and improved checkout procedures in libraries, which remove delay and thus excuses for failing to comply with rules for book borrowing (Boss, 1980; Greenwood and McKean, 1985). Finally, in *Case Study #23*, Shearing and Stenning (1984) provide a fascinating glimpse into the ways in which sophisticated crowd control and management — involving the use of pavement markings, signs, physical barriers (which make it difficult to take a wrong turn) and instructions from cheerful Disney employees — greatly reduce the potential for crime and incivility in Disney World.

Effectiveness of Situational Prevention

The examples of successful interventions mentioned in the course of describing the sixteen opportunity-reducing techniques, belong to its fourth component, the body of evaluated practice. This component also includes the evidence on displacement, but before moving to this topic it should be noted, in case a different message has been communicated through the cataloguing of successes, that situational prevention is not one hundred percent effective. Though reductions in crime may be considerable (often more than 50 percent), situational measures usually ameliorate, not eliminate a problem. In addition, situational measures do not always work as intended for a variety of reasons, including the following:

1. Measures have sometimes failed due to technical or administrative ineptitude, as when anti-climb paint to deter school break-ins was too thinly applied (Hope and Murphy, 1983), or when a scheme to defeat vandalism by replacing broken windows with toughened glass proved too complicated for school maintenance staff to administer (Gladstone, 1980).

2. Some measures have been too easily defeated by offenders, as in the case of the early steering locks in the U.S. and Britain which proved vulnerable to slide hammers (Clarke and Harris, 1992a), and that of the "smart" credit cards in France which could be disabled by stamping on the chip (Levi, 1992).

3. Too much vigilance has sometimes been assumed on the part of guards or ordinary citizens: Security guards rarely monitor CCTV systems as closely as designers expect; people pay far less attention to the street outside their homes than is sometimes assumed by neighborhood watch schemes and defensible space designs (Mayhew, 1979); and people rarely respond to car alarms so that the main result of their increasing use has been to reduce further the quality of life in cities (Clarke and Harris, 1992a).

4. Measures have occasionally provoked offenders to unacceptable escalation as in the case of the bullet-proofing of token booths on the New York subway which resulted in some attacks on booths with gasoline-fueled fires (Dwyer, 1991).

5. Some measures have facilitated rather than frustrated crime: Ekblom (1991) cites the example of pickpockets on the London Underground who stationed themselves near signs warning of theft to see which pockets were checked by passengers on reading the signs; and one result of introducing traffic bollards in Vancouver to frustrate cruising "johns" was to give prostitutes somewhere to sit when propositioning clients who had slowed down (Lowman, 1992).

6. In other cases, measures have been defeated by the carelessness or idleness of potential victims. Residents routinely frustrate entry control systems on apartment buildings by propping open doors to save themselves from answering the door bell. The preventive value of the early security-coded radios was reduced because car owners failed to enter their private codes, thus allowing the radios to revert to a standard code known to thieves (Braga and Clarke, 1994).

7. The preventive value of these radios was further reduced because thieves did not always know which were security-coded and continued to steal ones they could

not use; this flaw was remedied by a continuously blinking light fitted to indicate that the radio was security-coded (Braga and Clarke, 1994).

8. Some inappropriate measures have been introduced because no proper analysis of the problem was undertaken. For example, Harris and Clarke (1991) argued that the parts marking provisions of the federal Motor Vehicle Theft Law Enforcement Act of 1984 were bound to fail because parts marking was restricted only to "high risk" automobiles; leaving aside the resultant scope for displacement, most of the defined "high risk" models are taken not for dismantling and sale of their constituent parts, but for joyriding which will not be deterred by parts marking.

9. Other measures have proved unsuitable because insufficient thought has been given to users' needs. For example, one security innovation left senior citizens "trapped inside a fortress of heavy doors and electronic card-key devices which they found difficult to understand and to operate, while neighbors were no longer able to keep a friendly eye on them" (Sampson *et al.*, 1988: 484).

10. Finally, some measures have had a detrimental effect on the environment. Weidner (1996) argues that floor-to-ceiling turnstile railings installed at one New York City subway station did reduce fare evasion, but only at the cost of creating what was in many people's view "a draconian, prison-like environment." This could have been avoided had other, possibly equally effective measures, been taken instead.

These examples (as well as others provided by Grabosky, 1996) make clear that situational measures do not always work in intended ways. In addition, measures that work in one setting may not do so in another. An example is provided by helmet-wearing laws that dramatically (but fortuitously) reduced motorcycle theft in Germany (see below), but which had little effect in the United States. This was because the laws were not universally applied as in Germany, but were introduced in a piecemeal and inconsistent fashion (Mayhew *et al.*, 1989).

None of the failures of situational prevention seriously call into question the basic validity of the concept, but they suggest that matters may be more complex than those implementing measures sometimes appreciate. Measures must be carefully tailored to the settings in which they are applied, with due regard to the motives and methods of the offenders involved. Where the stakes are high, offenders must be expected to test the limits of the new defenses and to be successful sometimes in identifying vulnerabilities. This process may be assisted by the arrival on the scene of more resourceful or determined criminals than was previously the case. And this again may sometimes result in the greater use of violence. For the less serious forms of crime, measures that depend upon natural surveillance or the vigilance of employees may be expected to lose their value as people become more complacent.

That preventive measures may have a limited life is not a counsel of despair; rather, it is a fact that must influence the choice among preventive options of varying difficulty and cost. The challenge for research is to help practitioners avoid the pitfalls by providing a sounder base of knowledge upon which to act. All we know at present is that some measures work well in certain conditions. What we need to know is which measures work best, in which combination (Tilley, 1993c), deployed against what kinds of crime and under what conditions (Poyner, 1993). We also need to have much better information about the financial costs of particular crime prevention measures. As discussed below, this will require a greatly increased investment in evaluative research. It also means that the commitment to situational prevention has to be long term, which for many organizations and agencies will mean developing a permanent in-house capability.

Displacement of Crime

Under the dispositional assumptions of traditional criminological theory, situational variables merely determine the time and place of offending. Manipulating situations would thus simply cause offenders to shift their attention to some other target, time or place, change their tactics or even switch to some other categories of crime (Reppetto, 1976). Displacement has therefore been the Achilles' heel of situational prevention, but this has changed with the theoretical developments described above. Under the rational choice assumptions that now guide thinking about situational prevention, displacement is no longer seen as inevitable, but as contingent upon the offender's judgments about alternative crimes. If these alternatives are not viable, the offender may well settle for smaller criminal rewards or for a lower rate of crime. Few offenders are so driven by need or desire that they have to maintain a certain level of offending whatever the cost. For many, the elimination of easy opportunities for crime may actually encourage them to explore non-criminal alternatives. On the other hand, since crime is the product of purposive and sometimes inventive minds, displacement to other categories of offense would not be unexpected, so long as these new crimes served the same purposes as the ones that were thwarted.

Numerous examples of displacement have been reported, particularly in the early literature (Gabor, 1990). Street crimes increased in surrounding districts following a successful crackdown on these crimes in one New York City precinct (Press, 1971). The reduction in robberies following the introduction of exact fare systems on New York City buses was a accompanied by an increase of robbery in the subway (Chaiken *et al.*, 1974). In Columbus, a police helicopter patrol (Lateef, 1974) and, in Newark, a street lighting program (Tyrpak, 1975) appeared to shift crime to precincts not covered by the new measures. The reduced risk of theft for new vehicles fitted with steering column locks in Britain was found to be at the expense of an increased risk for older vehicles without the locks (Mayhew *et al.,* 1976). Gabor (1981) found that a property marking program in Ottawa may have displaced burglaries from the homes of participants to those of non-participants. Finally, Allatt (1984) found that the decrease in burglary on a British public housing estate which had undergone "target hardening" was accompanied by an increase of property crimes in adjacent areas.

Apart from these and other instances in which displacement was found, researchers may sometimes have failed to detect displacement that had in fact occurred. This is especially likely where the displacement involved kinds of crime other than the ones targeted. Thus, the reduction of aircraft hijackings in the 1970s achieved by baggage screening might possibly have resulted in an undetected increase in other terrorist activity, such as car bombings, assassinations and hostage taking. The methodological difficulty encountered in detecting such displacement has been explained as follows:

> If, in truth, displacement is complete, some displaced crime will probably fall outside

the areas and types of crime being studied or be so dispersed as to be masked by background variation. In such an event, the optimist would speculate about why the unmeasured areas or types of crime probably escaped displaced crime, while the pessimist would speculate about why they probably did not. No research study, however massive is likely to resolve the issue. The wider the scope of the study in terms of types of crimes and places, the thinner the patina of displaced crime could be spread across them; thus disappearing into the realm of measurement error (Barr and Pease, 1990: 293).

On the other hand, the uncritical acceptance of displacement might have meant that increases in crime, that would have occurred anyway, have sometimes been wrongly attributed to displacement. For example, London Underground officials believed that the appearance of a new kind of slug soon after ticket machines had been modified to prevent the use of an earlier, more primitive slug, was the result of displacement. However, Clarke *et al.* (1994) showed that the new slugs were found in different stations from the earlier ones, which suggested that different groups of offenders were involved. They concluded that, even if action had not been taken against the original slugs, the new ones might still have appeared.

With the development of rational choice analyses, evidence has begun to accumulate of the successful application of situational measures with few displacement costs. Thus, after reviewing 55 studies of displacement, Hesseling (1994) concluded that displacement was not found in 22 studies, and was never 100 percent in the remaining studies (see also Gabor, 1990, and Eck, 1993; Ferreira, 1995).

Much of this evidence on displacement comes from studies reproduced in this book. For instance, Knutsson and Kuhlhorn (1981) found no evidence of an increase in a range of "conceivable" alternative crimes as a result of the introduction of new identification procedures that greatly reduced check frauds in Sweden (*Case Study #7*). Following the re-arrangement of market stalls and improved lighting which reduced thefts at covered markets in Birmingham, England, no evidence was found of displacement of thefts to other nearby markets (*Case Study #4*). When Caller-ID became available in some parts of New Jersey, there was little evidence of an increase of obscene calls in other areas (*Case Study #5*), perhaps because obscene phone callers are generally not persistent random dialers, hoping to hit upon susceptible women. Rather, many appear to victimize only particular women of their acquaintance and, with the introduction of Caller-ID in their local telephone areas, these individuals are unlikely to have begun calling more distant parts of New Jersey where they knew no one. Finally, Matthews (1990) found little evidence that prostitutes simply moved to other locations following successful action to close down the red light district in Finsbury Park, which he explained by a relative lack of commitment to prostitution among many of the women involved (*Case Study #3*). As the environment in Finsbury Park became less hospitable "...it would seem that over a period of about one year, most of the girls gave up prostitution or moved back home or elsewhere. For many, their normal period of involvement in prostitution may have been three or four years and, therefore, the effect of intensive policing was to shorten that period for a year or two in most cases."[6]

In other cases cited above, the nature of the targeted offenses would have meant there was little point in looking for displacement. For example, it is unlikely that those deterred by random breath tests from drunken driving in New South Wales (Homel, 1993) or those deterred by speed cameras from speeding in Victoria (Bourne and Cooke, 1993) would have displaced these behaviors to some other time or place. People do not usually set out to commit these offenses, but will do so when circumstances dictate (Homel, 1993). One important circumstance is the perceived chance of arrest and, were the ubiquitous speed cameras or random breath testing patrols to be withdrawn, people would no doubt once again revert to their old ways.

Understanding Displacement

Deeper understanding of the motives and modus operandi of target groups of offenders, as obtained in Matthews' study, provides a way of dealing with the limitations of the statistical search for displacement discussed by Barr and Pease (1990). It may not always be possible to interview offenders, but in some cases insights into motivation and methods can be provided by closer analysis of patterns of offending. For example, Clarke and Harris (1992b) have shown important differences among automobiles in their risks for different forms of theft, which reflect the motives of offenders. Thus, new cars most at risk of "stripping" in the United States during the mid-1980s were predominantly European models with good audio equipment; those most at risk of "joyriding" were American-made "muscle" cars; and those at risk of theft for re-sale were mostly higher-priced luxury automobiles. These "choice structuring properties" (Cornish and Clarke, 1987) of the target vehicles are not difficult to understand in terms of the motives of offenders and would also help to direct the search for displacement if the security were improved for any sub-set of vehicles. Thus, if some "muscle" cars were made more difficult to take for joyriding it would make sense to confine the search for displacement only to others of the same group.[7]

Similar logic was followed by Mayhew *et al.* (1989) in their study of displacement following the reduction of motorcycle thefts in West Germany between 1980 and 1986, brought about by the progressive enforcement of helmet legislation. During this period, motorcycle thefts declined by more than 100,000 because the helmet requirement substantially increased the risks of opportunistic thefts for those offenders who were unable at the same time to steal a helmet.[8] Mayhew and her colleagues reasoned that since many opportunistic thefts would have been for purposes of joyriding or temporary use (for example, to get home late at night), the most likely result of the reduced opportunities for stealing motorcycles would be an increase in thefts of cars and bicycles. In fact, as shown by Table 2, there was little evidence of displacement to either category of target. Car thefts did rise over the same period, but only by a few thousand, while bicycle thefts declined (after an initial rise) to below their previous level. Bicycles may not usually provide a realistic or attractive alternative means of transportation, whereas cars may not provide the same joyriding thrills. They may also require more knowledge to operate and may be more difficult to steal.

A final illustration of the value of considering "choice structuring properties" is provided by the British gas suicide story (Clarke and Mayhew, 1988). The elimination of gas suicides in Britain in the 1960s and 1970s resulting from the introduction of natural gas (which contains no toxins) was not followed by substantial displacement to other forms of suicide. Consequently, the overall suicide rate for the country declined by about 40 percent. The lack of displacement was explained by Clarke and Mayhew in terms of the particular advantages of domestic gas as a form of suicide. It was readily available in every home, it was simple to use, and it was highly lethal. It was also painless, left no marks or blood, and required little courage. No other alternative possessed all these advantages and would therefore have provided an acceptable alternative for many people.

It has been argued that it will only be a matter of time before the suicidally-inclined in Britain displace to other methods and the suicide rate reverts to its former level. Indeed, there has been some increase in the suicide rate for males who have been making more use of other methods (including car exhaust gases, Clarke and Lester, 1987). However, there is substantial evidence that for many people the urge to kill themselves is in response to situational stress (such as a bereavement) and may dissipate as depression is alleviated. The gradual increase in the male suicide rate may therefore reflect, not "delayed displacement" by people prevented from killing themselves by the detoxification of gas, but an independent increase in the motivation to commit suicide.

This argument about the consequences of gas detoxification should not be taken to mean that longer-term adaptations never occur in response to situational measures. Indeed, it is widely believed that car thieves have gradually found ways to defeat steering column locks and support for this can be found in the somewhat higher than expected rates of car

TABLE 2
THEFTS OF MOTORCYCLES, CARS, AND BICYCLES:
FEDERAL REPUBLIC OF GERMANY, 1980-86

Year	Motorcycles	Cars	Bicycles
1980	153,153	64,131	358,865
1981	143,317	71,916	410,223
1982	134,735	78,543	453,850
1983	118,550	82,211	415,398
1984	90,008	72,170	376,946
1985	73,442	69,659	337,337
1986	54,208	70,245	301,890

Source: Mayhew *et al.* (1989).

theft in some countries, especially Britain, where the locks have been available for many years (Clarke and Harris, 1992a). On the other hand, the reduction in the rate of car thefts in West Germany, brought about by the introduction of steering column locks in the 1960s, has persisted to this day (*Case Study #1*). One possible reason for this (apart from the possibly higher quality of the German equipment) is that theft was greatly reduced almost overnight because the locks were made compulsory for all cars on the road. Consequently, neophytes were deprived of the example and tutelage of experienced car thieves. This affords a marked contrast to the situation in Britain where the locks were introduced only for new cars at manufacture. Consequently, car thieves could continue to operate so long as they concentrated their efforts on older vehicles. This meant they could gradually learn ways of defeating the steering locks and could continue to pass on the tricks of the trade to novices.

Diffusion of Benefits

Even when displacement occurs, it may sometimes be "benign" (Barr and Pease,

1990), as in the case of preventive measures which bring relief to repeatedly victimized groups although at the cost of an increased risks for others. This observation guided the design of an experiment to reduce burglary in Kirkholt, a public housing estate in the North of England (Pease, 1991). Target hardening priority was given to houses that had recently experienced a burglary, with the result that, despite their higher risks, few of these houses experienced a repeat burglary in the follow-up period. Pease also noted that these preventive benefits permeated, through what he called a process of "drip-feed," to other households that were not target-hardened so that the burglary rate for the whole of the Kirkholt estate declined dramatically.

The "drip-feed" effect is, of course, the reverse of displacement in that preventive action led, not to an increase, but to a reduction in crimes not directly addressed by the measures. As Clarke and Weisburd (1994) observe, similar effects have been noted under a variety of other names. For example, Miethe (1991) has referred to the "free rider" effect when residents benefit from the crime prevention measures taken by their neighbors and Sherman (1990) to the "bonus" effect sometimes observed in police crackdowns when there is a carryover of the preventive effect beyond the period when the crackdown is in force. Scherdin (1986) used the term "halo effect" when reporting that book detection systems prevented thefts, not just of the electronically protected materials, but also of other materials as well. In some cases, the phenomenon has been reported without giving it a name. Poyner and Webb (*Case Study #4*) found that measures to reduce thefts from shopping bags in particular city center markets seemed also to reduce thefts in other markets as well. In his evaluation of a CCTV system installed to reduce auto theft at a university, Poyner (*Case Study #11*) found an equal reduction of crime in the parking lot not covered as the ones that were covered by the cameras. In his study of CCTV on buses, he found that damage and other misbehavior was reduced, not only on five buses fitted with cameras, but throughout the whole fleet of 80 buses (Poyner, 1988).

Despite the variety of terminology, in all these cases the same phenomenon has been observed. That is to say, reductions in crime have occurred which are difficult to attribute to the direct action of situational measures. Clarke and Weisburd (1994) have argued that the generality of the phenomenon demands a standard term and they have proposed "diffusion of benefits," since the geographical and temporal connotations of this term parallel those of "displacement of crime." They have defined diffusion as:

> the spread of the beneficial influence of an intervention beyond the places which are directly targeted, the individuals who are the subject of control, the crimes which are the focus of intervention or the time periods in which an intervention is brought (Clarke and Weisburd, 1994:169).

They have also distinguished between two forms of diffusion which they call deterrence and discouragement. Deterrence was invoked by Scherdin (1986), for example, in explaining why the book detection system she studied also prevented thefts of items that were not electronically tagged, and by Poyner in identifying reasons for the general decline in damage to the fleet when only some of the buses were fitted with CCTV cameras: "The children have learned...that the cameras will enable misbehaving individuals to be picked out and that action will be taken..They appear to believe that most buses have cameras, or at least they are uncertain about which buses have cameras" (Poyner, 1988:50).

For diffusion by "discouragement," the key is not the judgment of risk, but the assessment of effort and reward. For example, one component of the successful action against burglary in Kirkholt was the removal of prepayment meters from many houses on the estate (Pease, 1991). This seems to have been enough to discourage potential burglars who could no longer be sure of finding a meter containing cash. Similarly, the drop in thefts at all Birmingham city center markets following the situational measures taken at only some of them may have been due to the fact that: "The general attractiveness of this area for thieves has reduced" (*Case Study #4*). Ekblom (1988b) accounted for the fact that anti-bandit screens in London post offices had produced a reduction, not just in over-the-counter robberies, but also in other robberies of staff and customers by speculating that would-be robbers may have received "the very general message that something had been done to improve security at the sub-post offices" (Ekblom 1988b: 39). Finally, Clarke *et al.* (1991) have suggested that an intensive target hardening program in Australian banks brought about a general reduction in robberies of all commercial targets (including convenience stores, gas stations and betting shops) because robbers began to believe that this form of crime was no longer worth pursuing.

It would be difficult to overestimate the importance of diffusion of benefits if the phenomenon is as common as these various examples suggest. By showing that the preventive benefits of situational measures extend beyond their immediate focus, the debate about their value is transformed. It is also clear that much more needs to be discovered about ways of enhancing diffusion. Sherman (1990) has suggested that the "free bonus" of crackdowns might be increased by randomly rotating crackdowns and back-offs across times and places so as to lead offenders to overestimate the actual levels of risk in force on any particular occasion. He also advocated the deliberate use of publicity about imminent crackdowns to promote this uncertainty in offenders' minds. Clarke and Weisburd (1994) argue that these strategies might be employed to diffuse the benefits of other forms of "situational deterrence" (Cusson, 1993) than crackdowns, and they also identify other possible means of enhancing diffusion, such as concentrating preventive action on highly visible or attractive targets, so as to lead offenders to think that preventive measures may have been more generally applied.

Since these various strategies depend upon influencing judgments made by offenders, we need to learn more about ways that offenders obtain and process information about preventive initiatives and what role is played in this process by their own direct observation, their relationships with other offenders and information obtained through the media. Whatever the practical pay-off from such studies, it is likely that diffusion of benefits will soon supplant displacement as the principal focus for theoretical debate about the value of situational measures.

A Prescription for Evaluation

Because diffusion has been overlooked, cases may already exist in which the effects of situational measures have been underestimated. Most existing evaluations have made use of "quasi-experiments," or "natural experiments," in which researchers have taken advantage of new preventive interventions to examine effects on crime through use of time series data, or a comparison with "control" data from an untreated site. Increased crime in the controls is usually attributed to displacement resulting from the situational measures, rather than to some extraneous increase in crime. On the other hand, decreased crime in the controls has not generally been attributed to diffusion, but to some overall, extraneous *decline* in crime.

Even without the difficulties of measuring displacement and diffusion, the interpretation of situational evaluations is problematic. Though declines in crime may be large, one cannot be confident about the durability of success because follow-ups are often brief, sometimes less than one year. In some of the studies, several preventive measures were deployed at the same time and their relative contributions to the outcome are unknown. For example, Felson *et al.* (1996) list eleven different measures that were introduced at the Port Authority Bus Terminal to deal with misuse of the restrooms. Finally, competing explanations for reported reductions in crime (other than as the result of the situational measures) have been insufficiently investigated in many of these quasi-experimental studies.

The weaknesses of quasi-experiments (see *Case Study #16* for a brief discussion), have led to calls for greater use of true experimental designs, involving random assignment of preventive measures between treatment and control groups (Sherman, 1996; Weisburd, 1997). However, while suited to the laboratory, these designs often involve serious ethical problems and are difficult and costly to implement in the real world (Clarke and Cornish, 1972; Farrington, 1983). These difficulties include: (i) attempts by practitioners, who may have their own views of the intervention, to subvert randomization; (ii) the reactive effects of the experiment, with the particular danger of "Hawthorne effects" resulting from the difficulty of concealing the fact that some areas or groups are receiving new treatments; (iii) the commitment of those administering the experimental treatment which may play an important role in the results; (iv) differential rates of attrition that may result in the non-comparability of randomly selected experimental and control groups; (v) changes over time in the intervention; and (vi) ethical problems involved in providing different levels of service to experimental and control groups or areas.

More serious than any of these difficulties is that crime prevention interventions are not like drugs, i.e. treatments with precisely measurable and controllable chemical constituents. Rather, they consist of a complex interaction of several related social and physical elements. This makes it impossible to be certain about the precise cause of any effect demonstrated by the experiment. One example is provided by a rare experiment concerned with shoplifting (Farrington *et al.*, 1993), in which three measures (electronic tagging, redesign of merchandise layout, and security guards) were systematically compared for effectiveness. Each measure was introduced in two stores selling electronic merchandise, while three other stores served as controls. It was concluded that electronic tags and store redesign were effective in reducing shoplifting (at least during the brief follow-up of three to six weeks), but that store redesign was undermined by further changes made by clerks to increase sales. The security guards, on the other hand, were not effective though the researchers acknowledged that this may have been due to store layouts which made it difficult to watch customers, or to the inexperience, advanced age, unimpressive physiques and lack of training of the particular individuals concerned.

It is most unlikely that these possibilities could be systematically explored within the confines of a rigorous experimental methodology. Few if any retail stores would tolerate the interference in their operations demanded by the experiments (or, more likely, series of experiments). Unless employed to do so, few criminologists would want to devote so much effort to sorting out the minutiae of security guard effectiveness in preventing shoplifting in just one kind of store. Many other, more rewarding problems beckon them. Add to this the difficulties of studying displacement and diffusion, which experimental designs do not necessarily solve and may even exacerbate because of the greater interference in the real world that may be required, and it becomes clear that these designs will have to be reserved for cases where it is imperative to achieve as much certainty as possible.

A more appropriate evaluative strategy for situational prevention will need to recognize that the value of particular situational measures is highly contingent on the nature of the problem and the circumstances in which it arises. Something that works in one situation will not necessarily work in another. What is needed is some quick, and occasionally rough, indication of whether a newly introduced measure is working. Since situational measures often achieve large reductions in crime, a simple time series or a comparison with a control group will frequently suffice. Where measures appear not to have worked, some possible explanations for this are also needed. Armed with this information, the action-researcher knows whether something else should be tried and, perhaps, what this should be.

Given the vast number of natural experiments being conducted in all manner of settings, the optimal strategy therefore seems to be: (1) to undertake as many evaluations as possible, (2) to compensate for weaker designs with detailed observation of the process of implementation (the value of which is illustrated by Farrington *et al.*'s observations about the caliber of their security guards), (3) to include as much information as possible about the costs and practicability of the techniques studied, (4) to conduct periodic meta-analyses of results (for examples see Poyner, 1993, Hesseling, 1994, and Eck, In preparation), and (5) to piece together the findings with reference to a systematic classification of situational techniques. This accumulating body of empirical results contributes to the development of robust principles of opportunity-reduction, which will help in developing tailor-made solutions for new problems arising in fresh circumstances. This strategy seems consistent with other recent writings about the need for theory-based evaluations of community initiatives (Connell *et al.*, 1995; Weiss, 1995).

The ultimate objective of the empirical evaluations is therefore not to document the precise value of particular interventions (say, security guards) observed under particular circumstances, but to build our detailed understanding of the principles of effective opportunity-reduction. Since situational crime prevention practitioners are constantly called upon to provide tailor-made solutions for new problems arising in fresh circumstances, they will be helped more by a robust and detailed theory of opportunity reduction, than by attempts to catalogue the effectiveness of a host of variations on specific crime prevention measures.

Implementation Difficulties

Crime prevention is no longer the inoffensive and neutral activity it once was in the days when it consisted purely of publicity exhorting people to lock it or lose it, and advice from the police on locks and bars. Now it involves the police and central/local government seeking to influence the civil behaviour of particular individuals, private companies and local authority departments responsible for the creation of criminal opportunities or motivation; instead of tackling the 'common enemy, crime', it cuts across conflicting public and private interests and policies, and has to compete for resources with other goals and needs, not always as a front runner. Reconciliation of all this conflict and competition means that crime prevention has to be slipped in by changing attitudes and expectations, by good salesmanship, clever design, close attention to cost effectiveness, sometimes piggybacking on other facilities and changes in an organisation, and using data recording systems developed and maintained primarily for other purposes (Ekblom, 1987a:11-12).

This extended quote may be a useful corrective to the case studies reprinted in this volume which are largely silent about the difficulties encountered in implementing situational prevention with the notable exception of *Case Study #21*. Rarely do the difficulties concern the identification of suitable measures since many alternative ways exist of blocking opportunities for specific classes of crime (cf. Hope, 1985; Smith, 1987). Rather, the difficulties of implementation usually concern acceptance of the responsibility for preventive action and issues of cost and coordination.

Because most situational prevention to-date has been undertaken in the public sector, discussion of implementation difficulties has focused largely on ways of achieving the necessary coordination among local government agencies (e.g. Gladstone, 1980; Hope, 1985; Ekblom, 1987a). Coordination is especially difficult when attempting to combine situational with "social" or "community" crime prevention measures (e.g. Blagg *et al.*, 1988; Sampson *et al.*, 1988; Liddle and Gelsthorpe, 1994; Gilling, 1996; Hughes, 1996; Sutton, 1996, Walters, 1996). However, with increasing recognition that much preventive action can be undertaken only by the private sector, for example by credit card companies, bus operators, offices and shopping malls (cf. Felson and Clarke, 1997a), more attention is being focused on issues of responsibility and costs. Those in the private sector tend to see crime prevention as a police matter and are rarely willing to "acknowledge that their property or operations are generating a substantial strain on police resources, accept that they have a duty, up to their level of competence, for the control of specific crimes, and take appropriate action" (Engstad and Evans, 1980:151). Acknowledging this responsibility would not only complicate the management task, but could involve the expenditure of significant resources. Analyses of these costs are therefore likely to play an increasingly important role in crime prevention (Burrows, 1991).

These points are illustrated by the familiar example of shoplifting, which is facilitated by some retailing practices including displays to encourage impulse buying. The risks of the ensuing "shrinkage" are accepted by most stores, which rely upon deterrence to contain the problem through the occasional arrest and prosecution of shoplifters. This results in significant costs being passed on to the criminal justice system, which are not borne by retailers except in an indirect way through taxation.

These practices will not be changed simply by government exhortation, which runs the risk of being dismissed as "blaming the victim" (Karmen, 1984). Nor could stores often be charged for police service when they have failed to adopt preventive measures (Pease, 1979). However, declining retail profits due to increased competition might force stores to take a more proactive role in prevention. This might also be facilitated by improved technology, which now permits instant credit checks (Levi *et al.,* 1991) and tighter stock control (Hope, 1991). The technology will always need to pass the retailer's cost-benefit scrutiny, but this will not take account of the criminal justice costs of failing to take preventive action. There will therefore be an increasing role for research such as that undertaken by Field (1993) on the costs of auto theft in the United States, which included analysis of criminal justice costs and of the potential savings that might result from government-mandated vehicle security standards.

Philosophical and Ethical Issues

When first introduced, the concept of situational prevention provoked fears about two unwelcome developments in society. In its more unattractive, "target hardening" forms (barbed-wire, heavy padlocks, guard dogs and private security forces) it suggested the imminence of a "fortress society" in which people, terrified by crime and distrustful of their fellows, barricade themselves in their homes and places of work, emerging only to conduct essential business (Davis, 1990). In its use of electronic hardware (CCTV, intruder alarms, x-ray scanning of baggage), it raised the specter of totalitarian, "Big Brother" forms of state control.

Experience of situational measures has dispelled some fears of the fortress society (though not all, cf. Bottoms, 1990). Many of the measures (such as parts marking of automobiles and the interior lighting of banks at night) are so unobtrusive as to be barely noticeable, while others (including street lighting, defensible space architecture, and uniformed security guards in shopping and leisure complexes) actually reduce the fear of crime. Yet other measures which enhance security, such as bar coding of merchandise and central locking of automobiles, also have the advantage of increasing the convenience of everyday life.

This very unobtrusiveness and convenience feeds the second fear — that it may not be the fortress society that is imminent, but Huxley's "brave new world." If America is the harbinger of change for the rest of the world, how much more true might not this be of Disney World? The unobtrusive yet powerful social control exemplified there (*Case Study #23*), under which people willingly accept being corralled and shepherded from place to place, may soon be shaping much of our leisure behavior, if not our lives! Add to this the astonishing growth in the technological devices now available to the "new surveillance" (Marx, 1986), and the potential for state control, not of the iron fist but of the velvet glove, seems frightening.

While credible under fascism or a dictatorship, this scenario of a sheep-like populace gives altogether too little credence to the power of democracy. Visitors to Disney World might temporarily surrender some autonomy, but only because they recognize that a degree of regimentation may be necessary if they are to enjoy the spectacles in safety and at reasonable cost. People may increasingly be willing to make this trade in their daily lives, but it will soon become apparent if they are not: Disney World will go broke. Moreover, while they may welcome powerful new forms of surveillance in guaranteeing national security or combating organized crime, they will fight its deployment in the everyday situations giving rise to most crime as soon as they perceive a threat to their civil liberties.

Nor is the vision, or perhaps nightmare, of a blanket application by the State of situational controls on behavior consistent with the essence of situational prevention: Situational measures cannot be applied wholesale; they need to be tailored to the particular circumstances giving rise to specific problems of crime and disorder. Moreover, unlike most other measures of crime control, situational measures are not the sole prerogative of the State, but need to be applied by particular private or business organizations. Far from being enthusiastically embraced, they may be strongly resisted. Indeed, the problem is less one of the sweeping application of situational measures, than of the failure to apply them when they should have been.

While ethical and legal questions surrounding particular situational measures, such as gun controls, have been extensively analyzed, there has in fact been comparatively little general discussion of the ethics of situational prevention. This is because both critics and advocates have been preoccupied with its effectiveness. As evidence accumulates of its preventive value in a wide variety of crime contexts, the focus of debate is likely to move increasingly to ethical and philosophical questions (Homel, 1996).

Fears will no doubt continue to be expressed about the fortress society and about Orwellian forms of surveillance, especially with the growing use of CCTV cameras in public places (Honess and Charman, 1992; Tilley, 1993c; Horne, 1996; Davies, 1996a,b). Because situational prevention sees everyone as susceptible to crime opportunities, it will continue to be criticized for its essentially cynical and pessimistic character, even though it seems more morally defensible than the traditional view of crime as the province of a small group of criminal individuals. This can provide a device for scapegoating particular individuals and groups and for justifying highly punitive or intrusive interventions (Seve, 1997). However, the debate about ethics in the next decade is likely also to encompass a broader set of issues relating to "victim blaming" and to distributive justice.

Victim blaming was mentioned above in the context of persuading businesses to modify criminogenic products and practices. Another vocal group on this subject are victim advocates who resist any imputation of victim responsibility because this might jeopardize the achievement of better rights and treatment for victims. However, most victims would no doubt prefer to have been protected from crime in the first place than to receive compensation or better treatment later. Most would also welcome sound advice on precautionary measures. Victim advocacy should therefore find a natural, symbiotic relationship with crime prevention, which neither compromises victim rights nor absolves offenders of responsibility. The position has been expressed as follows:

> The whole point of routine precautions against crime is that people can take responsibility without accepting criminal blame or even civil liability. Routine precautions by potential victims do not serve to exempt offenders from criminal responsibility. The citizen who reminds herself to lock her car door and does so still has a right to expect others not to steal that car, whether it is locked or not.... If crime opportunities are extremely enticing and open, society will tend to produce new offenders and offenses. By inviting crime, society will make it more difficult for the law enforcement system to prosecute and punish those who accept the invitation. With situational prevention, invitations to crime are fewer and hence it is more difficult for those who do offend to escape responsibility (Felson and Clarke, 1997b).

One of the topics arising under distributive justice is the risk of displacement following preventive action — particularly displacement from the rich, who can afford situational prevention, to the poor who cannot. This concern, often raised in the context of "gated communities" (wealthy residential enclaves), is related to a second concern that situational measures can be used by the powerful to exclude undesirables — such as the poor, minorities and young people — from public places such as shopping malls, parks, town centers and particular neighborhoods (O'Malley, 1994; White and Sutton, 1995).

On displacement from rich to poor, the issues are by no means straightforward. A wealthy neighborhood near to less affluent communities may provide a magnet for crime and, if it provides tempting targets and easy rewards for crime, may draw people into burglary who might otherwise not have become involved. On the other hand, reducing the opportunities for burglary may be unlikely to drive offenders back to the less wealthy areas where the pickings may be more meager. There is even the possibility that the preventive measures taken in one community might benefit a neighboring one through a process of diffusion. Measures taken by the wealthy may thus sometimes benefit the less affluent. A concrete example is provided by LOJACK, a vehicle tracking system that consists of a small transmitter hidden in a car that can be activated to facilitate recovery when the car is stolen. LOJACK is too expensive for everyone to buy, but a recent study suggests that it brings general benefits in terms of reduced car theft (Ayres and Levitt, 1996). One reason is that car thieves do not know whether any given vehicle is equipped with LOJACK because police have made this a condition of collaborating in the retrieval of cars fitted with the transmitters.

In addition, many so-called exclusionary measures are not the prerogative of the rich.It may be the case that in New York, doormen are found only in apartment buildings for the wealthy, but in Europe concierges are found in many middle- and low-income apartment blocks. Many public housing estates have manned entrances and some poor communities make use of street barriers to exclude drug dealers and others who might prey upon residents (Atlas and LeBlanc, 1994). Indeed, Oscar Newman's (1972) original "defensible space" work, the start of scientific interest in opportunity-reduction, was undertaken in public housing and makes use of design to help residents police the public areas of the estate. More recently, he has described how the use of gates to create "mini-neighborhoods" in a down-town low-income rental community in Dayton, Ohio, substantially reduced traffic and crime problems (Newman, 1996).

In some cases, cultural attitudes will prevent the adoption of particular situational measures, even though they might have been accepted elsewhere. Thus, photo radar is widely used in Australia, but was recently made illegal in New Jersey (Clarke, 1995), while a scheme to reduce fraudulent checks requiring a thumbprint has been adopted in New Jersey (*New York Times*, March 23, 1997, Sctn. 13, p. 1) when a similar scheme was rejected in Western Australia (Pidco, 1996). Even for the same population, what is found objectionable or intrusive can change over time. Witness changed attitudes to smoking or wearing seat belts.

Where situational measures are vetoed on ethical grounds or simply found objectionable, alternative situational measures can often be found that do not provoke these same reactions. Nevertheless, an improved understanding of ethical costs for the broad swathe of situational techniques would be of considerable value in planning interventions. Indeed, the greater attention being paid to these issues may result in general ethical guidelines, to be used together with improved information about the cost-effectiveness of particular measures, in tailoring responses to crime problems.

Political and Professional Constituencies for Situational Prevention

At the beginning of this Introduction, it was argued that situational prevention is a radically new form of crime control focused not on criminals, but on criminogenic situations, with all that implies for criminological explanation. Situational prevention can also be regarded, however, as a logical outcome of the precautions that people have always taken to protect themselves from crime and, seen in this light, it is little more than the systematization of a wide range of everyday, commonsense practices. That two such divergent views can be taken of situational prevention helps to explain why it is widely practiced in all but name, while at the same time it is resisted by many criminologists and politicians.

Its lack of political support may be surprising: The Left might have welcomed its focus upon local problems and local decision-making; Liberals might have been attracted to its essentially non-punitive philosophy; and Conservatives might have been attuned to its message concerning the need for agencies and communities to take the initiative in dealing with their crime problems. Perhaps the very breadth of this appeal means that situational prevention lacks a natural constituency among politicians, but they also have other reasons to resist it. It is too easily represented as being soft on crime and as blaming victims. It seems to demand new resources, in addition to those already allocated to the criminal justice system. It is easily characterized as demonstrating a failure of political will in dealing with the severe social and economic problems that confront society. Its essentially piecemeal approach affords little prospect of achieving immediate reductions in overall crime rates and its rational, analytic nature does not lend itself to eloquence in campaign speeches or political manifestos.

Politicians may indeed have a limited role in promoting situational prevention because particular measures often have to be initiated at a local level, sometimes by private sector organizations. The grass roots formulation of crime control must encourage cost-benefit appraisals of prevention and might result in more effective action, but it means that national politicians cannot claim the successes. When they do promote "situational" programs, such as neighborhood watch, there is the risk of this leading to the kind of unfocused efforts, out of keeping with the tenets of situational crime prevention, that result in disappointment and disillusionment. When central government intervention is indicated, as in the case of persuading vehicle manufacturers to improve security, this may not require laws enacted by politicians, but patient, "behind the scenes" negotiations conducted by civil servants to persuade reluctant parties to take preventive action.

Despite its lack of a political constituency, situational prevention has become a component, though a small one, of crime policy in some European countries (Willemse, 1994; Garland, 1996). This may be because civil servants can sometimes be more pragmatic than their political masters. Both in Holland and Great Britain, situational prevention is promoted by government crime prevention units and by a semi-autonomous governmental agency in Sweden. Its record of success and the resolution of ethical and theoretical dilemmas will mean that its policy role will grow, even in the United States where interest has been lagging. As mentioned above, this may be due partly to the disappointing results of attempts to implement CPTED in the 1970s. However, Bright (1992) has noted the absence of any crime prevention policy in America, which he attributes to a dislike of government intervention as well as to a strong ethos of personal responsibility that results in punishment being seen as the most appropriate response to law-breaking. Nevertheless, the recent federal government support for community and problem-oriented policing may signal a change, likely to benefit situational prevention.

Since the responsibility for much preventive action falls on the private sector, government officials promoting situational prevention will need to become familiar with a world that is now foreign to many of them. Their usual modes of governing, based upon fiscal control and parliamentary or congressional authority, will have to be supplemented by other change strategies, including negotiation and persuasion (Burrows, 1997; Travis, 1997; van Dijk, 1997). Some difficult issues, discussed above in the context of shoplifting, will also have to be addressed concerning the role of government in helping to prevent crimes that impact profitability and which businesses might be expected to deal with themselves. Without a lead from government, however, many crime problems bringing harm to businesses and their clienteles, or caused by business practices, might never be addressed. Without government research funding, it is also unclear how the requisite body of knowledge about preventing crime in commercial establishments would be accumulated (Felson and Clarke, 1997a).

While its role in policy now seems assured, situational prevention still lacks a strong professional constituency. Since it can be used by such a wide range of public and private organizations, it will never be of more than marginal interest to any particular group of managers. The security industry also may resist an approach which could reduce the demand for guards and security hardware, the industry's main staples. Finally, police interest in situational prevention is likely to be subsumed under problem-oriented policing.

At the same time, situational prevention expertise is increasingly being sought in a wide range of settings, public and private. Towns and cities in Britain and Holland are beginning to appoint crime prevention or "community safety" officers, and some criminologists are already employed in a preventive capacity in business and industry (Burrows, 1997; Challinger, 1997). In America, Felson (1994b) has proposed that university departments of criminology and criminal justice should operate a crime prevention extension service based on the successful agricultural model.

These developments offer considerable training and employment opportunities for criminologists, but not without some changes of attitude. More young criminologists will need to define their theoretical goals more in terms of control than enlightenment, and will need to define control more in terms of reducing opportunities than propensities. They will have to become familiar with a host of social institutions — schools, factories, hospitals, rail and bus systems, shopping malls and retail stores — beyond the courts and the prisons. They must no longer disdain the business world, but must recognize its central role in the production and control of crime (Felson and Clarke, 1997a). Their role models will increasingly need to become traffic engineers and public health specialists — professionals employed to improve everyday life — rather than academics and social commentators. In short, a more down-to-earth, pragmatic approach will be required.

Sutton (1996) and O'Malley (1997) have argued that such pragmatism conflicts with the philosophy and values of criminology students, many of whom aspire to be social reformers seeking a reduction in inequality and deprivation. While these are admirable ambitions, equally rewarding and challenging careers await those who can shift their professional goals from long-term social reform to making an immediate reduction in crime — which, after all, harms the very people they seek to help.

The Selection of Case Studies

Given the ever-present threat of displacement and the implementation difficulties discussed above, it should not be surprising that situational projects sometimes fail. Indeed, the history of Criminology is littered with failed attempts to reduce crime. What makes situational prevention interesting is that it so frequently works. This explains the present volume's emphasis on success. Many of the studies included report substantial reductions (often 50 percent or more) in the offenses addressed. Only the last case study, Shearing and Stenning's description of crowd management in Disney World, which includes no evaluation, falls outside this definition. However, there can hardly be a criminologist in the western world who has visited Disney World (and probably most of them have) who would not agree with the authors' conclusions about the security and safety of that environment.

The studies report deliberate efforts to prevent crime. Studies that have merely found a relationship between situational variables and crime have not been included. While some of the studies reprinted were not undertaken explicitly within a situational prevention context, their approach and methodology qualify them for inclusion.

As explained in the Preface, deciding which studies to include was more difficult for this second edition of the book than for the first one, because there are now so many more successful projects to choose from. In some instances, the measures were so straightforward and the evaluation so unproblematic that little academic purpose would have been served by reprinting the original paper. Where there was a choice between similar studies, those that dealt with displacement or that permitted comment (in the editorial note preceding each study) on some other important issue were selected. Some reports or articles on important successes, including the prevention of airline hijackings, could not be included without major editing which was not a practical possibility.

An important consideration governing the choice of studies among the remaining eligible ones was the need to demonstrate the generality of situational prevention by including studies that covered a variety of environmental contexts and offenses. Environmental contexts covered include private homes, shops, post offices, convenience stores,

TABLE 3
THE SIXTEEN OPPORTUNITY-REDUCING TECHNIQUES AND
ILLUSTRATIVE CASE STUDIES

The techniques	*The case studies**
1. Target Hardening	1, (15)
2. Access Control	2, (6), (11)
3. Deflecting Offenders	3, 4,
4. Controlling Facilitators	5,6,7
5. Entry/Exit Screening	8
6. Formal Surveillance	9, 10, 11, 12, 13, (3), (15), (21)
7. Surveillance by Employees	14, (7)
8. Natural Surveillance	15, 16, (4), (11)
9. Target Removal	(7),(14)
10. Identifying Property	17
11. Reducing Temptation	18
12. Denying Benefits	19
13. Rule Setting	20, (21)
14. Stimulating Conscience	22**
15. Controlling Disinhibitors	21
16. Facilitating Compliance	23

*Parentheses indicate secondary illustration.
**Case Study #22, concerned with the design of the Washington Metro illustrates use of all techniques.

parking facilities, public telephones, street markets, night life and red light districts, leisure complexes and different forms of public transport. The offenses covered include auto thefts, welfare fraud, toll fraud, burglary, robbery, employee theft and shoplifting, drunkenness and assaults, vandalism, graffiti, soliciting, fare evasion and obscene phone calling.

Finally, it was important to include examples of all sixteen opportunity-reducing techniques. All are in fact represented, though not equally. Not unexpectedly, it proved easier to find examples of the use of well-established techniques such as target hardening and formal surveillance than of the more recent techniques falling under the general category of "removing excuses." The sequence of studies in the volume was largely determined by the techniques illustrated (see Table 3).

Notes

1. Coleman (1985:16) is quite mistaken in describing the Home Office studies as being undertaken "to refute Newman's thesis." On the contrary, the limited support for his ideas provided by this research was a considerable disappointment to the researchers involved who included the present author.
2. The classification of 16 situational techniques makes a distinction between controls on facilitators and on disinhibitors (Table 1).
3. Partly due to concerns raised by Wortley (1996) and Newman (1997), some further changes have been made here in Clarke and Homel's classification. Specifically, "removing excuses" has been substituted for "inducing shame and guilt," and "stimulating conscience" for "strengthening moral condemnation."
4. This work on slug use was undertaken in the Criminal Law Education and Research Center of New York University, under the direction of my colleague, G.O.W. Mueller, now at Rutgers. Sitting in his office is one of the old parking meters without slug-rejecter or coin window. Would that more criminologists had such tangible evidence of the practical value of their work!
5. The Insurance Institute for Highway Safety (1995) has been pursuing an alternative solution to this problem with some success by lengthening the yellow signal and/or the period during which the light is red in all directions.
6. As mentioned in the editor's note to *Case Study #3*, Lowman (1992) found extensive displacement of prostitution into nearby streets when a similar street-closure scheme was introduced in Vancouver. This seems to have been due to the Vancouver prostitutes' need for money to support drug habits. The implication is that similar preventive actions may have different displacement effects depending on the precise nature of the settings and offenders involved (cf. McNamara, 1994). A further example is provided by Curtis and Sviridoff (1994) who argued that street-level drug enforcement undertaken by police in three different areas of New York City had varying displacement effects because of differences in the social organization of the drug selling enterprises.
7. In line with this reasoning, Eck (1993) has postulated that displacement follows a "familiarity decay" function, in that it is most likely to involve similar times, places, targets and behaviors to the offenses blocked. Bouloukos and Farrell (1997) have taken this line of reasoning one step further and have used the concept of familiarity decay together with that of "crime scripts" (Cornish, 1994) in arguing that displacement is less likely to occur when repeat victimizations have been prevented.
8. Similar reductions in motorcycle theft have been reported in Britain (Mayhew *et al.,*(1976), Holland (Van Straelen, 1978) and Madras, India (Natarajan and Clarke, 1994) following the enactment of helmet laws.

PART TWO

Case Studies

1. Steering Column Locks and Motor Vehicle Theft: Evaluations from Three Countries

Barry Webb

EDITOR'S NOTE: Evaluations of situational prevention are often short-term and little is known about the durability of its successes, which makes this case study particularly important. Originally published in Crime Prevention Studies *(Webb, 1994), it shows that the success of steering column locks in reducing auto theft has been maintained for a substantial time period — for nearly forty years in the case of Germany and for nearly thirty years in Britain and America where the locks were introduced later. The locks' effectiveness was first documented in* Crime as Opportunity *(Mayhew et al., 1976), the Home Office's initial venture in situational prevention. A journal reviewer of the publication said that the idea of reducing opportunities for crime would "never catch on;" Webb's case study shows just how wrong such predictions can be.*

Introduction

The introduction of car security devices into car design has become an important approach to the prevention of car theft. This has focused on two aspects of car design: improving perimeter security to prevent breaking-in to cars, and installing systems that disable the vehicle when parked to prevent it from being unlawfully driven away.

In the early history of the motor car, there was very little in-built security with the cabs of the first vehicles being completely open. Gradually, as glass windows and locks were introduced to doors, the level of car security increased. However, this was not always seen as beneficial. In London, obstructions caused by parked vehicles had become a serious problem by the 1920s due to increased vehicle congestion and the lack of any properly developed car parking strategy. Physically moving parked vehicles, facilitated by the open cab design of the early vehicles, had been an important method of managing this problem. The more secure vehicle design of the closed and locked cab prevented this, so between 1928 and 1932 car owners were prohibited by law from locking their vehicles when parking them in public places.

As attention focused more seriously on the growing problem of car theft and the need for car security, door locking systems and devices for protecting ignition switches were improved (Karmen, 1981). 'T' shaped door handles and locks were replaced with 'D' shaped handles to prevent the use of pipes to break the handles off. Eventually, locks were incorporated into the door itself. For many years vehicles were started using push-button ignition switches. These were protected in the early days by removing handles or plugs, but after 1910 locks were built into ignition switches. Chrysler has been attributed with pioneering the modern key-operated starter switch in 1949 (Harding *et al.*, 1987), a development which was quickly adopted by other manufacturers.

The growing problem of car theft, however, and the ease with which thieves were able to overcome the existing car security devices (see Karmen, 1981) led eventually to the introduction of legislation in Europe and the United States in the 1960s and 1970s which for the first time required manufacturers to fit cars with anti-theft devices. These regulations focused on preventing cars from being unlawfully driven away, and provided motor manufacturers with a number of options including transmission locks and devices to prevent the engine from running. The favored option adopted by nearly all manufacturers was the steering wheel or column lock, as this was considered to be more effective than the other devices.

The Introduction of Steering Column Locks in Europe and the United States

The Federal Republic of Germany (FRG) was the first country to make the incorporation of anti-theft devices in motor vehicle design compulsory. Regulations were drawn up on the design and fitting of protective devices against unauthorized use of motor vehicles in 1961, and these were included in the FRG Traffic Licensing Regulations in July of that year. The types of protective devices suggested by the regulations included gear box and gear lever locks and devices to prevent the engine from running. The vehicle manufacturers focused exclusively on the steering wheel lock.

The German regulations required all new cars and motor cycles capable of speeds of 25 km/h or more coming onto the road for the first time on or after the 1st July 1961 to be fitted with an anti-theft device that conformed to the standard. By 30th June 1962, all such vehicles on the road had to be so equipped. Stringent testing procedures were instituted to ensure locks complied with the recommended standard.

It was not until ten years later that motor manufacturers in Britain and the United States introduced steering column locks in their cars. In Britain, this was achieved through a voluntary agreement negotiated between the Home Office and the Society of Motor Manufacturers and Traders (SMMT) in which every motor manufacturer gave an undertaking to fit anti-theft devices according to the agreed specification. The specification was similar to that introduced in Germany and, again, manufacturers opted for the steering column lock. However, unlike the German legislation the British agreement applied only to new passenger cars and did not cover motor cycles. Steering column locks were to be fitted to all new car models from the 1st January 1970 and to all cars of existing models coming on to the road for the first time on or after the 1st January 1971.

In 1970, shortly after the British agreement had been reached, the United Nations Economic Commission for Europe agreed a similar standard for anti-theft devices in motor vehicles (ECE Regulation 18). This regulation, which applied to all four-wheeled motor vehicles, was accepted by the UK in 1972. Acceptance of the regulation did not have the force of legislation. What it provided was a standard, and in accepting this standard Governments were undertaking not to introduce more stringent regulations that would prohibit the use of vehicles on its roads which conformed to the ECE regulation. However, this standard was eventually incorporated into legislation. In 1973 it was issued as a European Community Directive (Council Directive 74/61/EEC) and the type approval regulations for Great Britain were accordingly amended in 1975 (The Motor Vehicle (Type Approval) (Amendment) Regulations 1975).

In the United States, concern in the mid-1960s about car theft was fueled by reports that so-called "joy-riders" were from 47 to 200 times more likely to be involved in a traffic accident than other drivers (Karmen, 1981). In 1966, Federal Motor Vehicle Safety Standard 114 was passed, although this was not to become effective until 1970. It required all manufacturers to equip new passenger cars with a key-locking system that prevented the car from being steered or driven forward without the ignition key. With the exception of SAAB, who focused on the prevention of forward motion, all of the major manufacturers selling cars in the US market began installing steering column locks in their vehicles in 1969 (Lee and Rikoski, 1984).

The Effect of Steering Column Locks on Motor Vehicle Theft in Germany

Shortly after the agreement between the SMMT and Home Office came into effect, doubt began to be expressed about the effectiveness of the steering column locks being fitted to cars. A report prepared by the Metropolitan Police in 1971 claimed that officers in the Traffic Division were able to overcome many steering column locks when trying to remove illegally parked cars. It was felt that, because there was no central testing of lock designs many were of inferior quality. The German regulations were considered much more stringent since these required the steering column locks to be approved by a central testing facility. In 1972, Metropolitan Police officers went to Germany to examine the methods used to test steering column locks and obtain views on the effectiveness of these locks and the standards set by ECE Regulation 18.

The report of that visit included an examination of thefts of all motor vehicles (including motor cycles as well as cars) in the Federal Republic of Germany between 1960 and 1970. The figures showed a reduction in thefts after the anti-theft regulations took effect in 1961 and that this lower level of theft was sustained until 1970 by which time theft figures had again reached pre-regulation levels. This pattern can be seen in figure 1 which shows thefts of motor vehicles in what was the Federal Republic of Germany between

FIGURE 1
NUMBER OF THEFTS AND UNAUTHORIZED TAKINGS OF MOTOR
VEHICLES IN GERMANY, 1957-1989

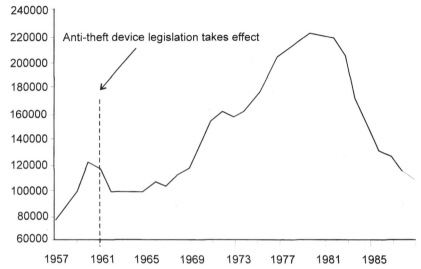

Source: Bundeskriminalamt, *Polizeiliche Kriminalstatistik*. Wiesbaden: Bundeskriminalamt
1960-1989.

Figure 1 shows a clear and immediate drop in thefts of motor vehicles after steering column locks were introduced in cars and motor cycles in 1961. Motor vehicle thefts in 1963, the first full year after steering column locks were fitted to all cars, were 20% lower than in 1960. This lower level of theft was sustained until the end of the decade. However, thefts began to rise towards the end of this period and continued to grow at a fast rate over the next decade. By 1980 the annual number of thefts and unauthorized takings of motor vehicles had reached twice that of 1960, the last year before steering column locks were introduced. The fall in motor vehicle thefts since 1980 is as dramatic as their growth during the previous decade, with thefts reducing to the numbers recorded 30 years ago. This sharp rise and fall in motor vehicle thefts is mainly due to changes in thefts of mopeds and motor cycles, which made up a substantial proportion of motor vehicle thefts. The drop in motor vehicle thefts in the 1980s follows the introduction of motor cycle helmet legislation in the FRG (Mayhew *et al.*, 1989). Thefts of mopeds and motor cycles are examined in more detail later in this section.

Figure 1 suggests that steering column locks had only a relatively short term beneficial effect on the motor vehicle theft statistics in the FRG. However, when the increase in number of motor vehicles on the road is taken into account a rather different and more encouraging picture emerges. Figure 2 shows the number of thefts and unauthorized taking of motor vehicles for every 100,000 registered vehicles in the FRG over the last 30 years. This figure also shows the rate of theft and unauthorized taking specifically of cars and other vehicles with four or more wheels (e.g. buses, lorries, coaches). In 1963 the Bundeskriminalamt began disaggregating their vehicle theft statistics to show thefts of these vehicles separately from thefts of mopeds and motor cycles. Lorries, buses and coaches were not included in the anti-theft legislation. However, these only made up a small proportion of "four or more wheeled vehicles." Most vehicles in this group are cars, so one might expect the pattern of theft for this group of vehicles to reflect theft of cars more

FIGURE 2

RATE OF THEFT AND UNAUTHORIZED TAKING OF MOTOR VEHICLES IN
GERMANY, 1957-1989 PER 100,000 VEHICLE REGISTRATIONS

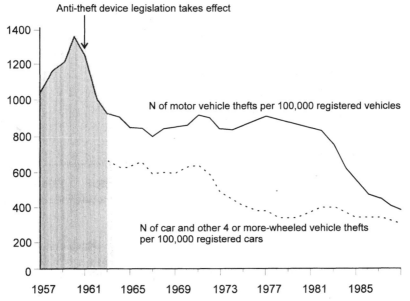

Source: Bundeskriminalamt, *Polizeiliche Kriminalstatistik*. Wiesbaden: Bundeskriminalamt.
United Nations, *Annual Bulletin of Transport Statistics for Europe*. New York: United Nations.

closely than theft of all motor vehicles.

Since 1957, there has been a five-fold increase in the number of vehicles on the road in the FRG. When this phenomenon is taken into account, a much more positive picture of the risk of vehicle theft over the last 30 years is revealed. Figure 2 shows that after the anti-theft device legislation took effect, the rate of motor vehicle theft steadily fell over following the six years. Throughout the 1970s, the rate of vehicle theft remained stable. Although the number of vehicle thefts increased by 92% between 1969 and 1980, the number of vehicle on the road also increased by 91%. A second period of reducing theft rates can then be seen during the 1980s.

The pattern of theft for "four or more wheeled vehicles" between 1963 and 1972 is very similar to that for motor vehicles as a whole. However, the rate of theft of these vehicles continues to drop throughout the following decade in contrast with the rate for all vehicles which shows no reductions until the early 1980s. These data therefore suggest that steering column locks have had a more beneficial long-term effect on car theft. Unfortunately, it is not possible to assess the immediate effect of steering column locks on car theft since the motor vehicle theft statistics have only been disaggregated since 1963. It had been thought that car theft had reduced substantially following the introduction of steering column locks. Mayhew *et al.* (1976) reported a crime reduction of 63% for thefts of cars in 1963 compared with 1960. However, it has subsequently been discovered that the Bundeskriminalamt report on which these data were based did not take into account the inclusion of motor cycles in the statistics prior to 1963 and their exclusion in this and subsequent years.

Although cars make up the vast bulk of motor vehicles in the FRG, they have not always been the main target of vehicle thefts. Since 1963, thefts of mopeds and motor cycles have made up between 40% and 70% of all motor vehicle thefts and unauthorized takings in the FRG. This, together with the much smaller number of mopeds and motor cycles on the road in the FRG compared with cars means that the risk of motor cycle theft is very much greater than that for cars. Figure 3 shows the rate of motor cycle and moped theft between

FIGURE 3
RATE OF THEFT AND UNAUTHORIZED TAKING OF MOPEDS AND MOTOR
CYCLES COMPARED WITH OTHER MOTOR VEHICLES IN GERMANY, 1963-1989

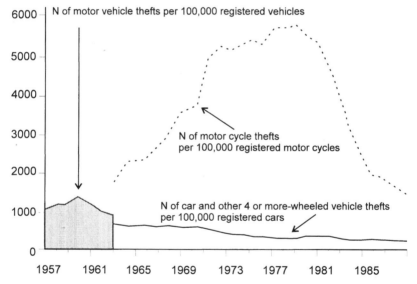

Source: Bundeskriminalamt, *Polizeiliche Kriminalstatistik*. Wiesbaden: Bundeskriminalamt
United Nations, *Annual Bulletin of Transport Statistics for Europe*. New York: United Nations.

1963-1989 compared with theft of other motor vehicles.

The growth in rate of moped and motor cycle theft between 1963 and 1980 is very marked, and reaches levels far in excess of the rate of car theft. Numerically, moped and motor cycle thefts had also grown to outnumber car thefts by 1973 and by 1980 made up 70% of all thefts of motor vehicles in the FRG. This is far greater than in Britain and the US where motor cycles have been found at various times to make up no more than 11% of vehicle thefts (Richards, 1993; Lee and Rikoski, 1984). The equally dramatic reduction in motor cycle theft that has taken place in Germany since 1980 follows the introduction of motor cycle helmet legislation (Mayhew *et al.*, 1989).

The rapid increase in the rate of theft of mopeds and motor cycles shown in Figure 3 suggests that steering column locks have been ineffective as a theft prevention device in these vehicles. Technically, the locks fitted to motor cycles and cars had to conform to the same standard. However, it may be easier to break steering column locks on motor cycles since handlebars enable much greater force to be applied to the lock than a steering wheel and the locks are more exposed to tampering. Motor cycles can also be moved by hand much more easily than cars. Even with the steering column lock applied, the front wheel can be raised so that the motor cycle can be wheeled away. It may even be possible to lift some light mopeds completely off the ground.

It is important to note, however, that Figure 3 shows thefts of all mopeds and motor cycles, including those with speeds of less than 25kmh which were not covered by the anti-theft device legislation. Transport statistics show that small mopeds make up a large proportion of the moped and motor cycle population in Germany. In 1967, 1972 and 1977 mopeds with an engine capacity of 50cc or less made up 72%, 86% and 77% of all mopeds and motor cycles on the road in Germany respectively.

Figure 4 provides further evidence that steering column locks have had a beneficial long term effect on theft of cars. This figure compares the pattern of theft of cars and other 4-or-more wheeled vehicles 1963-1989 with thefts from the inside of these vehicles.

The growth in theft from cars in the FRG over the 30 years since the anti-theft device regulations became effective is very striking, and bears resemblance to the pattern seen in Britain over the same period (Webb and Laycock, 1992a). Thefts of cars in the FRG, however, have remained at much lower levels throughout this period. This contrasts with the situation in Britain where thefts of and from cars were reported throughout the late

FIGURE 4
NUMBER OF THEFTS AND UNAUTHORIZED TAKINGS OF, AND THEFTS
FROM THE INSIDE OF CARS AND OTHER 4 OR MORE-WHEELED
VEHICLES IN GERMANY, 1963-1989

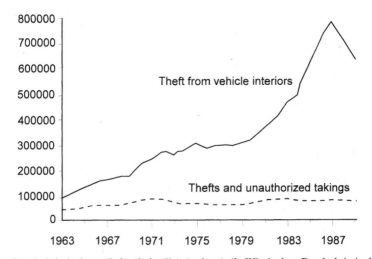

Source: Bundeskriminalamt, *Polizeiliche Kriminalstatistik*. Wiesbaden: Bundeskriminalamt

1960s and 1970s in very similar numbers. Together, Figures 2, 3 and 4 do seem to provide strong evidence that steering column locks helped to keep theft of cars in the FRG down to much lower levels than might otherwise have been expected in an environment where other forms of motor vehicle crime have been reported in large numbers.

The Effect of Steering Column Locks on Motor Vehicle Theft in Britain

In 1976 the Home Office published research which examined the effect of steering column locks on vehicle theft in Britain (Mayhew *et al.*, 1976). Unlike the situation in Germany, it was clear that the agreement negotiated between the Home Office and the SMMT had had little immediate impact on the overall vehicle theft figures. Thefts of motor vehicles in 1973, three years after the agreement had begun to implemented, were 42% higher nationally than in 1969, the last year before steering column locks began to be fitted. Since the British agreement only applied to new cars manufactured in or imported into Britain, it might perhaps have been unrealistic to expect an immediate impact on the national vehicle theft figures.

However, an immediate impact on theft of new motor vehicles was found. New cars in the study sample accounted for 20.9% of all vehicles stolen in 1969 but only 5.1% of vehicle thefts in 1973. The reason why this had not been reflected in the overall theft figures was that thefts appeared to have been displaced to older vehicles unprotected by steering column locks. The risk of theft to these cars had nearly doubled over the same period.

On the basis of these findings it was argued that overall vehicle theft figures might be expected to reduce as the proportion of cars on the road protected by steering column locks increased. In 1973, only 37% of cars in London were fitted with steering column locks. It was estimated that this would increase to 81% by 1980, and that at this point the more casual thefts of cars should show signs of reducing.

Figure 5 shows the rate of theft and unauthorized taking of motor vehicles in England and Wales between 1968-1990 compared with theft from vehicles. This rate is expressed as the number of thefts per 100,000 motor vehicles registered in Great Britain.

Figure 5 does not show any reduction in the rate of theft and unauthorized taking of motor vehicles in England and Wales after the anti-theft device agreement took effect. However, Figure 5 does show that as a proportion of all motor vehicle crime theft of vehicles has been reducing since 1980. Both theft of and from vehicles were reported in similar numbers between 1968 and 1980. Since 1980 thefts from vehicles have grown at a much accelerated rate, with the risk of this form of vehicle crime doubling between 1980 and 1990 from 154 thefts per 100,000 vehicles to 319 thefts. In contrast, the rate of theft of cars has stabilized since 1980 with very little increase over the following decade (169 thefts per 100,000 vehicles to 204).

These data do seem to provide evidence that the protection of a growing proportion of the motor vehicle population in Britain has helped to control vehicle theft. These data may also suggest, as in Germany, a displacement away from vehicle theft to other forms of vehicle crime, in this case stealing property from vehicles. However, some of the increase in theft from vehicles will be due to increased reporting. British Crime Surveys found that 30% and 40% of victims of such theft reported it to the police in 1981 and 1987 respectively (Mayhew, Elliott and Dowds, 1989). It is also likely that thefts from vehicles would have increased at the same rate even if theft of vehicles had remained unchanged. Webb and Laycock (1992a) suggest that the increase in theft from cars is partly due to the increased presence and attractiveness of in-car entertainment systems in cars.

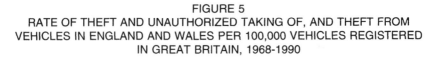

FIGURE 5
RATE OF THEFT AND UNAUTHORIZED TAKING OF, AND THEFT FROM
VEHICLES IN ENGLAND AND WALES PER 100,000 VEHICLES REGISTERED
IN GREAT BRITAIN, 1968-1990

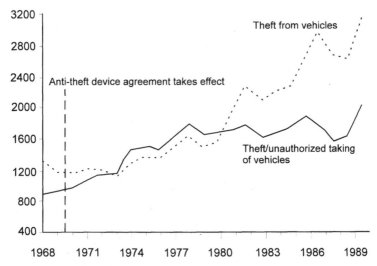

Source: Home Office, *Criminal Statistics England and Wales*. London: HMSO
Department of Transport, *Transport Statistics Great Britain*. London: HMSO

There is further evidence of a change in the nature of vehicle theft in Britain that may
be attributable to steering column locks and which may explain why the effect on national
statistics is not as dramatic as might have been hoped. It has long been recognized that
vehicle theft is a complex phenomenon, made up of a number of quite distinct problems.
A key distinction is between the taking of vehicles for temporary personal use, and the theft
of vehicles for financial gain. At the time of the original evaluation it was felt that steering
column locks were most likely to deter the more casual and less determined thief who takes
the vehicle for temporary personal use. In Britain, the national motor vehicle theft statistics
do not distinguish these different types of theft. However, data are available which show
whether stolen vehicles were subsequently recovered or not and these may distinguish
thefts for temporary use from more professional theft for financial gain. Figure 6 shows
these data. Thefts of vehicles which are not recovered will also include some insurance
fraud where the owners are involved in the disappearance of their vehicle.

Most vehicles that are taken illegally are recovered some time later. Unrecovered
vehicles make up the minority of thefts. However, Figure 6 shows that the balance between
these two types of theft has been steadily changing over the last 10-15 years with an
increasing proportion of stolen cars remaining unrecovered. This suggests that the vehicle
theft problem in Britain is becoming less dominated by more casual thefts for temporary
use and involves more theft for financial gain, with more professional theft or insurance
fraud. These data support the view that the steering column lock policy in Britain has helped
to reduce more casual thefts of vehicles. Clearly, however, these devices are less effective
at controlling more determined theft which has increased.

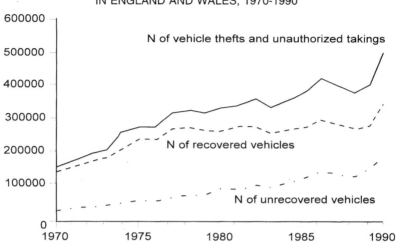

FIGURE 6
NUMBER OF RECOVERED AND UNRECOVERED STOLEN VEHICLES
IN ENGLAND AND WALES, 1970-1990

Source: Home Office

The Effect of Steering Column Locks on Motor Vehicle Theft in the United States

Concern about the increasing problem of motor vehicle theft in the USA led the FBI to conduct a national survey on behalf of the Vehicle Theft Committee of the International Association of Chiefs of Police (FBI, 1975). The survey was carried out during the months of September and October 1974 and collected data on 85% of all vehicles reported stolen nationally in that period. The information requested in the survey included location, time and place of theft; type, year and model of vehicle stolen; and details of offenders arrested. The data on type and year of passenger cars stolen were examined for evidence of the impact of the steering column locks which motor manufacturers had been fitting to new cars since 1969. Table 1 (next page) presents this analysis.

The data shown in Table 1 were interpreted as evidence that steering column locks were having a beneficial effect on vehicle theft. Cars protected by steering column locks made up nearly 58% of cars on the road in the US in 1974 but only 45% of vehicles stolen in that year, suggesting that they were less at risk than might have been expected.

No data were collected on the situation before steering column locks began to be fitted by motor manufacturers, so the conclusion that Table 1 shows the effect of steering column locks must be treated cautiously. Houghton (1992) reports that older cars are more at risk of theft in Britain than younger models, despite having steering column locks, and that similar results have been found in Australia. Although newer cars are more likely to have better security, there may also be other reasons why older vehicles are more at risk of theft. For example, since older cars are more likely to be owned by poorer sections of the population, they are more likely to be parked in high crime areas and less likely to be garaged.

TABLE 1
TYPE AND YEAR OF PASSENGER CARS STOLEN
IN THE UNITED STATES SEPTEMBER-OCTOBER 1974

	1968 and older models	1969 and newer models
As a proportion of all vehicles on the road	42.1%	57.9%
As a proportion of all vehicles stolen	54.7%	45.3%

Source: FBI (1974), *Crime in the United States: Uniform Crime Reports 1974*. Washington, DC: US Department of Justice.

Figure 7 shows the rate of theft of and from all motor vehicles in the US per 100,000 registered vehicles between 1960-1990. This graph shows a rapid growth in the rate of auto theft in the four years before the anti-theft device regulations became effective in 1970. This is followed by an immediate reduction in the rate of theft. How far this can be attributed to the introduction of steering column locks in new cars is uncertain. The same pattern can also be seen for theft from vehicles, which would not be expected to be affected by steering column locks. In addition, the British data suggest that one would not expect to see such an immediate reduction in the rate of auto theft as the legislation only affected new cars.

FIGURE 7
RATE OF AUTO THEFT AND THEFT FROM VEHICLES IN THE USA PER 100,000
REGISTERED VEHICLES, 1967-1990

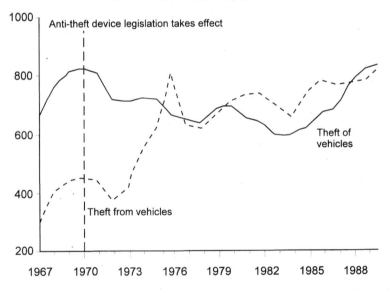

Source: US Department of Justice, *Sourcebook of Criminal Justice Statistics*. Washington, DC: US Department of Justice

However, the rate of auto theft continued to drop throughout the 1970s until 1983 when it began to grow rapidly. Theft from cars increased enormously during this period. This does provide much stronger evidence that the protection afforded to an increasing proportion of the US vehicle population by steering column locks has had a beneficial effect on auto theft, at least for a decade.

Further support for the view that steering column locks reduced the risk of auto theft in the US comes from work which has examined the impact of more general social factors on the US automobile theft rate (Cohen *et al.*, 1980). It was found that the automobile theft rate between 1973-1977 was much lower than would have been expected on the basis of population density, unemployment rate, proportion of population aged 15-24, and number of automobiles per capita. It was felt that this lower rate of theft was due in part to the introduction of improved vehicle ignition security systems.

The data from Britain suggest that, since only new vehicles were fitted with these devices, one might not have expected to see any impact on national figures for some years. However, Table 1 suggests that the vehicle population in the US is fairly young with only 42% of cars on the road being six or more years old. Also, in the eight years following the introduction of steering column locks the number of registered vehicles increased at an average annual rate of 4% in the US and 2.5% in Britain suggesting that the size of the new vehicle population was increasing faster in the US than in Britain. In this context, introducing steering column locks in new cars may have had a faster impact on the general security level of the US vehicle population.

It has also been suggested that the higher level of vehicle ownership in the US compared with Britain means that more potential offenders may have legitimate access to a car (Clarke and Harris, 1992a). Increased car security may have a greater impact under these circumstances where young people have less need or are less motivated to steal cars for temporary use.

British data presented earlier suggested that steering column locks had helped to reduce theft of vehicles for temporary use but not theft involving permanent loss of the vehicle which had been increasing. Clarke and Harris (1992a) report that the same trend may also be taking place in the US, with reductions in the proportion of arrests for vehicle theft involving juveniles, auto theft clearance rates and recoveries of stolen vehicles. However, Clarke and Harris conclude that the evidence for such a change in the nature of auto theft in the US is not very strong, pointing out discrepancies between two sources of data on recovery rates and the fact that changes in arrests and clearance rates may be explained by changes in enforcement priorities.

Conclusions

There is a considerable amount of evidence that action taken by Governments leading to the introduction of steering column locks by motor manufacturers has had a beneficial effect on motor vehicle theft. Data from three countries show that overall motor vehicle theft rates either reduced or stabilized after anti-theft device legislation and agreements became effective, and that this effect was sustained over long periods. British data suggest that these locks have had most effect on the more casual takings of motor vehicles for temporary use.

Variations in the vehicle theft patterns in the three countries examined reflect the speed with which vehicle populations were protected by steering column locks. Only in Germany has an immediate reduction in vehicle theft been found which is clearly associated with the anti-theft device policy requiring all cars and motor cycles to be fitted with steering column locks within a very short period. Car theft has continued to reduce to rates which are much lower than in either Britain or the US. The stronger effect of steering column locks on the vehicle theft rate in the US, where only new cars were fitted with these devices, compared with Britain appears to be related to the faster renewal of the vehicle population in the US.

It has been suggested that, by requiring cars to be fitted with anti-theft devices within a very short period the FRG legislation helped to destroy a car theft "culture" amongst juveniles (Clarke and Harris, 1992a). The immediate effect of the FRG regulations specifically on cars is not known. However, this view is supported by data suggesting displacement of theft away from cars to unprotected mopeds but no displacement back to cars after helmet legislation reduced moped and motor cycle theft. Evidence of displacement was also found in Britain, but this involved thieves focusing on other cars not fitted with steering column locks rather than on other types of vehicle, so that there was less dramatic impact on the car theft culture.

Since the anti-theft device regulations were introduced, the motor vehicle crime problem has changed considerably in nature in all three countries. This may partly be due to the improved protection of cars from being unlawfully driven away with criminal activity focusing on other forms of motor vehicle crime. It may also reflect changes in availability and demand for vehicles and vehicle parts. Theft from vehicles has grown rapidly in all three countries studied here to become, in numerical terms, one of the biggest crime problems faced by these countries. Webb and Laycock (1992a) suggest that, at least in Britain, the growth in theft from vehicles is associated with the fitting of radio-cassette players as standard equipment in mass market cars. There is also evidence from Britain, and perhaps the US, that theft involving permanent loss of the vehicle, either through thieves stealing for financial gain or insurance fraud, is growing. Anecdotal evidence suggests that this is also a growing problem in Germany involving cross-border trafficking of stolen vehicles into eastern Europe. Clearly, attention now needs to focus on these aspects of the motor vehicle crime problem which lie outside the scope of the anti-theft device regulations introduced in the 1960s and 1970s.

2. An Evaluation of Walkway Demolition on a British Housing Estate

Barry Poyner

EDITOR'S NOTE: As explained in the Introduction, *Oscar Newman's "defensible space" work has powerfully influenced public housing in many parts of the world. His influence is evident in this study, first published in* Crime Prevention Studies *(Poyner, 1994), of measures taken on a housing estate in London to exclude predatory offenders — the provision of entry phones to enable residents to screen visitors' access and the demolition of walkways linking the buildings which were thought to provide access for criminals. The study has two important lessons for evaluation, the first of which is to treat cautiously any claims of success not supported by careful research. Poyner shows that, contrary to press reporting of police data, no general reduction in crime followed demolition of the walkways, though some specific effects were evident. The second lesson is that detailed analysis of time series of disaggregated crime statistics can help to unravel the preventive effects of a package of measures. In this case, Poyner shows that more effective than walkway demolition was the earlier (and cheaper) installation of entry phones.*

Background to the Evaluation

A characteristic feature of much British medium-rise high-density public housing built in the 1960s and 1970s was the overhead walkway system (see Figure 1). The concept of "streets in the air" seems to have derived from the ideas of the famous French architect Le Corbusier in his utopian vision of the *Ville Radieuse*. Instead of housing blocks being isolated from each other, they were connected by a network of walkways and corridors on several levels or decks above ground. This enabled pedestrians to move around the estate without the need to return to ground level.

By the mid-1980s, these walkway systems had become associated with many of the problems of run down public-sector housing. In particular, they were being blamed for increasing crime and residents' and visitors' fear of being attacked.

In her book *Utopia on Trial*, Alice Coleman (1985) listed walkway systems as one of the main conditions allowing incivilities and crime to develop in housing schemes. She described them as one of the "ringleaders of the anti-social design gang" (p.80). She found that a number of other "bad" design features such as a large number of apartments per entrance and variables to do with pedestrian access were associated with the presence of overhead walkways.

Coleman summed up her view of walkways as follows.

> All these things add up to the undesirability of anthill designs riddled with walkways, passages between exits, lifts, staircases and ramps. Fortunately, however, the worst excesses of all these variables can be cut by a single solution: the removal of overhead walkways (1985:67).

These comments should not be dismissed as merely the overstated views of an academic geographer. Her ideas were taken up enthusiastically by a number of politicians in Britain. The following extract from *The London Standard* (Friday, January 17, 1986) illustrates the strength of feeling. Mrs. Kirwan, the chair of Westminster City Council's housing committee, was reported to have said: "We have to remove or block these walkways. They are a design disaster and lead to mugging and other crimes. They can be dark and fearsome places to go. Often tenants won't use them at night for fear of mugging."

Mrs. Kirwan went on to say:

> The walkways on some estates in Southwark and Haringey were used by rioters as they fought with police. At the Broadwater Farm Estate in Tottenham, where P.C. Blakelock was killed, police were bombarded by missiles thrown from walkways. And at a smaller riot in Peckham police refused to venture into a Southwark Council estate for fear of having petrol bombs dropped on them from the walkways.

By the end of 1985, a research team, led by the author, decided to explore the effects of walkway removal on crime, and set about finding a suitable example for evaluation. At the time, the Westminster City Council was removing walkways on its Mozart Estate. It was clearly too early to evaluate walkway removal on that estate as demolition was still in progress. However, it was discovered that seven walkways had been removed on the nearby Lisson Green Estate in 1982, three years earlier, and this seemed an ideal time to assess the effects.

The Lisson Green Estate was being held up as an example of what could be achieved by removing walkways. Mrs. Kirwan publicly claimed that crime on the Lisson Green

Estate had been "drastically cut" as a direct result of the removal of walkways. The member of parliament for the area, Kenneth Baker MP, said that the structural changes at Lisson Green had reduced crime on the estate. He took credit for this improvement, saying he had been a pioneer in the field of "creative demolition" (*Architects' Journal*, March 26, 1986). Under the headline "End of walkways cuts crime" a national newspaper claimed that crime and vandalism on the estate had been reduced by 50% after the walkways were removed.

The Lisson Green Estate

Our first task in the evaluation was to find out more about what had happened on the estate. Experience of previous evaluations had led us to recognize the danger of attributing changes in crime patterns to the one intervention that was the focus of the evaluation. It might have been that other changes had more significant effects than the removal of seven walkways.

The most obvious source of information of changes on the estate was the estate management team. Therefore, contact was made with officials from the City Council's housing department and the estate management office. They were willing to help with the evaluation, but it proved difficult to find precise information about earlier changes on the estate. Officials were aware of the demolition of the walkways, but they could not provide precise dates when work had been done.

In an attempt to locate more precise dates, the research team decided to make a search of back issues of the local weekly newspaper *The Marylebone Mercury*. An estate manager at Lisson Green had mentioned the extensive press coverage given to the estate, and since a complete microfiche record was available at the Marylebone Public Library, it was a comparatively easy task to track down events occurring on the estate. Indeed, the newspaper turned out to be a rich source of information about the estate, and notes were made from a review of five years back issues from 1981-1985.

FIGURE 1
OVERHEAD WALKWAY SYSTEM ON THE LISSON
GREEN ESTATE, LONDON

It was also possible to talk to a reporter on the paper who had taken a special interest in the estate over the years, and who helped form a clear picture of the problems and changes over the five-year period.

The estate has been built from 1972 to 1975. It contains nearly 1,500 apartments in 23 medium-rise six-story blocks. Originally, all blocks were connected by a walkway system at two levels on the 3rd and 5th levels (see Figure 1). One newspaper cutting described the walkways as "an almost uninterrupted run of three-quarters of a mile from one end of the estate to the other."

By the time the evaluation was made, the estate had experienced many of the problems common to large, rundown housing estates in Britain. Examples reported in the local newspaper included: unruly children; problems of rubbish disposal; a spate of muggings; concern about asbestos in the building fabric; inadequate heating; blocked sewers; leaking roofs; problems with elevators; Tenants' Association squabbles; speeding cars on estate roads; congested parking; drugs: and concern over the structural safety of the apartment blocks.

The City Council had responded to many of these problems. A great deal of money had been spent tackling the rubbish disposal problem, overhauling the heating system, removing walkways, installing entry phones and removing the asbestos from inside apartments. The opening of a full-time estate office to deal with management and maintenance problems was considered a particular achievement.

The Removal of Walkways

Walkways were first identified as a problem by the newspaper when a front-page headline read "Skaters and cyclists turn estate into hell" (June 5, 1981). Kids were riding bicycles, skateboards and even motorcycles along the walkways and generally being a nuisance. Residents had suggested the installation of entry phones, which could be fitted to enclosed sections of the walkway system where it passed through the central corridor of some blocks. They had also suggested blocking off or removing sections of the walkway system. The housing department of the City Council responded by saying that walkway removal was too costly, but they did promise to install some entry phones on the estate.

At the same time, mugging was developing into a serious issue, as reported by *The Marylebone Mercury*. The newspaper ran a special campaign in July 1981 highlighting the problem. The estate was described as a place "where elderly live in fear." The blocks were described as "diabolical hell holes," and the newspaper urged the City Council to "close those muggers alleys."

In the year that followed, the City Council was subjected to some considerable pressure from the local member of parliament, Kenneth Baker, who had just been made Minister of State for Industry and Technology. He pressured for the cleaning up of the estate and the installation of entry phones and removal of walkways. The council had already agreed to entry phones, and had made several attempts to clean up rubbish on the estate. Finally, in October 1982, the seven walkway bridges were removed at a cost of nearly £100,000.

The walkway system was cut at both walkway levels at four points. Figure 2 is a photograph of one of these points. Originally there were bridges at both levels between the building on the left and the lift tower in the center of the photograph.

FIGURE 2
WALKWAY SYSTEM WHERE WALKWAYS WERE REMOVED

FIGURE 2
WALKWAY SYSTEM WHERE WALKWAYS WERE REMOVED

Crime Data

The next task was to find out what were the recorded crime problems on the estate. The sources of data were the crime books kept at Paddington Green Police Station. Access to police files was arranged through previous research contacts with the Metropolitan Police.

We had learned from other work that simple "before-and-after" data on a crime prevention intervention was not a reliable way to judge its impact, particularly when other changes were occurring in the period of study. Under these circumstances, it is more revealing to look at the changing pattern of crime over a period.

The effort required to abstract data for an extended period was considerable. It was not possible to use the police computer-based data because the estate boundaries did not coincide with police beat boundaries. In the hope of being fairly economical with research resources. It was decided to restrict crime data for the estate to years 1982, 1983 and 1984. Because the walkway bridges were removed in October 1982, it was hoped that the three years of data would show the levels of crime prior to their removal and the pattern thereafter. It was thought that a period of two years after the demolition was necessary to establish that any change in crime pattern was relatively permanent. Other evaluations had shown that the impact of crime prevention interventions can peak and decay quite quickly (see, for example, Laycock, 1991).

It was not clear which kinds of crime would be most affected by walkways. The local police had based most of their assessment of problem housing estates on the work of their Burglary Analysis Unit, and Lisson Green remained at the top of their list. Mugging had also been referred to on the walkways, but this meant assembling information on "robbery" and "theft from the person," which were recorded in different places, as well as from the "serious crime book" and the "beat crime book." Previous experience of evaluations had shown that auto crime can be a sensitive measure of changes on a housing estate. Thus, it was decided that the analysis would need to include all reported crime.

The first surprise to emerge from the data as it was assembled, was that there were very few burglaries from apartments. On the other hand, there were a large number of robberies and snatches at the beginning of 1982. Both these findings raised questions which could only be answered by going back further to see what crime was like on the estate in 1981 (which were the oldest data available since police records are only kept for five years).

From a cursory analysis of the auto crime data for the four years 1981-1984, it seemed that there was a reduction in thefts from cars in the year after the removal of walkways, but that these had begun to increase in 1984. This led us to decide to extend the analysis of auto crime into 1985, and eventually we decided to extend the whole data collection to cover the five-year period. This gradual expansion of the database extended the number of crimes included in the analysis from a first estimate of 500 to a total of 1,340 for the full five years.

The Overall Pattern of Crime

Table 1 presents a classification and analysis of crime on the estate recorded by the police during 1981-1985. The categories are only roughly based on official police crime definitions, but they were thought to be more useful in understanding how crime was affected by removing walkways.

Looking at the overall crime levels, the total numbers of crimes for each of the five years are fairly stable. There is a slight reduction in the 1983 figure, but there is no major reduction following the removal of the walkways during 1982.

The rate of crime per household was also not as large as on some inner-city problem estates. The rate at Lisson Green averaged about 15 crimes per 100 households. Although this was about twice the average for residential areas in Britain (see, for example, Poyner and Webb, 1991:13), it was comparatively moderate for problem housing estates. The annual rate of recorded crime in other inner-city estates had been known to reach 50 crimes per 100 households and more.

It is often argued that reported crime statistics can be biased in favor of high-profile crime prevention initiatives. One possible way this can be done is for the police to reject more reports as "no crimes." For example, reports of theft or damage may, on investigation, be considered no more than accidental losses and damage. Since the reports which were subsequently "no crimes" were also recorded in the police crime books, it was possible to establish the rate at which reports were "no crimes." The table shows a very stable "no crime" rate at about 20%. If anything, the rate decreases after the walkway removal. If the police had been trying to distort the record, albeit subconsciously, the rate might be expected to rise. From this and the analysis that follows it is unlikely that the police record was biased to support crime prevention programs on the estate.

Looking in more detail at the various types of crime, there are one or two lines in the table which suggest that some crime reduction has taken place. There is an apparent reduction in break-ins and other burglary of apartments in 1982. More dramatically, there is a large reduction in robberies and snatches in 1982 and 1983. The two other categories to show reductions in 1983 are thefts of and from cars and vans. Each of these is discussed in turn.

TABLE 1
A CLASSIFICATION OF RECORDED CRIME ON THE LISSON
GREEN ESTATE DURING 1981-1985

	1981	1982	1983	1984	1985
Break-ins to apartments	21	5	10	13	11
Other apartment burglary	2.1	8	10	16	22
Non-residential burglary	13	21	12	24	28
Damage to apartments	27	20	16	16	40
Other estate damage	9	15	13	6	13
Robberies and snatches	33	17	7	7	11
Other assaults	9	8	8	10	4
Theft (non-auto crime)	13	17	23	18	16
Drug offenses (arrests)	0	4	7	4	5
Theft of cars and vans	23	31	16	11	21
Theft from cars and vans	19	51	37	54	41
Other auto crime	15	21	23	25	27
Other crime	8	4	6	7	6
All Recorded Crime	211	222	188	211	245
Crimes Per 100 Households	14.4	15.1	12.8	14.4	16.6
Reports "No crimes"	54	61	44	48	56
"No crimes" as % of crimes	20%	22%	19%	19%	19%

Burglary of Apartments

It might be imagined that one effect of breaking up the walkway system would be to discourage access by potential burglars, particularly if they were local youths wandering about the estate in a relatively aimless way. To look more closely at the drop in crime shown in Table 1, the research team examined the monthly pattern of break-ins to see if this could be related to the removal of walkways. Figure 3 shows these data slightly simplified into three-month periods through the five years of crime data.

It seems clear from the histogram that the demolition of walkways had no major effect on break-ins to apartments. We could find no explanation for the relatively large number of break-ins for the first quarter of 1981. This peak of activity appears to be due to eight break-ins during March, which could easily have been the work of one active burglar and could not be considered as a significant pattern of crime.

Robberies and Snatches

A similar analysis of robberies and snatches, shown in Figure 4, produced a more interesting picture. It showed that the estate certainly suffered from the "spate of muggings" reported in the local newspaper. Although the graph shows the number of incidents fell to a low point immediately after the demolition of walkway bridges, the problem seems to

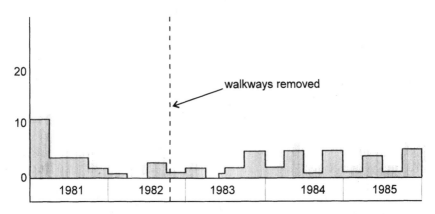

have greatly reduced during the two quarters before demolition began.

The research team sought an explanation for this drop in muggings before demolition. It was then realized that other changes on the estates reported in the local newspaper might be relevant. It was known that some entry phones had been installed in some blocks before the walkway demolition, and so efforts were made to identify which blocks were involved.

FIGURE 4
NUMBER OF ROBBERIES AND SNATCHES ON THE LISSON GREEN ESTATE IN
EACH THREE-MONTH PERIOD, 1981-85

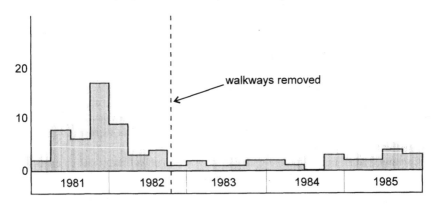

It was discovered from staff at the local estate office that four blocks near the main entry to the walkway system, at point A in Figure 5, were the first to be protected by entry phones. The main pedestrian access to the walkway system is via a ramp from the main street neighboring the estate at point A. Since the main line of the walkway system passed through the central corridors of two of these blocks, it seemed very likely that this would have closed direct access to the walkway system from this main street entrance.

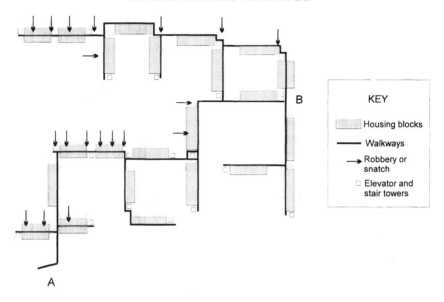

FIGURE 5
LOCATIONS OF ROBBERIES AND SNATCHES ON THE WALKWAY
SYSTEM ON THE LISSON GREEN ESTATE IN THE SIX MONTHS
BEFORE CHANGES WERE MADE

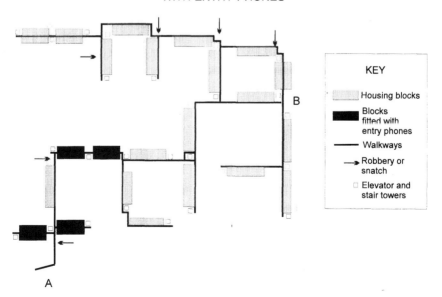

FIGURE 6
LOCATIONS OF ROBBERIES AND SNATCHES ON THE WALKWAY
SYSTEM ON THE LISSON GREEN ESTATE IN THE SIX MONTHS BEFORE
DEMOLITION BUT AFTER THE FIRST FOUR BLOCKS WERE FITTED
WITH ENTRY PHONES

To try to understand the influence of the installation of the entry phones, robberies and snatches that had occurred on the walkways were plotted onto the walkway diagram for three periods of six months: before the entry phones were installed (Figure 5) and after installation of the entry phones but before walkway demolition (Figure 6). There were no incidents in the third six month period. The results were very clear. Figures 5 and 6 show that nearly all the attacks (shown by arrows) occurred before the first entry phones were fitted. A few (three) occurred in the next six months. By the time the seven walkway bridges were down, no more attacks were reported on the walkway system.

While it is clear that the changes to the walkway system have been successful in removing the problem of attacks, it could be claimed that the removal of walkways played a relatively minor part. Closer examination of the distribution of attacks as shown in Figure 5, before any changes were made, revealed that most of the attacks took place on the parts of the walkway which pass through the central corridors of some blocks. These are the parts of the walkway system which most lacked surveillance. Other parts of the walkway system were either on bridges or in long galleries or balconies along the side of blocks (see again Figure 1).

The effectiveness of the entry phones was not only to block the walkway but also to exclude access to the least supervised parts of the walkway system. These more detailed findings suggest that it was not just the walkway that was the problem, but that parts of it lacked surveillance from neighboring buildings and ground level. It is easy to see when visiting the estate that much of the walkway system can be seen from the windows of surrounding apartments, as well as from elsewhere on the walkway system and from the access roads at ground level.

A footnote on the reduction in robberies and snatches might be added. The preoccupation in criminology with the problem of displacement might lead some to assume that the robberies and snatches would be displaced elsewhere. Surely, since it was the walkway system that was blocked, one might expect robberies and snatches to be displaced to the ground level on the estate. In fact, the number of attacks elsewhere on the estate was small and remained at about the same level throughout these changes. In the six months before entry phones were installed, there were six attacks at ground level, in the six months between entry phone installation and the demolition there were four attacks elsewhere, and in the six months after demolition there were three attacks not on the walkways. There is certainly no evidence here to support the displacement theory, but equally no real evidence for a "diffusion of benefits."

Vehicle Crime

The other two crime categories which needed some further investigation were thefts of and from cars and vans. The histogram for theft from cars and vans, shown in Figure 7, indicates a dramatic reduction in offenses in the quarter during which the walkway demolition took place.

Although this reduction in theft from vehicles looks encouraging to anyone hoping to see benefits from the demolition, it seemed to the research team somewhat surprising that these changes should have such an immediate and significant effect on such thefts. It might have been expected that vehicle crime would not be so strongly influenced by the walkway system since car parking is at ground level. The removal of the walkways would have little effect on access to parking areas.

FIGURE 7
NUMBER OF THEFTS <u>FROM</u> CARS AND VANS ON THE LISSON GREEN ESTATE
IN EACH THREE-MONTH PERIOD, 1981-85

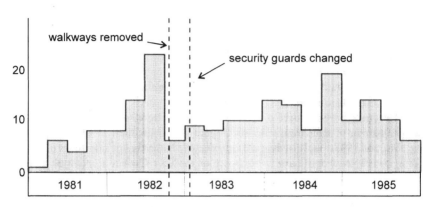

Inquiries were made of the estate management staff to see if they might know of an alternative explanation for this dramatic change in the pattern of thefts from cars. The estate manager was amused to hear of the research team's finding because it immediately reminded him that during the demolition contract it had been necessary to enforce very stringent parking restrictions on the estate roads. Roadways were blocked off and cars removed if they got in the way. Apart from the disruption of car movement and access, it was clear that far fewer cars were able to park on the estate during the last quarter of 1982.

FIGURE 8
NUMBER OF THEFTS <u>OF</u> CARS AND VANS ON THE LISSON GREEN ESTATE IN
EACH THREE-MONTH PERIOD, 1981-85

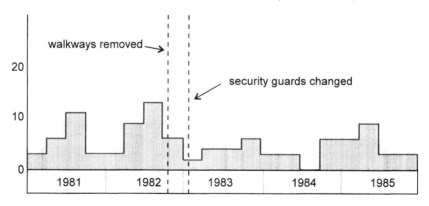

It was clear that such a disruption of parking arrangements and a reduction in the number of cars able to park on the estate could readily account for this change in pattern of theft. However, the pattern of theft of vehicles, presented in Figure 8 shows that the reduction occurs even more strongly in the first quarter of 1983, the quarter after the demolition took place.

Further questioning revealed that shortly after the demolition of walkways the contract for the security guards, who controlled vehicle access to the estate, was changed. Because the estate is close to central London, and particularly close to the business district to the south and east of the nearby Marylebone Station, it had from the start suffered from parking by commuters. To deal with this problem, vehicle access to the estate had been restricted to one entrance at point B on estate layout diagrams. A security point with a kiosk and vehicle barriers had been installed, which is staffed during weekdays by a security guard. In 1982, the City Council became dissatisfied with the performance of the security guards and a new contractor was brought in.

The new guards began work in January 1983 almost three months after the demolition work. The pattern of theft from vehicles (Figure 7) and the theft of vehicles (Figure 8) during 1982 and 1983 could also be partly attributable to the change in security guards. The outgoing contractor would have been aware of the City Council's intention to end its contract, and this could be part of the reason for the peaks of vehicle crime in the second and third quarters of 1982. It could also be the main reason that vehicle crime remained under some control throughout 1983.

The conclusion from these arguments seemed to be that the dip in vehicle crime following the walkway demolition was the result of both the restriction of parking during demolition work and the introduction of a new security guard contract at the beginning of 1983. It seems much less likely that the removal of seven walkway bridges had any direct influence on vehicle crime.

Conclusions about Changes in Crime

The first conclusion is that the evaluation did show that changes to the walkway system had some beneficial effect on crime. However, the effect appears to have been very specific and limited. It appeared to be almost entirely related to robberies and snatches that had been taking place on the walkways, particularly where the walkways were enclosed. Other hoped-for effects, such as on burglary, did not materialize.

The success in reducing robberies and snatches was due to a change in the pattern of use or misuse of the walkways. When the system was complete, it would have been possible for prospective muggers to wander along the full length of the walkways in search of a victim. There would be little to stop this behavior, as the design encouraged anyone to enter from the street via a ramp at point A and walk the whole length of the system and back without appearing suspicious in any way. Once the seven bridges were removed, this pattern of behavior would have become impossible, but even the introduction of the entry phones (as seen in Figure 6) would have made it just as difficult.

A second important conclusion was that by looking at crime data over a long time period, it is possible to explain many of the variations in the pattern of crime in terms of changes in the environment. Providing there is enough information, it should be possible to understand most of the variations in crime. For example, information emerged which may explain the tendency for the overall level of crime on the estate to rise in the fifth year of the study. During 1984 and 1985, the City Council ran a program for the removal of asbestos from inside the apartments. This involved the progressive emptying and renovation of apartments. This was a major program, and while the work was in progress there was an increase in criminal damage to empty apartments, which can be seen in the numbers of crime shown in Table 1 (page 65).

Where Did a 50% Reduction in Crime Come From?

The evaluation revealed only small changes in crime levels. The reduction in crime was in no way of the order originally claimed in the press reports. It seemed important to find out why this was the case, and why the newspapers had reported such grossly inaccurate information.

During the evaluation work, the research team looked at the police file on the estate. It contained several brief notes on crime figures which, no doubt, had been communicated at various times to the housing department. The City Council had asked the police for crime figures on the Lisson Green Estate. The police were unable to provide figures for the estate because their crime data were calculated for police-beat areas. The beat area containing the estate was considerably larger than the estate itself. However, they did provide some figures for the beat area as a whole.

These police figures do not show a crime reduction. However, in an attempt present a positive message, they do claim a reduced annual rate of increase in crime. The figures on the file were:

1981 .... 379 crimes
1982 538
1983 558
1984 560

What appears to have been done with these figures was to calculate the percentage increase for each year, which produced the following percentages as noted on the file:

81 to 82 up by 42%
82 to 83 up by 27% — wrongly calculated; it should have been 3.7%
83 to 84 up by 0.4%

What appears to have happened is that someone had interpreted the change from a 42% increase to a 27% increase as good news, and then described it as reducing the increase in crime by half. Hence someone has ended up quoting a 50% reduction in crime.

To further confuse the popular view, a journalist was reported to have asked a question at a public meeting on crime prevention on a neighboring estate, which was quoted as: "Since a 60% crime reduction had been achieved on Lisson Green, could similar reductions be expected on Mozart?" The figure of 60% was taken for a fact in all subsequent reporting of the issue.

Lessons for Other Evaluations

This was not the first evaluation in which the research team had examined crime data over an extended period (see also Poyner and Webb, 1987b; Poyner and Woodall, 1987), but it was perhaps the clearest demonstration of how crime levels can be influenced by environmental and other changes. It is clear from this kind of study that time-series data are much more sensitive in assessing the effects of crime prevention interventions than the more conventional "before-and-after" studies.

If a "before-and-after" study had been made of vehicle crime on the estate, it would have provided overwhelming evidence to support the idea that walkway removal reduced car crime. Again, an evaluation of the effect on break-ins might have taken 1981 as a "before" condition and 1983 data as an "after" condition. Such a study would indicate a marked improvement, but the evidence of Figure 3 shows that it is very unlikely that the walkway demolition had anything to do with the difference.

A further conclusion can be drawn from such doubts about "before-and-after" comparisons. Many criminologists argue that crime surveys of potential victims give a more accurate indication of crime levels. From this there is a common tendency to disregard police-reported data as unreliable. Of course, doubts can be raised about most sources of data, but if time-series data are necessary for effective evaluations, survey techniques would have to be greatly elaborated to obtain usable data. Not only would this make survey techniques inordinately expensive, but they would become increasingly invasive and no doubt begin to influence criminal behavior on an estate.

FIGURE 9
PHOTOGRAPH OF WALKWAY ON THE
LISSON GREEN ESTATE IN 1993, ABOUT
NINE YEARS AFTER DEMOLITION

A further corollary follows from the use of time-series data. The evaluation shows that much of the effect of walkway improvement came from the introduction of entry phones. As Figure 6 indicates, most of the robberies and snatches on walkways had stopped before the walkways were removed. There seems to be a lesson here. Perhaps all large-scale and expensive proposals for intervention should be carefully monitored before a final decision is made to spend large sums of money. No doubt the City Council's housing committee would have thought twice about embarking on £100,000 expenditure if they had been monitoring crime as in Figure 4 in the months before the demolition contract was let.

Finally, this study demonstrates very clearly the mistake of relying too closely on conventional crime categories. The police were monitoring this estate for its domestic burglary problem, and certainly (as shown in Table 1) there had been some reduction in this offense. But the main effect of changes to the walkway system was to a mixed category of "robbery" and "theft from the person." There is always a need for researchers to go back, wherever possible, to the original crime reports to identify relevant categories for any particular study. Unfortunately, this is becoming ever more difficult with the computerization of records, which can impose rigid structures on the classification of crime information.

Postscript

The overall impression of the findings from this evaluation was that the threat of robberies or purse snatches on the walkways had virtually disappeared. In preparing this rewriting of the original paper, the author revisited the estate and found further evidence that residents' feelings of security along the walkways had continued to increase. Whereas in 1986 the walkways were bleak and uncared-for, in 1993 they were becoming more personalized or territorialized. As can be seen from the photograph in Figure 9, there is now clear evidence that residents feel able to decorate their part of the walkway with planters and hanging baskets.

There are, of course, additional reasons why these improvements may have been made. There has been a continual change in resident population, with a noticeable increase in the proportion of Asian residents. Many of the apartments are now leased rather than rented. Also, now that the cleaning services have been placed with outside contractors, uniformed cleaners can frequently be seen at work on the walkways. All of these developments reemphasize the need for long-term monitoring of change. Perhaps, the reduction in crime was a necessary ingredient in these later improvements.

3. Developing More Effective Strategies for Curbing Prostitution

Roger Matthews

EDITOR'S NOTE: The process by which a red light district in North London was transformed into a tranquil residential area in less than two years is described in this case study, first published as a Security Journal *article (Matthews, 1990). The measures taken against street prostitution and associated problems of cruising consisted of intensive policing against prostitutes and pimps and a road closure scheme which severely restricted the opportunities for cruising. Not only were these measures highly successful, but they also produced some other benefits, in terms of reductions in auto theft and burglary, presumably because fewer offenders were being attracted to the district. Perhaps the most unexpected result concerned the apparent lack of displacement. The surrounding streets were unaffected and there was little evidence that the prostitutes had moved to nearby red light districts. It appears from interviews with the women involved, that many of them, especially the "away-day" girls who travelled to London each day by rail, may have simply desisted from an occupation to which they were only marginally committed (Matthews, 1986). The most frequent reason for involvement in prostitution given by 68 percent of the 70 women interviewed was: "Because you can earn better money than elsewhere." However, they seemed not to be so dependent on these earnings as the prostitutes studied by Lowman (1992) in downtown Vancouver, who were frequently supporting drug habits. Consequently, a scheme to discourage cruising johns, similar to the one described here, merely resulted in displacement of the prostitutes to nearby locations. Other more recent schemes to discourage street prostitution in England reported by Matthews (1993), did achieve similar results to those in North London, though in each case the combination of measures varied because of local circumstances. Matthews (1993: 33) concludes: "... it is not enough to simply combine certain elements...What is critical is how such measures are combined and implemented...if (interventions) are to produce the maximum benefits, then they have to be implemented in a particular sequence with a great deal of thought, care and commitment." In other words, effective situational prevention is rarely a matter of using off-the-peg solutions; instead, it nearly always has to be carefully tailored to the specific problem and its setting.*

THE PROBLEMS associated with curb-crawling (i.e. cruising or seeking prostitutes) and prostitution have become a major concern among a wide range of communities in a number of countries in recent years (Cassels, 1985; Levine, 1988; Lowman, 1986; Shaver, 1985). In each of these countries, the problem may display different characteristics, but usually involves a number of predictable attributes. Primarily, it tends to heighten the level of harassment and intimidation on the street, particularly for the female population living in the area. Relatedly, this harassment is often compounded by other forms of nuisance and disturbance associated with a continuous stream of traffic throughout the day and night. The combined effect of these pressures is to heighten the general sense of insecurity, to fragment community networks, and to limit personal mobility and restrict freedom of movement. In London, it was found that many residents living in the inner city refrain from going out because of the fear of crime (Jones *et al.*, 1986). Among women, this results in what amounts to an informal curfew. In "red-light" districts, these problems and restrictions tend to be compounded. In poorer neighborhoods characterized by high levels of incivilities, the result is often, as Wilson and Kelling (1982) have suggested, a spiral of decline in which the message is transmitted that the area is a legitimate target for a variety of crimes.

It is not only that curb-crawling and prostitution are simply the causes of decline, but it may well be that they are attracted to areas where decline and social disorganization are already taking place. The important point is that, once curb-crawling and prostitution become established in an area, the rate of decline is almost invariably accelerated. Even though the problem tends to have a relatively low priority nationally, it can become the major concern in the specific areas in which it occurs (Pease, 1988; Jones *et al.*, 1986).

It is significant that the degree of concern that residents in "red-light" areas have expressed in relation to this problem has increased significantly in recent years. This is not simply a matter of the objective problem itself becoming more pronounced. Changing attitudes appear to involve changing levels of public tolerance, growing demands for greater freedom of movement, as well as changing conceptions of the division between public and private space. Therefore, not surprisingly, the demands to do something about these problems have come, as it were, from "below." Often, however, residents have found that their demands have been dismissed and law enforcement and other agencies have chosen to concentrate on various other, more "serious" problems.

When the police have responded to the problem, they have normally organized their intervention through vice squads, which have focused predominantly on the street prostitutes, arresting them for soliciting and related offenses. This form of policing, which is currently in operation in many urban centers in England, has, however, been shown to have limited effectiveness.

Traditional Policing Methods

The traditional method of policing street prostitution in English towns and cities is to conduct a series of sweeps through the area. Most of the policing is done by car, and girls are followed, cautioned, or arrested, taken to the station, and prosecuted, and normally within a few days, they appear in court, pay a fine, and then are back on the streets working "overtime" to pay it off. Some prefer to opt for short prison sentences if they are unable or unwilling to pay the fine.

Curb-crawlers (male clients) pose a slightly different problem. Because the current legislation places the onus on the police to prove "persistence," it means that the police feel obliged to follow suspected curb-crawlers for a considerable period of time before stopping them and questioning them. Most at this stage receive a warning, and very few are prosecuted. Thus, the police find that dealing with curb-crawlers is a very time-consuming and unrewarding task.

In periods of heightened pressure, the police tend to "crack down" and swamp the area by throwing all available manpower into repeated sweeps. The effect of such a strategy normally is to provide a temporary reduction while police resources remain available. Inevitably, however, the police presence diminishes and the problem reemerges. This cycle can be maintained for many years. It is an extremely limited, time-consuming, and expensive operation. The end result is the creation of a "manageable" level of prostitution and curb-crawling in which the problem is continuously recycled rather than removed.

This recycling process tends to be reinforced through the informal relations that are built-up between the police and the prostitutes over a period of time. The police and prostitutes may soon be on a first-name basis, and a "working relation" is established. The police are, therefore, able to give the impression, both to their superiors and local residents, that they are doing something by showing lengthy arrest sheets, while maintaining both their own position and that of the more persistent prostitutes by organizing the rates and distribution of arrests for soliciting.

Changes in public attitudes have, however, meant that the traditional style of policing is becoming widely viewed as inadequate. Local residents have increased the pressure on the police to work out a more effective and enduring solution. It was these pressures that surfaced in the Finsbury Park area of North London between 1980 and 1986 and that underpinned what was to prove one of the most effective attempts to combat the problems associated with prostitution and curb-crawling in England. It involved a multi-agency approach, in which the police worked closely with the local residents and the local authority to develop a response that involved new styles of intensive policing, combined with a traffic-management scheme that was designed to remove, or at least significantly reduce, the incidence of curb-crawling and soliciting in the area.

Multi-agency Policing

It became increasingly apparent during the 1980s that the police operating in isolation were likely to have only a limited effectiveness (Burrows and Tarling, 1985). The employment of more police or more comprehensive forms of policing would be only of a marginal benefit if the targets of crime were left unprotected. On the other hand, the adoption of locks and bolts and other security devices was seen to have limited effectiveness if not supplemented by other interventions (Safe Neighbourhood Unit, 1985; Forrester *et al.*, 1988; Lea *et al.*, 1988). The necessity of developing a more comprehensive approach to crime reduction was clearly recognized by Sir Kenneth Newman, who wrote that

> My strategy continues to reflect the fact that the force cannot provide tidy solutions to the many problems that confront Londoners and impair their quality of life. Indeed, it would be a monstrous deceit for anyone to attempt to sustain such a fiction. The major resources of crime reduction are to be found in the community itself and in other public and voluntary agencies (Newman, 1986:7).

The former Commissioner of the Metropolitan Police clearly saw that if police effectiveness was to be noticeably improved, it would need to develop relations with the community organizations and with a range of relevant agencies. As Kinsey *et al.*, (1986) have argued, a multi-agency approach involves two things: first, a shift from reactive to proactive policing, and second, a sharing of the responsibility for crime prevention and control with other agencies.

Fortuitously, the growing interest in multi-agency initiatives in London coincided with the growing demands in the Finsbury Park area of North London for an effective police response to the problem. The police attended meetings set up by the Finsbury Park Action Group (FPAG), which facilitated better links between the police and the public.

Residents had also approached the local authority and asked them to restrict access into the area in order to deter curb-crawlers. Again, by good fortune (rather than good will), the local authority was planning a traffic management scheme for the area and was able to incorporate the suggestions of the FPAG in a way that rationalized its own proposals.

Within a relatively short period of time, agreement was reached through a series of regular meetings among the police, the local authority, and the local residents. It was decided that a combined offensive, involving more intensive forms of policing on one hand, should be combined with a traffic management scheme on the other.

Intensive Policing

In the period prior to the implementation of a road-closure scheme, the police implemented a diverse range of interventions directed not only at the prostitutes and the clients, but also at the pimps and the local landlords, who made short-term accommodation readily available for purposes of prostitution.

During 1982, the number of women charged with soliciting was 181, and in the year prior to the implementation of the road-closure scheme (1983), it rose to 666. During this period, a number of women were repeatedly arrested. Prostitutes on the streets were a relatively easy target for the police. But during this period the police also began to turn their attention to the curb-crawlers. In this period, which preceded the passing of the Street Offences Act (1985), which made curb-crawling an offense, the police gave a mixture of formal and informal cautions to suspected curb-crawlers. In the vast majority of cases, this level of intervention appeared to be very effective in deterring the clients. According to police records, very few reappeared in the area after having received a caution.

During 1984, 12 pimps were arrested, together with five brothel keepers. Although the numbers involved were relatively small, these prosecutions were to prove significant, since they involved the closing of various houses on which the prostitution trade was dependent.

A critical factor during this period of intensive policing was the vastly improved flow of information from the public to the police. This created greater efficiency and the more effective deployment of police resources. This relationship was sustained and developed before and after the road-closure scheme was implemented.

Designing out Curb-crawling

By the time that the road-closure scheme came into effect, the 16-strong vice squad had effected a considerable reduction in the problem and brought it down to manageable proportions. Intensive policing, however, was sustained for a period following the implementation of the road-closure scheme.

The volume of traffic — both during the day and throughout the night — had been extremely high for a residential area. Heavy traffic was often accompanied by horn blowing and by drivers leaning out of car windows and calling to or shouting at women on the streets. Occasionally bitter interchanges between curb-crawlers and local residents took place.

Although the vast majority of the residents in the immediate area supported the road-closure scheme, there were objections from some residents — particularly from those who lived in the surrounding streets. The nature of the objections to the scheme was two-fold. On one hand, local residents were concerned that a road-closure scheme may act to design "in" rather than design "out" the problem — that is, by placing physical barriers around the area, the enclosed area might become a home for a range of criminal activities and attract a number of "undesirables" who might see the enclosed area as affording them some degree of protection from the police who would have difficulty pursuing them in police cars.

The second major concern particularly evident among the residents in the surrounding streets was the fear of displacement. Prostitution, after all, it was argued, was the "oldest profession" and was therefore unlikely to disappear. Also, although it may well be the case that certain "opportunistic" crimes may be reduced through environmental changes, prostitution was unlikely to be significantly reduced by such a method. Such attitudes are widespread, and as Ronald Clarke has pointed out:

> The dispositional bias of criminological theory has tended to reinforce popular beliefs in the inevitability of displacement ("bad will out"). People find it hard to accept that the occurrence of actions with often momentous consequences for both the victim and the offender can turn on apparently trivial situational contingencies of opportunities or risks (Clarke, 1983:245).

The expectation held by many was that prostitution would be displaced in some form to neighboring areas or that the clients and the prostitutes would find alternative, and possibly even more, undesirable methods of "doing business."

Despite these objections, the scheme eventually came into operation early in 1985, and within a relatively short period of time, a remarkable transformation occurred. Soliciting and curb-crawling virtually disappeared, and the area was transformed from a noisy and hazardous "red-light" district into a relatively tranquil residential area. Not only that, but many of the fears and anxieties about the possible negative effects of this strategy did not occur. Instead, the overall result appeared extremely positive and superseded even the most optimistic expectancies. The significant benefits that resulted from this multi-agency initiative included the following:

(a) *An increased sense of security.* This was particularly evident among the female residents of the area. But it was not only the women, for whom harassment and intimidation had almost become a normal part of life, who benefited from this intervention. Many of the male members of the community of all ages undoubtedly felt less constrained and more secure.

(b) *A reduction in the volume of traffic.* The volume of traffic circulating in the area — particularly late at night — declined considerably. This, in turn, reduced the level of noise and congestion and made the streets safer for all members of the community.

(c) *A reduction in the number of crimes reported.* Table 1 shows that in the 6-month period prior to the implementation of the road-closure scheme, the number of crimes reported to the police in the area was 475, of which 110 were motor vehicle crimes, 121 involved burglary, and the rest involved a range of serious crimes. In the corresponding 6-month period after the scheme was implemented, the total number of reported crimes decreased to 275, with the number of serious crimes going down by almost 50%. These figures are extremely significant, since the expectation would be that improved police-public relations would result in a *higher* level of crime being reported to the police.

TABLE 1
RECORDED INCIDENCE OF CRIME IN FINSBURY PARK 1984/5 - 1985/6

Type of Crime	Sept/Feb 1984/5	Sept/Feb 1985/6
Motor Vehicle Crime	110	74
Major Crime	76	40
Burglary	121	97
Total Crime	475	275

Source: Matthews (1986)

(d) *An improved relationship among the police, the public, and the local authority.* As a result of the links that were developed among the police, the public, and the local authority during the implementation of this successful strategy, more meetings were set up to devise coordinated ways to deal with other problems in the area. Prior to this initiative, the public's confidence in the police was extremely low. However, as a result of taking the residents' concerns seriously, police-public relations improved considerably.

(e) *The anticipated level of displacement did not occur.* The expectation that prostitutes and their clients would move to surrounding areas was not borne out. The surrounding streets remained unaffected, and the evidence gathered from a nearby "red-light" district indicated that few of the women who had been operating in Finsbury Park had moved to new locations.

The apparent lack of displacement, more than any of the other positive effects of this initiative, is probably most remarkable. The belief in the inevitability of displacement, however, seems to be bound up with a conception of motivation of the prostitutes and the clients that may be unrealistic. An examination of the prostitutes and the clients provided some indication of why the anticipated level of displacement did not occur.

The Prostitutes and their Clients

The prostitutes who worked in Finsbury were not a homogeneous group. They expressed a variable commitment to "the game" and operated under different levels of pressure and incentives. Taken very broadly, the large number of women who worked in the Finsbury Park area between 1983 and 1986 can be divided into three groups. The first group comprised a "hard core" of about 30 women who lived fairly locally, had a long-term commitment to prostitution, and had been in the game for a number of years. The second group involved women and girls who came to London principally for the purpose of practicing prostitution. This group, often referred to as "away-day" girls, came to London, and Finsbury Park in particular, either because they had heard that it was a good area to work or they had a contact address. The ready availability of cheap accommodation that was let out to prostitutes by local landlords undoubtedly provided an attraction to women who were thinking of working as prostitutes in London. It is estimated that there were about 200-300 "away-day" girls engaged in prostitution in Finsbury Park over this period. The third category involved a number of women who engaged in prostitution on a much more sporadic and temporary basis. Many of these women drifted in and out of prostitution and were on average much younger than the other two groups. The very fact that they drifted in and out of prostitution and were sometimes involved for only very short periods makes any estimation of their numbers extremely difficult, but they almost certainly constituted the largest group.

Research carried out in 1983 by Valerie Dunn involved interviews with seventy prostitutes working in Finsbury Park. Most of this sample were drawn from category two and a few from the third category. The vast majority were between 20 and 35 and most of them had been on "the game" for 2-3 years. Table 2 shows answers to the question: Why do you do prostitution?

TABLE 2
ANSWERS BY 70 PROSTITUTES IN FINSBURY PARK TO THE QUESTION:
"WHY DO YOU DO PROSTITUTION?"

a.	Because you can earn better money than elsewhere	68%
b.	You like meeting different men	54%
c.	You like the independence	49%
d.	To supplement social security	45%
e.	There is no employment available	40%
f.	To get your own back on men	35%
g.	Because it fits with your family commitments	31%
h.	To pay for addiction	18%
i.	Because somebody forced you	12%

Source: Dunn (1984)

These alternative replies obviously were not exclusive and many of the women expressed mixed and sometimes conflicting reasons for why they had taken up prostitution. This complex mixture of responses is, however, probably not very dissimilar to the type of responses which most people would give for explaining their occupational choices.

It was evident that the intensive policing in the area prior to the implementation of the road-closure scheme had deterred many of those women whose commitment to the game was sporadic. The "away-day" girls, on the other hand, were, over this period, subject to systematic surveillance and arrest, which made soliciting increasingly difficult to pursue. As the level of fines were also increased during this period, the activities of the local courts provided a further disincentive. It would seem that over a period of about 1 year, most of the girls gave up prostitution or moved back home or elsewhere. For many, their normal period of involvement in prostitution may have been 3 or 4 years, and, therefore, the effect of intensive policing was to shorten that period by a year or two in most cases. Most importantly, the message was undoubtedly transmitted to other potential "away-day" girls that working in Finsbury Park was becoming extremely difficult. There did remain a "hard core" of about 20 women operating in the area, but most of these found it more congenial to work from home via advertisements or from the local public house (The Finsbury Park Tavern).

As for the clients, their level of motivation was also much lower than was generally assumed. Most of them seemed to be deterred by a police caution. The profile that emerged of the average "punter" (John) was that he was between 35 and 45 years of age, married, and living in surrounding suburban areas. The vast majority were, according to police classifications, "white Europeans" or of "Mediterranean appearance." The occupational distribution of the 79 curb-crawlers for whom formal cautions were issued was that 15 were unemployed, 14 were manual workers, five were from service occupations, 10 were salesmen, 23 were tradesmen (many of whom worked in the building industry), and 12 were from the managerial and professional classes.

Thus, it transpired that the motivation of both the prostitutes and their clients was highly differentiated, and, in many cases, they exhibited a much lower level of commitment than was expected. Through a combination of interventions that embodied proactive, attritional, and deterrent elements, the problem was reduced with an apparently low level of displacement.

Conclusions

There can be little doubt that the problems associated with prostitution and curb-crawling could have been effectively overcome only through a multi-agency initiative. A comprehensive resolution to the problem required not only a diverse police initiative aimed simultaneously at soliciting and curb-crawling as well as pimps and brothel keepers, but also required environmental changes. It is also essential to have an organized residents association able to initiate, coordinate, and monitor the various processes. The interventions of the police and the council proved to be mutually reinforcing. It became apparent after a year or so that the police on their own may well have been able to maintain the problem within reasonable limits, but the situation required a more permanent disincentive if it was to achieve a satisfactory long-term solution. By the same token, the road-closure scheme on its own, without any organized police presence, may have created a more entrenched and contained "red-light" district. Thus, the sequence of intervention is crucially important, since it seems necessary to establish a police presence in the area *before* the environmental changes take place. If the initiatives occur in the reverse order, prostitution could take forms that might aggravate and intensify the problems.

Clearly, implementing such a multi-agency offensive does not guarantee automatic and inevitable results. The context in which the strategy is implemented may well affect the manner of intervention and the possibilities of obtaining a positive outcome. Therefore, if this type of approach is to be replicated, there are a number of questions that require more detailed examination. First, we need to find out how this strategy needs to be adapted in order for it to be effective in different situations. Second, the issue of displacement requires further investigation. Displacement is clearly the Achilles' heel of crime prevention initiatives. It is therefore important that more extensive measures of displacement be developed and employed in future studies of this type. Third, we also need to know more about the commitment to prostitution and curb-crawling of the men and women involved. The indication is that it is a great deal less than most people believe. Any comprehensive theory of crime prevention must incorporate an assessment of the motivation of offenders and examine the relationship between victims and offenders in more detail. The evidence from Finsbury Park certainly indicates that curb-crawling and prostitution may be far more "opportunistic" crimes than is generally imagined. It appears to be not so much the outcome of a fixed biological need meeting an ineluctable economic force as that of a relatively contingent and flexible arrangement that is certainly reducible and may well be removable. If we are to respond constructively to growing community pressures to deal with this problem, then it seems we need to develop and refine the type of multi-agency approach that proved so successful in North London.

4. Reducing Theft from Shopping Bags in City Center Markets

Barry Poyner and Barry Webb

EDITOR'S NOTE: This case study first appeared in a Tavistock Institute of Human Relations' publication (Poyner and Webb, 1987a) and has been edited by the authors for inclusion in this volume. It developed from an earlier study of "street attacks" (violent and sexual assaults, robbery and thefts from the person) in Birmingham and Coventry, two large cities in England, which found that many of these incidents were thefts from shopping bags occurring at markets in the city center (Poyner, 1981). Because of their concentration in the central part of the city, with excellent rail and bus connections, these markets attracted thieves like bees to a honey pot. Conditions at the markets also facilitated theft. In the covered markets the lighting was so poor and the shoppers so close-pressed by the arrangement of stalls that it was easy for thieves to remove purses from shopping bags without being noticed. According to the evidence of the case study, the installation of improved lighting (to enhance natural surveillance) and the widening of spaces between stalls (deflecting offenders) in the worst affected markets substantially reduced these thefts. There seems also to have been some diffusion of benefits in that thefts in nearby markets also declined, perhaps because: "The general attractiveness of this area for thieves has reduced." Finally, a note on terminology: "Shopping bags" are large cloth or plastic bags with handles to carry purchases; "purses" and "handbags" in common American parlance would be, respectively, "coin purses" and "pocketbooks."

ONE OF THE clear findings to emerge from an earlier study of street attacks in the city center of Birmingham was the existence of a large number of thefts of purses from shopping bags, usually carried by women (Poyner, 1980, 1981, and 1983). These thefts were concentrated almost exclusively in the Birmingham Bull Ring, well known as the center of one of the largest retail markets in England. In all there are well over a thousand stalls some occupied six days a week selling fresh food of all kinds, clothing, household goods and even antiques. There are four main market areas: two Bull Ring Markets open six days a week, an indoor market hall where most of the meat, fish and poultry are sold and the Bull Ring Open Market which has many fruit and vegetable stalls. The other two markets open three days a week. They are the Rag Market which is under cover and the Flea Market which is outdoors. These markets concentrate more on clothing, household goods, antiques, toys, etc.

The crime which is the subject of this case study is not a specific crime as defined in police statistics but is a sub-group of "thefts from the person of another." In the earlier study it was found that there was a clear set of thefts which involved the offender removing a purse or wallet from the top of an open shopping bag or from a side pocket. The victim often claimed that the shopping bag must have first been unzipped by the thief, but often it was possible to observe women with purses or wallets pushed into the top of shopping bags or plastic carrier bags. Thefts of this type only occurred in crowded places and the victim was not aware of the theft happening until shortly afterwards. The result was that few offenders were ever seen by victims and few caught.

Because these thefts occurred mainly in the market areas of the Bull Ring, it was hypothesized that offenders would probably follow likely victims, usually older women, around the market stalls and while the victim was preoccupied with her search for suitable purchases or while waiting to be served, the offender would take her purse.

Two particular features of this type of crime were identified which were believed to offer approaches to the prevention of the theft. Firstly, the offenses occurred in a very specific area of the city center and at remarkably specific times. Not only did these thefts tend to occur on three days in the week — on Tuesday, Friday, and Saturday, the busiest three market days — but they also tended to be restricted to quite narrow periods, i.e., between midday to 2:00pm on Tuesdays and 1:00-4:00pm on Fridays and Saturdays. It also seemed that the crime was seasonal, occurring mainly in the summer months. These factors together suggested that some form of intensive policing of the markets where theft occurred would discourage would-be thieves.

The second feature of this crime was that it was found to occur most in the two markets with the more densely packed stalls and less in the other market areas with a more spacious layout. The study proposed that as an alternative to intensive policing, it may be that changing the layout of the market stalls so that they were all more spaciously arranged would reduce this kind of theft. It was suggested that the gangway widths might be increased from about 2 meters to 3 meters. It was hypothesized that wider access ways made it more difficult

FIGURE 1
EFFECTS OF DIFFERENT GANGWAY WIDTHS ON MARKETS

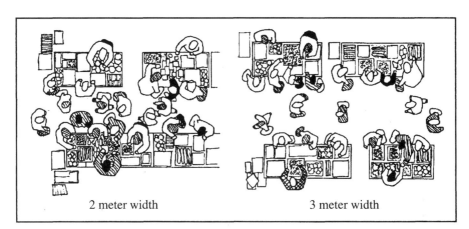

2 meter width   3 meter width

for offenders to steal without being noticed by other shoppers in the crowded gangways as Figure 1 illustrates.

At the time these proposals tended to be treated as an academic exercise and the research team had little expectation that any action would be taken. However, a visit to Birmingham in the summer of 1984 revealed that one of the markets with a high level of theft had been replanned and the narrowest access ways between stalls had been increased to a design width of 10 feet, which was exactly the dimension (i.e. 3 meters) proposed in the earlier study. In addition the area had been planned more spaciously in other ways such as providing more space behind the stalls and wider cross accessways. It was therefore decided that a study would be made of the effect of these changes.

It was only later when data were being collected from police records that the research team discovered that in 1982 (probably beginning in late 1981) the police had set up a Divisional Support Unit to deal with street crime in the city center. Two teams were formed, one of which had the specific brief to look into the problem of theft from the person in the markets. The policing work was a covert operation with officers not normally wearing uniform. Several techniques were tried by this team including using a policewoman dressed as a woman shopper as a decoy. This approach was felt to be unsuccessful and so forms of detection were used. The Bull Ring Open Market, which was the area later replanned was observed from nearby roofs by some of the team to try to identify intending offenders. These officers then directed some officers on the ground to follow likely suspects. In the opinion of the sergeant in charge of the team the exercise was successful, but not in terms of many arrests. A few arrests were made, but it soon became known that the police were making observations because details had to be given in court. He felt that it soon became a game. The offenders and police knew who each other were and so the offenders gave up offending while the police were about. Nevertheless, the police action was seen as a strong deterrent to this kind of theft. The Unit was disbanded by the end of 1982. This was about the same time as the Open Market was being replanned.

Although the police action did not acknowledge any influence from the original research study, it is very hard to believe that none of the senior officers who set up the Divisional Support Unit knew of the study. The research findings had been formally presented to a group of senior officers of the West Midlands Police in 1980 and the report made available to the Chief Constable and other senior officers. The work was also reported in the autumn 1981 edition of *Police Research Bulletin* (Poyner, 1981). The publication of this article and the setting up of the Division Support Unit seem to have occurred within weeks of each other. The influence on the new market layout is much less certain. It is quite possible that the designer made the decision to increase the design width of gangways to 10 feet for other very good reasons than to reduce crime.

The Data

The crime type that was the basis of the original work was not a recognized police crime category but a sub-set of "theft from the person," with a few incidents categorized as "other theft." Because the coding of crime used by the police does not specifically identify these thefts, it was not possible to obtain data on this crime pattern from any computer search through police data sources. The only way to identify reliably all the crimes which occurred in these market areas was to go back to the original police files and select incidents by hand.

This task of working through all available crime files of a busy city center police sub-division is a very time consuming and dusty business. It had been found in the original study that 75% of the thefts occurred in the six months April to September. It was decided that only searching files for these six month periods would reduce the search time by 50% but would still provide a 75% sample of each year's thefts.

Apart from the practical difficulties of handling box files scattered around a police station undergoing extensive refurbishing, it was very easy to identify the thefts required and the authors are quite confident that the selection work was accurately carried out.

In the event, data on these thefts were obtained for four complete summer periods (1982-1985). These data are presented alongside the analysis from the original report in Table 1.

TABLE 1

THEFTS FROM SHOPPING BAGS IN BIRMINGHAM MARKETS (FIGURES FOR THE PERIOD OF MARCH TO AUGUST IN EACH YEAR)

	1978	1982	1983	1984	1985
Rag Market	52	82	54	17	12
Open Market	54	21	45	33	12
Market Hall	20	4	11	12	9
Flea Market	—	—	2	2	—
Totals	126	107	112	64	33

Discussion

First, looking at the totals in Table 1 there is very clear evidence of progressive significant reduction in the crime from 1983, the year in which the layout of the Open Market was changed. There seems little doubt that whatever the precise details of the changes which have taken place the markets area is no longer seriously plagued by this particular crime. The crime reduction from 1983 to 1985 amounts to a 40% reduction in the first year and over 70% reduction in two years.

Policing. Having recognized that the overall figures show a very substantial reduction in thefts, it is even more interesting to look more closely at the analysis in Table 1. If we compare 1982 data with the data from the original study, we find that overall there is a roughly similar level of crime but that the distribution between market areas is quite different. The Bull Ring Open Market and Market Hall have much lower levels of theft while theft increased in the Rag Market.

From what is now known of the activity in the Markets this appears to be the result of the intensive policing by the team from the Divisional Support Unit. Their impact on the Open Market and its immediate neighbor the indoor Market Hall is clear. However, the overall picture does not seem to justify the claim of crime reduction. On the face of it, police action seems to have redistributed much of the crime rather than prevented it. For the most part these thefts had been *displaced* into the Rag Market. The Rag Market was the largest of the markets with smaller stalls than the Bull Ring Open Market but with the same narrow gangways. The more important difference is that the Rag Market is a large shed structure. It would not have been so easy for the police to make observations as in the Open Market which is partly surrounded by buildings with many vantage points for observation. As the sergeant of this team explained, the would-be offenders became fully aware of what the police were doing, and so it can only be assumed that the offenders adapted by operating in more, for them, congenial surroundings.

Markets management. If the policing had not reduced the overall level of these crimes, what did? It was clear from the figures in Table 1 that from 1983 crime did drop in both the Rag Market and the Open Market and some clarification of what changes might be responsible was required. To do this a meeting was held with the General Manager of the City of Birmingham Market Department. The result of this meeting and a further interview with a member of the Markets own security staff revealed that there were a number of factors that may have contributed to the decline in theft. These are best discussed under a series of separate headings.

Density of use and congestion. The Birmingham Markets had been long regarded as a thriving business and the improvements already mentioned to the Bull Ring Open Market had also been accompanied by a number of other improvements. Over the last few years the number of market stalls had been increased substantially. Most of these changes had been to extend the Flea Market. In fact when the original study was made in 1978/9 this market comprised only a few stalls. The number of stalls at April 1985 are given in Table 2. The figures for the Rag, Open and Indoor markets are little changed since 1979, but the Flea Market has become a major element of the market complex. Like the Rag Market the Flea Market only operates on Tuesdays, Fridays and Saturdays.

TABLE 2
NUMBER OF RETAIL MARKET STALLS
AVAILABLE IN APRIL 1985

Rag Market	552
Flea Market	231
Bull Ring Market Hall	197
Bull Ring Open Market	158

While the increase in the size of the markets area has taken place, many traders have commented that trade has reduced. Unfortunately, by the very nature of the organization, there are no reliable statistics for the amount of trade, but it does seem that either due to the increased number of stalls or because of a decrease in trade combined with the increase of stalls, the general impression is that the markets are not quite so busy as they used to be. If this is the case, this in itself could account for some of the reduction in theft. It is clear that thefts from bags relies on the existence of crowded areas and if these are reduced so is the opportunity to steal.

Design changes. Apart from the development of the Flea Market, the main design changes that had taken place in the markets since the original study had been made, were the replanning of the Open Market, part of which is now roofed over, and the up-grading of the building that houses the Rag Market. In this case the front of the building was given a face lift and inside a ceiling was added with an improved lighting system. It is worth noting that the lighting system was not a minor improvement but one carefully designed for modern conditions. It won a certificate of commendation in the "Energy Management of Lighting" Award Scheme. This scheme is administered by the Electricity Council and the Lighting Industry Foundation, designed to encourage the most effective use of electricity.

The redesign of the Open market came first and was carried out within the first three months of 1983. Although the upper part of the old layout was a series of free standing hexagonal stalls with 10-feet between stalls the lower and busiest area (adjacent to the Woolworth store and the Indoor Market Hall) had stalls with 8-feet gangways often further narrowed with boxes. The new layout has a similar number of stalls but the space around the stalls is more evenly distributed. The minimum gangway width between stalls is 10 feet and some are a little wider. There are also more cross access ways. The design also gives more space for the traders to stow the stock and this has helped to reduce the obstructions in the gangways. The overall effect is much more space and less congestion and for the most part movement around the stalls is much more free (see Figure 1).

At first sight the increase in crime in the Open Market from 1982 to 1983 could indicate that the new layout had no impact, but it must be remembered that the policing team were at work in 1982. In fact if 1982 is ignored, the pattern of theft in the Open Market is consistently down from the original study through 1983 (when the layout was changed), and 1984/5. The crime reduction over the first two years of the new layout amounts to well over 70%, which is the same proportion as the reduction for the markets area as a whole. It seems quite reasonable to claim that the new layout with wider gangways has reduced crime.

The Rag Market also shows a significant reduction in theft. But here there was no change in the layout of the stalls. The most significant change was the new lighting system. As can be appreciated from Table 2, the Rag Market is a very large shed with over 550 stalls. These stalls are little more than trestle tables used mainly on Tuesdays, when it is particularly crowded around lunchtime. Being in a relatively poor standard of accommodation compared with the Bull Ring Market Hall, the general level of lighting was poor and the combination of moderate levels of illumination and narrow crowded gangways seems to have been attractive to thieves. The improvement to the lighting seems to have made the difference. The new lighting system was installed towards the end of 1983 which accounts very well for the considerable drop in crime in this market between the summers of 1983 and 1984. This is the first clear evidence found by the authors to show that improved illumination levels reduce crime. It is perhaps paradoxical that the crime concerned only occurs during daylight hours!

Conclusions

There is little doubt that the two original hypotheses about policing in the markets and about the increasing of gangway widths have been proved to a considerable extent. In addition to this it has been found that increased levels of illumination appear to have deterred would-be thieves. This finding fits in very well with the ideas of the original study which emphasized the importance of would-be offenders being exposed to the view of other shoppers as a means of preventing crime. Both reducing congestion around the stalls and increasing the illumination increases the risk of thieves being seen to steal by other members of the public.

The problem with the use of intensive policing appears to be that it has not reduced crime overall but merely redistributed it. However this is not the case for the design changes to the markets. There was no evidence of displacement of theft to other markets or shopping areas. Indeed, quite the opposite has happened. The reductions in the Rag and Open Markets were accompanied by smaller reductions in the surrounding area. What seems to have happened is that by improving the worst areas of risk, the whole markets area has benefited. The general attractiveness of this area for thieves has been reduced.

Of course, those who believe unswervingly in the universality of the displacement theory will claim that the thieves have merely gone elsewhere. However, if they have gone elsewhere they will almost certainly have had to adopt other forms of theft because the original study showed very clearly that this type of crime occurred almost exclusively in these market areas, and there was no evidence to the contrary in the more recent review of crime files.

One final point, the markets security staff had a clear view that congestion was one of their main problems with crime. Apart from the more dramatic changes referred to above, they also felt that it was possible to manage the markets in such a way to reduce congestion. Apparently a few years ago the back of the Rag Market was particularly crowded because groups of stall holders used a particular sales approach. They liked to gather a large crowd around and make a direct sales pitch rather than wait for customers to approach their stall. To reduce this congestion these stall holders were moved and dispersed to less congested locations.

5. Deterring Obscene Phone Callers: The New Jersey Experience

Ronald V. Clarke

EDITOR'S NOTE: Not so long ago, telephone calls were placed through an operator who might know the caller's identity and telephone number. This imposed a significant control on the telephone as a facilitator of crime. As soon as callers could dial their own numbers, however, and could therefore be anonymous, phones could be used for all manner of offenses such as fraudulent sales, bomb hoaxes, and false fire alarms. In particular, they could be used to make obscene calls, which are considered by victims to be a serious form of sexual harassment, not the trivial behavior sometimes portrayed. This case study, first published as a Security Journal *article (Clarke, 1990), finds that obscene phone calling declined in New Jersey soon after the introduction of Caller-ID, a device that displays the caller's number to the person answering. With this demonstration of effectiveness, it might have been expected that Caller-ID would be eagerly adopted elsewhere. Instead, its introduction has been opposed by civil libertarians who have argued in the courts that Caller-ID is an unwarranted intrusion on the privacy of telephone callers, unless it is made available with a blocking option that prevents the calling number from being displayed (Temple and Regan, 1991). Given that obscene phone calling is one of the most prevalent forms of sexual harassment, it is ironic that Caller-ID's opponents have included advocates for women concerned that the device would compromise the security of women's refuges. This concern can be addressed by the selective provision of the blocking mechanism and solutions also exist for most of the other privacy concerns. Nevertheless, Caller-ID has generally been allowed in other states only with a blocking option for all subscribers, which under-mines its crime prevention value. New Jersey has also been forced to make the blocking option generally available, but, in the latest technological twist, has recently intro-duced a new service known as Anonymous Call Rejection (New York Times, February 6, 1997, p. C12), which rejects calls when display of the number has been blocked!*

OBSCENE PHONE CALLS are a particularly troublesome form of crime. They are common, can cause considerable distress to victims and are hard to prevent or prosecute. Ten percent of women questioned in the British Crime Survey (Pease, 1985) and about fifteen percent of households polled by New Jersey Bell reported that they had received at least one such call in the previous year (New Jersey Board of Public Utilities, 1989). Victims often report anger, shame and disgust, feelings which may persist for weeks or months (Savitz, 1986). Some may change their telephone numbers or obtain an unlisted number, while those who think the caller knows where they live may keep their doors locked and not go out alone.

These consequences belie the common attitude, especially among men, that the offense is a comparatively trivial one. Indeed, Pease (personal communication) reports that a Gallup poll conducted in 1989 for a British television program found marginally higher levels of worry, upset and fear among victims of obscene phone calls than among victims of burglaries, robberies and snatch thefts. Moreover, if obscene phone calls included a threatening component (which about a third did) they attracted seriousness ratings equivalent to those of a domestic burglary.

Because of the anonymity presently afforded to the caller by the phone, it is very difficult for the victim (almost always a woman) to protect herself from the isolated call, especially as she may initially assume that it is from someone she knows (Warner, 1988). For repeated calls, various steps can be taken such as blowing a whistle down the phone, installing an answering machine, having someone else answer or changing one's number. The police or telephone companies can take effective action only in more persistent cases. For these, a device called a "trap" can be physically placed on the incoming line to record all calling numbers, which, together with the customer's log of obscene calls, may permit the originating phone to be identified. This is an expensive and cumbersome procedure. It also results in few convictions of offenders,[1] though a warning delivered by the police will often be enough to stop the problem.

The New Technology

As in so many other areas of modern life, developments in technology are now changing the picture. Essentially, these remove some of the anonymity afforded the caller by making it much easier to identify the calling number. Various systems are being developed, but in the New Jersey Bell area, the first to deploy the technology, two such systems are now available in districts where the central office exchanges have been technically equipped.[2] The first, "Caller-ID," is a device attached to the customer's telephone with a modular jack which displays the incoming call's number and keeps a record of these. The display unit costs at present about $70 and residential customers are charged $6.50 per month for the service. The second, "Call Trace," is a service through which customers can punch in (or dial) a simple code to have the number recorded of the last telephone call received. Unlike Caller-ID, this service requires no special equipment nor payment of a monthly charge. Instead, there is a $1 charge for each use of this service. A further difference between the two systems is that with Call Trace the number is made available not to the customer, but only to "legally constituted authorities."

These situational preventive measures (Clarke, 1983) promise to undermine the opportunity structure for obscene phone calling since they greatly increase the attendant risks, even for isolated acts.[3] This assumes that many such calls are opportunistic and are made from home or business phones. Although little is known about the circumstances of obscene phone calling — most studies are based on very small samples of men under treatment for compulsive calling (e.g., Goldberg and Wise, 1985; Dalby, 1988) — this seems a reasonable assumption as it is difficult see how a public telephone would allow repeated dialing of victims or the drinking and masturbation which frequently seem to accompany the offense (Savitz, 1986).

The introduction of the new technology should therefore result in a marked decline of obscene phone calls and, indeed, this was reported for Hudson County, New Jersey, where Caller-ID was first offered on trial to about 200,000 customers at the end of 1987. Though less than 1% of the customers in Hudson County had subscribed to Caller-ID in the first six months of the service, traps set by the New Jersey Annoyance Call Bureau declined by a third compared with an equivalent period in the previous year. At the same time, demands for traps in the remainder of New Jersey increased by more than 50 percent (New Jersey Board of Public Utilities, 1988).

Unfortunately, the Hudson County results do not prove that Caller-ID is an effective deterrent to obscene calls. First, traps can be requested to deal, not just with obscene calls, but with a variety of other annoyance calls involving pranks, threats and harassment; it is possible that the decline in traps may principally reflect a decline in these other kinds of annoyance calls rather than obscene calls *per se*. Second, any initial deterrent effect of Caller-ID may dissipate as obscene callers discover that the risk of chancing upon someone with the device is in reality rather small. An analogous result was found following the introduction of the breathalyzer in Britain, where an initial sharp decline in drunken driving rapidly dissipated, presumably as offenders made more realistic assessments of their chances of detection (Ross, 1973). Third, the fact that demands for traps in other parts of New Jersey increased so greatly during the trial may be indicative of displacement of annoyance calls away from customers in the Hudson County area to those elsewhere. Fourth, there may have been little or no decline in obscene calls, but a change in the way that telephone company employees handled complainants; it is likely, for example, that victims may have been given the option of purchasing Caller-ID when they might previously have been advised to apply for traps.

It would be difficult to check the latter possibility without surveying customers in exchange areas with and without Caller-ID (see below). However, the fact that Caller-ID has now (i.e. November 1989) been more widely available in New Jersey for nearly a year permitted the present investigation of the possibilities that: (i) Caller-ID may deter some kinds of annoyance calls more easily than others, (ii) its deterrent effect might be short-lived, and (iii) it might displace annoyance calls into adjacent exchange areas without Caller-ID. Two separate analyses were undertaken using records maintained by the New Jersey Bell Annoyance Call Bureau to consider the effect of the new technology on, (a) the *volume,* and (b) the *nature* of complaints about annoyance calls.

The Volume of Annoyance Calls

In considering the effect on the volume of annoyance calls, it was necessary to take account of the fact that wherever Caller-ID has been made available, so has Call Trace[4] which can be used by any customer without special equipment or payment of a monthly fee. This makes it impossible to distinguish the effects of the two separate systems. It also makes it necessary to examine not just the volume of traps (as was done for the Hudson County trial), but also the volume of "call trace cases" which the Annoyance Call Bureau can now establish instead of traps for customers in areas with the new technology.[5]

Annoyance Call Bureau monthly records of "traps" and "call trace cases" were compared for two sets of exchange areas: (i) 57 areas where Caller-ID and Call Trace were available to customers during June-September 1989 and, (ii) the remaining 155 New Jersey Bell exchange areas without the new technology.[6] The comparison was made for two periods of time: June to September 1989 and the same months for the previous year. A limitation of this comparison is that six of the 57 areas (i.e. the original six central office exchange areas of the Hudson County trial) were already equipped with the new technology in June to September 1988 and, presumably, had therefore already obtained whatever benefits were to be had. This somewhat contaminates the design; the practical consequence is that any decline observed in the second period in the number of traps and call trace cases established for the 57 areas by the Annoyance Call Bureau would underestimate the technology's true effect by about 10 percent (i.e., the six Hudson County trial areas constitute about 10% of the total).

The results (Table 1) indicate that the sharp decline (of the order of 70%) in the number of traps placed in Caller-ID/Call Trace areas was accompanied by a large increase in the number of call trace cases established, from an average of around 10 per month during the three months in 1988 to about 300 per month in the same three months in 1989. However, the *combined* count of traps and call trace cases for the 57 Caller-ID/Call Trace areas still shows that there was an overall decline of approximately 25% in action taken by the Annoyance Call Bureau. (As mentioned above, this decline would have been greater had it been possible to exclude the original six areas of the Hudson County trial from the group of 57.) For the remainder of New Jersey there was also a decline, but a much smaller one of only about 4 percent, in the number of traps and call trace cases established. That there was no *increase* for the remainder of New Jersey, rules out the possibility of displacement of annoyance calls to areas without the new technology.

The Nature of Annoyance Calls

The second analysis, concerned with the *nature* of complaints about annoyance calls compared information about all traps placed in Caller-ID/Call Trace areas between March 1, 1989, and April 14, 1989, with a one-in-three sample of traps placed in the remaining areas of New Jersey. This yielded 352 cases for Caller-ID/Call Trace areas and 359 for the other areas of New Jersey.

TABLE 1
COUNT OF CUSTOMERS FOR WHOM TRAPS AND CALL TRACE CASES WERE
ESTABLISHED, NEW JERSEY, JUNE-SEPTEMBER 1988/89*

| | Non-Caller ID/Call Trace Exchanges (N=155) | Caller ID/Call Trace Exchanges (N=57) | | |
	Traps	Traps	Call Trace Cases	Traces + Traps
June 1988	701	689	4	693
July 1988	664	649	12	661
Sept 1988	732	665	11	676
Total	2097	2003	27	2030
June 1989	750	241	351	592
July 1989	693	203	298	501
Sept 1989	573	178	254	432
Total	2016	622	903	1525

*Because of a work stoppage, figures for August 1989 were incomplete.

TABLE 2
NATURE OF CALLS FOR WHICH TRAPS ESTABLISHED, NEW JERSEY,
MARCH AND APRIL 1989

	Non-Caller ID/Call Trace Exchanges	Caller ID/Call Trace Exchanges
Ring/Hang-ups	120	124
Threatening	87	100
Harassing	71	73
Obscene	68	40
Other/No Information	13	15
Total	359	352

$\chi^2 = 8.31$, N.S.

Table 2 shows that there was no statistically significant difference between the Caller-ID/Call Trace areas and the remainder of New Jersey in the nature of requests for traps. This suggests that the technology has had no more effect on some kinds of annoyance calls than others. The analysis also reveals that, for both areas combined, obscene calls constitute about 15% of the grounds for requesting traps, a smaller proportion than either harassing (20%) or threatening (26%) calls. The biggest single category were ring/hang-ups (34%).

Summary and Discussion

The present study has found that action taken by the Annoyance Call Bureau in response to complaints about annoyance calls (15% of which were obscene calls) has declined in one year by at least 25% for those areas in New Jersey with the new telephone technology. This suggests that the similar result achieved earlier in the Hudson County trial was not due simply to the novelty of the technology. Furthermore, the fact that (unlike in the Hudson County trial) there was almost no change in the number of traps for other areas suggests that not only was the technology responsible for the decline, but there was no displacement of annoyance calls to areas without the technology. Finally, it appears that the technology may have had an equal effect upon all forms of annoyance calls.

These are encouraging results, though, unfortunately, they do not permit a judgment to be made concerning the comparative effectiveness of the two forms of the new technology, nor do they prove that the technology has led to a decline in annoyance calls. It may not be the volume of such calls that has been affected, but only the means of dealing with them. There are several ways in which the latter could result. For example, rather than establishing a trap, the telephone company employees could advise complainants to purchase Caller-ID or to use Call Trace. Alternatively, instead of reporting the call, a customer with Caller-ID could tell the caller that if he persisted with the behavior his number would be reported to the authorities, or customers could satisfy themselves by establishing a trace in the knowledge that, were the call to be repeated, they could make a complaint with more confidence that something would be done. In October 1989, customers activated Call Trace on 23,728 occasions.

It is unlikely that a choice could be made among the various possibilities discussed above without mounting a survey of subscribers in areas with and without the technology. This would seek to establish the incidence of obscene and other annoyance calls, as well as differences in the ways of dealing with them. Even if the only result of the new technology were found to be that customers dealt differently with annoyance calls, this may still be considered a considerable benefit, not just for the phone company which is thereby saved the cost of dealing with such calls, but also for customers who have been "empowered" to take effective action themselves.

Whatever the benefits of the new technology, it is not without its critics (Marx, 1989). It is argued that Caller-ID significantly infringes the privacy of those making telephone calls; that it may violate some state wiretap laws and federal privacy legislation; that it can reveal unlisted telephone numbers as well as the numbers of those, such as battered women in refuges, with legitimate needs to keep their whereabouts secret; and that it may inhibit use of hotlines and the anonymous passing of information. Further, it does inhibit small deceits such as claiming to be at the office when in reality at a bar, though it facilitates some others such as ignoring an unwanted call on the pretext of being absent from home.

In response to some of these concerns, it has been suggested that Caller-ID be made available only with a facility that alerts the caller that his or her number is being displayed. Another possibility would be to provide Caller-ID only with a facility which enables callers to block display of their numbers. New Jersey Bell has claimed that the latter option would not only be expensive to provide (of the order of $9-15 million), but would be detrimental to the community at large since it would undermine Caller-ID's ability to deter annoyance and obscene calls (New Jersey Board of Public Utilities, 1988). It would certainly detract from the benefits of Caller-ID for businesses such as pizza delivery outlets for whom immediate display of the calling number has great advantages. The blocking option is also resisted by the police, fire companies and emergency service providers, although, for them, urgent calls are increasingly received via the new 911 system which also displays the calling number. Many of these objections could be met by providing the blocking option on a selective basis and, indeed, the Pennsylvania Public Utility Commission ruled in November 1989 that Caller-ID be made available in the commonwealth with a per call blocking option for "at risk" customers, such as those in women's refuges or in some law enforcement positions.

A more radical step would be to make only Call Trace available since numbers identified under this system are not directly accessible to the customer. This would still allow annoyance calls to be dealt with more effectively than by setting "traps," but without infringing the caller's rights to privacy. This is resisted by the telephone companies, not just because of the potential loss of revenues associated with Caller-ID, but because both marketing studies and take-up of the new service shows that Caller-ID is much in demand (New Jersey Board of Public Utilities, 1988). In other words, the telephone companies believe that Caller-ID is what the public wants.

With so much at stake, the competing costs and benefits of Caller-ID, Call Trace and other systems that reduce the anonymity of telephone callers need to be more clearly established. This will require a much greater investment in research by the telephone companies and the public bodies charged with their regulation. Such research should include carefully designed comparative surveys of customers in areas with and without the new technology to identify differences in the experience of receiving and dealing with annoyance calls; without such surveys the deterrent value of the new technology may be difficult to prove.

Notes

1. For example, of 52,334 "abusive" phone calls (including 11,793 obscene calls) reported by customers to the Bell Telephone System in October 1967, only 78 resulted in court convictions (U.S. Congress, 1968)
2. A third service, "Call Block," prevents receipt of calls from up to six designated numbers.
3. Offender's who know their victims may also know whether they possess Caller-ID. (Pease, personal communication, reports that about 25% of the British recipients of obscene calls identified in the poll referred to above thought they knew the identity of the offender).
4. This appears also to have been true for the Hudson County trial though the facility was not publicized at the time.
5. A "call trace case" has to be initiated by the police on the basis of a complaint made by a telephone customer. Unless there is a threat to life, three to five successful traces usually have to be made by the complainant before the police will initiate a "case." While call trace cases and traps are alternative methods now open to be used by the Annoyance Call Bureau for customers in areas with the new technology, it should be noted that there are important differences in the administrative and physical procedures involved. Caution is therefore needed in comparing statistical counts of traps and call trace cases.

6. The 57 areas with the new technology serve approximately 1.6 million customers, about half of all New Jersey Bell's subscribers.

ACKNOWLEDGMENTS. This study could not have been accomplished without the help of Dory Dickman and information obtained from Ellie Schollmeyer, Kathi Peters and their colleagues at New Jersey Bell. The Annoyance Call Bureau in Elizabeth, New Jersey, kindly provided access to records.

6. Eliminating Pay Phone Toll Fraud at the Port Authority Bus Terminal in Manhattan

Gisela Bichler and Ronald V. Clarke

EDITOR'S NOTE: Sloan-Howitt and Kelling have told the remarkable story in Case Study #19 of the successful attack on graffiti in the New York City subway. In an equally compelling account, too long for reprinting in this volume, Felson et al. (1996) have described another success obtained in a New York transit facility — the huge Port Authority Bus Terminal in Manhattan. Adjacent to Times Square, the terminal was a by-word for disorder and crime during the 1980s and early 1990s. It was a refuge for the homeless and a haven for all manner of hustlers and petty criminals who existed by drug dealing, prostitution, mugging and a variety of scams perpetrated on the hapless commuters. One of the scams involved "shoulder surfing," surreptitiously obtaining calling card numbers used by commuters at the terminal's pay phones. These numbers were then sold to people wishing to make cheap long distance calls who would come to the terminal for this purpose. The scam was a multi-million dollar business involving many thousands of calls annually to such countries as the Ivory Coast and Gambia, which rather few commuters would need to call. This case study, first published in Crime Prevention Studies *(Bichler and Clarke, 1996), describes how the building managers set about eliminating the problem. It shows that the different recommendations made by two separate consultants — reducing access to banks of phones outside commuting hours, and reprogramming pay phones to prevent unauthorized access to long distance lines — were equally effective in reducing the problem, but with different levels of inconvenience for management and commuters. It also shows how the scam was resistant to conventional policing methods. If the police had employed problem-oriented methods, they, rather than the building's mangers, might have been able to claim credit for the success captured in this headline from a* New York Times *(August, 6, 1995: A16) story describing the terminal's transformation: "Croissants? A Clam Bar? Is this the Port Authority Terminal?"*

Introduction

The telephone system has an important dual role in the production of crime both as crime target and crime facilitator. Its pay phones are the target of theft and vandalism and its long distance calling facilities are subject to wide scale "toll fraud." It facilitates a variety of serious offenses, such as kidnapping and criminal conspiracy, and also makes possible a vast number of more everyday offenses of prostitution ("call girls"), drug dealing and obscene phone calling.

Apart from the usual array of criminal justice responses (police crack-downs, task forces, stiffer penalties and the like), some specific counter measures have been developed, frequently by the phone companies themselves, to deal with these various crimes. Illegitimate access to toll lines has been made more difficult and pay phones have been target-hardened to prevent theft and vandalism. To prevent their use in drug dealing, they have also been removed from some neighborhoods or their capacity to receive incoming calls has been blocked. In addition, "traps" to identify the source of obscene phone calls and wire-tapping equipment to listen into the phone conversations of known racketeers have been developed (Natarajan *et al.*, 1995).

Little of this activity, whether crime or counter-measure, has attracted the interest of criminologists though some early research was undertaken on specific crimes. This included small scale studies of obscene phone callers or their victims (e.g. Savitz, 1986; Dalby, 1988) and exploratory work on the environmental correlates (neighborhood characteristics, natural surveillance, usage levels, etc.) of vandalized pay phones (Mawby, 1977; Mayhew *et al.*, 1979).

Stimulated by the development of situational prevention, there have recently been signs of an awakening interest in the effectiveness of some specific counter measures. Analyses undertaken in Australia (Wilson, 1990; Challinger, 1991) and England (Markus, 1984; Bridgeman, 1997) have documented successful measures involving re-design, re-siting and target hardening to reduce theft and vandalism associated with pay phones. In New Jersey, the introduction of Caller-ID (a device that displays the telephone number of an incoming call) was found to have reduced the incidence of obscene phone calls (Clarke, 1990), while an analysis of obscene phone calling patterns led to the conclusion that such devices would probably also be effective in Britain (Buck *et al.*, 1995). Finally, the introduction of a new computerized phone system on Rikers Island (a New York City jail) was shown to have reduced jail phone costs by half as a result of eliminating fraudulent access by inmates to toll lines (La Vigne, 1994) .

The new phone system at Rikers Island also led to fewer fights between inmates because removing the scope for fraud eliminated much of the competition for access to the phone. In addition, as all inmates were issued with personal identification numbers (PINs) linked with their commissary accounts, it was possible to identify any excessive phone use by particular inmates (La Vigne, 1994). The reduction of violence was an unexpected benefit and shows how the previously insecure phone system "created" additional crime beyond the fraudulent use it permitted.

The present study also documents successful efforts made to deal with toll fraud, and the additional problems created, but this time at the pay phones of the Port Authority Bus Terminal at 42nd Street in Manhattan where international toll fraud was a highly organized business involving millions of dollars. There was also inconvenience to commuters, who often found it difficult to find a phone not in use. More seriously, the fraudsters attracted to the bus terminal and, possibly also some of those using their services, constituted a pool of criminals who preyed upon commuters and other terminal users. In short, the opportunities for toll fraud helped to produce the more general crime problems at the terminal, documented by Felson *et al.* (1996), which made it notorious throughout the Northeast of America (Baehr, 1992; Meier, 1992; Myers, 1992).

The precise nature of the problem involving the telephones was not immediately apparent to management and emerged only in the course of the successful effort to tackle the more general crime problems at the terminal (Felson *et al.*, 1996; Lambert, 1995). This paper describes the efforts made to understand and deal with the pay phone problem and evaluates the effects of the measures adopted. First, however, a brief description is provided of the bus terminal.

The Port Authority Bus Terminal

The Port Authority Bus Terminal (PABT) is the primary ground transportation facility for the New York metropolitan region. Commuter buses arrive at the terminal in midtown Manhattan from New Jersey and the nearby counties of New York State, and travelers can obtain direct bus service between the terminal and the three international airports serving the region. Bus service can also be obtained to the Atlantic City casinos, the Meadowlands sports complex, Monmouth Park and Aqueduct racetracks and the New Jersey shore. In addition, the terminal provides direct and connecting bus travel throughout the United States, Canada and Mexico. The terminal currently handles about 55 million passengers annually and on a typical weekday approximately 7,000 buses use the terminal.

The terminal is a large and complex structure consisting of two wings. The south wing of the building occupies an entire city block between West 40th and 41st Streets, from Eighth to Ninth Avenues. The north wing occupies about half the block between Eighth and Ninth Avenues, from West 41st to 42nd Streets. Above and below street level, the north and south wings are connected by corridors, walkthroughs and bus roadways, and direct underground passageways connect the terminal with the 8th Avenue and 42nd Street subway station. The terminal has three separate loading levels capable of handling about 220 buses simultaneously. A three-story structure above the terminal roof has more than 1,100 auto parking spaces. Ticket plazas, waiting areas, restrooms, restaurants and other services are located throughout the building.

Crime at the Terminal Pay Phones

While it had been apparent for some years that the PABT pay phones were the locus of criminal activity, the precise nature of the problem was unclear. Despite there being nearly 350 of these phones, they were always busy with people lined up to use them, even on weekends and outside rush hours when few commuters were using the terminal. People were loitering around the phones who police suspected were drug dealers and prostitutes using the phones to make contact with their customers. Some phones were clearly "controlled" by particular individuals who were occasionally involved in violent territorial disputes with interlopers.

In addition, from at least 1987, the PABT was widely known to be a place where toll fraud was rife. People who wanted to make calls to anywhere in the world could do so at a fraction of the usual cost by making contact with a "hustler" at the terminal who would place the call for them. Certain banks of phones were reportedly "reserved" for calls to particular countries, for example, China at one carousel and India at another. According to newspaper reports of the day (e.g. McFadden, 1987), the hustlers were obtaining illegal access to the international lines through two methods. The first was by "shoulder surfing" which involves the "hustlers" positioning themselves to hear the number spoken by a legitimate user or to see it entered on the telephone keypad. Many hustlers became very adept in this method of obtaining numbers which they could then use to gain illegal access to the long distance lines. A second method of obtaining these access numbers was by purchasing these from "middlemen" who were in contact with hackers who had penetrated the computers of corporations to "steal" the calling card billing numbers issued to executive employees.

The loitering and criminal activity surrounding the phones contributed to the terminal's threatening and unsavory atmosphere. The Port Authority Police had made various efforts to deal with the problem, but it proved difficult to gather sufficient evidence for an arrest[1] and, when this was possible, the offender was often back in the terminal the next day having been released on bail. Consequently, the police became frustrated and assigned low priority to dealing with the activity which continued unabated, sometimes in the full view of police officers (Holloway, 1992).

Only in 1990, when a task force was created to improve the environment and atmosphere of the bus terminal did the nature and the scale of the toll fraud really become clear. The activity related to pay phones was specifically targeted by the task force. Resolution of the problem took three years and involved the implementation of recommendations made by two different groups of consultants. The task force received little help from the telephone companies providing service to the pay phones.[2] Moreover, The Port Authority absorbed major losses in pay phone revenue in order to prevent their customers from being victimized from toll fraud. The following sections describe the two stage process by which toll fraud was eliminated.

Stage One — The Project for Public Spaces, Inc.

The task force first contracted with the Project for Public Spaces, Inc. (PPS) to undertake an analysis of the misuse of pay phones and to recommend solutions. PPS is a non-profit corporation specializing in the planning, design and management of public spaces. Founded in 1975, the organization grew out of the work of William H. Whyte's Street Life Project, with the objective of improving problematic public spaces so as to make them more attractive, enjoyable and, ultimately, more active. In developing their recommendations, PPS projects employ a variety of observational and survey techniques in analyzing how people use the public spaces concerned.

ANALYSIS

As a first step in their analysis of the problem, PPS located every pay phone in the building. It was found that the PABT had many more of these telephones (347) than the two large railway stations in Manhattan, each of which has considerably more commuter traffic than the PABT — Pennsylvania Station (with 96 pay phones), serving New Jersey and Long Island rail commuters as well as AMTRAK long distance travelers, and Grand Central Terminal (with 210 pay phones), serving commuters from Connecticut and other points north. PPS also found that the PABT pay phones generated more than twice as much income ($210,954 in April 1990) than the combined revenue ($87,880 for April 1990) from the pay phones at two of the region's major airports, LaGuardia and JFK International.

These findings prompted the following observations:

> ... the current situation at the PABT is such that it functions as a comfortable communications/transportation hub for illegitimate as well as legitimate uses and that a part of the problem is an excess of pay phones... This excess of telephones allows ample telephones for other uses, many of which are not ones the Port Authority wishes to support. This is a clear repetition of an issue found with other aspects of the Bus Terminal; where there is a vacuum of desirable activity, other activities, potentially undesirable, will fill the space (PPS, 1990:2).

In order to target pay phones for removal, as well as to identify the precise nature of the misuse, PPS undertook more detailed studies, one of which involved systematic observation of particularly active phones to identify "illegitimate" users. This study proved abortive because there was no reliable way of distinguishing illegitimate from legitimate callers, though the "hustlers" were more readily identifiable. Another study involved a survey of more than 300 commuters waiting in line for buses during the evening rush hours, which revealed that pay phone use by commuters was largely confined to calling their homes or offices to report on delays and estimated times of arrival. These were usually collect calls or made by coin and were approximately four to five minutes in duration.

This information about commuter calling patterns enabled PPS to identify phones plagued by misuse through examination of revenue patterns for each pay phone for a period of three months. "Hot spots" of misuse were identified by disproportionately large revenues from credit card calls and were found to be "... most heavily concentrated on the floors nearest the ground level, where the heaviest circulation occurs" (PPS, 1990:2). Also, "...clusters of phones appear to facilitate illicit use, allowing for multiple sales without having to move around" (PPS, 1990:2).

RECOMMENDATIONS

Since they believed that no single strategy could resolve the illicit phone use, PPS advocated a multi-dimensional approach (PPS, 1990:5). They argued that a comprehensive approach must be adopted and that "..failure to do so may lead to a decrease in one pattern of criminal behavior, and a concomitant increase in another, as criminals try to make up for lost income by re-channeling their efforts" (PABT Internal Memorandum, 1991:2).

Their recommended courses of action included (PPS, 1990:5):

1. Reducing pay phones to the number needed to accommodate legitimate patrons.
2. Relocating the phones to serve legitimate patrons more adequately.
3. Centralizing the location of phones in a supervised location.

4. Limiting phone calls to those reflecting the bulk of legitimate uses to be achieved, a) by allowing only brief, coin calls to specific area codes and, b) blocking international calls.

5. Developing a detailed data base in order to monitor pay phone activity.

IMPLEMENTATION

By December 31, 1990 the "01" and "011" international dialing capabilities of all pay phones at the bus terminal had been blocked. The hustlers left the building but were soon back, apparently having discovered that they could still gain access to international lines by first calling the access codes of individual companies such as MCI and AT&T. Federal regulations prohibited blocks on these codes in the interests of fair competition.[3]

Reducing the absolute number of pay phones and relocating some to serve legitimate users more adequately and to increase supervision was the next course of action. An internal report indicates that between December 1990 and September 1991, 90 telephones were removed from the bus terminal, reducing the total to approximately 250. A memorandum circulated on September 23, 1991, detailed plans to relocate another 77 pay phones and reduce the total number to 148 — though, as of March 1995, 198 pay phones remain at the Bus Terminal.

Despite these efforts, illicit activity involving the phones continued and the management resorted to gating-off 110 problematic phones outside rush hour times (PABT Internal Memorandum Nov. 6, 1991).[4] As will be shown below, this somewhat crude method of restricting access to the phones was highly effective in reducing fraudulent use.

Stage Two— Telecommunications Expertise

Despite its effectiveness, physically blocking access to the pay phones was not satisfactory in the long-term since the gates were unsightly and the labor costs involved in removing and re-erecting them on a daily basis were not insubstantial. Moreover, in using the gates, the Port Authority was in violation of its contract with the companies owning the pay phones, since the contracts stipulated unrestricted access to the phones.

Serendipity played a part in the final solution which involved more sophisticated changes to the dialing capabilities of the pay phones. The leader of the task force created to improve the terminal, Bob Williams, became aware that a contract was being negotiated with Teleport Communications Group Inc. (TCG) for forty-eight Elcotel "smart" phones to be installed on a trial basis in the World Trade Center, another large Port Authority facility in Manhattan.[5] Williams realized that if these "smart" phones were placed instead at strategic locations in the PABT, they could be used to gather better information about ways in which the hustlers were subverting the blocks on international dialing and he succeeded in getting the new phones installed at the PABT.[6] In December 1991, Williams also engaged John Gammino, a telecommunications expert with John Richard Associates, Inc. (a management consulting firm specializing in the communications industry) to analyze the data produced by the smart phones, to define the precise methods used in committing toll fraud and to devise solutions (Guhl, 1993).

PROBLEM RE-IDENTIFICATION

Gammino began by examining calls placed through AT&T, the main long distance carrier connected to PABT pay phones during 1990 (i.e. pre-blocking). He found that calls from PABT pay phones were much longer, with an average time of 15-20 minutes, than the four to five minutes that is usual for such calls from pay phones. His examination of call destinations showed an enormous volume of international traffic with calls to virtually every country from Algeria to Zimbabwe (see Table 1), whereas the commuters serviced by the terminal should have been making very little use of the pay phones for international calls.

In addition to these findings from the AT&T records, 1991 and 1992 data from the smart phones revealed temporal patterns of calling which did not correspond to the travel patterns of PABT's primary users. Of the 185,000 travellers who use the terminal each day, about 65,000 are round-trip commuters who travel during the morning (07:00-10:00) and evening (16:00-18:00) rush hours. It might therefore be expected that most pay phone calls would be made during these times. In fact, Gammino found that a substantial proportion of calls were made during evenings and weekends and, moreover, that many of these calls were being made to individual businesses, at times when these businesses were not open. After speaking with the businesses concerned, Gammino confirmed that many unauthorized international calls were being placed during non-business hours through the company's telephone system or "Private Branch Exchange" (PBX).[7] Fraudulent operators were accessing the PBX's through voice mail and other automated systems to place long distance calls. The numbers to access these systems had been purchased from hackers who had broken into the PBX systems to acquire the dialing codes that permit employees to make long distance calls through the company's phone system when they are away from the office.

Gammino's examination of telephone call reports generated by the 24 "smart" phones confirmed that there were three other ways in which toll fraud was being perpetrated. First, instead of directly dialed long distance calls, many calls were being made via the 5-digit access codes of major carriers such as AT&T (10288), MCI (10222), and Sprint (10333). The second method of gaining access to the toll lines was through 1-800 carrier numbers (similar in function to the five digit access codes) such as 1-800-877-8000 (Sprint) and 1-800 corporate or business numbers.[8] The third method involved gaining access through the 950 (MCI) codes. Once the fraudulent operators gained access to the telecommunications network by any of these routes, they would connect calls using stolen calling card numbers. Many of these numbers were known to be obtained at the bus terminal itself by "shoulder surfing" (Baehr, 1992; Guhl, 1993; Hoey, 1992a,b; Telecom & Network Security Review, 1995).

RECOMMENDATIONS

Gammino's proposed solution involved developing an algorithm to re-program the pay phones so as, (i) to block all international calling capabilities (but not interstate calls which were prohibited from being blocked by federal regulations and which were not subject to fraud at the PABT) and, (ii) to prevent subsequent re-dialing by disabling the keypad for calls placed to corporate PBX systems.

In order to block access to PBX systems without blocking access to long distance carriers using 1-800 or 950 calling programs, Gammino developed a data bank of frequently called 1-800 business numbers, for which subsequent re-dialing capabilities were blocked. This modification would mean that voice mail systems and beepers at these numbers could no longer be accessed through the pay phones except by using coins. The PABT management was concerned about the loss of these customer services, but the PPS

TABLE 1
DESTINATIONS OF AT&T INTERNATIONAL DIRECTLY DIALED CALLS PLACED
FROM PABT PAY PHONES, 1990

Country	Total Calls	Min per Call	Revenue	Country	Total Calls	Min per Call	Revenue
Algeria	5,492	18	$140,855	Jordan	379	49	22,631
Argentina	531	32	21,749	Kenya	352	18	10,214
Australia	1,747	21	50,774	Kuwaiti	1,210	23	37,418
Austria	283	16	4,866	Liberia	591	14	12,786
Bang.	538	70	61,552	Macao	458	28	20,970
Belgium	876	26	30,515	Malaysia	577	28	25,669
Belize	1,127	19	24,750	Morocco	437	46	22,101
Brazil	478	37	22,783	Nepal	266	17	9,014
Cameroon	543	16	12,941	Netherlands.	1,211	19	24,594
C. Verde	407	19	13,456	Niger	531	15	16,762
Chile	1,541	20	38,410	Norway	538	17	10,315
China	8,255	43	431,581	Oman	293	29	10,462
Colombia	1,495	28	56,087	Pakistan	2,586	58	245,060
Czech.	365	38	15,509	Panama	12,847	18	271,915
Ecuador	1,893	56	125,007	Paraguay	876	25	28,459
Egypt	2,536	72	59,431	Peru	3,445	40	236,204
England	6,465	16	101,780	Phil.	383	23	15,277
Ethiopia	3,785	22	137,401	Poland	24,743	17	516,490
F. Antilles	583	19	12,296	Portugal	268	11	4,588
France	9,942	16	174,982	Qatar	390	23	12,307
Gabon	1,756	13	36,795	Romania	1,438	32	70,344
Gambia	31,404	5	310,195	Sing.	1,579	18	44,569
Ghana	5,096	18	150,403	Spain	1,306	15	24,320
Guinea	2,062	18	72,287	Surinam	4,480	22	141,321
Guatemala	257	30	8,396	Sweden	1,118	18	22,028
Guyana	6,594	30	262,726	Switzerland.	529	14	8,874
Honduras	651	26	17,464	Taiwan	3,520	19	105,482
H. Kong	7,513	16	120,746	Tanzania	271	18	7,690
India	1,699	50	186,623	Togo	751	15	17,847
Indonesia	9,564	18	201,187	Tunisia	1,433	17	34,733
Ireland	392	14	5,955	Turkey	6,089	18	138,135
Israel	41,483	8	457,179	Uruguay	2,293	27	73,932
Italy	1,256	14	20,528	W. Germ.	5,368	18	107,628
I. Coast	18,063	14	296,456	Yugoslavia.	558	22	16,654
Japan	1,309	17	31,978	Other	8,069	n/a	284,395
				Total	269,164	n/a	6,456,833

NB. Countries with less than 250 calls during 1990 have been consolidated into the "Other" category. These figures do not include calls placed through 1-800 numbers.
Source: Gammino, 1992b.

TABLE 2
SOFTWARE TRIAL RESULTS ON 24 "SMART" PHONES
(TWO 12-DAY PERIODS, PRE- AND POST-IMPLEMENTATION)

	Pre-test Period (Feb. 1992)			Post-test Period (April 1992)			Change Between Periods (%)	
	Calls per Day	Minutes per Day	Avg. Call Length	Calls per Day	Minutes per Day	Avg. Call Length	Change in Calls	Change in Minutes
All Phone Calls	548	4,900	9	344	1,377	4	-37	-72
Frequently Dialed Calling Card Numbers								
MCI access	73	918	13	17	82	5	-77	-91
MCI calling cards	72	543	8	34	133	4	-52	-76
MCI operator	75	1,443	19	10	15	1	-86	-99
Sprint calling cards	51	302	6	24	62	3	-54	-79

analysis had shown that most legitimate callers used coins or called collect and, after balancing the needs for service and security, the management consented to a trial of the software solution.[9]

TESTING THE SOFTWARE

Testing of the disabling software algorithm began in March 1992 on the 24 smart phones selected on the basis of high levels of suspected fraud. A comparison of calls made from these phones one month prior to implementation (February) with one month post-implementation (April), showed a dramatic change in calling profiles (see Table 2). The number of calls and duration of calls were significantly reduced. Calling patterns became normal for pay phones, with primarily interstate and local calls, four to five minutes in length, more frequently made during rush hours. Additional analyses showed that the numbers of calls lasting more than ten minutes and those lasting more than one hundred minutes had been nearly halved.[10] Police confirmed that the hustlers and their customers had abandoned the re-programmed test phones within a short period of time.

FULL IMPLEMENTATION

Following this successful trial, the software solution needed to be implemented on the remaining pay phones in the terminal. Officials from the telephone company providing the pay phone services initially resisted this action on grounds that it would cost them $350,000 to alter the phones. They also argued that the only result of changing the terminal's pay phones would be to displace the crime to other locations. However, they were persuaded to take action following higher-level intervention and by June 1992 all the PABT phones had been changed.

Once the solution was implemented throughout the terminal the fraudulent activity disappeared and there was a dramatic improvement in the atmosphere of the building. Due to the nature of the fraud, any breach of pay phone security would be immediately noticed as the fraudulent operators would undoubtedly return in force, just as they did after discovering ways of subverting the blocks on "01" and "011" dialing. Customer surveys conducted after the changes have uncovered few complaints regarding inability to access voice mail or pagers (Port Authority of New York and New Jersey, 1994).

Evaluative Data

The effectiveness of action taken against toll fraud is reflected in monthly gross revenue data aggregated for all pay phones, from October 1989 to December 1994 (See Figure 1).[11]

Figure 1 shows a sharp increase in gross revenues during the latter part of 1990, peaking in November. The decline in December 1990 coincides with the blocking of "01" and "011" calls, while the severe drop between January and February of 1991 coincides with the use of gates to restrict access to 110 problematic phones outside rush hours. Between February 1991 and June 1992 when gating was in force, there was a further slight decline in revenue (with some apparent seasonal fluctuation), which may have been due to reductions in the number of pay phones.

FIGURE 1
AT&T MONTHLY GROSS REVENUE FOR THE PORT AUTHORITY BUS TERMINAL
PAY PHONES, OCTOBER 1989 AND DECEMBER 1994*

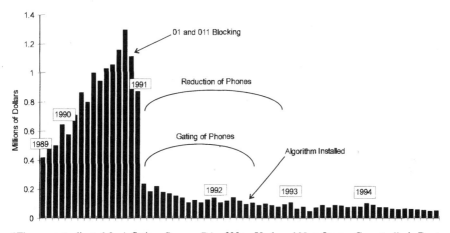

*Figures not adjusted for inflation. Source: PA of New York and New Jersey, Comptroller's Dept.

Following full implementation of the algorithm in June 1992 (and the removal of all gates), there is evidence of a further slight decline in gross revenues.[12] It is quite evident from these patterns that both the gating-off solution and the software solution were effective in dealing with toll fraud. However, the software solution seems to have been somewhat more effective than the gates, as well as having aesthetic and other advantages.

That this reduction in revenues is largely the result of the blocks on international calling is supported by data provided by Teleport Communications Group, Inc (TCG) on international calling on the twenty-four original smart test phones during July 1994 to March 1995. Results indicate that not a single international call was made from any of the twenty-four phones.[13]

Displacement of toll fraud to other Port Authority facilities was not a particular concern to management. This was because the World Trade Center had also been equipped with "smart" phones, while the three airports were not thought to be conveniently enough located for fraudulent operators to develop a profitable trade there, even though the

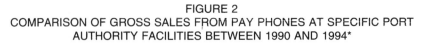

FIGURE 2
COMPARISON OF GROSS SALES FROM PAY PHONES AT SPECIFIC PORT
AUTHORITY FACILITIES BETWEEN 1990 AND 1994*

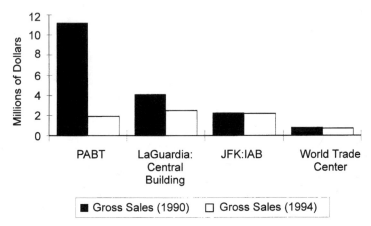

*Figures not adjusted for inflation. Source: PA of New York and New Jersey, Comptroller's Dept.

international clientele prevented blocks on international access codes for the pay phones.

Analysis of gross revenue by facility confirms these assumptions; Figure 2 shows there has been no increase in revenue at the other facilities.[14]

It also seems unlikely that there was significant displacement of pay phone toll fraud to the nearby Time Square area (where pay phones have been altered to prevent fraud) or to the other large commuter terminals in Manhattan. A search of Lexis/Nexis for 1992 through 1995 found a dramatic decline in coverage of toll fraud at the PABT, Grand Central Station and Pennsylvania Station and the focus of the coverage was on the efforts that had been made to rid each terminal of the problem. In 1994, only one story was uncovered by the search relating to toll fraud at Pennsylvania Station. In addition, a number of news reports were found indicating that a number of New York businesses had adjusted their PBX systems so as not to accept calls from the PABT and the other terminals.

Concluding Remarks

Brantingham and Brantingham (1993b) distinguish between hot spots of crime that are "crime generators" and ones that are "crime attractors." The former are places such as shopping malls or parking lots that become hot spots simply because so many people pass through them, of whom a proportion will be offenders. The latter, which may include red light districts or drug markets, become hot spots because the many opportunities for crime they provide attract the presence of predatory offenders. It is clear from the analysis of calling patterns that the PABT pay phones were crime attractors; the hustlers preying upon them and the customers availing themselves of cheap calls where mostly not the commuters who comprised the bulk of the bus terminal's legitimate users, but instead were people who came specifically to the terminal because of the opportunities for toll fraud. Moreover, the criminals attracted to the phones seem to have engaged in a number of other crimes such as purse-snatchings and muggings that further contributed to the lawless and unsavory atmosphere in the terminal.

Why the PABT became the principal venue for toll fraud in New York is unclear, but the large concentration of pay phones and the fact that these went unused for much of the day must have played a part. The terminal is also well known in the region, is close to centers of poor immigrant populations, and is easy to reach via the subway and bus lines. In addition, it provides a comfortable environment for the hustlers who must hang around for long periods of the day because it gives them shelter from the weather and access to restrooms and fast food outlets. It also provides them with many entertainment opportunities, both on-site (a bowling alley and an off-track betting office) and nearby (with a concentration in 42nd Street and Times Square of liquor outlets, drug markets and porno movie theaters).

Whatever the terminal's "attractive" properties, it is clear that the hustlers were not much deterred by the regular presence of large numbers of police. While the police were understandably frustrated by their inability to deal with the problem through conventional means of surveillance and arrest, they missed the opportunity to take the lead in finding more creative solutions to the problem by applying the principles of problem-oriented policing (Goldstein, 1979, 1990). It was only when the building managers decided that the problem must be solved were solutions identified and a spectacular crime prevention success achieved. This is reminiscent of another notable crime prevention project in New York — the successful effort to rid the subway of graffiti (*Case Study # 19*). Here again, management stepped in to develop solutions to a problem that the police had failed to control by conventional patrolling and investigative methods. This is further evidence of just how much the police must change if they are to take advantage of the potential afforded by problem-oriented policing.

Despite this potential, the difficulties of this kind of problem-solving work should not be underestimated. These have less to do with developing solutions (two very different solutions were found to the toll fraud problem though with different costs and benefits), than with implementing them. The PABT management received little cooperation from the major telephone service providers who, in general, were not bearing the costs of the fraud since they passed these on to customers, either directly or in the form of increased charges. Indeed, solving the problem of toll fraud resulted in a substantial loss of revenue from the pay phones for the Port Authority.[15] What appears to have motivated management to improve the situation is not profit, but pride. It was recognized that travellers deserved a better facility and it was humiliating to be responsible for so notorious a crime location as the bus terminal.

This suggests, finally, that there might be other occasions when corporate pride could be tapped in the interests of preventing crime, especially when the responsible institution is large and important enough to be susceptible to public "shaming." There are many corporations and businesses, such as the automobile manufacturers and insurance companies, that fit this definition and that could do more to prevent crime by closing the opportunities provided by their products and services. "Shaming" these institutions into action may provide large dividends for criminal justice policy.

ACKNOWLEDGMENTS. While we as its authors are responsible for the content of this report and the opinions contained, it could not have been produced without the cooperation and assistance of Daren Krebs, Account Manager of Public Communications, Teleport Communications Group Inc., and Janice Sazallai, Senior Researcher in the Accounting Division of the Port

Authority of New Jersey and New York. We are also most grateful for the assistance given by the consultants whose recommendations provided,the basis for the successful action taken against toll fraud — John Gammino, President of John Richard Associates Inc., and Fred Kent and Steve Davies of the Project for Public Spaces, Inc. Ken Philmus, the Manager of the Port Authority Bus Terminal, and the leader from the end of 1991 of the task force to improve the terminal, provided us with invaluable assistance and much useful advice. Professor Marcus Felson also gave us many useful suggestions.

Notes

1. The work of the police in arresting offenders was hampered by cumbersome and inadequate technology. Pen registers (that record all calls made on a particular phone line) were available, but could only be effectively used when it was possible to match pen register records with the results of direct surveillance of the phone concerned.
2. Dated tariff legislation regulating the industry limits the common carriers liability for fraud thereby distorting normal market incentives to resolve the problem. In particular, the current legislation absolves from liability those with the ability to prevent fraud — equipment manufacturers, vendors, carriers, and customers. For example, AT&T has a clause in its contract stipulating that any breach of security and the associated costs are the responsibility of the company on whose property the PBX switch is located. Major components of the industry are currently trying to sort out liability concerns in the courts (Federal Communications Commission Hearing, Oct. 9, 1992).
3. Each phone company offering long distance calling in the United States has a five digit access code or carrier identification code. These codes were not disabled by the block on 01 and 011 calling. This meant that fraudsters at the PABT could simply dial the access code, then 0 + area code + number sequence. By blocking the "01", "011" calls, only directly dialed calls were being prohibited (01+country+city+number).
4. All phones in the ticket hall area and 6 units next to the parcel check were gated-off all day on Sunday and on Monday to Saturday during 10:00-6:00 hours and 20:00-06:00 hours. In addition, all phones adjacent to the bowling alley were gated-off from 20:00 Friday-06:00 Monday.
5. "The 'Smart Phones' (Elcotel Units) are programmable units capable of logging and manipulating a variety of data such as: area codes accessed, telephone numbers accessed, duration of calls and time of calls. The units can identify calling patterns, block calls by individual phones and alert the responsible party if the unit has been damaged. The information the unit captures can either be down loaded to Teleport, Big Apple (the Teleport service provider) or to the client (PA)." (PABT Internal Memorandum, Sept. 1991:3).
6. Elcotel smart phones were installed during September 1991 at the following sites, determined largely on the basis of the PPS analysis (PABT Internal Memorandum, September 23, 1991: 1-2):

North Wing:
      Subway Level

a) on tenant storage wall across from M.P. Cozzoi Co.	7
b) on wall next to doors leading to south wing	2

      Main Concourse

a) next to 42nd St. exit	6
b) on M.E.R. Wall	5
Second Floor — by escalator and newsstand	6
Total North Wing	26

South Wing:
    Main Concourse — next to escalator   12
    Second Floor
        a) fronting poppers   5
        b) opposite escalator near bowling center   2
    Fourth Floor
        a) opposite gates 403, 411and 420   3
Total South Wing   22
Grand Total of Smart Phones   48

7. PBXs or PABXs are "private" switches that are purchased by businesses and located on their property. A recent service offered by the telecommunications industry to market these switches allows traveling employees to access messages, and to punch in an access code to get a second dial tone upon which they can place another call. While this system saves money by consolidating all long-distance traffic, it provides hackers with an avenue into the PBX system. Hackers use "auto-dialers" or "war-dialers" to uncover corporate telephone access codes. Auto-dialers randomly call various numbers and when answered by a PBX system the hacker's computer generates different combinations of digits until it gets a second dial tone, whereupon it prints out the circuit number.

8. 1-800 calling had provided many options for calling international and interstate available to the business community. Businesses bought into these two options en masse without realizing how insecure the systems were.

9. Apart from the new algorithm, Gammino suggested some other possible counter measures, including: the installation of credit card phones that allow international calling with a card only; the installation of debit cards or cash cards where individuals prepay for calls and use the card as credit cards at the phone; and the construction of a centralized long distance phone facility with attendants and security so that legitimate users could access the phones.

10. In a period of twelve days pre-implementation there were respectively 713 calls over ten minutes in duration and 92 over 100 minutes, compared with 388 and 48 in a comparable post-implementation period.

11. During 1992 the Port Authority changed the telephone carrier serving the pay phones, though this change seems to have had little effect on gross revenues because the difference between gross revenue and net revenue remained constant throughout the period. Another factor complicating interpretation of Figure 1 is that the Elcotel "smart" phones choose the most profitable route for each call. This may have resulted in some small increases in revenue for the pay phones that is masked by drops due to the interventions.

12. Some uncertainty exists regarding the full implementation of the algorithm. By June 1992 all the pay phones had the algorithm in place, but not all had been replaced by smart phones until the end of 1992. (Internal reports also indicate that the contract with Teleport Communications Group Inc., was not finalized until January 1993). In addition, tests of the blocking capabilities in August of 1992 found inconsistencies; some international calls were still being connected. Given this extended period of implementation, it is possible that the full effects of the algorithm were not obtained early in 1993.

13. It should be noted that the gross revenue data in Figure 1 include only AT&T revenue and not that from TCG because monthly data for the latter were unavailable. However, estimates of the monthly values for 1993 and 1994 on the basis of annual TCG totals did not significantly alter the curve in Figure 1.

14. The drop in overall pay phone revenue at the PABT between 1990 and 1994 was significantly greater than the decline in revenue from AT&T international calling alone (see Figure 1). This apparent discrepancy may result from a combination of other circumstances, including: a decline in fraudulent international calls made through long distance carriers other than

AT&T; a decline in fraudulent interstate calls; a decline in local calls to PBX and voice mail systems; a decline in local calls made in furtherance of drug-dealing and prostitution; a decline in the number of pay phones; and a very large reduction in the homeless population (see Felson *et al.*, 1996).

15. Net profits accruing to the PABT from its pay phones in 1990 were $2,556,458; in 1994 the net profits were $748,183 (figures not adjusted for inflation).

7. Macro-measures against Crime: The Example of Check Forgeries

Johannes Knutsson and Eckart Kuhlhorn

EDITOR'S NOTE: This case study, first published by the Swedish National Council for Crime Prevention (Knutsson and Kuhlhorn, 1981), is distinguished by its particularly careful study of displacement. Having established that the abolition of the bank guarantee for bad checks in 1971 together with new identification procedures had reduced check frauds in Sweden by 80-90 percent in subsequent years, the authors found that other crimes, which could provide alternative sources of income and which might therefore have been expected to increase as a result of displacement, had also somewhat declined after 1971. This more general fall in crime was thought to be the result of a decline in drug abuse in 1973 and 1974. As the crime statistics did not permit firm conclusions about displacement, the authors adopted another approach. They followed up the subsequent criminal careers of a sample of those convicted of check fraud before the introduction of the new procedures. They were still unable to find any evidence of a systematic switch to other forms of crime. More particularly, they were unable to find any evidence of "escalation" which is frequently supposed to be the result of situational impediments: Not one of the sample was convicted of robbery in the two years following their convictions for check fraud. Currently, there is less concern about the fraudulent use of checks than of credit cards. Between 1988 and

1990, credit card sales doubled worldwide and in 1990 MasterCard's worldwide fraud losses were $240.8 million and those of Visa were $355 million (Levi et al., 1991). This might seem to be a form of "displacement" except that most of the credit card offenders are probably responding to the opportunities created by the proliferation of credit cards rather than being diverted from check fraud (Tremblay, 1986). As shown by Webb (1996), these opportunities for credit card fraud are themselves amenable to situational prevention.

Check Abuse

Various changes that have occurred in society have had an impact on the structure of opportunities for committing crimes. In general, these changes have been to the detriment of obedience to the law. Obvious examples of this trend may be seen in the introduction of the self-service principle in department stores and the advent of the automobile era.

In the present article, we intend to report on one type of crime which arose during the 1960s: check forgery. In contrast to most other types of crime, however, efforts to halt this accelerating criminality by means of preventive measures proved successful. Indeed, this case represents one of the few examples in which crime prevention measures have been successful.

Check forgeries became increasingly common in connection with the introduction of the check as a means of payment in the 1960s. In Stockholm, the number of such crimes sextupled between 1965 and 1970, growing from 2,663 crimes in 1965 to 15,817 in 1970. Nationwide, the increase in such crimes was not as dramatic. The number of crimes grew from around 10,000 to around 40,000, i.e., a fourfold increase (Table 1).

TABLE 1
NUMBER OF REPORTED CHECK CRIMES IN STOCKHOLM
AND IN ALL OF SWEDEN, 1965-1970

Year	Stockholm		All of Sweden	
	No. of crimes	Index	No. of crimes	Index
1965	2,663	100	10,019	100
1966	4,785	180	13,001	130
1967	5,127	193	13,952	139
1968	9,182	345	21,808	218
1969	7,236	272	23,210	232
1970	15,817	594	39,337	393

The attention of the police was directed to this problem primarily as a result of the fact that they began to be burdened with an increasing volume of investigations of crimes involving check forgeries. In many cases, police departments had to add new staff to the fraud division.

The immediate background to the crime was usually that the criminal in one way or another, generally by theft, gained possession of checkbooks. The checks were then used as means of payment in stores or banks as a way of obtaining cash. In the majority of cases, the checks were used in stores. In addition, these checks were often used as means of payment in "the underworld." Most frequently, they were used in this way by drug addicts in their attempts to settle debts or buy drugs. This trade was concentrated in Stockholm in notorious spots frequented by drug addicts.

In purchases of goods or services in stores, restaurants and similar places, the amount of the check was generally under 300 Swedish kronor. The existence of this particular limit was closely connected to the basic precondition for check forgeries in Sweden, the so-called *bank guarantee*. Under the terms of the bank guarantee, any person accepting false checks was indemnified by the drawee bank up to a maximum of 500 kronor per check if the person paying by check had been required to show identification. For amounts under 300 kronor, the person accepting the bad check would be indemnified even if no identification had been required. In other words, for amounts under 300 kronor, the store, etc. accepting the check had no interest in determining whether or not the checks were good, since the store could not suffer a loss in any event. The banks collected the bad checks and then reported the case of check forgeries to the police.

The police, in turn, often had whole series of crimes to work with, since each check used was counted as one crime. A single missing checkbook could, as a result, give rise to many separate crimes. From the strictly investigative angle, these crimes had some relatively positive aspects, since there was often some bit of evidence that could be pursued. Various clues in the form of fingerprints, signatures or notes concerning identification documents played an important role. In many cases, the same criminal had used all of the checks in a checkbook. Thus, if the police could link him to any one of the checks, they could clear up all the crimes connected with that book. The simultaneous solving of a series of crimes in this manner was relatively common. These were undoubtedly the factors which accounted for the high general rate of cleared crimes, which was always over 50%.

The police responded quickly to the increase in crime. At an early stage, they initiated negotiations with representatives of the banks and the retail trade in an attempt to cope with this accelerating form of crime. The discussion centered on two points. The police called, first of all, for the removal of the bank guarantee. Secondly, they wanted it to be required for check-users to show proof of identification. These proposals met with relative indifference on the part of both the banks and the retailers. The negotiations drew out in time. The banks tended to play down the situation from the beginning, arguing that this was actually an information problem which could be resolved with the help of information campaigns. Meanwhile, check fraud shot up. Not until 1970 did the parties manage to reach an agreement which stipulated that the bank guarantee would cease to apply from July 1, 1971, and that henceforth check users would be required to present identification when paying by check or cashing a check.

The adoption of these measures led to a lively debate on the possible consequences of the action. Many observers feared that check forgers would be "forced" to commit other, more serious crimes in order to obtain compensation for their loss of income. Some people even feared that robberies would increase. However, no really serious attempts were made to study the actual consequences of the measures.

The question of displacement effects, i.e., the switch by criminals to other types of crime when they are prevented from committing a particular category of crime, is not a simple matter. From the purely theoretical standpoint, it might be expected that there is a great risk if, on the one hand, the criminals have a great "need" for crime, owing to drug addiction, for example, and, on the other hand, if the crimes that have been prevented are critical for the criminals' "livelihood." If the "need for crime" varies in strength and the crime is more of a "peripheral" nature, the risk of displacement effects is less.

Effects of the Measures

In the years immediately following the new measures, checks virtually disappeared from the retail trade. When they subsequently did return to the scene, identification was required of persons using checks. This represented a change in the opportunity structure as well as in the social control. The opportunities for crime decreased at the same time that a situational control was introduced. The positions were advanced from the traditional formal control after the fact in instances when a crime had been committed and detected to a type of control in the situation which affected everyone who used checks.

The effects of the measures against check forgeries could soon be seen in the crime statistics (Table 2). From a peak level in 1970, the number of crimes reported dropped to a level which has since been around 10-20% of these former figures. Thus, the efforts have to be considered a success as far as the prevention of this type of crime is concerned.

Society's traditional measures proved to be ineffective in combatting and preventing these crimes. The rate of cases solved was constantly very high, and most of the relatively active check forgers were caught and sentenced to various penalties. What this policy of deterrence failed to achieve was attained rapidly by the crime prevention measures which were implemented. An expensive and ineffective system of formal controls was supplemented by an inexpensive and effective situational control.

What, then, was the effect on other crimes? An examination of conceivable alternative crimes, e.g., burglary from homes, basements, and attics and thefts of and from cars, shows that they *declined* in the two years immediately following the implementation of the measures. This downward trend during 1972 and 1973 applies to all crimes of theft. Based on a simple notion of displacement effects, the results are surprising, since one would have expected to see an increase. During 1974 and 1975, the figures for these other crimes did in fact increase.

What can be the explanation for the decline in reported crimes of theft in 1972 and 1973 and the renewed rise in 1974 and 1975?

One explanation might be that it is not actually a question of real changes in crime rates, but rather a change in the rate of reporting crimes. Closer examination indicates, however, that it is difficult to find factors that might yield such results. It is most likely that these variations of reported crimes do reflect genuine changes in crime rates.

However, there is a possibility that these variations are due to changes in the narcotics situation. We know that many of the criminals are drug addicts. Moreover, most drug addicts are criminals. Criminals who are drug addicts have a higher crime intensity than criminals who do not use drugs. Under these conditions, it is conceivable that the scope of the drug abuse may influence the crime level in such a way that when the abuse is of a greater extent, criminality is also greater. The data indicate that drug abuse in Stockholm declined in 1972 and 1973 and that it increased in 1974 and 1975. It therefore might be these changes which explain the recorded variations in the number of reported crimes. We would, however, like to stress that this line of thought is of a speculative nature.

However, it can be asserted that the crimes would have been reduced less in 1972 and 1973 and would have increased more rapidly afterwards if the possibilities of check fraud had not been largely eliminated.

These arguments show that the question of displacement effects cannot be decided with data of this type. What is required is information on the crime repertoire of check forgers and how it was changed after the measures were taken. This information is provided in the following individual-based analysis.

TABLE 2
NUMBER OF REPORTED CHECK CRIMES IN STOCKHOLM AND IN ALL SWEDEN,
1970-1978.

	Stockholm		All of Sweden	
Year	No. of crimes	Index	No. of crimes	Index
1970	15,817	100	39,337	100
1971	7,835	50	23,810	61
1972	2,198	14	7,315	19
1973	1,668	11	4,926	13
1974	1,496	9	5,800	15
1975	1,867	12	7,069	18
1976	2,548	16	8,279	21
1977	3,107	20	9,228	23
1978	2,066	13	5,667	14

The Check Forgers

The purpose of the individual study is to shed light on the career of the check forger. Our analysis is based on two populations — persons who had committed such crimes during the heyday of check forgery before the elimination of the bank guarantee on July 1, 1971, and persons who had committed such crimes after this measure, i.e., when this type of criminality had been reduced to a fraction of its former level.

The target population was the 1970 check forgers in Stockholm (all persons apprehended for check forgery), while the 1975 check forgers constituted a comparison group. However, it is difficult to determine whether any differences between the 1970 and 1975 populations can be traced back to the elimination of possibilities of check forgery. They may also have their roots in altered police routines, changes in legal practice, etc. In order to bring these factors under control, we chose two additional comparison populations: persons who had been sentenced for crimes of appropriation of property in 1970 and 1975 (all crimes under Chapter 8 of the Swedish Penal Code).

After having identified the individuals behind the crimes, we decided to conduct the investigation in such a way as to ensure an equal number of persons in the groups. To do so, we took 1/17 sample of the 1970 group of persons who had committed crimes of theft and a 1/23 sample of the corresponding 1975 group.

The persons identified in this manner were then studied with respect to *convicted criminality* in the police files (including cases in which prosecution was waived, etc.). If, during a one-year period from the time of the crime in question, they had been convicted of a criminal files crime, they were included in the target population. In this manner, the populations were made comparable with one another.

The first conclusion that could be drawn was that the check forgers criminality during the period in question (the one-year period before and after the crime) included many types of crime. More than half of the check forgers had also committed crimes of theft of property during the period in question, and over a third of the appropriation criminals had committed check forgeries. Thus, there is no such person as a typical check forger with chronic recidivist tendencies for only check forgery.

The age of the offenders was around 30 years at the time the crime was reported. Approximately 15% were women. Over two-thirds of criminals investigated had been previously convicted of crimes.

Recidivism

Since the possibilities of continued criminal activity were to some extent blocked for the 1970 check forgers, we attempted to answer the following two questions:

1. To what extent did the 1970 check forgers become involved in new crimes, especially in unpleasant types of monetary transactions such as robbery?

2. What is the pattern of recidivism for the 1970 check forgers?

We investigated the involvement of the four groups in different types of crime both during a two-year follow-up period after the crime and during the entire decade of the 1970s after the crime. We were unable to detect any trend towards a systematic switch to other types of crime. Not one of the 1970 check forgers had been convicted of robbery during the two years following their original crime — a fact which ran directly counter to the assumptions made in the debate on this topic.

Generally speaking, the 1975 check forgers — an important comparison group — committed somewhat more serious crimes (especially crimes of violence) during the two-year follow-up period than did the group of 1970 check forgers. Thefts were an exception in this respect. A greater number of the 1970 check forgers were convicted of grand larceny and fewer of theft than the 1975 check forgers. Since a similar trend exists for the corresponding groups of persons convicted of crimes of theft of property, it is likely that this can be ascribed to a change in legislation and in legal practice.

We also analyzed the offenders' repertoire of crime before the period in question and during that period. The results of this analysis suggest that check fraud should be viewed as a form of supplementary criminality which varies with the opportunity structure. Hence, we were unable to find corroboration for the thesis of a switch to more serious crime.

To offer a correct answer to the rate of recidivism of the 1970 check forgers as compared to that of the other groups, consideration has to be taken of the individual's prognosis. We therefore calculated such a prognosis, using multiple regression analysis and available data, on the client's previous criminality and personal data such as age and sex. On the basis of this prognosis, we could establish that the group of 1970 check forgers with the most serious criminal records had a lower rate of recidivism during a three-year follow-up period than did individuals in the other three groups with corresponding records. These results corroborate previous findings: the elimination of possibilities for check fraud seems to have been more effective in reducing crime than in displacing it.

We would, however, like to register certain general observations. The methods employed here are fairly rough ones, whereas the changes in crime which may have occurred are relatively minor. Further, we do not know whether or not the 1970 offenders may have sought compensation for loss of income from check forgery by stealing larger amounts, for instance, without this being reflected in the number of crimes and the categorization of the crimes.

On the other hand, the sources of error in the other direction are not to be neglected, either. Waivers of prosecution under Item 2, Article 7, Chapter 20, of the Code of Legal Procedure have increased considerably. These crimes, which are stricken from the police files after a short period, are thus on the rise. Further, it is probable that the number of crimes per conviction or item in the individual's criminal record has increased. In addition, the risks of detection have declined substantially during the 1970s. All of these factors suggest that actual differences in rates of recidivism between the check forgers from 1970 and 1975 are larger than reported. Finally, one should not lose sight of the fact that the number of check forgers dropped considerably between the two years.

The Multiplier Effect of Drugs

We also studied the role of drug abuse. We investigated two populations — the 1970 and 1975 check forgers — with respect to the occurrence of drug abuse. The data for this part of the investigation was taken from a file which includes all of the approximately 7,500 persons who at any time between April 1965 and December 1979 in the Stockholm Remand Prison showed needle marks from injection abuse. This file was set up by Professor Nils Bejerot, a social medical officer in Stockholm, and it also contains information on the individual's debut with respect to drug abuse. It would appear that this file contains the great majority of injection addicts in Stockholm. Despite the fact that only around 0.5% of the adult population of Stockholm belongs to this category, they accounted for around 50% of the two check forger populations. These 50% accounted for two-thirds of the crimes recorded during a three-year follow-up period after the one-year base period.

The significance of narcotics for continued criminality was approximately as great as that of all other data on previous criminality, age, sex, etc. together.

Approximately half of the drug addicts had had their crime debut before their first injection. However, it should be noted that these data are very rough. The first instance of injection abuse may have been preceded by a more or less lengthy period of drug abuse with other modes of administration of the drug. Furthermore, the debut crime in the police files is not infrequently the visible tip of a "criminal iceberg" which has been recorded by the child welfare authorities. An analysis of these rough data does, however, indicate that drug abuse and criminality tend to accelerate one another and pave the way for recidivism.

Drug addicts have crime rates which are two to three times as high as those of other criminals who are not addicted to drugs, and this goes for virtually all types of crimes. However, this is only a rough estimate of the multiplier effect of narcotics, although it does agree with international findings.

Better knowledge of the multiplier effect of drugs requires more information than that available to us. (An investigation with this aim in mind is currently being planned). However, it is certain that narcotics do accelerate the type of crime being studied here and drug abuse is of tangible significance for the overall crime levels in Stockholm.

Concluding Comments

There is little doubt that the measures taken — the elimination of the bank guarantee and the introduction of identification requirements — were effective.

It is important to remember that they were implemented on the macro-level and not, as is customary, on an individual level. The measures meant that everyone who used checks was affected. The great majority of legal checking account users had to put up with increased restrictions so as to make it possible to cope with the abuses of a relatively small group.

Beginning in the late 1970s, a new type of crime has arisen. Charge account and credit card frauds have begun to spring up in the wake of these cards. There are many parallels to the case of check forgeries (Knutsson, 1980). The police have initiated negotiations with the credit card companies in an attempt to develop measures which can stem the new forms of criminality. The aim of the police is to avoid, in so far as possible, contacts with credit card abusers, i.e., to avoid micro-measures of the traditional type. It remains to be seen whether a regulation of the type studied in the present report can be achieved.

In addition to the conclusion regarding the effectiveness of the measures, this study also contains important implications for two scientific theses which, although unproven, are often presented in connection with discussions on anti-crime measures: the thesis of "objective interests" and the thesis of "the constancy of vices."

The thesis of "objective interests" states that established social institutions are interested in maintaining certain types of crimes in order to justify their own existence and/ or to reap economic gains. The showpiece example is the alleged interest of the insurance companies in the continuation of crimes against property. As far as the police are concerned, certain criminologists have asserted that the police maximize their profits by taking measures against minor offenses of a traditional nature while avoiding conflicts with the establishment. Taking action against minor offenses is ineffective but visible. Since criminality of this kind is constantly growing, the resources and power of the police will also continue to grow. Since the perpetrators of such crimes are among the weakest members of society, the risk of effective protests against police injustices and false priorities is minimal.

Judging by the current study, the thesis of "objective interests" would appear to be incorrect. According to this thesis, popular in many circles, the police ought not to have attempted to persuade the banks to alter their routines in order to cope with check forgeries. The police should instead, according to this notion, have stuck to traditional action against these crimes — which, from the standpoint of police investigation, are quite convenient — in order to become more powerful.

With respect to the banks, another observation can be made. They were prepared to accept the losses occasioned by the check forgeries. The check system apparently yielded such large earnings for them that this expense was negligible.

In a cost analysis, however, the costs incurred by society must not be ignored. The judicial apparatus is highly expensive for the taxpayer. The extra efforts on the part of the police, the courts and the correctional system which were caused by the check forgeries also have to be taken into consideration.

The second thesis can be summarized in the formula that "the sum of vices is constant." Once such a thesis is accepted, it is easy to end up in a fatalistic attitude; it is useless to try to prevent crime, since the criminals will seek compensation by committing other crimes. Our findings, in any case, show that this thesis does not hold in the example of check forgeries. There was no increase in other forms of crime. We were unable to establish a switch from check forgery to other, more serious crimes. Rather, forgers with the most serious criminal records appeared to have reduced the level of their criminal activity. Furthermore, the thesis of the constancy of vices has been cast into doubt in an earlier NCCP report relating to an analysis of crime trends in Stockholm after implementation of police measures (Kuhlhorn, 1976).

The inadequacy of the thesis of the constancy of vices is exemplified in no area more clearly than that of alcohol policy. It would appear that many people do believe in the thesis of the constancy of vices. It is asserted that reduced legal availability of alcohol — for instance, through the use of some form of rationing cards — would be compensated for by bootlegging, smuggling or "perverted stimulation" (forbidden fruit tastes sweetest). But it can be shown that after the introduction of rationing cards in Sweden in the early years of this century, alcohol consumption did decline, while home distilling and bootlegging did not develop into Sweden's leading national disease. It was also possible in the context of alcohol policy to demonstrate that the sum of vices could be increased without difficulty. The alcohol policy effort to get Swedes to drink wine instead of stronger alcoholic beverages met with notable success as far as a sharp increase in wine consumption was concerned; however, there was no offsetting decline in liquor consumption so as to result in a constant level of vices.

Another example which tends to refute the thesis of constancy of vices may be found in the area of traffic law. Speed limits, for instance, have proved to be effective as regards the prevention of accidents. But there are no indications that motorists have — in accordance with the thesis of the constancy of vices — attempted to obtain compensation by running through red lights or by always driving the shortest route, even if it means driving the wrong way down a one-way street.

In conclusion, we would like to state once again that this investigation lends support to the notion of macro-measures. The fact that macro-measures apparently can be effective must not, however, be interpreted as proof that they can replace individually oriented measures. We have, for instance, shown that drugs have a strong crime-generating effect. This effect is so strong that our social welfare authorities should seriously consider which methods can best stimulate drug addicts to seek immediate treatment for their drug problems.

8.   The Economic Benefit of Electronic Article Surveillance

Robert L. DiLonardo

*EDITOR'S NOTE: Few published evaluations exist of the security industry's staples —
guards and hardware — reflecting a lack of professionalism not just among the
providers of these goods and services, but also among business and corporate consumers. It also reflects unwarranted neglect of business by criminologists and a lack of
government sponsorship of research into private security. Given the millions of dollars
involved, this situation cannot continue indefinitely and there are some encouraging
signs of change, particularly in the recent establishment of two academic journals to
promote more rigorous analysis of security work —* Journal of Risk, Security and
Crime Prevention *and* Security Journal. *Indeed, this case study, undertaken by a
security professional, Bob DiLonardo, first appeared in* Security Journal *(DiLonardo,
1996) and is one of the first evaluations to be published of merchandise tags, used since
the 1980s as a deterrent to shoplifting in apparel stores worldwide. It shows that the
tags can achieve significant reductions in shortages of the order of 35-75%. Particularly convincing is the demonstration that when the tags were removed from a store where
they had proved effective, shortage increased and then declined again when they were
re-introduced (see Figure 2). No doubt, these kinds of results would be obvious to many
users. That they have not been previously published is not simply due to lack of
professionalism, but also to fear of benefiting the competition. Ways of reconciling the
conflicting needs for more published evaluations and for maintaining competitive*

advantage will have to be found by the leaders of the security industry if it is to attain the professional status that many of them desire.

Introduction

Electronic article surveillance (EAS) is the term used to describe retail anti-shoplifting protection systems for both apparel and packaged products. These systems have been successfully implemented in tens of thousands of stores worldwide. They were introduced in 1968-69, and have been in widespread use since the mid-1980s.

In essence, an electronically detectable element (tag) is either pinned onto a garment or affixed via adhesive to the item to be protected. Transmitters and receivers are placed at store exits in order to detect the presence of the tags as shoppers leave the stores. At the point of purchase, these tags are either removed or rendered inoperative (deactivated) so that the purchaser may exit the premises without setting off an alarm. If a shoplifter were to attempt to leave the store while carrying items which contained the "live" electronic elements, the detection equipment at the exit would sound an alarm, and appropriate security counter measures could be taken.

These systems have proved to be an effective psychological and physical deterrent to shoplifting, and in recent years technological improvements have provided more reliable, smaller, and less expensive products. In concert with the social benefits of shopping in stores which are relatively free from crime, the use of EAS provides some very real and quantifiable economic benefits to the user retailer. The scope of this paper is to define these benefits; describe the major methods of statistical analysis; and demonstrate, via case studies, how very large EAS users use the data in order to provide a basis for a return on investment calculation.

The primary benefit earned through the use of security systems like EAS is the reduction of inventory shortage ("shrink"), which is the money lost when a retailer compares the amount of merchandise which is physically present in the store at a given time to the amount of merchandise that the statement of accounts shows should be present. This calculation is routinely made on a semi-annual basis in order to include shortage as a component of gross margin and, eventually, profit and loss. Accurate inventory reconciliation statistics are readily available, though propriety to each retailer. Most of the larger American retailers assign inventory reconciliation duties to a specific group of accounting personnel. These statistics, as with most retail data, are generally reported in dollars and as a percentage of sales.

Over the years, the power of the economic arguments for EAS has dominated the decision process. While there exists an abundance of internal data prepared by retailers and EAS manufacturers which proves the economic effectiveness of EAS, almost none of it has been published. One small study on the effects of the psychological deterrence of EAS systems was conducted at the University of Wisconsin-Whitewater (Scherdin, 1986). This attempted to quantify whether there was a significant difference in the rate of book theft before and after installation of an electronic security system, and concluded that theft levels were reduced for both books, which were protected by EAS, and audiovisual materials, which were not protected by EAS.

A Brief History of the Development of the Measurement Techniques

In the 1970s, retailers used EAS as a means to apprehend shoplifters. As more and more large chains began to install EAS systems, the focus changed to deterrence rather than apprehension. Retailers began to recognize that it was more beneficial to stop shoplifters from attempting to steal, and they began to employ EAS more fully and completely. Concurrently, EAS technology began to become much more user friendly, specifically by becoming smaller and less expensive.

At that time, it was relatively simple for a retailer to cost justify an EAS expenditure. The systems were installed in stores which generated the highest inventory shortages. The products deterred shoplifters, and shortage levels began to fall rapidly, so a strictly constructed financial analysis was not required. Beginning in 1982-83, however, as economic conditions became more competitive, as inventory shortage became somewhat more manageable, and as store operating expenses started to rise, retailers began openly to question the investment in EAS equipment. While knowing intuitively that the product was working because sales associates were finding less evidence of theft, retailers began to demand a hard-and-fast cost justification. Since the dynamics of this process were not well understood, the initial response from EAS vendors was to discount the cost of the equipment, which by definition would improve the cost justification, instead of trying to demonstrate some sort of economic benefit - such as measuring the depth and breadth of the reduction in shortage.

Additionally, the complexity of retail inventory shortage became a factor in choosing EAS as a security solution. While there may be only three generally accepted causes of inventory shortage — shoplifting, internal theft, and poor transaction control — it is nearly impossible to establish a proportion for each. Each retail environment has its own dynamics. One store might have exceedingly poor document control, while the adjacent store has more dishonest employees. Though retail accounting rules may be somewhat standardized under generally accepted accounting principles, there is wide latitude in the application of those standards. Consequently, it became almost impossible for EAS vendors to prove that reductions in inventory shortage were a function of a successful EAS program. In some cases, EAS was unfairly blamed for rises in shortage!

Around 1983, Sensormatic Electronics Corporation (the world's largest EAS manufacturer) made a significant investment in a program which helped its clients actually measure the performance of EAS products. At that time, my role at Sensormatic was that of a national account sales manager with responsibility for large West Coast clients. Because of my retail, financial, and security industry background, I was given the responsibility to design and build this program from inception in an effort to stimulate sales and to understand better the customer base.

During the mid- to late- 1980s more than 30 statistical studies were conducted using actual inventory reconciliation data. Access was given to the inventory reconciliation data in order to assist store management in gaining an understanding of the dynamics of inventory shortage. All of this work was undertaken with the full cooperation of, and for the sole benefit of the retail chains which participated. Today, cost-benefit analyses of this type are routinely performed by Loss Prevention, Internal Audit, Shortage Control, or other retail financial executives. Enlightened EAS sales people are also conversant with the techniques employed.

On the strength of these studies, some very strong conclusions can be drawn regarding EAS as a profit producer in the retail environment. The primary conclusion is that the use of EAS equipment can successfully reduce shoplifting and total inventory shortage anywhere from 35 to 75%, depending upon the type of retail environment and the thoroughness of the system's usage. This reduction translates into increased profitability - all other factors being equal. Second, EAS equipment can be cost justified using traditional methods of financial analysis, such as comparing economic costs to benefits. Third, preserving the heart of a merchandise assortment by preventing theft can improve sales, and this improvement can be measured.

The three brief case studies which follow illustrate methods used to collect and examine data in order to address the three following questions:

- Will EAS reduce inventory shortage, and if so, by how much?
- What is the effect on shortage if EAS is removed and subsequently re-installed?
- How can the effects of EAS be measured if the equipment is installed in different locations over a period of years?

Will EAS Reduce Inventory Shortage, and If So, by How Much?

This is the single most important question, and it can be answered precisely and with the certainty of over 15 years of experience with the shortage statistic analysis. In this first case, the client was a large department store chain with 16 locations, which was an operating division of a nationally prominent holding company with over 200 locations. The operating division had introduced EAS in eight stores, and was attempting to quantify its results in order to decide whether to expand EAS into the rest of the chain.

The use of EAS is determined generally by two factors. Of primary concern is the level of inventory shortage which has been incurred. Typically, the retailer chooses to use EAS on items with high shortages because an appropriate return on investment can be achieved. Of secondary concern is whether or not there exists an appropriate EAS product to protect the desired merchandise category. In the late 1960s and early 1970s , apparel was virtually the only type of merchandise which could be protected. As time passed, EAS companies designed adhesive label-like products which could be affixed to packaged products, thereby opening up many more merchandise categories to adequate protection. As of today, several high shortage merchandise categories remain inadequately protected by EAS. The most common example is fashion jewelry. Most rings, watches, and necklaces are locked in security fixturing rather than protected by EAS.

The information provided in this case demonstrates a critical idea regarding EAS performance measurement. The gauge of the success or failure of the EAS program should be a function of shortage results in those departments which use the system, and not necessarily a function of total store (overall) shortage. Management procured EAS in order to curb shoplifting in approximately 40 men's and women's apparel departments, where inventory shortages exceeded 3.5% of the sales, and represented about 60% of the chain's sales volume and over 70% of its shortage. Shortage in other departments, like children's shoes, housewares, and others, was not considered a problem and was not singled out for EAS use. In fact, shortage in these other areas did not exceed 2% of sales. When combining the statistics to examine the overall shortage in a department store, they masked the serious situation in the apparel departments. Senior management tended to take a macro viewpoint and focused upon the overall shortage which was equal to or below the industry average. A detailed micro analysis was required in order to fund any additional anti-shoplifting programs.

The primary goal of the analysis was to isolate the inventory shortage statistics so that EAS user stores could be compared to non-user stores, and EAS user departments could be compared to non-user departments. Additionally, statistics were developed which compared the shortages before and after the use of EAS. When the analysis was completed, management could examine the statistics from the apparel departments in the eight EAS user stores in order to determine: (1) whether shortage correlated with the same data from the eight non-EAS stores; (2) whether shortages dropped during the time period where EAS was introduced; (3) whether the same statistical tendencies were exhibited in the merchandise departments which did not utilize EAS; and (4) whether there was any correlation to overall shortage statistics (see Figure 1).

The graph in Figure 1 demonstrates some key points. First, shortage in the apparel departments (EAS users) dropped steadily since year 1, while shortage in the apparel departments in the eight non-user stores rose during the same time period. Second, overall shortage in the user locations dropped at a slower rate than in the user departments - indicating that shortages rose in other departments within the same locations. In these cases user departments represent about 60% of the stores' total sales, so the entire overall shortage reduction was attributable to the performance in the EAS tagged departments. Third, overall shortage in the eight non-EAS stores rose steadily, while falling in the EAS user stores. Performance of this nature was common, and is characteristic of retail chains which stagger installation of EAS over a period of years. This topic is to be covered below in the third case study.

FIGURE 1
SHORTAGE COMPARISON BETWEEN STORES WITH AND WITHOUT EAS

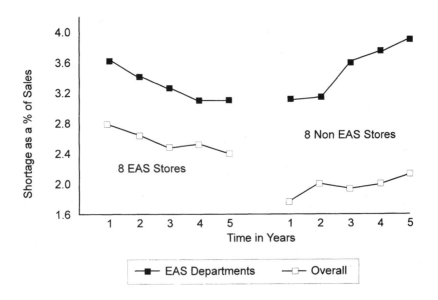

In summary, shortage in EAS user departments in user stores decreased about 17% during the 5 years of the study. Shortage in the same departments in the non-EAS user locations rose 30% during the same time. Overall shortages decreased in EAS user stores strictly on the strength of the shortage improvement in the user departments.

The introduction of EAS was the only security measure that was introduced selectively in this department store chain. All other security programs were evenly applied across all stores. Because of the accuracy and thoroughness of the study, management drew two conclusions. First, the results in the EAS user departments and stores were clearly superior to results in non-EAS locations, and second, that EAS would be introduced into all remaining stores. As of this writing, the chain continues to use EAS in all stores.

What is the Effect on Shortage if EAS is Removed, then Reinstalled?

This next case describes a 9-year experiment with EAS in a prominent West Coast department store division of a nationally recognized chain (not the same as in the case mentioned above). In the late 1970s, EAS was installed in seven of 12 stores with great success. Before the equipment was installed, the EAS user locations incurred overall shortages of about 4.0% as a group. These stores were in predominantly urban locations. The fashion apparel departments were the designated EAS user departments. Before installation, the aggregate shortage of this group exceeded 7.0% of sales. During the first year after the installation, shortage in the EAS user departments dropped 47%, and the shortage in these departments in one particular store (store 360) dropped over 80%.

Management was pleased with the decision to install EAS, but because store 360's shortage dropped precipitously (to 1.4% of sales), they decided to remove the EAS

FIGURE 2
EFFECTS ON SHORTAGE OF REMOVAL AND INSTALLATION OF EAS IN ONE
STORE (360) COMPARED WITH OTHER USER AND NON-USER STORES

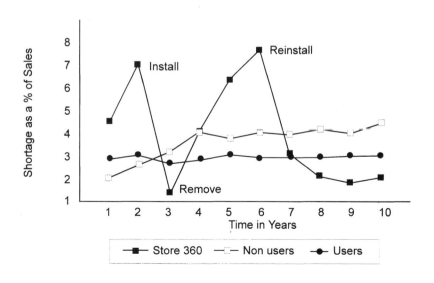

equipment and place it in another location with high shortage. It was thought too costly to maintain the EAS system in a store with such a low shortage, and it was doubted that shortage levels could possibly return to the previous high. In order to add some deterrent qualities to this situation, it was agreed to leave the electronic detection equipment positioned in the store's exits, but to remove all plastic tags and accessory devices.

The EAS equipment was removed in early 1980. Immediately after its removal, shortage began to rise quickly. Between 1980 and 1982, shortage in the EAS user departments rose from 1.4% of sales to 7.7%. Based upon the disastrous 1982 results, management decided to reinstall EAS.

The information contained in Figure 2 demonstrates another key point regarding the use of shortage statistics to establish an economic benefit for EAS systems. The removal of the EAS equipment resulted in a large and immediate rise in inventory shortage. The subsequent re-installation of the equipment resulted in another dramatic shortage reduction. These data provide some statistical verification of the value of the system. Additionally, many of the same patterns of shortage performance chronicled in the first case study have been repeated in this case. Most notable is the idea that shortages in user stores can sustain a gradual reduction over an extended time, while shortages in non-user stores tend to rise during the same period.

As in the first case, comparing shortage results before and after the installation of EAS equipment demonstrates the pivotal economic benefit to the retailer. To illustrate the point, in the last year before the re-installment of EAS, store 360's annual sales in the EAS user departments were approximately $8 million. A 7.7% loss equaled $616,000. During the next year, after the re-installation of EAS, shortage dropped to 2.9% on sales of $8.2 million, or a loss of only about $238,000. The difference of $378,000 (reduced to its cost complement) is the pool of money which is used to cost justify the equipment purchase. The cost of re-outfitting the store and managing all aspects of the EAS system was only about $105,000, thereby providing a highly beneficial return on the investment.

How Can the Effects of EAS be Measured if the Equipment is Installed over a Long Period of Time?

Most multi-store users of EAS equipment install it in groups of stores over time (usually years). Characteristically, EAS is first installed in stores with shortages at crisis levels. As shortages drop in the initial installations, other stores became candidates and the process repeats itself until either all stores become users or the economic situation in the remaining stores does not warrant EAS.

The following third case is taken from a large East Coast department store division of a nationally prominent chain. Over a period of nine years, the division installed EAS in six different groups of stores until about 45% of the stores were equipped (21 of 46 stores). Each group contained between two and five locations. The EAS-user stores represented about 62% of the division's sales volume. Senior management was accustomed to reviewing overall shortage data on a chainwide basis, and since these figures remained fairly constant, they questioned whether EAS had any positive economic impact.

In reviewing the shortage data, it became clear that the piecemeal installation of EAS had little impact upon the chainwide overall shortage for two reasons. First, the shortage and sales in each group of EAS user stores represented only a small fraction of chainwide shortage. Since these groups were installed over a long period of time, the net effect of any shortage improvement was hidden by the magnitude of the chainwide numbers, and by the fact that the reductions took place over such a long time period. Second, inventory shortages were rising chainwide in the apparel portion of the business, the departments in which EAS was installed, while shortage performance in hardlines was improving. The net result was that overall shortages were unchanged even though each user store had shown dramatic improvement in its apparel shortage.

FIGURE 3
SHORTAGE COMPARISON (USING THE SHORTAGE PERFORMANCE MATRIX)
OF EAS USER STORES (21) WITH NON-USER STORES (25)

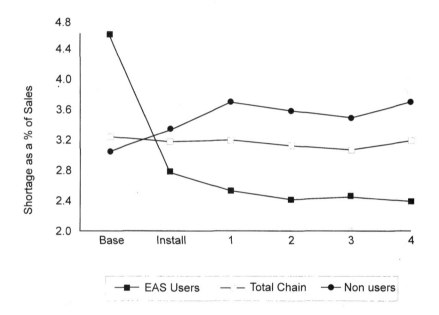

In order to clarify the situation, the same statistical techniques described in the first two cases were applied here. Statistics from EAS user and non-user stores and departments were isolated and the installation dates for EAS were obtained. Individual store statistics were accumulated and analyzed, but due to the staggered installations, no clear picture existed of the size or rate of impact that EAS may have had on the profitability of the company. In order to solve this problem, a *shortage performance matrix* (DiLonardo, 1985) was designed which provided a method with which to align the statistics regardless of the year of installation. Starting with the pre-installation base year, the matrix measures shortage performance in stores as if EAS had been installed simultaneously in all of them. For example, assume that three stores installed EAS in 1982, four stores in 1983 and five stores in 1984. The base year for statistical purposes is the last full year of shortage data before the EAS installation. As in the other cases mentioned above, this is when high shortages force management into making decisions. In our example, 1981 is the base year for the stores which had EAS installed in 1982; 1982 is the base year for stores installing

EAS in 1983, and so on.

Figure 3 illustrates this idea graphically. The X-axis is the time function which plots the base year, the year EAS was installed, and the subsequent four years- providing a composite performance over an extended period of time. Since all data begin with a base year instead of a chronological year, groups of stores installed at different times can be treated statistically as a unit. This method can be employed to study overall shortage or shortage within merchandise categories. An analysis of this type is not complex because inventory shortage is reported in dollars and as a percentage of sales. Therefore, the shortage percentage for the composite base year is simply the accumulation of the shortage dollars divided by sales dollars in the same departments or stores.

In Figure 3 shortage in EAS user stores dropped from 4.5% to 2.75% in the first full year after the installation, a reduction of about 39%. Shortage continued to drop for the next four full fiscal years. For the non-user stores, shortage rose about 13% over the 6-year period which was during a similar time as the user stores. It is interesting to note that the shortage performance of the entire chain barely changed. Inventory shortages dropped significantly in the apparel departments of the EAS user stores, while rising in non-user stores. The matrix helped to quantify the aggregate amount of the savings, and the results supported a decision to install EAS in the remainder of the stores.

The Relationship Between Shortage and Sales

It is worth noting that the amount of inventory loss has a direct and measurable impact upon a store's sales. If an item is stolen from a store, the opportunity to sell it for a profit is lost forever. Additionally, all of the costs incurred to bring that item to market are lost. If enough items are stolen rather than sold, the retailer suffers because of an increase in shortage and because he has fewer items left to sell. To illustrate, assume that a fruit stand contains ten apples which are to be sold for $1.00 each. If all are sold, the retailer realizes $10 in sales and zero in shortage. If two are stolen and eight are sold, sales drop to $8, and inventory shortages rise to $2, or 25% of sales. The costs associated with bringing all ten apples to market are the same in both cases. Over time, the combined losses can have disastrous effects on the profitability of the store.

As has been shown in the above cases, the typical EAS user installs equipment in high volume, high shortage stores because the financial payback from shortage reduction is earned fastest. Additional stores are protected as shortage rises to crisis levels. Some enlightened retail chains install EAS equipment in all new stores as each is opened as "insurance" against high shortage. Historically, however, the primary reason for the application of EAS has been to stimulate a reversal in deteriorating shortage results.

A look at the merchandise assortment planning process provides a more positive view of EAS as a management tool. Successful stores, whether a single or multiple unit operation, prepare and execute model stock plans based upon sales projections. They begin with a revenue forecast and work backwards to the number of units required to be sold at a given price in order to achieve the plan. In general, a high volume store receives a better selection and more depth of stock. A medium-sized store receives a slightly narrower selection, with some marginal styles excluded. A small store receives only the most marketable items even though it is generally accepted (Poisson theory of distribution) that small stores require a higher percentage of total stock in order to generate a smaller percentage of sales. Each style, size, and color in the small store's assortment is critical to sales performance. Even a small amount of shoplifting of key items will negatively impact a small store's merchandise assortment, and the net result is higher shortage and lower sales. Little work has been done in studying this aspect of the potential economic benefits of security devices like EAS.

Conclusions

Retail inventory reconciliation statistics clearly show that EAS has been, and continues to be, an effective anti-shoplifting tool. Historically, almost all retailers have used the retail method of accounting, which records almost everything as a percentage of sales. The consistency of this method of reporting makes comparison studies between retail organizations relatively easy to accomplish. Until the mid- to late- 1980s, the industry had some difficulty isolating and reporting the relevant statistics, but since that time the methods explained in the cases above have become standard operating procedure for retailers around the world.

The most important methods of measurement are comparative in nature. Shortage in EAS user stores should be compared to non-user stores. As mentioned previously, overall shortage is not necessarily the best indicator of performance. Shortage statistics in the EAS user departments should be compared to those in non-user stores. Finally, the best yardstick for economic measurement compares the performance before EAS was installed to results afterwards.

9.   The Care of Public Transport in The Netherlands

Henk van Andel

EDITOR'S NOTE: One of the studies included in Crime as Opportunity *(Mayhew et al., 1976), the Home Office's first venture into situational prevention, dealt with vandalism on double-deck buses. Its findings suggested that bus conductors perform a valuable crime prevention role because vandalism was much greater on buses operated without them. Dispensing with conductors was a cost-saving measure, and public transit systems throughout the world have employed the same rationale to shed staff such as porters, guards, and ticket collectors who exercise an informal surveillance function. It may not be extrapolating too far from the Home Office study to suggest that the almost universal increase of crime and vandalism on public transport may have been the result of this policy. This case study, first appearing as an article in the* British Journal of Criminology *(van Andel, 1989), reports an enlightened attempt by the government of the Netherlands, influenced by the important crime prevention work of Jan van Dijk and others in the Dutch Ministry of Justice, to reverse the damage. Public funds were provided to permit the employment of some 1,200 individuals to serve as "VIC's" (the Dutch acronym for "safety, information and control" officers) on the tram and metro systems in three major cities. Together with a new boarding procedure for buses which meant that passengers had to show their tickets to the driver, this led to a substantial decline in fare evasion and some reduction of vandalism. While the resultant savings did not pay for the new positions, these were filled by unemployed young people, especially by women and minorities and, van Andel argues, these important social benefits have to be part of the cost-benefit calculation. The successful experience with VIC's on public transport has resulted in the concept being extended so that "city guards," as they are known, now operate in more than forty towns and cities in Holland, with useful results in terms of the reduction of fear and crime (van Dijk, 1997).*

AN EXPERIMENT has been carried out in the Dutch public transport system to tackle fare-dodging, vandalism, and aggression. On the tram and metro system the level of inspection has been increased by employing about 1,200 young people. On buses the boarding procedure has been changed. The results show that the percentage of fare-dodgers fell after the introduction of the measures. The number of incidents decreased during the project; feelings of insecurity did not decrease. Damage experts, passengers, and staff agree that the measures put a halt to the increasing trend in vandalism. Given costs and benefits, the measures made an important contribution to cutting petty crime on public transport and thereby improved the quality of service.

Introduction

When the present government came to power in the Netherlands it expressed concern that the massive scale of minor traffic offences, petty offenses against property, and other forms of minor vandalism were seriously endangering safety on the streets. The response of the minister of justice was to set up a special committee in September 1983. The minister took the line that petty crime not only had a negative impact on the quality of life in the Netherlands but also placed enormous demands on the police and courts.

The committee's first report, published in December 1984, contained an attempt to apply the theory of situational crime prevention to the phenomenon of petty crime.[1] According to this theory, certain forms of crime are committed simply because numerous opportunities for doing so present themselves (Mayhew *et al.*, 1976; Clarke, 1983). It is not poverty or a personality defect that makes the thief, but opportunity.

In addition to the question of whether the temptation does or does not exist, there is the importance of security measures. In view of the limited success of technical security measures (Mayhew, 1984), the committee recommended tackling petty crime by reinstating service personnel (instead of machines) to perform supervisory functions in otherwise impersonal situations (the concept of occupational surveillance).

One of the areas considered by the committee was public transport. The increase in fare-dodging and vandalism on Dutch public transport is a good example of petty crime which can largely be attributed to a decline in functional supervision (i.e. the theory of opportunism). Conductors disappeared for economic reasons as long ago as 1963. This entailed a change in procedure on boarding a bus or tram: the driver was now responsible for selling and checking tickets. The introduction in 1966 of automatic machines to stamp tickets relieved the driver of some of this responsibility but at the same time increased opportunities for fare-dodging. In the case of trams the problem was compounded by the introduction of a new design of vehicle with more than one door. Responsibility for ensuring that passengers had a valid ticket shifted from driver to individual passenger, and contact between the two parties was reduced; supervision of passengers in bus or tram largely disappeared (Hauber, 1977).

In response to these developments, the minister of transport and public works announced in December 1984 the introduction of two measures: one for the tram and metro system and one for the bus system. The public transport companies operating tram and metro services in the three major cities (Amsterdam, The Hague, and Rotterdam) were thus authorized to take on, as an experiment for a period of three years, approximately 1,200 unemployed young people to tackle fare-dodging, vandalism, and aggression on the tram and metro system and to improve the information and service available to passengers. These new officials are known in Dutch as VIC (corresponding to *Veiligheid, Informatie, Controle* — safety, information and control). A sum of 33 million guilders was set aside each year for this purpose, reflecting the government's concern with combating petty crime and with practical steps to reduce youth unemployment and for opening up employment opportunities for women and members of ethnic minorities. In calculating this sum, allowance was made for some 13 million guilders per year in extra revenue for the public transport companies and a saving of 3 million guilders on the costs associated with vandalism. Thus the total budget for the tram and metro experiment was 49 million guilders per year. The second measure introduced involved changing the procedure when boarding a bus. All passengers must now walk past the driver, who checks their tickets to see if they are valid and sells them a new one if necessary.

The two measures — the VIC project (tram, metro) and the change in the boarding procedure on buses — have been jointly evaluated by the Ministry of Transport and Public Works, the Ministry of Justice[2] and the public transport companies of the three cities. This article briefly assesses the extent to which the goals of the project were realized in the first two years of operation. The following questions are considered. Have the appointment of VICs and the change in the boarding procedure on the buses reduced fare-dodging and thus increased public transport revenue? Has vandalism in vehicles, at bus and tram stops, and in metro stations declined? Has passenger information improved? Do passengers and employees feel more secure? Discussion of the results is preceded by a brief description of the measures themselves and the design of the evaluation.

Description of the Measures

VIC project. In autumn 1984, the public transport companies of Amsterdam, Rotterdam and The Hague were given permission to recruit 1,200 new VIC employees as a way of increasing safety, information, and control. The companies were allowed to organize the project as they considered appropriate for their own situation.

The recruitment campaign was geared to employing unemployed people aged 19-28 and every effort was made to ensure that women and ethnic minorities were well-represented in the intake. There was a good response to the campaign. Requirements were low, but employees had to be able to cope with unfriendly passengers and fare-dodgers: in the end, only one in ten applicants could actually be recruited as VIC, many proving unsuitable for lack of the required social skills. Of those taken on, 50 percent had been unemployed, 30 percent were women, and 25 percent came from ethnic minority groups (blacks, Mediterranean, etc.).

On January 1, 1987, 535 VICs were employed in Amsterdam, 375 in Rotterdam and 230 in The Hague. All VICs received short (2-3 month) training comprising a number of courses in criminal law and legal theory and practical exercises in ticket inspection. In general the VICs performed well in their new function.

VICs are deployed in different ways in the three cities. In Amsterdam and Rotterdam they are authorized to impose fines. In Amsterdam they work in groups of 2-4, checking trams and the metro system on a random basis. Once they have checked a tram or metro train they get out and board another one. In Rotterdam the VICs check trams on a random basis, but man the metro stations permanently. However, their role in the metro stations is not to check passengers but to provide information and fulfill a preventive function. The Hague opted for a "ustomer friendly" approach. VICs travel in pairs the full length of the tram route and are not authorized to impose fines. Passengers caught without a valid ticket are given the choice of buying one from the driver or leaving the tram.

In the event of problems with passengers, VICs in all three cities can obtain support from a special team or from the police as the tramdriver can use his radiotelephone to summon assistance which should arrive within minutes.

Change in boarding procedure on the buses. Until the 1970s, responsibility for both ticket sales and ticket inspection rested with the bus driver. Automatic machines for stamping tickets were introduced as a means of speeding up the service and improving punctuality. This reduced direct contact between the driver and passengers and was followed by an increase in fare-dodging. After a successful pilot project in which all passengers were required to board the bus at the door nearest to the driver and show their tickets or buy a new one, the new procedure was introduced on a permanent basis in Amsterdam in 1985 and in Rotterdam and The Hague a year later. The automatic machines for stamping tickets in buses have been taken out of service or removed altogether.

Design of the Evaluation

The research was designed to be quasi-experimental, involving both a pre-test and a post-test (Cook and Campbell, 1979) and comprised three elements:

1. *Quantification of the extent of fare-dodging.* The purpose of this was to discover the extent to which the number of people illegally using public transport has fallen since the deployment of VICs and the introduction of the new boarding procedure for buses. For this purpose, the public transport companies carried out a series of counts, making random checks on all passengers in a tram, bus or metro train.[3] These took place in March 1985 (base figure), November 1985, March 1986, and November 1986.[4]

2. *Following trends in the costs associated with vandalism.* This research used the costs of repairing damage and drew on the opinions of damage experts, passengers, and staff.

3. *Interviews with passengers and staff.* The measures taken were expected to make public transport safer and more attractive. In order to ascertain whether this was indeed the case, a survey was carried out among passengers and staff (including VICs). A representative sample of public transport users (N=900) were asked before and after the introduction of the new measures to assess a large number of aspects of the public transport system.[5] They were also asked about their experiences as regards safety, vandalism, information, and inspection. The first survey was conducted in November 1985, the second in September 1986. A

preliminary survey revealed that passengers regarded safety as the most important of the three VIC responsibilities for ensuring a high standard of public transport. A questionnaire was also carried out in September 1986 among regular staff and VICs. The survey among VICs was useful for determining whether they considered their job worthwhile and whether they were motivated.

Results

Fare-dodging. It is clear from the counts that the percentage of fare-dodgers fell in all three cities after the introduction of the VICs and the change in the boarding procedure for buses (Fig. 1). The decline was most pronounced during the rush hour on weekdays, largely because of the hours worked by the VICs: a 32-hour week with a heavy bias towards normal

FIGURE 1
PERCENTAGE OF FARE-DODGING:
BEFORE AND AFTER THE NEW MEASURES

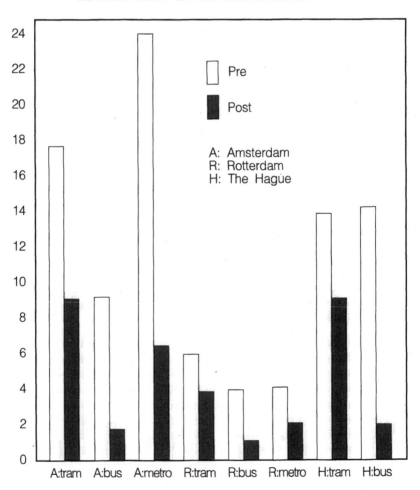

working hours; deployment is less at weekends and late at night, and this is reflected in the higher percentage of fare-dodgers at these times.

In Amsterdam the introduction of the VICs produced a sharp fall in the percentage of fare-dodgers on the tram (from 17.7 percent to 9.0 percent) and the metro (23.5 percent to 6.5 percent). The largest drop occurred in the first year. The publicity surrounding the intensification of ticket inspection probably led to a sharp initial decline in fare-dodging which subsequently stabilized. The new boarding procedure on the buses also led to a sharp decline (from 9.2 percent to 1.7 percent).

A reduction in fare-dodging was also evident in Rotterdam, despite the fact that the percentage of fare-dodgers before the introduction of the measures was already low. On the trams the percentage of fare-dodgers fell from 5.8 percent to 3.7 percent, on the metro from 4.0 percent to 2.6 percent, and on the buses from 3.8 percent to 1.3 percent. The Hague experienced an initial decline in the percentage of fare-dodgers on the trams (from 13.7 percent to 9.5 percent), but this was not followed by any subsequent drop. The change in the boarding procedure on the buses produced a large drop (from 14.1 percent to 2.4 percent).

The survey carried out among passengers revealed that they had noticed an increase in ticket inspections, more so in Amsterdam and The Hague than in Rotterdam. This can be explained by the proportionately greater increase in the number of ticket inspectors in these two cities. Rotterdam already employed a relatively large number of inspectors before the introduction of the VICs. The changes have produced a significant, across-the-board increase in passenger satisfaction on this issue. In the 1985 survey passengers often awarded a low score to the transport company for the frequency of ticket inspection, a year later most considered this aspect highly satisfactory. Passengers apparently like being asked to show their tickets. The increase in passenger satisfaction is connected with passengers' impression that fewer people are dodging fares than they used to before the VICs. However, a quarter of passengers still think that fare-dodging is acceptable in certain situations (e.g. for people on low incomes).

As a result of increased ticket inspection, respondents claim that they no longer dodge fares or that they do so less than before. There seems to be a strong correlation between behavior and a person's views on fare-dodging: those who regard it as acceptable show a greater tendency to dodge fares.

A closer analysis of fare-dodgers as a group reveals the following:

- Young people dodge fares more often than old people and have been least influenced by the new measures; the average age of the fare-dodger has fallen in the period covered by the evaluation. Old people are apparently more afraid of being caught without a ticket or take being caught more to heart.

- Men dodge fares more often than women; however, the difference has become less pronounced as a result of a more marked decline in fare-dodging among men aged 25-40.

There remains, therefore, a specific group of young passengers who are little affected by the increased controls.

Safety. The number of violent incidents on public transport has fallen during the project. In 1985, 11 percent of passengers reported having seen someone attacked or harassed in the three months preceding the survey, and 5 percent had themselves been the victim of such an attack. A year later, in 1986, the percentages had fallen to 3 percent and 2 percent respectively.

One in three passengers thinks that safety has improved because of the increase in the number of staff. However, the level of feelings of insecurity has declined only slightly and such feelings remain common: 24 percent of passengers sometimes feel unsafe, and 13 percent occasionally avoid public transport for this reason (the corresponding figures before the changes were 27 percent and 15 percent). Clearly, feelings of insecurity are influenced by many social factors, and being the victim of an incident makes a lasting impression on a person's perception of the situation (Heijden, 1984).

Vandalism. In the years preceding the new measures, public transport companies were faced with ever-rising costs as a result of vandalism. Deploying VICs to combat vandalism is just one of many projects which have been started in response to this problem. Municipal authorities, for example, have initiated various projects to tackle vandalism and apprehend young vandals, and public transport companies have invested large sums in materials designed to withstand vandalism.

A slight reduction in repair costs for vehicles and rolling stock was evident in Amsterdam in 1986 after the introduction of VICs,[6] but there was no noticeable difference for metro stations. The reduction in the other two cities was less marked. The figures show no consistent trend.

A study was carried out in Amsterdam into cleaning times for two virtually identical tram routes. For a three-week period, VICs were present in the trams on one line for 29 percent of the time but never boarded trams on the other line. All trams on both lines were inspected every night and cleaned and repaired as thoroughly as possible ready for reuse. Trams on the line without VICs took roughly 15 percent longer to clean than those on the line patrolled by VICs. In Rotterdam and The Hague, the decline in damage and graffiti in buses and trams does not show up in the figures, but experts and depot managers nevertheless have the impression that less time has been spent on vehicle repairs and cleaning to remedy the effects of vandalism.

Since VICs have been on duty in the metro stations in Rotterdam the amount of graffiti on external walls has remained virtually unchanged, but the amount inside the stations has fallen by roughly 30 percent.[7] There has also been a decline in the number of broken windows in metro stations. At tram and bus shelters at street level, however, the number of windows that had to be replaced in the same period doubled.

Passengers reported seeing fewer cases of people damaging or defacing property in 1986. In the survey they expressed greater satisfaction with the appearance and cleanliness of the public transport system.[8] As would be expected, vandalism usually occurs out of sight of employees, but a quarter of the staff interviewed did discover at the end of the shift, anything from several times a week to every day, that something had been damaged or defaced. However, at least half the staff felt that vandalism had declined since the introduction of VICs.

It is impossible on the basis of the various figures available to draw any firm conclusions about the impact on costs associated with vandalism. The variations are too marked, and vandalism also depends on other factors. However, damage experts, passengers, and staff unanimously agree that the VICs and new boarding procedures on the buses have stemmed the long-standing increase in vandalism.

Information. Passengers' assessment of the information provided on public transport has been almost unaffected by the measures, although they are pleased that there are more opportunities for asking staff questions. The proportion of people dissatisfied on this score has fallen from 37 percent to 26 percent. The proportion of people who regularly ask employees questions inside the vehicles has increased from 9 percent to 28 percent.

What the changes mean to passengers and staff. The introduction of VICs and the change in boarding procedures on buses have not gone unnoticed among passengers and have improved the image of public transport. Passengers now give a higher rating to many aspects which affect the quality of public transport. Aspects which were rated unsatisfactory before the introduction of VICs (such as ticket inspection) are now judged satisfactory.

Despite the fact that passengers give a positive verdict on the performance of the VICs and have noted a number of improvements, this has not led to an increased use of public transport in Amsterdam and Rotterdam. Only in The Hague do 7 percent of respondents now claim to use the system more frequently. On the other hand, there is no indication that former fare-dodgers have abandoned public transport: it can therefore be inferred that they are now more likely to buy a ticket.

Employees are in general well disposed to the new measures. A large percentage of the staff believe that thanks to VICs the number of fare-dodgers and incidence of vandalism have decreased and information on services has improved. Tram drivers do not feel that their personal safety has improved, but do feel less lonely. There has been no change in the level of aggression by passengers against tram drivers. Bus drivers feel that they now have more authority and are in favor of the new boarding procedure.

The VICs themselves take a positive view of the project. They think their work is effective and have a high opinion of the co-operation and supervision from the public transport companies. The VICs feel that they have managed to establish a clear role in the eyes of the passengers. Their only regret is that they cannot devote more time to the safety aspect of their work which, they feel, has yielded the fewest results.

Evaluation

Deployment of VICs. The public transport companies have adopted different policies as regards the powers allocated to VICs and the way in which they are deployed. The principal differences relate (a) to whether they are authorized to impose fines and (b) to whether they carry out random checks or travel on particular vehicles.

One of the most important tasks of the VICs is to inspect tickets on trams and in the metro. Counts show that the percentage of fare-dodgers have fallen sharply on all three public transport systems. In The Hague, however, the percentage soon stabilized at a relatively high level. Passengers, and fare-dodgers in particular, quickly realized that the VICs in The Hague were not authorized to impose fines, and this has undermined the effectiveness of the checks. People would pay only if confronted by a VIC, and even then would not receive a fine. Further, the disadvantage of the system of assigning VICs to particular trams is that passengers can see whether there are VICs on board and decide to wait for the next tram instead. With 250 VICs working in pairs, it is never possible to man more than 20 percent of the tram services in The Hague.[9]

The greatest improvement in safety seems to have been achieved in those places where staff (VICs) monitor the situation for longer periods of time. In particular, the passengers on the trams in The Hague, where VICs accompany particular vehicles, and on the metro in Rotterdam, where they are deployed in a particular metro station, feel that safety has improved.

The decrease in graffiti and damage in the metro stations in Rotterdam which are permanently manned by VICs and the lower cleaning costs on tram lines in Amsterdam which are inspected by VICs suggest that VIC presence over a longer period of time has a stronger preventive effect on vandalism.

The foregoing suggests that from the point of view of ticket inspection, VICs who accompany particular trams for the length of their journey are less effective than those who carry out random checks, because their movements are more predictable. On the other hand, the presence of VICs in a particular place for longer periods improves safety and reduces vandalism. If VICs are to carry out their inspection duties effectively they must be authorized to impose fines.

Financial costs and benefits of the VIC project. Deploying the VICs costs 49 million guilders per year: 43 million guilders for wages; 2.5 million guilders for management costs; and 3.5 million guilders for overheads.

The benefits which the public transport systems derive from the deployment of VICs may be classified as follows:

- A significant decline in fare-dodging. Depending on the type of journey and the sort of ticket bought, the extra revenue from ex-fare-dodgers on the trams and metro is estimated at between 12 and 14 million guilders.

- An increase in the number of fines imposed. The extra revenue generated (for the Ministry of Justice) is estimated at 1 million guilders per year.

- Costs associated with vandalism have stabilized or even fallen slightly. However, these changes cannot be ascribed exclusively to the introduction of VICs, as other measures to tackle vandalism have undoubtedly also played a part. A sum of 1.5 million guilders has been credited on the benefit side of the project: this does not represent an actual cost reduction but a leveling off of the trend of increasing costs.

Given that the benefits to the public transport systems are worth between 14.5 and 16.5 million guilders and total costs are 49 million guilders, the VIC project in its current form covers roughly one third of its costs. This is more or less what was expected when the project was started.

Financial costs and benefits of the new boarding procedure on the buses. Reactions to the new boarding procedure have been overwhelmingly positive, even though buses are delayed longer at the stops as a result. This has forced the bus companies to put on extra buses on some routes, given that passengers regard punctuality as the most important criterion in their assessment of public transport.

The new boarding procedure entails costs of 6.1 million guilders. The benefits take the form of increased revenue because fewer people are dodging fares. One obvious difference between this and ticket inspection by VICs is that everyone boarding the bus is checked. The benefits for the three cities together are estimated at 3.6 million guilders. In Amsterdam and The Hague the new boarding procedure almost completely covers its costs. In Rotterdam, where an effective inspection system already operated so that the percentage of fare-dodgers was relatively low in the first place, the costs were relatively high.

Social benefits. In addition to the financial costs and benefits, which are important for the public transport companies, the measures also have a social significance. As in most cases it is impossible to place a monetary value on the social benefits, they are described below largely in qualitative terms:

- The measures have made an important contribution to cutting petty crime on the public transport system. This improves the quality of public transport.

- The VIC project has created approximately 1,200 new 32 hour-per-week jobs. Savings on unemployment benefits amount to some 21 million guilders per year. Many of the new jobs have been taken by young unemployed people, who thereby gain work experience and training.

- The VIC project has provided an opportunity for putting into practice the government's policy of opening up employment opportunities for women and members of ethnic minorities.

Discussion

In the light of the results, the increased level of ticket inspection achieved by the deployment of VICs on trams and metro and the introduction of tighter controls when boarding buses may be said to have succeeded in the short term in reducing petty crime on public transport. Increased staff presence did not, however, reduce passengers' feelings of insecurity, although safety in a number of places did improve. Certain other effects may become apparent in the longer term. Feelings of insecurity, for example, might still diminish. Passengers think that fewer people dodge fares, and this may lead to a shift in norms: fare-dodging may come to be seen as less acceptable. The employees' positive attitude towards the VIC project probably has an effect on their manner towards passengers, which can in turn improve relations between staff and passengers and increase social control. So the results can be seen as a confirmation of the close link between the concepts of situational crime prevention and occupational surveillance. Shaw (1986) came to similar conclusions in evaluating the effect of crime-prevention projects: employing caretakers is more effective in preventing crime than any amount of hardware.

Notes

1. The Committee defines the term "petty crime" in its first report (p. 12) as follows: "punishable forms of behavior occurring on a large scale which can be dealt with by the police on a discretionary basis or, in the case of a first offence, are generally handled by the Public Prosecutor or are dealt with by the courts at the most through the imposition of a fine and/or a conditional custodial sentence and which — mainly because of the scale on which they occur — are a source of nuisance or engender feelings of insecurity among the public."
2. Following its first report the committee received funds to carry out a number of experiments. These built on the recommendations to the minister of justice made in the plan for fighting crime entitled *Crime and Society* (Bottomley, 1986). The evaluation of the VIC project is just one instance of this.

3. The research used a national registration system in which the public transport network was divided into a number of equal areas/routes. For each area and time of day (peak hours, off-peak hours, and evening), a sample was taken among those passengers who had their tickets checked.
4. In Rotterdam the measure for the base figure was taken in November 1985.
5. The study began at a time when the change in boarding procedure had been operating for over six months in Amsterdam and only one month in The Hague. Some transport companies had already recruited the full number of VICs on certain sections of the system. Because of this, and because changes in attitude and behavior take much longer to manifest themselves than the period covered by the counts, the results do not convey a complete picture. The results should be seen as an indication of what actually happened.
6. The damage repair costs represent the adjusted calculations of damage clearly identified as being the result of vandalism. Repair costs are calculated on the basis of repair work and replacement costs using new and old parts which are still in stock and in working order. In some cases repairs are combined with regular servicing. Not all costs are recorded immediately. Damage to vehicles and street furniture as a result of football hooliganism or squatters' riots is included in the general figures.
7. However, most graffiti is done after 23:00 hours when VICs are no longer on duty in the metro stations.
8. In Amsterdam in particular, it was found that benches, arm and back rests, and seats were damaged less frequently. This is partly connected with the fact that seats with padding, which are easily slashed, have been replaced by hard, polyester ones that are less easily vandalized.
9. The Hague has since experimented with a new approach. At the end of 1986, in an effort to increase the surprise factor in inspections, the transport company started to deploy VICs on particular sections of a route; on certain sections of a tram route all vehicles are manned by VICs.

ACKNOWLEDGMENTS. Thanks are due to Marianne Hoekert, Corina de Jongh, Liesbeth Nuijten, Jan van Dijk, Guus Roell, and Gert Jan Veerman for their contribution.

10. Preventing Auto Theft in Commuter Lots: A Bike Patrol in Vancouver

Paul Barclay, Jennifer Buckley, Paul J. Brantingham, Patricia L. Brantingham and Terry Whin-Yates

EDITOR'S NOTE: Figure 3 in this case study, an edited version of one first published in Crime Prevention Studies *(Barclay et al., 1996), raises some intriguing possibilities. It strongly suggests that the publicity surrounding proposed bike patrols for a commuter parking lot produced a steep decline in auto thefts about one month before the patrols began. This provides another example of the crime prevention power of publicity (see Case Study #17), and underlines the need for better understanding of ways to exploit this power. However, the graph raises the additional possibility that previous declines in crime noted before the introduction of preventive measures might also have been due to publicity, and might not just have been evidence of the fact, as sometimes was claimed, that crime was declining anyway. If this is indeed a more general phenomenon, perhaps it should be known as "anticipatory diffusion," since it probably relies for its effect on the same mechanisms of deterrence and discouragement underlying diffusion of benefits.*

Introduction

In recent years public policy in British Columbia, as in other developed and urbanized jurisdictions, has placed strong emphasis on reducing the flow of automobiles into city centers by improving public transit in ways that will attract commuters out of their cars and onto mass transit vehicles. One feature of this policy has been the introduction of free "park-and-ride" parking lots for commuters at suburban transit nodes. Commuters from the dispersed bedroom communities of the "divergent metropolis" (Felson, 1994a) can drive to these suburban transit nodes, park their cars for free, and ride high-speed transit the rest of the way into the city center (Mancini and Jain, 1987; Webb *et al.*, 1992). British Columbia Transit (BC Transit) is the Crown corporation responsible for operation of the public transit system in greater Vancouver. Vancouver's mass transit system is, at present, essentially a bus system with one high-speed, elevated automated rail transit line (SkyTrain) and one high-speed commuter ferry (SeaBus) (DesChamps *et al.*, 1991). Park-and-ride lots are associated with suburban SkyTrain stops and a number of major suburban bus interchanges. The park-and-ride lots create concentrations of parked, unattended cars at most hours of the day and night.

Contemporary theoretical work in environmental criminology (Brantingham and Brantingham, 1991) and in routine activities theory (Felson, 1994a) suggests that such concentrations of unattended vehicles should also create hot spots of vehicle crime. And indeed, such commuter parking lots seem to generate disproportionate shares of suburban auto theft in the United States (Mancini and Jain, 1987), in Australia (Geason and Wilson, 1990) and in England and Wales (Webb *et al.*, 1992).

Automobile theft is a high-volume crime in British Columbia generally and in the greater Vancouver area in particular. Within greater Vancouver, automobile theft seems to concentrate near major activity centers and along major transit routes (Fleming *et al.*, 1994; Weigman and Hu, 1992; Brantingham *et al.*, 1991). Studies of this crime in Vancouver strongly support the rational choice theory of offending (Cornish and Clarke, 1986), routine activity theory (Felson, 1994; Cohen and Felson, 1979) and pattern theory (Brantingham and Brantingham, 1993). In particular, there appears to be a strong relationship between auto theft and place (Eck and Weisburd, 1996; Fleming et al., 1994). The majority of British Columbia auto thieves appear to be juveniles who steal for joyriding and transport purposes and who are attracted to malls, large parking lots, and other easily accessible locations that feature concentrations of older vehicle makes and models that are technically easy to steal (Fleming, 1993; Fleming *et al.*, 1994).

BC Transit operates park-and-ride commuter parking lots in association with many of its bus interchanges and SkyTrain stations. The largest of its park-and-ride facilities is located at the Scott Road SkyTrain station in the suburban city of Surrey. The Scott Road facility is comprised of four separate parking lots with a rated capacity of 2,411 parking stalls. This is an enormous concentration of parked cars. The second largest park-and-ride facility in the BC Transit system has a capacity of 400 cars. The Scott Road facility is more than eight times larger than the commuter car park studied by Laycock and Austin (1992:156), more than ten times larger than the average of the 19 suburban London commuter car parks studied by Webb *et al.* (1992:25), and more than 30 times larger than the average of 72 Connecticut commuter car parks studied by Mancini and Jain (1987:544).

Figure 1 is a schematic map of greater Vancouver showing the location of major municipalities, the approximate route of SkyTrain between downtown Vancouver and suburban Surrey, the approximate location of the Scott Road SkyTrain station, and the approximate location of two probable displacement sites.

FIGURE 1
GREATER VANCOUVER REGIONAL DISTRICT
SKYTRAIN, SCOTT ROAD, SURREY CITY CENTRE AND GUILDFORD LOCATIONS

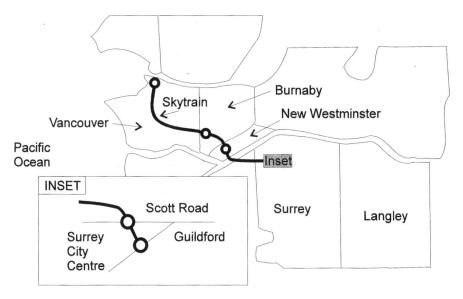

Such a massive park-and-ride facility should, theoretically, constitute a major crime generator (Brantingham and Brantingham, 1995). By the fall of 1994, the Scott Road facility had developed both a public and a police reputation as one of greater Vancouver's crime hot spots (Spinks *et al.*, 1995; Zyartuk, 1994). Auto theft was seen to be one of its major problems.

This article presents the results of a limited natural experiment in which formal surveillance in the form of a security bicycle patrol was introduced into the Scott Road park-and-ride facility for the single month of April 1995. Following completion of this experiment, we were asked by BC Transit Security to help assess the crime prevention impact of the bicycle patrol.

The Scott Road Facility

British Columbia Transit (BC Transit) is the Crown corporation (government-owned, independently incorporated operating authority) responsible for operation of the public transit system in greater Vancouver. The Insurance Corporation of British Columbia (ICBC) is the Crown corporation holding a monopoly over issuance of mandatory motor vehicle liability insurance. It also writes most of the comprehensive vehicle insurance policies that provide theft coverage. The two Crown corporations have a mutual interest in reduction of auto theft. BC Transit must make park-and-ride facilities safe places for transit customers to park if it wishes to increase transit ridership. ICBC must typically pay out about $3,500 per stolen vehicle to repair damage done during the course of the theft (Fleming *et al.,* 1994).

The Scott Road SkyTrain Park-and-Ride is accessible twenty-four hours a day and experiences high traffic, except during the early-morning hours. It is unfenced and most of the lots have multiple entries and exits (see Figure 2). There are no shops in the Scott Road facility and visibility from the SkyTrain station into the parking lots is poor. In terms of the correlates of high-crime car parks identified by Webb *et al.* (1992:25), the Scott Road park-and-ride facility would appear to be an ideal location for the crime of vehicle theft. Moreover, its location near major roadways, with easy transit access and with an absence of formal guardians has been shown to be strongly associated with high crime rates at other suburban locations in greater Vancouver (Brantingham and Brantingham, 1995). It is, however, in an open, flat area. An official guardian, if elevated, would have a broad viewing range across the park-and-ride lots. Actual formal surveillance is possible.

The Bike Patrol

In September 1994, BC Transit Security proposed a comprehensive prevention plan for Scott Road. Consistent with recommendations found in the limited literature on car park security (e.g. Mancini and Jain, 1987: 546-549; Geason and Wilson, 1990: 36-39; Poyner,

FIGURE 2
SCOTT ROAD STATION PARK-AND-RIDE

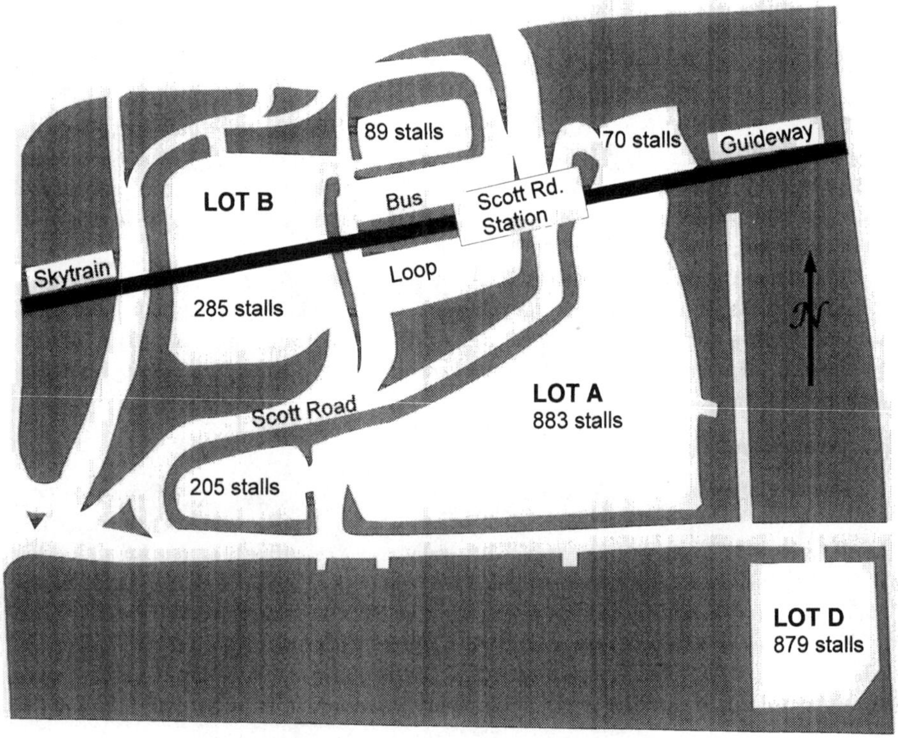

1991; Eck and Spelman, 1992; Laycock and Austin, 1992; Webb *et al.*, 1992) and in line with recommendation made by Seattle Transit security on the basis of Seattle's experience with problems in commuter park-and-ride lots, this plan included fencing the perimeter of the parking lots and limiting access through a single main entrance/exit for each lot; upgrading lighting, trimming shrubs that were blocking sightlines, and introducing a CCTV surveillance system; installing emergency phones throughout the lots; introducing a mobile security guard patrol from 9:00 to 24:00 hours each day, 7 days a week; and instituting a pay parking system coupled with a staffed collection kiosk at the single entry/exit to each lot.

Although this proposal received conceptual support within BC Transit, the large start-up costs required for implementation, together with issues ranging from jurisdictional questions to the relative contributions that might be reasonably expected from other agencies, delayed implementation of any part of the plan until well into 1995 when only the mobile security patrol recommendation was implemented. And that implementation was temporary, operating for the single the month of April 1995. At the completion of the test month, the program was closed while BC Transit looked for some way to assess its impact.

The mobile security patrol "experiment" was designed by BC Transit security. The Insurance Corporation of British Columbia, which was averaging insurance payouts in excess of $40,000 per month as a result of Scott Road vehicle thefts, provided $15,000 to support a one-month test implementation. A private security firm was retained to supply the security personnel utilized in the test. The mobile security patrol took the form of a bicycle patrol that circulated through the Scott Road park-and-ride lots. Four security guards, dressed in bright yellow jackets, helmets, and other gear very similar to that worn by police bicycle patrol constables in greater Vancouver, patrolled in pairs and in irregular patterns during the hours of 7:00 A.M. to 7:00 P.M., Monday through Friday.

Mobile security by bicycle has good surveillance potential at the Scott Road park-and-ride lot. The elevation of bicycle riders is sufficient to allow security personnel a much better view of the lots than would be possible from a vehicle or on foot. Bicycle-mounted security personnel were also highly visible to people using the park-and-ride lot. Bicycles offer another advantage as well. Access to different points in the very large area covered by the park-and-ride lots is quicker by bicycle than by motor vehicle or by foot. Patrol on bicycle, in a high visibility lot with few points of refuge (Nasar and Fisher, 1992, 1993), has the potential of increasing perceived risk on the part of potential offenders.

While the limited and post hoc nature of this study did not make it possible to observe the bicycle patrol or to interview people using the Scott Road SkyTrain station, we believe that such a patrol is more like a security guard at an entrance to a building than it is to a mobile police patrol. Everyone using the SkyTrain station during the hours the bicycle patrol operated would be likely to see the guards on their bicycles even when they were in a different lot.

The introduction of the bicycle patrol was preceded by a media campaign which resulted in extensive coverage in local newspapers and in the major regional daily newspapers starting March 11, 1995. Headlines such as "Bike squad gears up to squelch car break-ins" and "Yellowjackets invade SkyTrain station" capture the flavor of this coverage (Spinks *et al.*, 1995). The Scott Road bike patrol was given coverage on local television news shows on April 1, the day it started. There were also several follow-up stories about the bike patrol in the local press during mid-April.

The Study and its Objectives

In late April, as the test project was coming to a close, one of us was contacted by BC Transit security and asked whether it would be possible to have a team of students from a Simon Fraser University crime prevention course attempt to assess the impact of the bicycle patrol on the auto theft problem at Scott Road despite its short duration and despite limited availability of comparison data.

The initial student study of the bicycle patrol (Spinks *et al.*, 1995) focused on changes in the average number of vehicles stolen from the Scott Road park-and-ride lots for short periods before, during, and after the bicycle-patrol test, utilizing Scott Road park-and-ride vehicle-theft data obtained from the Surrey RCMP detachment. The results of the project indicated that there was a large reduction in vehicle thefts at the Scott Road park-and-ride lots during the test month. During the eight-month pre-test phase, 192 cars were reported stolen. This was an average of 24 cars per month. During the test month (April), only three cars were reported stolen. Theft of autos remained lower than average during the post-experimental phase, with only three cars reported stolen during May and 13 stolen reported in June, indicating a possible diffusion of benefits. (Spinks *et al.*, 1995) .

The student project focused on the Scott Road site alone. As a result, the question of whether there had been any diffusion of benefits from the bicycle-patrol intervention or whether there had been any displacement of vehicle thefts to other locations within Surrey was left open. In addition, it appeared that the media coverage that accompanied the introduction of the bicycle patrol at Scott Road might have enhanced its effect (see Laycock, 1991, and Poyner, 1988, on the interaction of crime prevention initiatives and media coverage). This research attempts to explore both the preventive impact of the bicycle patrol and its attendant media coverage, and displacement and diffusion of benefits effects in more detail using police data on vehicle theft for all parts of Surrey.

Motor vehicle theft data used for this study were obtained from the Surrey RCMP detachment. A differently constructed experiment conducted over a longer time span and situated in a jurisdiction where geographically coded crime data were available for a longer pre-experiment time period would have been better from a scientific point of view. However, the Scott Road park-and-ride bicycle patrol test was run at a crime hot spot by an operating agency that is subject to the pressures and constraints that always limit courses of action outside the laboratory. The police data covered a thirteen-month period, from August 1994 through August 1995. Thefts were recorded by date and for a small spatial unit called an atom. It was impossible to conduct analyses on data for the period prior to August 1994 because the city of Surrey was not divided into small-area atoms for purposes of police record keeping until then.

The test period extended for only a single month. Follow-up data were collected for a period of four months following the experiment.

The Local Backcloth: Broader Trends around the Intervention Site

Although the vehicle theft trends in British Columbia as a whole appeared to be headed downward in 1995 following an extended period of increase (Fleming *et al.*, 1994) the general trend in Surrey and adjacent municipalities appeared to be upward from 1994 or leveling off.

Table 1 compares reported motor vehicle thefts for the first eight months of 1994 and

1995 for Surrey and four adjacent municipalities. Motor vehicle theft was increasing or leveling off in all of these municipalities over the time frame of this study. While there was a downward trend in the province as a whole, there was no general downward trend in the large municipalities that form the Vancouver suburbs in and around Surrey. Any decrease in vehicle thefts at the Scott Road park-and-ride occurred against this general local trend.

TABLE 1
MUNICIPAL MOTOR VEHICLE THEFTS
(EIGHT-MONTH COMPARISONS, 1994 AND 1995)

Municipality	Total Vehicle Thefts January-August, 1994	Total Vehicle Thefts January-August, 1995
Burnaby	1,419	2,329
Langley City	205	212
Langley District	307	314
New Westminster	563	664
Surrey	2,567	3,151
British Columbia Totals	17,238	14,943

The Scott Road experiment was played out against this general backcloth, but requires a more-detailed spatial and temporal analysis to provide a basis for estimating the impact of the natural experiment.

A Site-Specific Analysis

We examined the more specific context of the Scott Road park-and-ride bicycle patrol test and vehicle-theft changes at other Surrey motor vehicle theft hot spots. Two of these hot spots (Block, 1990), Surrey City Centre and Guildford, stood out both because they appeared to be likely displacement locations on theoretical grounds and because, together with the Scott Road park-and-ride facility, these atoms accounted for about 16 percent of all motor vehicle thefts occurring across the 113 Surrey police atoms in the period before the bicycle patrol test took place. Table 2 focuses on the crimes occurring at these four locations before, during, and after the bicycle-patrol test.

TABLE 2
VEHICLE THEFTS BEFORE, DURING, AND AFTER THE
SCOTT ROAD PARK-AND-RIDE BICYCLE-PATROL TEST

Police Small Area	Before Total	Before Column %	During Total	During Column %	After Total	After Column %
Area Surrounding Scott Road	82	13.2	12	8.2	47	18.2
Scott Road	192	30.0	6	4.1	34	13.2
Guildford	159	25.8	69	47.3	88	34.1
Surrey City Centre	189	30.4	59	40.4	89	34.5
Surrey Total	3,116		686		1,056	

As is apparent from Table 2, the Scott Road park-and-ride site dropped from a position as the single hottest vehicle-theft hot spot in Surrey in the pre-test period to a position as a cold spot during the test. In the eight months preceding the test, Scott Road averaged 24 vehicle thefts per month. During the test month and the month immediately following, Scott Road averaged three vehicle thefts per month. In the three months following that, vehicle thefts at Scott Road climbed back to an average of 11.3 per month.

Time series analysis (Barclay *et al.,* 1996) on vehicle-theft data aggregated into weekly counts established that, except for the reduction at Scott Road, there was no significant trend in the level of motor vehicle thefts in Surrey during the test period. The Scott Road vehicle-theft reduction is so large that if it is included in the analysis, there is a mild (but not statistically significant, r = .09) downward trend in auto thefts for Surrey as a whole across the test period. The Scott Road reduction cannot be attributed to seasonal effects. Although there are very strong seasonal effects on vehicle theft in the northern parts of British Columbia (Fleming, 1993), the mild and stable climate of greater Vancouver does not appear to impose climatic fluctuations on vehicle theft in Surrey. A standard seasonal decomposition run on six years of monthly Surrey vehicle theft counts collected for an earlier project (Fleming *et al.,* 1994) found no seasonal effects in the data in the greater Vancouver area.

The magnitude and timing of the impact of the introduction of the bicycle patrol at the Scott Road park-and-ride lot is tracked in Figure 3 using reported vehicle-theft counts. The data have been aggregated into two-week units for the purposes of this figure. The curve has been smoothed using a moving-average procedure to accentuate trends.

FIGURE 3
SCOTT ROAD AUTO THEFT TRENDS

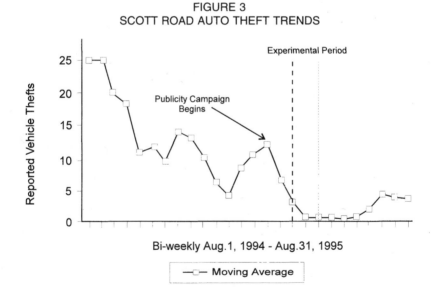

Bi-weekly Aug.1, 1994 - Aug.31, 1995

—□— Moving Average

Three things are apparent in Figure 3. First, the publicity campaign that preceded the actual introduction of the bicycle patrol at Scott Road appears to have had a substantial impact almost immediately. A short upward trend in reported vehicle thefts was reversed, and counts dropped sharply. Second, the actual introduction of the bicycle patrol accelerated the reduction in reported vehicle thefts. Third, the reduced levels of reported vehicle thefts continued at Scott Road for many weeks and were still relatively low at the end of the study period. Note that both the publicity campaign and the bicycle patrol appeared to contribute to this reduction. This combined effect appears to be consistent with similar interactive crime prevention effects reported in crime prevention interventions in England (Laycock, 1992; Poyner, 1988) and reinforces the notion that multiple types of situational interventions can have a cumulative impact in reducing crime at a particular intervention point.

While we have no actual counts, we have been told by BC Transit that there were many telephone complaints about motor vehicle theft at Scott Road prior to the introduction of the bicycle patrol and an inordinate number of complimentary calls after its introduction. The bicycle patrol appears to have had positive impact on transit riders in general, as well as a crime prevention impact. While this cannot be studied because of the post hoc nature of the research, it seems reasonable to us that the high visibility of private security on bicycles (putting the riders at a level from which they could be seen from a distance) may have had a general fear-reduction impact.

The introduction of bicycle patrol at Scott Road appears to have reduced the average motor vehicle theft counts at that park-and-ride facility by some 87.5 percent and this reduction was maintained for some time following termination of the experiment: a clear example of situational crime prevention at an established hot spot and an example of a diffusion of benefits over time at that location.

Displacement and Diffusion of Benefits

Displacement of crime can take a variety of forms (P.L. Brantingham and P.J. Brantingham, 1984; Barr and Pease, 1990). Spatial displacement might move offenders into adjacent areas or to more distant crime generators or crime attractors (Brantingham and Brantingham, 1995). Temporal displacement might move offenders into different time periods at the same location. The Scott Road bicycle patrol operated from 7:00 A.M. to 7:00 P.M., Monday through Friday. A functional displacement might cause offenders to take up some other crime. We are not currently in a position to address the latter possibility, but we can say something about spatial and temporal displacement of motor vehicle thefts.

Diffusion of benefits from a situational crime prevention intervention can similarly take several forms (Clarke and Weisburd, 1994). Benefits can diffuse spatially to other areas, preventing crime at locations that have not experienced the intervention. Such a diffusion is likely when a prevention program is widely advertised, but its spatial boundaries are not made clear. Potential offenders are likely to avoid the general area where the prevention program is implemented rather than just the specifically protected location. Moreover, because much crime is a spatial by-product of travel to some specific destination point, if the destination point is protected and therefore avoided by potential offenders, the nearby areas into which crime might spill over from the destination end up protected as well (Brantingham and Brantingham, 1991, 1995; Langworthy and LeBeau, 1992b).

Benefits can diffuse in time, preventing crime during hours when an intervention, such as the bicycle patrol, is not actually operating and continuing for at least a while after a program stops (Clarke and Weisburd. 1994). This sort of diffusion of benefits in time has been documented as a "residual deterrence" effect from small-area police "crackdowns" by Sherman (1990) and by Kohfeld and Sprague (1990). Short-term, small-area concentrations of police patrol and arrest activity not only suppress crime in the target area during the police action: those reductions appear to continue for a time after the police concentration is withdrawn. A similar effect ought, in principle, to be seen in places where a private security "crackdown" raises the risk of offending. This appears to have happened at Scott Road.

Benefits can also diffuse functionally, preventing other types of crime than those specifically targeted by the situational intervention (Kohfeld and Sprague, 1990). In principle, increasing the risks of committing one type of crime at a specific location could increase the risks of committing other types of crime (Clarke and Weisburd, 1994). In practice, techniques that work well in preventing vehicle thefts do not necessarily work well in preventing thefts from vehicles. At present we do not have sufficient data on the incidence of other types of crime at Scott Road and other parts of Surrey to address this issue.

No Temporal Displacement at Scott Road

We undertook a temporal displacement analysis at Scott Road, exploring whether times at which motor vehicle thefts were reported to the police, and therefore, presumably, the times at which the thefts occurred had changed in any substantial way. No change appears to have occurred. Prior to the introduction of the bicycle patrol, 39.6 percent of all motor vehicle thefts were reported to the police between the hours of 6:00 A.M. and 9:00 A.M. In the period after the experiment started, 41.7 percent of all Scott Road motor vehicle thefts were reported between the hours of 6:00 A.M. and 9:00 A.M. No temporal displacement had occurred.

This is particularly interesting because a substantial proportion of the Scott Road motor vehicle thefts occurred outside the hours during which the bicycle patrol was actually operating. Yet car thieves did not change their temporal patterns to adapt, they reduced their activities instead. This may suggest another diffusion of benefits in diurnal time. If so, then it also suggests that publicity campaigns should be imprecise about the exact hours when a preventive intervention might operate. A crime attractor such as a large parking lot with no surrounding activities requires an affirmative decision to go there to look for a target. While this was not part of the research, it is possible that most of the motor vehicle thieves going to the Scott Road park-and-ride were persons looking for low-risk opportunities. British Columbia motor vehicle thefts are a youth crime aimed at older vehicles (Fleming, 1993). The Scott Road park-and-ride is deserted at night after the trains stop running. The vehicles parked there over-night are exposed without guardianship. Their owners are somewhere else, without their vehicles. Thieves who went to Scott Road at night would probably expect to see no guardians (either official or unofficial) at all. They may have been the ones who keyed on low-risk opportunities in selecting suitable targets (Felson, 1994a; Clarke, 1992). They must have traveled to Scott Road by car (also common in British Columbia for even the theft of old cars (Fleming, 1993)) and, with an expectation of a bicycle patrol, may have been easily deterred. The remaining motor vehicle thefts were probably persons, caught at Scott Road station when the SkyTrain and busses stopped for the night, who stole a vehicle to get home. We have found a similar late-night theft of motor vehicles near bars in another municipality. Bar closing hours are close to bus stopping hours. Bar patrons often miss the last bus home.

We now look at three additional displacement and diffusion areas: the area surrounding Scott Road; Surrey City Centre; and Guildford.

THE AREAS DESCRIBED

The area immediately surrounding the Scott Road park-and-ride atom is mixed industrial and residential. Adjacent atoms are largely lower-income, single-family residential.

Surrey City Centre is a regional shopping center. There is a large grocery store, a library, a few retail stores, a public recreation center, a SkyTrain stop and a bus interchange - all located next to an anchor mall. East of the Surrey City Centre mall are located high-density, lower- and middle-income residential areas. This mall is also located along an arterial highway that runs parallel to the SkyTrain route.

Guildford is a very busy retail-commercial area comprised of numerous fast-food restaurants, video-rental businesses and other "chain" retail shops. Directly adjacent to the area's anchor, Guildford Mall (and directly across the street from some of the parking lots), is a high-density, low-income, older residential area. The residential area is comprised mostly of low-rise apartment buildings and has a palpable "run-down" ambiance.

THE SCOTT ROAD SURROUNDS

We explored the trends in reported motor vehicle thefts at four police atoms that generally surround the Scott Road park-and-ride. The average number of cars stolen per month in this group of atoms was 38. The number of vehicles reported stolen in these atoms during April 1995, the experimental month, was 12.

The atom which immediately surrounded the Scott Road SkyTrain Park-and-Ride may have been directly affected by the bicycle patrol at the park-and-ride. While the total number of thefts for this area for the month of March 1995 was 23, during April, the number of reported auto thefts dropped to four and, in May, only eight thefts were reported. By June the number of reported motor vehicle thefts rose to 17, perhaps indicating the temporal limit of a diffusion of benefits in time and space from a short-term intervention such as the Scott Road bicycle patrol. The numbers were small, however. The limited time for the study makes it show no statistical increase or decrease in the nearest atom during the test period. There was a decrease in the weeks following the test period, perhaps a slow diffusion of benefits.

The other three atoms adjacent to Scott Road had a consistent combined pattern of nine or fewer offenses per month and, because of the small numbers of crimes, analysis of a possible displacement effect was difficult. However, a consistent pattern was apparent in all of these atoms, which were comprised of a mix of both residential and commercial land use: the number of reported auto thefts in April 1995 was near the lowest observed during the thirteen months of the study period.

SURREY CITY CENTRE

An average of 26 stolen vehicles was reported at Surrey City Centre each month over the thirteen-month study period. The average number of reported vehicle thefts for the months preceding April 1995 was 24, while the average for the months following was 29. The number of vehicles reported stolen at Surrey City Centre during the month in which the bicycle patrol was operating at Scott Road was 34. While at first glance this seemingly high number may seem to indicate a displacement effect, a closer examination of the actual pattern of offenses for the thirteen-month period reveals that this is probably not the case. A detailed time series analysis reported in Barclay *et al.* (1996) indicates that there was no measurable displacement to Surrey City Centre.

Temporal displacement analysis was conducted to see whether there was any appreciable change in the times at which Surrey City Centre motor vehicle thefts were reported to the police. Displacement from Scott Road would presumably be reflected in a rise in the proportion of offenses reported at Surrey City Centre during the key reporting times at Scott Road. There was no change in the proportion of offenses reported at Surrey City Centre during the early-morning hours. There was some modification in the pattern of reporting during the early afternoon, but it seems unlikely that Scott Road auto thieves displaced both spatially and temporally. All indications are that the bulk of Scott Road park-and-ride thefts probably involved late-night joyriding or theft for transportation purposes after the SkyTrain and busses stopped running. It seems unlikely that joyriders and thieves trying to get home after a night out on the town would alter their activity patterns to steal cars from Surrey City Centre at midday.

GUILDFORD

The average monthly number of reported motor vehicle thefts for the thirteen-month study period was 24. The average number of thefts for the months preceding April was 20 while the average number for the following months was 30. The number of thefts of auto at Guildford for the test month of April was 38.

The time series analysis (see Barclay *et al.*, 1996)) suggested that there was a partial displacement of Scott Road vehicle thefts to Guildford. This finding is tempered by the temporal displacement data, which showed no substantial modification in the times at which Guildford motor vehicle thefts were reported to the police during and after the Scott Road experiment. This suggests that there was some displacement of opportunistic vehicle theft to Guildford but little or no displacement of planned vehicle theft.

This is consistent with police perceptions: Surrey constables we interviewed informally indicated a belief that a substantial proportion of the vehicle thefts at Scott Road had been opportunistic joyriding and transportation-related thefts by residents of the Guildford area. To the extent that this perception is true, it would explain why some displaced vehicle thefts would occur at Guildford, but not at Surrey City Centre. The geometry of home location (Brantingham and Brantingham, 1991) and routine activities (Felson, 1994a) would dictate this particular displacement. Offenders look for things to steal either relatively near to home or at crime generators such as transportation nodes or at crime attractors such as very large concentrations of unguarded targets (Brantingham and Brantingham, 1995). If police perceptions are correct, Guildford would be a displacement area for Scott Road because it would be close to offenders' homes. Surrey City Centre would not be a displacement area because it would require a trip outside the offenders' normal activity spaces.

Summary of Results

Table 3 contains a summary of the results of the time series analysis reported fully in Barclay *et al.* (1996). As can be seen from Table 3, the time series analysis found that Scott Road had an overall decrease during the study period and showed a sharp drop during the bicycle-patrol period. There was also a decrease from the overall trend that continued after the bicycle-patrol experiment ended, but compared to the experimental period this constituted a small increase. Vehicle thefts still remained well below the pre-bike-patrol period during the post-experimental period.

TABLE 3
VEHICLE THEFT TRENDS AT SELECTED SITES IN SURREY

Time Frame	Scott Road	Scott Road Surrounds	Surrey City Centre	Guildford	Surrey as a Whole
Full study period	decrease	no trend	no trend	no trend	no trend
During experiment	sharp decrease	no trend	no trend	increase	borderline decrease
After experiment	small increase	small decrease	no trend	increase	no trend

In the area adjacent to Scott Road there was no statistical upward trend over the entire study period, or during the experiment, or during the period following the experiment. This indicates that there probably was no major spatial displacement to the areas adjacent to the Scott Road park-and-ride, but also indicates that the thefts in the surrounding areas were low enough that there was no possibility of any strong diffusion of benefits into the surrounding neighborhood.

At Surrey City Centre there was no statistical upward trend over the entire study period, or during the bike patrol experiment, or following the experiment. Surrey City Centre is the next large node on the SkyTrain system. This suggests that there was no spatial displacement to the next similar cluster of criminal opportunities and indicates that something besides riding the SkyTrain contributes to target selection by the offenders who steal vehicles at Scott Road.

In contrast, there was an increase at the Guildford shopping center both during and after the Scott Road bicycle-patrol experiment, suggesting some displacement to this alternative high-activity center. This is consistent with the idea that at least some of the Scott Road park-and-ride vehicle thieves live in or use the Guildford area.

Most importantly, Surrey as a whole reflected the bicycle-patrol reductions at the Scott Road park-and-ride. While borderline ($r = .09$), there was a clear drop in the weekly totals for Surrey during the bicycle patrol. Such displacement as did occur was not substantial enough to negate the positive impact at the park-and-ride. The net effect of the park-and-ride bicycle patrol was a reduction in the total auto thefts experienced in the city.

Overall, the time series analysis supports the idea that there was a strong reduction in vehicle theft at Scott Road both during and after the experiment, and that there was little or no displacement into contiguous neighborhoods or to the next nearest crime-generator site. It suggests that there was some displacement, but not complete displacement, to an alternative crime-generator site.

Conclusion

It is always impossible to determine conclusively the exact amount of displacement of a crime. Crime is a dynamic behavior, and while there are definite patterns to any criminal behavior, rarely (if ever) is crime predictable with a 100 percent degree of accuracy. Given the preceding analysis, it is apparent that the bicycle patrol which was implemented for a one-month period at the Scott Road park-and-ride did, indeed, prevent some thefts of motor vehicles. It would also seem that there were some displacement effects from this location to one other well-known problem area in the city of Surrey, but not to another established problem spot. The evident diffusion of benefits in temporal form at Scott Road, and the positive impact for Surrey overall, further strengthens the idea that there was only partial displacement of the offenses actually prevented at the park-and-ride by the bicycle patrol. As is stated by Hesseling (1995), to fully understand displacement, more needs to be studied than just the areas adjacent to where the program was implemented and a variety of data sources must be used.

It would be interesting to analyze the results of a longer period of patrolling. This would likely give a clearer picture of what exactly the effects of formal guardianship would have on auto theft in a specific location such as the park-and-ride, as well as the locations surrounding such a place. A longer study period of a few years would also have been advantageous. An exploration of data for other types of crime would also be very useful, but was not possible in this particular post hoc study. Moreover, the results of the initial student study (Spinks *et al.,* 1995) were sufficient to permit BC Transit to plan to initiate a more-extensive bicycle patrol at the Scott Road park-and-ride lots, at new park-and-ride lots serving a commuter train service; and at other smaller park-and-ride lots. We hope that there will be a follow-up study looking at the impact of this expanded bicycle-patrol program.

ACKNOWLEDGMENTS. The authors gratefully acknowledge the efforts and assistance of Inspector Jim Good and Corporal Doug Semple of the Surrey detachment, Royal Canadian Mounted Police; Larry Ward, President and Chief Executive Officer of SkyTrain and Director of Security, BC Transit; Andy Patterson, Supervisor of Physical Security, BC Transit; and the Insurance Corporation of British Columbia. The student team that took the initial look at the Scott Road bicycle patrol was comprised of Paul Barclay, Ralph Jahn, Shelley Pitman, Karpal Singh and Patrick Spinks. Judy Reykdal, Senior Policy Analyst at the Police Services Division, Ministry of Attorney General, Province of British Columbia, supplied specially retrieved monthly motor vehicle theft data for municipalities adjacent to Surrey.

11. Situational Crime Prevention in Two Parking Facilities

Barry Poyner

EDITOR'S NOTE: This case study, originally published as a Security Journal *article (Poyner, 1991), is the third reprinted in this volume directed by Barry Poyner. As in Case Study #4 dealing with sneak thefts in markets, it provides some evidence of diffusion of benefits. Security improvements made to the parking facilities studied appear also to have benefited other nearby lots. The case study also shows, once again, how specific situational measures need to be. While theft of cars was reduced at a city center parking garage by preventing unauthorized access and improving natural surveillance at the exit, these measures had little impact on theft from cars. As Poyner notes, stealing gasoline or tires would not be difficult for people entering and leaving the garage by car. In the university parking lots, theft of cars was not as much of a problem, because the lot entrances were supervised by a manned security barrier. On the other hand, theft from cars from these lots had been a persistent problem, probably because of poor surveillance. This was successfully remedied by the installation of CCTV manned by security officers, which quickly resulted in arrests of some offenders and presumably in the deterrence of others.*

PERHAPS THE simplest way to demonstrate the effectiveness of situational measures for crime prevention is to introduce them into an otherwise stable setting and monitor the effect on crime. This paper summarizes the effect on auto crime of introducing measures in two car parking lots in England.

Two kinds of auto crime are considered: stealing cars and the theft of items from cars. What the two case studies show is that these two types of auto crime require quite different preventive measures.

A Town Center Parking Garage

The first case study is a public parking garage in the town center of Dover in Kent. It is situated close to the main shopping street and next to the bus station and provides both short- and long-term parking. There are five floors of parking (11 split-levels) with about 400 parking places. There is only one entrance/exit for vehicles and one pedestrian access with a lift and staircase, as shown in Figure 1. The method of payment is "pay-and-display," which requires drivers to buy tickets from machines on each floor and display them inside the windshields of their cars. Such a payment system also means that there is no mechanical access control on entering or leaving the garage.

The building had suffered from vandalism and theft for a long time. Security for the garage had been provided by a private security company that patrolled at night, whereas inspectors from the town authority randomly visited the garage during the day. By 1983, it was recognized that this approach to security was not working. Vandalism had become a major problem with graffiti and frequent damage to windows, lifts, doors, and fire extinguishers. The staircase area was often used as a public toilet.

Auto crime was also a problem, with many thefts of and thefts from cars being reported to the police. Many of these thefts involved the cars of vacationers visiting the town, and this proved a serious embarrassment to local officials who became concerned about the image the parking garage presented of the town. There was also concern about the loss of revenue from local people who were not using the garage because of its reputation.

Improving security of the parking garage. A package of measures was developed by local officials in consultation with a police crime prevention officer. It was believed that much of the problem stemmed from the use of the parking garage by youths who could readily gain access by climbing over ground level walls along two sides of the building and who also hung about in groups in the stair and lift lobby.

To discourage this use of the building, the gaps above the low-level walls at ground level were filled in with wire mesh. The pedestrian entrance by the stair and lift lobby was fitted with a self-closing steel door so that it could only be used as an exit, making the only pedestrian entrance via the main vehicle entrance. Two further measures were used to enhance the surveillance of the main entrance/exit: The lighting was improved at the main entrance and the pedestrian exit door, and an office was constructed next to the main entrance and leased to a taxi company to operate from the parking garage. This taxi business has been able to operate from 8:00 a.m. to 12:00 midnight on 5 days a week and from 8:00 a.m. until 2:00 a.m. on Fridays and Saturdays. The effect of this package of measures was to restrict entry to the main vehicle entrance, which was well lit and provided with indirect surveillance for most of the 24 hours of each day.

Effect of the measures. The security measures were introduced during the last 3 months of 1983. Officials considered the measures a success because they saved in maintenance and repairs the cost of the improvements within the first year. In other words, damage to lifts, doors, lighting and windows, and graffiti was greatly reduced by the security package. Furthermore, the impression of greater security had begun to encourage greater use of the

FIGURE 1
PLAN OF THE ENTRANCE FLOOR OF THE PARKING GARAGE
IN THE DOVER TOWN CENTER

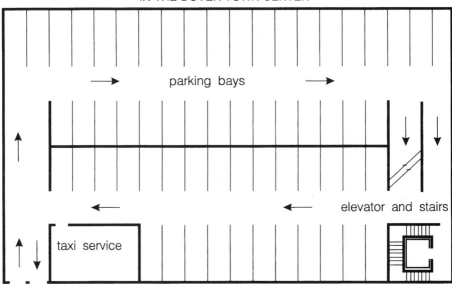

main entrance

parking garage by the public. However, no formal assessment was made of the effect on auto crime.

To do this, permission was sought and gained by the author to access police records. Manual searches were made through crime reports from the relevant police subdivision that covered the town center, and notes were made of all crimes reported during the years 1982, 1983, 1984, and 1985 in the parking garage and in two nearby open parking lots that had a similar number of car parking places and that were operated by the same pay-and-display system. The 4 years chosen for the evaluation were the 2 years prior to the measures being installed and the 2 years after installation.

Table 1 summarizes the crime recorded in the three car parking facilities during these 4 years. It is quite clear that the parking garage had a more serious crime problem than did the two open parking lots, having a total 96 crimes compared with totals of 17 and 26 for the two parking lots. It is also clear that in the 2 years following the new measures crime in the parking garage was reduced to about half the level it had been in the 2 years prior to the measures being introduced.

No displacement of crime. Since displacement is often assumed to occur with situational crime prevention, it is always useful to seek ways of testing this assumption. Here, the two nearby parking lots show no sign of crime being displaced from the parking garage. Indeed, there is some evidence of a reduction in crime in the two parking lots. The crime level in all three car parking lots was reduced even though no security initiatives were taken in the open parking lots. If the displacement theory is correct, it would be reasonable to expect at least some increase of crime in surrounding car parking lots

TABLE 1
ALL CRIME RECORDED IN THREE TOWN CENTER PARKING FACILITIES

	Parking Garage	Parking Lot 1	Parking Lot 2
1982	43	11	9
1983	53	6	17
Total crime before measures	96	17	26
1984	24	5	8
1985	25	8	4
Total crime after measures	49	13	12

following a reduction in the parking garage. The evidence here does not support the displacement theory.

Effects on car theft. Although the figures in Table 1 refer to all crime, including criminal damage to both the facilities and to vehicles, the main categories of crime were the theft of cars and the theft of items removed from vehicles (components such as wheels, radios, or personal property left inside vehicles). The number of incidents of these two types of theft are given in Tables 2 and 3.

These crime data show a considerable difference in reductions for the two types of car theft. Both theft of cars and theft from cars were a problem in the parking garage before the new measures were introduced. However, the measures appear to have reduced the theft of cars far more effectively than they did the theft of items from cars. Indeed, the level of theft of cars in the parking garage was reduced to the low levels already existing in the open parking lots. The theft of items from cars was reduced only by a small number.

TABLE 2
THEFT FROM CARS RECORDED IN THREE TOWN CENTER
CAR PARKING FACILITIES

	Parking Garage	Parking Lot 1	Parking Lot 2
1982	19	4	4
1983	23	2	8
Total crime before measures	42	6	12
1984	17	0	4
1985	16	3	2
Total crime after measures	33	3	6

TABLE 3
THEFT OF CARS RECORDED IN THREE TOWN CENTER
CAR PARKING FACILITIES

	Parking Garage	Parking Lot 1	Parking Lot 2
1982	19	4	4
1983	19	3	6
Total crime before measures	38	7	10
1984	3	2	2
1985	4	3	2
Total crime after measures	7	5	4

Conclusions. Perhaps the first and most obvious conclusion is that parking garages are much more susceptible to crime than are open parking lots. Although the measures introduced concentrated on reducing accessibility, it seems unlikely that accessibility is the main reason why a parking garage is so vulnerable, because the parking lots are equally accessible. The real reason seems to be the lack of surveillance in a parking structure with 11 different levels. It must be comparatively easy for potential offenders to search upper floors for insecure or vulnerable cars without being observed. By comparison, the open parking lots can receive far more surveillance both from those using them and from people in adjacent streets and buildings.

Much more difficult is the explanation as to why the measures reduced the theft of cars but not theft from cars. The measures were designed to limit access by nonusers of the parking garage and to give some informal surveillance to the one entrance/exit. If these measures reduced the theft of cars, it could be that the main reason why car theft had been a problem was that youths hanging around the park had been tempted into stealing vulnerable cars. By making it more difficult to gain access, this would reduce the number of youths hanging about the parking garage, and by providing surveillance of the exit, it would increase the risk of a thief being seen and being recognized driving a car out of the garage.

If the measures did discourage the theft of cars but not the theft of items from cars, there must be some important difference in the methods used to commit these two crimes. What the author suspects is that much theft of items from cars actually requires a car to carry out the crime. Some of the reported thefts involved the removal of wheels and suitcases and the siphoning of gasoline. It would arouse suspicion to carry these out of a car garage on foot, but once loaded into a car, there would be no reason to suspect the driver of theft, as he or she would be driving the car in and out of the garage quite legitimately. The lack of surveillance on upper floors and the lack of entry and exit controls in a pay-and-display system makes this kind of criminal activity comparatively easy, with little risk of being caught.

A University Parking Lot

The second case study is of security measures introduced to car parking at the University of Surrey at Guildford, England. Parking is generally located in several large parking lots located along a perimeter roadway around the campus some distance from the university buildings. Access to these perimeter parking areas is via the perimeter road that has a manned security gate close to the campus entrance. Nevertheless, the perimeter parking lots suffered a considerable amount of crime.

Following the arrival of a new chief security officer in 1980, a new system was introduced for recording incidents of crime, antisocial behavior, and safety problems on the campus. It was soon recognized that auto crime was one of the main security problems facing the university. It was proposed that measures be introduced to increase surveillance of the three main perimeter parking lots in the form of improved lighting (which had earlier been reduced as part of an energy-saving program) and by cutting back or pruning of

FIGURE 2
PLAN OF SURREY UNIVERSITY CAMPUS
SHOWING THE LOCATION OF THE MAIN PARKING LOTS

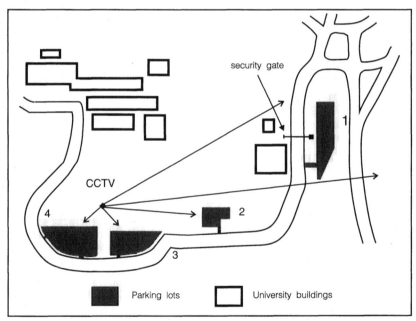

landscape planting and trees in and around the parking lots. In addition, a CCTV camera would be set up on a tower overlooking the two largest and adjacent parking lots. It would be able to scan most of the parking facilities and was equipped with infrared sensing and loudspeakers through which the security guards could give warnings or provide information. A diagrammatic plan of the campus showing the location of the CCTV tower and the main parking lots is shown in Figure 2.

The improvements to lighting, which involved extending the period during which the lighting was switched on, and the cutting back of landscape foliage was done in September 1985, in preparation for the return of students in October. The tower for the CCTV installation was erected in January 1986, but the actual installation of the camera and monitoring equipment was delayed for technical reasons until March 1986.

Effect of the security measures on auto crime. The crime records for the university provided readily available information about auto crime for the whole campus. The data in Table 4 show the recorded incidents in 1984, 1985, and 1986. The figures show an increase in crime experienced in 1985 and a much lower number of incidents for 1986, suggesting that the measures had been partly successful. However, the figures also show important differences for the different types of crime.

First, theft from cars was a much more frequently reported problem and it also produced the most dramatic drop, from 92 in the year when measures were introduced to 31 in the year following the introduction of security measures. The other two kinds of auto crime were not so frequent, and the degree of reduction much less certain.

Following from the findings in the Dover parking garage, it might be argued that the reason for relatively few thefts of cars was because the access to the campus was supervised by a manned security gate, and this might effectively reduce the risk of cars being illicitly driven off the campus past this security point. However, it is clear that the measures have been more effective in reducing the theft from cars.

TABLE 4
AUTO CRIME RECORDED BY THE SECURITY ORGANIZATION
AT SURREY UNIVERSITY

	1984	1985	1986
Theft from cars	61	92	31
Theft of cars	5	15	12
Damage to cars	16	31	22
Total incidents	82	138	65

The two largest parking lots (1 and 4) provide enough incidents to enable a more detailed month-by-month analysis of the theft from cars. Furthermore, it is interesting to compare these two parking lots because only one could be supervised by the CCTV camera. Lot 4 was easily covered by the camera, but lot 1 was out of sight of it (see Figure 2). Figures 3 and 4 show histograms of the pattern of thefts from cars during the 3 years 1984-86.

It is very clear from both histograms that in the period immediately following the installation of the CCTV system the level of thefts had been dramatically reduced, with many months having no reported incident. However, it is also clear that the cutting back of landscape foliage and increased lighting times had no apparent impact on this crime problem. Some might argue that these were necessary conditions for the CCTV surveillance to work effectively, but they are clearly not effective measures by themselves.

What is much more interesting is that parking lot 1, which could not be monitored by

FIGURE 3
NUMBER OF THEFTS FROM CARS IN PARKING LOT 4 AT
UNIVERSITY OF SURREY IN EACH MONTH OF 1984, 1985, 1986

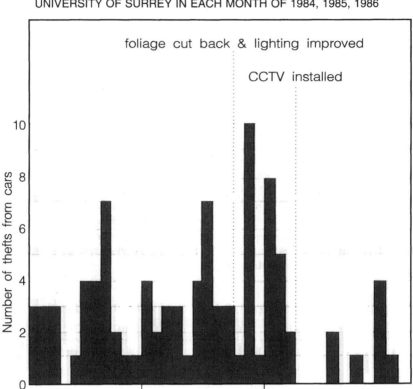

the surveillance camera, still seems to have been effectively protected by it. The reason for the immediate drop in thefts for parking lot 1, even though it could not be viewed by the camera, is probably because the CCTV system enabled the security guards to make three arrests immediately after the system became operational and three further arrests and two specific loudspeaker warnings in the following 3 months. In one incident a man was seen removing hubcaps from a car and putting them in his own car, an observation that supports the conclusion about these thefts suggested above.

Again, the fact that crime was reduced in a parking lot without the benefit of the surveillance system but close to areas with surveillance sheds doubt on the theory of displacement. Rather than displace crime to less well protected targets on the campus, the "good effect" has spread out beyond the immediate area of application. This is very reminiscent of the findings from another case study of surveillance on buses in the North of England by the same research team (Poyner, 1988). In that study, it was found that the impact of video cameras fitted to a few buses affected vandalism on the whole bus fleet. Indeed, although the data in Table 1 are rather weak for the two open parking lots in Dover,

FIGURE 4
NUMBER OF THEFTS FROM CARS IN PARKING LOT 1 AT
THE UNIVERSITY OF SURREY IN EACH MONTH OF 1984, 1985, AND 1986

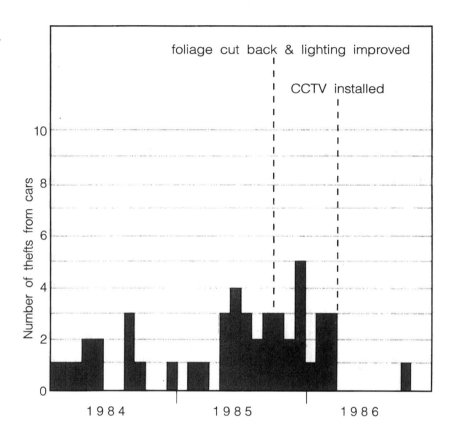

that case study also appears to reflect the same idea of the "good effect" of measures spreading beyond the immediate situation in which they were implemented. Is this not a cue for an alternative theory to displacement?

Conclusions from Both Case Studies

It is clear that the design and management of parking facilities has a crucial influence on the risk of auto crime. It would appear that surveillance, whether formal or informal, is probably the most effective situational measure at reducing both kinds of auto crime. The open parking lots in Dover that had more natural surveillance had less crime of both kinds than did the multilevel parking garage. It was also found that surveillance of the entry/exit points at the university and the modified parking garage seemed to keep the theft of cars down to a low level, and no doubt much tighter controls on access and exiting would have a more complete effect.

The lesson from this must be that secure car parking must permit a good deal of surveillance. This is easiest to achieve with parking lots that, if not naturally supervised by frequent movements of legitimate users or by being overlooked from surrounding streets and buildings, might be satisfactorily covered by properly monitored electronic surveillance. Security would be enhanced against the theft of cars by supervision of access and exit points.

If multilevel parking structures are to be used, the solution is more difficult. Certainly, what should be avoided is creating a large number of relatively small parking floors that are likely to be deserted for most of the time. How far electronic surveillance can be successfully adapted to multilevel parking garages is unclear. Surveillance might be achieved by a mixture of strategies to increase informal surveillance. Floors might be designed to be as large as possible to maximize the presence of legitimate users and to be as open as possible to maximize visibility across the floor. Other strategies might be to link garages at upper levels to other facilities such as restaurants or department stores to increase the presence of legitimate users. It may be that much tighter control of the entry and exiting of cars would limit the attraction of the garage for drivers intending to steal items from other cars.

ACKNOWLEDGMENT. The research from which this paper was prepared was originally funded by the Home Office in London.

12. CCTV in Three Town Centers in England

Ben Brown

EDITOR'S NOTE: CCTV, or video cameras, have been used in many business and other semi-private settings, including stores, banks, ATM machines, buses (Poyner, 1988), parking lots (Tilley, 1993c) and subway systems (see Case Study #22). They have also been used successfully in residential accommodation for seniors to reduce burglary and frauds by unsolicited callers (Chatterton and Frenz, 1994), and in schools to help keep order in cafeterias and sports stands (New York Times, January 31, 1996, p.A15). Their more widespread use in city streets and centers has been resisted by civil libertarians, alarmed by the specter of intrusive State control (New York Times, February 7, 1996, p.A12). In Britain, however, they are beginning to be used more widely in these settings and, as mentioned in this study, condensed by Helen McCulloch from a Home Office report (Brown, 1996), they have generally been welcomed by the public. The evidence in Brown's report of their effective use in Newcastle-upon-Tyne city center will undoubtedly accelerate their use elsewhere, but less satisfactory results from two other cities studied should sound a warning: The cameras will only be effective if systems are designed with close attention to the setting and its specific crime problems.

Introduction

Closed circuit television (CCTV) cameras are becoming a common feature of public life in Britain. They can be found in shopping facilities, town center streets, banks, building societies, car parks, schools and colleges, transport facilities and housing estates. The presence of CCTV cameras within shopping centers is common. Center managers often install cameras as part of an overall management package which deals with a range of activities, including criminal and anti-social behavior. In an attempt to match the standards set by shopping centers, many local authorities have installed or are planning to install CCTV cameras in their town center streets. A recent estimate indicated that over 200 areas across the country, ranging from metropolitan cities to small market towns, have installed or are planning CCTV systems (Clarke, 1994).

Despite early fears concerning civil liberties, the general public, at the moment, does not appear to be concerned about the proliferation of such schemes within the public domain. Research conducted for the Home Office in 1992 showed that very few people — 6% of respondents — were worried about the presence of CCTV cameras (Edwards and Tilley, 1994).

The success of cameras in reducing overall crime levels within different locations, however, has rarely been assessed (or indeed questioned). In their recent survey of retailers carried out on behalf of the British Retail Consortium, Speed *et al.* (1995) found that this lack of empirical evidence concerning the effect of cameras on overall crime levels is causing some concern. Although retailers have contributed considerable sums of money to support public CCTV schemes, they remain unconvinced about the effectiveness of cameras (for example, on apprehension for theft). They also do not believe that CCTV schemes in public areas have increased either turnover or profits. The lack of empirical evidence for the effect of CCTV, therefore, may affect the willingness of retailers to fund such schemes in the future.

There are a few small scale evaluations that have attempted to assess the impact of security cameras on crime and disorderly behavior within different locations. Van Straelen (1978) claimed that the installation of CCTV cameras in a large French supermarket had reduced losses by 33 percent. More recently Tesco launched an internally-developed security package known as the "Totally Integrated Security System" (TISS) to tackle losses incurred at their stores. Although TISS involved changes in store design and procedure, its main component was the provision of CCTV which allowed the monitoring of all vulnerable areas both within and outside the store. When TISS was first introduced into an existing "problem" supermarket, unknown losses dropped from some $12,000 a week to $5,000 a week (Burrows, 1991). In addition cash losses from tills dropped considerably and violent incidents almost disappeared. This indicated that when CCTV was installed within a shop as part of an integrated security package, it deterred crime within this environment. There were also other benefits in that

> ... the "quality" of arrests of more professional thieves is improved and that taped evidence increases the likelihood of "guilty" pleas in the courts. (Burrows, 1991:9).

In 1985, a bus company in the North East of England launched a security program aimed at deterring vandalism on buses (Poyner, 1988). Initially, one bus was equipped with a CCTV camera on the upper deck. In the first month of operation, this camera filmed a number of incidents involving damage caused to the upper deck of the bus. The bus company, with the assistance of a local school, soon identified the perpetrators and took action against them. The success of the video bus was well publicized in the local media. Staff from the bus company visited schools and demonstrated the effectiveness of the system by filming pupils on the top deck of buses and then showing them the tapes. More buses were then equipped with video equipment and incidents of vandalism decreased further.

CCTV cameras can also reduce crime in car parks. Poyner (1991) showed that when security staff at the University of Surrey installed CCTV cameras in their car parks, car crime (especially theft from vehicles) declined. The author suggests that this effect was because the system had been used to arrest and take action against offenders and that these successes were publicized in the local press. It is important to note that other improvements were made to the car parks at the same time: the lighting was improved and bushes were pruned in order to improve the opportunities for surveillance. Tilley (1993c), in possibly the most thorough evaluation of the effect of CCTV on crime to date, also found that the presence of CCTV cameras within car parks could reduce car crime. He too remarked that:

> The effect of CCTV appears to be enhanced when it is installed alongside other complementary measures, raising its credibility as a source of increased risk to the offenders. (Tilley, 1993c:23).

However, he also discovered that the systems did not have to be technically sophisticated or monitored continuously to have an impact on car crime in car parks. Since he found that very few arrests took place in the car parks included in the study, he concluded that the

> ... removal of offenders does not constitute the mechanism through which CCTV currently reduces car crime. (Tilley, 1993c: 23).

This failure to apprehend offenders might have affected the long term effectiveness of some of the camera systems evaluated by Tilley. In some cases the cameras became less effective at deterring crime as time passed, an effect that is common to many crime prevention efforts. Regular publicity concerning the role of the cameras in apprehending suspects was recommended to maintain the perceived effectiveness of the system amongst offenders.

Both Webb and Laycock (1992b) and Mayhew *et al.* (1979) found that installing CCTV cameras as part of a general security package at selected London Underground stations had reduced the number of robberies within these premises. Webb and Laycock found that after 12 months the effect of the project began to wear off, possibly because offenders realized that the risk of being caught had not increased. Mayhew *et al.* also found that the number of thefts from the person had declined, but their data indicated that these offenses might have been displaced to neighboring stations.

One of the main arguments against the effectiveness of cameras is, indeed, that they simply displace rather than deter or prevent crime. Evidence indicates, however, that cameras within some locations may in fact lead to a "diffusion of benefits." For example Poyner (1988, 1991) found that the presence of cameras within one location had a beneficial effect on the number of offenses within another, unprotected location. When cameras were introduced to reduce vandalism on buses, reductions in the incidence of vandalism occurred on all buses and not just those which had cameras. When cameras were installed at University of Surrey parking facilities, car crime decreased not only in the car parks that were covered by cameras, but also a nearby car park where there was no camera coverage.

How Might CCTV Cameras Reduce Crime?

Installing CCTV cameras to tackle criminal and disorderly behavior is an example of what Brantingham and Faust (1976) refer to as primary crime prevention, and what Clarke (1992) refers to as situational crime prevention. The theoretical approach to this type of crime prevention refers to the reduction of criminal opportunities, and so

> ... has turned to theories of the crime *event* rather than the motivated offender, for its inspiration. (Pease 1994: 662).

Cohen and Felson (1979) in their routine activities theory state that for an offense to occur three elements must converge in time and space during the course of people carrying out their routine activities. These are a motivated offender, a suitable victim and the absence of a capable guardian. As Tilley (1993c) points out, it is possible that the presence of CCTV cameras may deter crime by impinging on any one of these elements. For example, the presence of cameras may remove the motivated offender by increasing the perceived risk. Alternatively, the cameras may allow the police and/or other security agencies to respond more quickly to an offense therefore introducing the presence of a capable guardian. Another possible alternative is that the presence of CCTV cameras may remove suitable victims by making potential victims more security conscious and therefore less vulnerable to crime. However, the lack of empirical evidence means that is impossible to say which of these three elements is affected by the presence of CCTV cameras within an area.

A complementary theoretical approach is provided by the rational choice theory of Clarke and Cornish (1985). This suggests that offenders are involved with making decisions and choices, and these choices exhibit a measure of rationality. The focus of this approach is on both the offender and the immediate situational context of crime. Installing CCTV cameras within an area increases the opportunities for surveillance and thus the risk associated with offending. Offenders would be deterred by cameras only if they interfered in some way with the likelihood of offenders benefiting from this behavior within that particular context. In Felson's language, this is equivalent to de-motivating the offender.

Different groups of people may have different ideas about how CCTV might affect criminal behavior. As part of their research into the acceptability and perceived effectiveness of CCTV, Honess and Charman (1992) found that the public believed that the main purpose of camera systems was to help with the detection and investigation of crime. Honess and Charman also asked the managers of various different types of schemes (such as car park, shopping center and town center schemes) what they perceived the use of the camera systems to be. For managers, crime prevention rather than detection was the dominant aim of CCTV.

Aims of the Research

Although CCTV is also used in town centers to supervise internal and external private areas such as inside shops and in shopping malls, the focus of this report is on schemes that cover external public town center streets. It looks at how the police and other agencies use CCTV systems to tackle crime and disorderly behavior within town center streets. It also examines the effect of installing cameras on the number of incidents that occur within the town center and surrounding areas. In doing this, we may begin to understand the circumstances and conditions that are needed for CCTV to have the greatest impact on these types of behavior. Three cities were looked at in depth; Newcastle, Birmingham and King's Lynn although only the experience in Newcastle is discussed fully in this paper.

Newcastle upon Tyne

Newcastle upon Tyne is a large provincial city situated on the mouth of the river Tyne in north east England. The city center is typical of large English metropolitan city centers, if a little more compact. The area has a low resident population but has many public houses, night clubs, restaurants, shops and offices. It also plays host to a number of major events, including royal visits. In addition, St James's Park, the football ground for premier league Newcastle United is situated near to the center. The city center, therefore, attracts large numbers of people and vehicles, and the police officers working here face a number of problems, including those associated with public order, personal safety, property crime, traffic congestion and terrorism.

To help the local commander deal with these problems, a 16-camera monochrome CCTV system was installed in December 1992. All the cameras have a pan, tilt and zoom function. Images from these cameras are transmitted by microwave to four monochrome monitors which are located in the front desk area of the local police stations. Two of these monitors are split screen and two are single image. The system records images in time lapse mode but operators can switch to real time recording if required. Attached to the monitors is a facility for producing hard copies of images which are used to provide additional evidence for prosecutions.

The initial funding for the system came from the City Center Partnership Security Initiative, a corporate initiative set up using a grant from the Department of the Environment and funds from the local private sector. Northumbria Police Authority is responsible for paying the on-going maintenance cost and that of the salaries and costs relating to the civilian operators who monitor the system.

Camera positions were selected using crime pattern analysis. The area covered by the cameras contains a number of major vehicular thoroughfares, is partly pedestrianized and is made up of shops, commercial and financial properties, and an extremely high number of licensed premises. There is also a large covered shopping mall within Newcastle city center — Eldon Square — which has its own privately operated camera system.

Newcastle city center is highly conducive to camera surveillance. The streets are wide and relatively straight; there are few pedestrian underpasses and few obstacles which block the view of the cameras. The area covered by each camera is considerable and overlaps with those areas covered by neighboring cameras. Very few streets within the city center do not have some form of camera coverage. Most vulnerable premises are located in the streets that have full camera coverage.

THE AIMS OF THE SCHEME

The main aim of the system is to support the operational policing of the city center area. The system is therefore used as part of a wider policing package to tackle burglary (including ram-raiding, i.e. use of a vehicle to break through a shop front), public disorder, theft from the person, robbery, the selling and using of hard drugs, traffic congestion, security and terrorism. In general terms:

The purpose of the use of the CCTV to monitor public places, by a police approved system, is to assist with the prevention and detection of crime. Closed circuit television will also assist greatly in the maintenance of public order, reducing nuisance and vandalism offenses and enhancing a sense of safety by members of the general public. (Use of closed circuit television system, codes of practice for Newcastle city center, paragraph 2.1).

OPERATIONAL PROCEDURES

The system is controlled entirely by the police. All monitors are located within the front desk office in the police station. The team of police officers and civilian staff who work in the office are responsible for monitoring the cameras 24 hours a day. They work on exactly the same shift pattern as the operational officers and so form part of a wider operational policing team. Although there is always one member of staff who is designated as the CCTV operator working at any one time within the front office, any member of the front desk team can and does operate the camera system. This ensures that the system is monitored constantly and helps to reduce fatigue in the operators. Each member of staff will sit with a more experienced operator until he or she learns the basics of the system.

When the scheme was first launched, it had a radio/phone link to the area operations room at Byker. However the staff who monitor the system now have their own personal radios which they can use to communicate directly with officers on the beat. The operators believe that this is a great improvement because it provides the facility for immediate communication. This allows them to co-ordinate a much quicker response to an incident. There is also a separate radio link to local retailers and to the operators of the privately owned and monitored system in the Eldon Square shopping center.

HOW THE CCTV SYSTEM IS USED

The operators use the cameras to "patrol" the city center, in much the same way as would an operational officer: they search for suspicious incidents, monitor potentially difficult situations as they happen and keep an eye on the local "characters." The know that there are likely to be problems in certain areas at certain times. During the day, they tend to concentrate on the busy shopping areas whereas during the evening and night they tend to concentrate on those areas where the majority of the pubs and nightclubs are located. They also know that certain areas are associated with different types of crime. Licensed premises within a particular street, for instance, tend to be the location of many public order problems; a park area is often used by certain members of the public to roll and smoke cannabis cigarettes; there is also a certain area there children and youths tend to congregate which leads to problems of criminal damage. Even more organized criminal activity may be linked with a particular location and these problems can be tackled with the help of the camera system.

The operators also make use of local intelligence information. This may include keeping an eye out for wanted persons. Intelligence reports may also indicate that a certain area may be suffering from a spate of certain types of offenses. The camera operators can then be on the look out within these areas for these types of offenses. The police can also use the camera for gathering evidence as part of organized surveillance operations.

THE EFFECT OF CCTV ON CRIME INCIDENTS

The police in Northumbria made available final incident code data from a number of areas which allowed an assessment of the effect of installing the cameras in Newcastle city center. Final incident code data refer to incidents that the police have responded to and have assigned a code to. They are therefore similar to recorded crime as represented in recorded crime statistics.

The data examined in the study relate to 20 different types of incidents which took place in the following areas:

- **CCTV area** — this is made up of four police beats of the Newcastle Central area. These beats cover the shopping, business and financial areas of the city center. Fourteen of the 16 cameras installed in the city center are located within these beats. The coverage of this area is very extensive and is integrated, i.e. the field of view for each camera overlaps.

- **No CCTV area** — this is made up of the seven remaining beats of the Newcastle Central area which surround the central CCTV area. The area mainly consists of the two universities and the riverside district. St James's Park (the football ground of Newcastle United) is also located within this area. Only two of the 16 cameras are located within these beats.

- **Byker** (Newcastle East) — this is one of Newcastle Central's neighboring divisions and consists mainly of residential housing. There are no cameras in this area.

- **Force** — Data for all other divisions within the Northumbria force were collated and used to provide an additional control measure.

Table 1 shows the average monthly totals for the 26 months before the cameras became fully operational in March 1993 and for the 15 months following this date. Only those offenses which show significant decreases or increases have been included in this table.

The most marked results are for burglary. Although there is no change in the number of burglary incidents in Byker and the rest of the force, the numbers of such incidents in both the CCTV and No CCTV areas of the Newcastle Central division have dropped significantly. The greatest reduction is within the CCTV area where there has been a 56 percent drop in the average monthly figure for burglary incidents. There has also been a similar pattern in the number of criminal damage incidents. Within Byker and the rest of the force the number of criminal damage incidents rose but in the two central divisions it fell significantly. Once again the greatest reduction of 34 percent occurred within the CCTV area.

The numbers of vehicle crime incidents have dropped in all the areas. The most marked reduction however is within the CCTV area where the average monthly numbers of incidents for both theft of and theft from vehicles have almost halved, although it is important to note that the numbers for these incidents are small. "Other" thefts (i.e. other than vehicle-related) also fell significantly in the Central division, but in this case the greatest reduction of 18 percent occurred in the No CCTV area. Finally, there is some evidence for an effect on juvenile disorder. Although there was no reduction in the numbers of these incidents for the Central division areas, there were significant increases in Byker

TABLE 1
AVERAGE MONTHLY TOTALS AND PERCENTAGE CHANGES FOR INCIDENTS
BEFORE AND AFTER THE CAMERAS BECAME FULLY OPERATIONAL

	CCTV		NO CCTV		BYKER		FORCE	
	Before CCTV	After CCTV	Before CCTV	After CCTV	Before CCTV	After CCTV	Before CCTV	After CCTV
Burglary	**40**	**17**	**75**	**46**	110	107	2307	2260
% change	*-57%*		*-39%*		*-3%*		*-2%*	
Criminal Damage	**32**	**21**	**111**	**83**	217	225	**4107**	**4441**
% change	*-34%*		*-25%*		*+4%*		*+8%*	
Theft of Motor Vehicle	**17**	**9**	**168**	**100**	141	122	**2590**	**2298**
% change	*-47%*		*-40%*		*-13%*		*-11%*	
Theft from Motor Vehicle	**18**	**9**	**106**	**65**	110	98	**2146**	**1803**
% change	*-50%*		*-39%*		*-11%*		*-16%*	
Other Theft	**223**	**198**	**197**	**161**	153	154	2437	2233
% change	*-11%*		*-18%*		*+1%*		*-8%*	
Juvenile Disorder	13	15	19	20	**158**	**204**	2601	3185
% change	*+15%*		*+5%*		*+29%*		*+22%*	

1. Figures in bold indicate a significant difference in the incidence of offenses, p=0.05.
2. Where the base figure is low (i.e. less than 20), the percentages are expressed in brackets).

FIGURE 1
BURGLARY INCIDENTS, JANUARY 1991 - MAY 1994, FOR NEWCASTLE AND
NORTHUMBRIA POLICE REGIONS

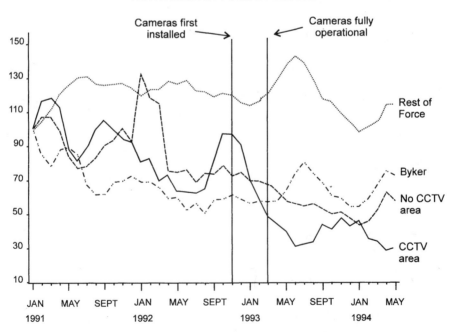

FIGURE 2
TRENDS IN THE NUMBER OF CRIMINAL DAMAGE INCIDENTS, JANUARY 1991 -
MAY 1994, FOR NEWCASTLE AND NORTHUMBRIA POLICE REGIONS

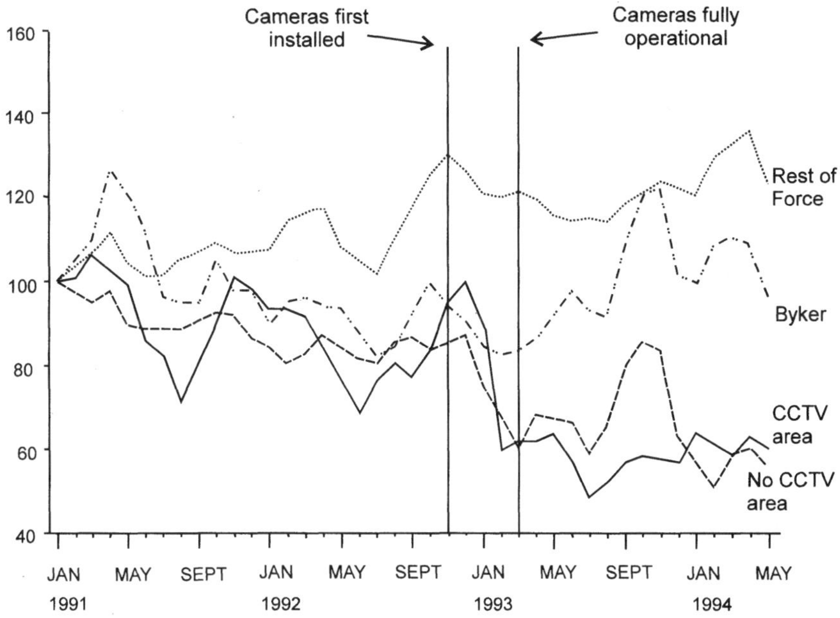

and the rest of the force.

By plotting the monthly figures for these offenses we can obtain a better idea as to how CCTV has affected these types of incident. Figures 1 and 2 refer to burglary and criminal damage respectively. In the graphs, each month's figures are represented as a percentage of the base figure, which for these charts is the number of incidents that occurred during January 1991. To make the comparisons clearer, quarterly moving averages of the monthly indices have been represented. The graphs show that for the CCTV area, the No CCTV area and Byker, the numbers of burglary and criminal damage incidents were all declining before the cameras were installed. After the cameras were installed, the rate for these incidents fell dramatically within the CCTV area. There have also been reductions in the No CCTV areas, but these reductions are more gradual, especially in the case of burglary. It is particularly interesting to note that the fall within the CCTV areas occurred after the cameras were installed but before they became fully operational. This suggests that in the first instance the presence of cameras was deterring crime. Unlike many other crime prevention initiatives, however, the effect has been sustained which suggests that further action has consolidated and continued the initial effect.

The effect of cameras on vehicle crime is harder to discern (data can be found in Brown, 1996). Thefts of and from vehicles were declining in the CCTV area, the No CCTV and the Byker division prior to installation of the cameras. After the cameras were installed, thefts of vehicles have continued to decline sharply within the whole of the central division whereas the vehicle theft rate for Byker seems to have stabilized. In the CCTV area, however, this effect appears to fade after 8 months and the number of thefts of vehicles rises sharply. After September 1993 the trend for the CCTV area becomes similar to that in other areas.

The effects of cameras on juvenile disorder incidents and 'other' thefts are not as clear as for burglary (see Brown, 1996, for data). Incidents of juvenile disorder were increasing sharply in the CCTV and No CCTV areas of the central division prior to installation of the cameras. Such an increase is not evident in the figures for Byker, or indeed the rest of the force. When the cameras became fully operational, juvenile disorder incidents fell very sharply in the CCTV area, despite a sharp increase in such incidents prior to Christmas 1993, the figures have continued to fall. During the same period, there have been gradual increases in the numbers of this type of incident within Byker and the rest of the force. There has also been a sharp decrease in juvenile disorder in the No CCTV area, but the reduction does not coincide very well with either the installation or operational use of the cameras. Other thefts also appear to have decreased in the CCTV area since the installation of cameras despite a rise in the number of offenses prior to Christmas 1993. However, evidence for the effect of cameras is weaker.

EFFECT OF THE CCTV SYSTEM ON ARRESTS AND INVESTIGATION

In order to look in more detail at how the cameras may be affecting crime rates within the Newcastle Central area, figures concerning arrest rates were made available to the researchers. Unfortunately these figures were only available on a divisional basis and could not be broken down into the CCTV and No CCTV areas. Moreover, there were no directly comparable categories for 'other' thefts and juvenile disorder. However, they can be used to give some indication as to whether or not the camera system is helping to improve the arrest rate for some types of offense.

Table 2 shows that the average monthly number of arrests for both burglary and criminal damage have fallen since the cameras became fully operational, In both cases, however, the reduction in the arrest rate is considerably lower than the decrease in the number of incidents. This means, therefore, that for burglary and criminal damage the risk of arrest has increased since the cameras were installed within the central division.

For theft of and from vehicles, arrests and incidents have dropped by similar amounts, which indicates that the risk of arrest for these offenses has remained more or less stable. It is interesting to note that the number of arrests for drunken offenses has increased sharply despite a small drop in the number of incidents. This means that the risk of arrest for drunken offenses has increased considerably since the installation of the cameras.

The personal experience of one of the five current camera operators supports these data. Between March and November 1994, one operator was directly responsible for just over 100 arrests. Almost half of these arrests were for drunken offenses, public order offenses or assault offenses. This shows how useful the cameras can be in controlling disorderly behavior, especially that fueled by alcohol. It is important to bear in mind that public disorder and assault incidents within town centers can have serious consequences. In late 1994, the operator noticed and alerted police officers to an assault which subsequently became a murder investigation. Just after 11:00pm one Sunday evening the operator saw a person lying in the street. He looked around the area and then noticed two people who appeared to be attacking members of the public indiscriminately. One of the assailants then walked up to another person at a bus stop and hit him. The victim fell over and, as he fell he knocked his head on the curb. At this moment a bus drew up. The assailants then got on the bus, but by this time the CCTV operator had alerted police officers. The officers arrived on the scene just as the bus was leaving and they managed to stop the bus and arrest the assailants. The victim later died of his injuries.

TABLE 2
AVERAGE MONTHLY ARREST RATES FOR NEWCASTLE CENTRAL BEFORE
AND AFTER THE INSTALLATION OF CAMERAS

	Average monthly number of arrests			Number of arrests per 100 incidents	
	Before CCTV	After CCTV	% change in arrests	Before CCTV	After CCTV
Burglary	24	18	-25%	21	28
Criminal Damage	22	21	-4%	16	20
Theft of Vehicles	22	14	-36%	12	13
Theft from Vehicles	8	5	*(-37%)	7	6
Drunken offenses	101	127	+26%	65	85

*Base figure is less than 20

Two important points are raised by this particular case. The first is that officers have to be able to respond to incidents very quickly. Without a rapid response, the assailants may have escaped on the bus before officers attended the scene. It would then have been more difficult and more time consuming for investigating officers to identify the assailants from the pictures recorded by the system.

The example also illustrates the evidence gathering properties of the system and its value in directing investigations. Even though many people witnessed this event, the availability of a tape recording of the incident is estimated to have saved the force thousands of pounds in resources and time spent investigating the case. Recordings of disturbances, which sometimes involve several people, are especially useful because they provide the police with hard evidence which can be used to resolve discrepancies raised by the accounts of an incident given by different people.

Summary of Experience with CCTV in Newcastle

The findings presented here provide compelling evidence that initially the presence of CCTV cameras within Newcastle city center had a strong deterrent effect on the incidence of a number of offenses. However, there is also evidence to suggest that the effect of the cameras on some offenses began to fade after a period of time, although it is important to note that the central division is faring better than the control division and the rest of the force. The use of cameras has had a lasting effect on burglary and criminal damage. This may be due to the increase in risk of detection associated with these two types of offense in the central area.

On the basis of the evidence presented here, the number of public disorder incidents has remained unchanged since the installation of the cameras. But as the case study and arrest data show, the strength of CCTV systems might lie less in preventing these offenses (which, it is argued, will occur regardless) than with coordinating a quick, effective response and gathering evidence should it be required. A quick response may mean that officers are able to diffuse a situation before it becomes serious, or at least reduce the harm done to one of the participants. Providing evidence can direct investigations, saving officers both time and money.

It was not possible as part of this study to collect any data concerning the use of CCTV evidence in the prosecution process. Peter Durham, the local police commander claims that:

> Almost all of the 400 people arrested as a direct result of the scheme admitted guilt after being shown video footage, therefore avoiding the considerable costs associated with contested trials. (Durham, 1995: 20).

Although it is impossible to say how many of these 400 would have been arrested and then gone on to plead guilty in the absence of any video footage, the indication is that the system has contributed significantly to the prosecution process.

For all the offenses examined above, there is little evidence to suggest that crime has been displaced either to other locations or from one type of offense into another. In fact there is some evidence that there has been some "diffusion of benefit" to the No CCTV area especially for criminal damage and burglary offenses, i.e. the beneficial effect of CCTV extends beyond the area immediately supervised by cameras to neighboring areas which are not directly covered.

Summary of Experience with CCTV in Birmingham

Self report data concerning victimization indicated that crime had been reduced in streets where there was a good CCTV view. Moreover evidence from an analysis of crime data suggested that the presence of cameras had had most effect on robbery and theft from the person. There was also evidence to suggest that the cameras may have acted in conjunction with pedestrianization and other traffic calming measures to reduce the incidence of burglary within the city center.

Both the survey data and the recorded crime data indicated that offending had increased in areas where there was partial or no camera coverage which suggests that some locational displacement of crime may have occurred. This was most evident for robbery and theft from the person. It is unclear, however, how far the increases in these offenses in surrounding areas are a direct result of crime displacement, or of an increase in opportunities within these areas. It is possible that the extensive redevelopment that had taken place within areas outside the central zone, which had resulted in an increase in the number of entertainment venues, may have increased the number of potential targets for this type of offense.

Evidence from an analysis of recorded crime data, however, does point more convincingly to displacement of criminal activity to theft from cars and, in particular displacement of offending from robbery and theft from the person into theft from cars. The charts for these two offenses are almost mirror images of each other. In one area, robberies and thefts from the person remained relatively stable, whereas thefts from vehicles increased significantly; for the surrounding areas the opposite is the case.

It appears that the presence of cameras had a distinct and complex effect on the pattern of local offending. Within the city center area, the system had perhaps acted to curb the increase in certain types of offense, namely robbery and theft from the person, rather than reduce their overall incidence. It had achieved this by reducing crime in those areas with good camera coverage but there was also considerable evidence that offending was more common in those areas where there was little or no coverage.

A number of factors may have been responsible for the apparent effects. The city center, unlike Newcastle, covers a wide area and extends well beyond the area covered by the cameras. There are also a greater number of natural obstacles, such as street furniture and trees. This presented a difficult environment for effective CCTV surveillance and meant that there were a number of locations that crime could be displaced to, and as crime was displaced over time from one area to another, it changed in nature. For example, the cameras may have helped to prevent crime, predominantly robbery and theft from the person, on those streets with camera coverage within the city center core area. However, crime may have been displaced to other local areas, such as the recently developed convention area of the city and car parks. Within the convention center area, robberies and thefts have apparently increased. Because of local circumstances, the displacement of offending to car parks has manifested itself in theft from rather than of vehicles.

It is also important to recognize that because Birmingham was one of the first city center schemes in the country, the police and county council could not learn from the experience of others and this may have been reflected in the way that they set up the scheme in the first place. Citywatch recently commissioned a review of the system which recommended that camera positions should be modified in the light of changes suggested by Aldridge (1994).

The failure of the camera system to reduce directly overall crime levels within Birmingham city center does not detract from the other less evident benefits of the system. The system has helped police officers working within this area deal with many problems, most notably a wide range of public disorder/public safety problems. It has also increased the public's feelings of safety when using the city center at night, and this may be as important for the city center as an area as any real reduction in crime.

Summary of Experience with CCTV in King's Lynn

There was evidence to suggest that the use of cameras within King's Lynn had reduced the incidence of various types of offenses, most notably burglary, but to a lessor extent assaults and possibly vehicle crime. The fact that the cameras had been involved in over 80 arrests for property offenses and almost 100 arrests for public order offenses reinforced the point that it was action precipitated by cameras which led to these effects.

The findings illustrate the extent of surveillance that the CCTV systems can provide in towns like King's Lynn. Operators noticed over 2000 incidents in a 32-month period, of which only 16% resulted in police officers contacting a suspect. In most of these cases, the police chose not to respond. There were also a similar number of incidents where the movements of people were monitored at the request of staff from other agencies.

The results illustrate how useful the camera system can be in helping the police carry out their day-to-day duties. Demands on the police are considerable but officers are often alerted to many incidents where a police response, especially an immediate police response, is inappropriate or unnecessary. Moreover, by the time many incidents come to the attention of the police, they cease to require a police response.

In an environment such as King's Lynn, the cameras were very helpful in determining whether an incident required a police response and what that response should be. In this respect, the system helped manage police resources more effectively.

The findings reinforce the point raised by the Newcastle case study, that the cameras were at their most effective in dealing with crime when they were integrated into a command and control strategy, and were used to discover incidents and coordinate an appropriate police response. It was often the case that incidents occurred within range of the cameras but were not noticed by operators. In these cases, investigating officers viewed tape recordings of the area where an incident had taken place. Although these tapes were viewed regularly during the course of an investigation, they only provided useful information very occasionally.

Conclusions

THE POLICE USE OF TOWN CENTER CCTV SYSTEMS

The police use town center camera systems in a number of ways to tackle criminal and anti-social behavior. The primary use of camera systems within town centers is as a tool to "patrol" these areas effectively and discover incidents as they occur. The police use the information provided by the cameras to coordinate suitable responses to these incidents, whilst gathering evidence that can direct the investigation of an offense and secure the swift conviction of an offender. Although camera footage is used in helping detect an offender after an event has occurred, this is a less common and less effective way of having an impact on crime.

Overwhelming evidence from the case studies indicates that cameras are used most often to deal with conspicuous anti-social and criminal behavior, most notably various small scale public order problems, ranging from unruly nuisance behavior to fighting and assaults. Even though many of these offenses may appear trivial in nature, they can be a significant problem for town center management. If problems such as littering, vandalism and loitering within town centers are not tackled responsibly and effectively, they may get worse. A town center may the be perceived as dirty and/or dangerous which, in turn, not only deters legitimate users (URBED, 1994) but also may attract potential offenders (Kennedy, 1990; Murray, 1983). It is also important to remember that a significant minority of arrests attributable to the camera systems relate to other types of crime such as robbery, theft and burglary.

The information provided by camera systems is also very useful in helping the police to manage their resources more effectively. Almost one third of all calls to the police are false alarms (Waddington, 1993; Ekblom and Heal, 1982). Camera systems, therefore, can give some indication as to whether or not a police response is require at all.

THE EFFECT OF CCTV ON PROPERTY CRIME IN TOWN CENTERS

The findings from the case studies indicate that CCTV camera systems can help reduce the incidence of property crime within town centers. In Newcastle and King's Lynn, and to a lesser extent Birmingham, property crime has reduced in those areas covered by cameras. This refers mainly to the burglary of shops, but also to theft of and from vehicles.

The evidence from the Newcastle and King's Lynn case studies suggests that initially the presence of cameras deterred all the types of property crime examined. It also appears that the effect of the cameras on some of these crimes may have faded over time to a certain extent. Within the time period examined, however, there were net reductions in these offenses in areas with camera coverage.

What appears to be the important factor in sustaining the effect of cameras on property offenses is that the risk of arrest for these offenses in increased. In Newcastle, for those offenses where there is evidence for a sustained effect, the risk of arrest is increased. This suggests that the presence of cameras within an area may initially deter criminal behavior, thus accounting for dramatic reductions in crime often observed and widely publicized for schemes around the country. What sustains this effect, however, is a real increase in arrest rates for certain offenses.

THE EFFECT OF CCTV ON PERSONAL CRIME IN TOWN CENTERS

The effect of cameras on personal crime is less clear. In the large metropolitan districts, the cameras seem to have had considerably less impact on overall levels of public order and assault offenses. Within King's Lynn, a smaller market town, there is evidence to suggest that cameras have reduced assaults in those streets covered by cameras, but the numbers of incidents are small and this reduction occurred after the cameras had been operational for some months.

The benefit of the camera systems in dealing with offenses such as assault, however, may lie less in their deterrent effect but more in the way they help officers deal with such offenses. Camera systems can benefit police officers in dealing with assaults and disorder in two ways. First, they can help to coordinate a quick and effective response which may reduce the seriousness of the incident. Second, they can be used to gather evidence that might be used in the investigation of an offense and the swift conviction of an offender. Such evidence might be otherwise difficult and resource intensive to collect. In areas such as King's Lynn, where these types of offenses are relatively rare and where resources are less stretched at the relevant times, the incidence for these types of offenses may eventually decrease in areas covered by cameras.

The presence of CCTV cameras within the study areas has had little overall impact in the incidence of robbery and theft from the person. The rates for these types of offenses did not decrease after the cameras were installed in either of the two areas where these types of offense were examined. However the findings from the Birmingham case study suggest that the cameras have helped to contain the problem of robberies and personal thefts within an area, possibly by reducing their incidence in areas where there is a good camera view. The fact that the system in Birmingham has led to the arrest of offenders for these types of offense supports this notion. However, it seems as though these offenses are more easily displaced to town center areas or streets that are not covered by cameras, but are still routinely used by members of the public.

DISPLACEMENT AND DIFFUSION

The displacement of crime is a major issue in the evaluation of any situational crime prevention measure. It is very difficult, especially using quantitative crime data, to identify displacement correctly. To identify displacement (or even the effect of cameras on offending behavior) using these data, one has to infer the intentions and beliefs of offenders (Gabor, 1990).

There is evidence to suggest, however, that some displacement of crime has taken place. The findings that the likelihood of crimes being displaced by the cameras depends on the nature of the offense, the types of area the cameras are located in and the extent of the camera coverage within this area. Personal crimes such as robbery and theft from the person appear to be more easily displaced. This may be because the number of "suitable" victims is greater than for property crime, especially in locations where the town or city center extends beyond the area covered by cameras and the layout is complex.

As evidence of this, some displacement of robbery and theft from the person seems to have occurred in Birmingham. In this location, the city center area extends into a neighboring police division, well beyond the area covered by cameras. There are many places within the town centers that have no camera coverage but are still used by potential victims; consequently offending may move from those areas that have coverage to that areas where there is partial or no coverage. Moreover in Birmingham, as crime has been displaced to different areas, it has manifested itself in different forms, especially theft from vehicles.

Property crime on the other hand, is easier to control using cameras and because of its nature is less likely to be displaced within town centers. In Newcastle, where the extent of camera coverage within the town center is high, there is no evidence which indicates that property crime has been displaced, either by location or offense type. In fact, it appears that there may have been some diffusion of benefits.

The implications of these findings are that in order for a camera system to be effective within a town center, there needs to be a high degree of coverage. There is also no guarantee that acquisitive personal crimes such as robbery will not be displaced to surrounding areas, especially if these areas are routinely used by both potential victims and motivated offenders. If a town center area has many side streets and other premises such as car parks, it will require many cameras and several operators to make such a system effective. This has obvious resource implications. However, the cameras can in some instances liberate resources by cutting down considerably on the number of false alarms that police patrols are required to attend.

A number of issues also emerge from this and other studies which have looked at the effect of CCTV on crime. The first is that CCTV seems to work best when it is part of a package of measures, which in this case is a general command and control strategy. With packages of measures it can be difficult to separate any individual element and point to it as a source of success, and so in this case simply installing cameras is no guarantee that crime will reduce in the long term. What is important is the way in which CCTV is used as part of an overall strategy for policing town centers. Secondly, as is common with many crime prevention efforts, the effectiveness of packages that include CCTV may wear off over time. In order to sustain an effect, the cameras must play a part in the apprehension of offenders, and other conditions must be altered to improve the potential of CCTV to have this effect. Camera successes can then be publicized, reinforcing the message for offenders that there is an increased risk of being caught.

13. Reduction of Employee Theft in a Retail Environment: Displacement vs. Diffusion of Benefits

Barry Masuda

EDITOR'S NOTE: The work undertaken by the security departments of large business-es and corporations generally consists, on the one hand, of detecting dishonest employ-ees and, on the other, of ensuring that standard security practices and hardware are in place. Too little of their work consists of the detailed analysis and solution of specific problems in the manner advocated by situational prevention. The present study, first reported in Security Journal *(Masuda, 1992), constitutes an important exception. Detailed analysis of theft patterns from the distribution center and stockrooms of a New Jersey discount electronics retailer, undertaken by the director of security, Barry Masuda, revealed that thefts were concentrated on certain high-risk items, in particular camcorders and VCRs. The "low tech" solution was to introduce a regimen of repeated counting of the stock of these items so that any shortages could be linked directly to the presence of particular employees. Not only did theft of the items plummet, but thefts of other items, not repeatedly counted, also declined. The study therefore provides some of the first and clearest evidence of diffusion of benefits. It may be no coincidence that this early application of situational prevention principles in retailing was in a highly competitive sector with narrow profit margins. As competition becomes increasingly fierce in all sectors, as it must, the scope for situational prevention will also grow. In turn, as situational prevention is applied increasingly in commercial contexts, the calculation of the costs of prevention, as well as its benefits, will become more sophisticated. There is a natural symbiosis, therefore, between situational prevention and the work of business and corporate security departments.*

Introduction

The profit motive often conspires to create trade-offs that adversely affect the purpose of a retail entity's system of internal controls and overall security plan. Moreover, the geographic selection of sites (highly trafficked areas with many access points) and the dwindling quality (marginally literate) of entry-level labor resources tend to exacerbate the external and internal factors that have an impact on shrinkage, the financial term that represents the unexplained loss of physical inventory. The need to sell combines with negative environmental factors to exert constant upward pressure on shrinkage, wherein the retailer is often more part of the problem than part of the solution. How to balance the retailer's need to merchandise, maintain adequate levels of inventory, and expedite the flow of goods with the corresponding need to prevent losses represents a complex and traditionally antagonistic dilemma for the loss prevention expert.

The following case illustrates how a focused strategy employing intensive intervention techniques reversed the historical losses of a major electronics and appliance retailer and yielded substantial "diffusion of benefits" (Clarke, 1992) for a wide variety of nontargeted inventory products.

The Problem

This study examines the loss history of a New Jersey-based discount electronics and appliance retailer between 1989 and 1991. During this 3-year period, the company employed a total of 1,500 persons at four retail locations (superstores) and one distribution center.

Sales floor area of the four retail locations averages 40,000 square feet and each location has its own warehouse averaging another 40,000 square feet. The corporation distribution center encompasses 342,000 square feet. The distribution center and each superstore carries approximately $40 million in physical inventory, though seasonal fluctuations alter this number significantly (see Table 1).

Stores are open 10-15 hours per day, 7 days a week; the distribution center never closes. It ships two-to-four tractor trailer loads of merchandise to each store daily, as well as processes store returns, receives all purchases generated by corporate buyers, and prepares the routing and loading of customer deliveries. Interstore transfers are trucked in-house, while deliveries are shipped by an external contractor that administers its own traffic operation and truck fleet from within the distribution center.

Annual sales for 1989 were $300 million. End of the year shrinkage was reported at 1.5% of the cost of goods sold.

From a physical security perspective, retail and warehouse operations present access control problems (stores have four-to-five entrances and exits; the distribution center, 39) and merchandise control problems (the product line consists of over 7,000 different "brown" goods (electronic products) and "white" goods (appliance products).

Decentralized security staffs are supported by centralized investigative and audit divisions. The employee-to-security ratio is 61 to 1.

Prior to 1989, the company experienced rapid growth and the corresponding lack of organizational stability that it brings. The Management Information Service Department was not structured to accommodate the increase in capacity generated by exploding sales; operations was not accustomed to receiving, transferring, and delivering large quantities of goods quickly and efficiently; and security was, in short, overwhelmed.

These structural faults were eventually corrected but inventory shortages began to increase at a higher rate than previous trends. In addition to taking an end-of-the-year physical inventory, management required its inventory control department to take intermittent cycle counts (i.e. physical counts of particular product categories) of all product lines.

TABLE 1
INVENTORY BREAKDOWN FOR FIVE LOCATIONS

Location	Inventory at Cost*
Distribution Center	$24 million
Store 1	$3 million
Store 2	$8 million
Store 3	$3 million
Store 4	$3 million

* Not adjusted for seasonal variance.

Cycle counting is a sampling process designed to test the accuracy of known (or believed to be known) inventory levels. It obviates the costly and time consuming need to take repetitive physical counts of retailer's entire stock without abandoning the need to obtain reliable information about the accuracy of on-hand quantities of merchandise (Jannis *et al.,* 1980). Table 2 shows the cycle count results for eight "shrinkage sensitive" categories for the sixteen-month period between September 1989 and December 1990.

TABLE 2
CYCLE COUNT RESULTS FOR EIGHT PRODUCT CATEGORIES
PRIOR TO INTERVENTION

Count Date	Merchandise Category	Unit Shrinkage	$ Shrinkage in %
09/16/89	Car stereos	94	9.0
05/06/90	Camcorders/VCRs	475	6.1
05/19/90	Big screen TVs	13	1.9
05/27/90	Electronics	245	1.4
08/31/90	Car stereos	62	10.8
10/03/90	Tapes and batteries	6,273	8.2
11/30/90	Portable CDs	10	9.8
12/13/90	Radar detectors	46	2.7
12/31/90	Movie video tapes	287	2.1

The variance in the percent of shrinkage reported for each category is a function of each product's relative distribution within the overall inventory. Ninety-four units of car stereo, for example, represents a loss of 9.0% of the entire stock in this product that was on hand at the time. Theft aside, factors influencing shrinkage rates are per unit costs and quantity. The relatively low rates of shrinkage for electronics and radar detectors are due, in large part, to the lower per unit costs and larger stocking levels. Higher priced products (car stereos and portable CDs), with lower relative unit losses, tend to correspond with higher rates of shrinkage expressed as a percent of dollar value at cost, while lower priced products (electronics and radar detectors), with high unit losses, tend to correspond with lower rates of shrinkage (even despite losses sustained from vigorous pilferage, shrinkage rates for these products have still not pierced the 2% threshold). The exception to this rule, as evidenced by both the high unit losses and high rates of shrinkage, was demonstrated by the camcorder and VCR product category. Strong consumer demand dictated that large quantities of these costly products always had to be kept in inventory.

By mid-year 1990, losses[1] had risen to unprecedented levels. In response, management took decisive steps to counter this problem by adjusting its focus and moving toward the development of an effective action plan that stressed intervention and prevention.

Methodology

Prior to the adoption of new intervention measures, the protection of merchandise consisted of a strategy that relied primarily on maintaining the physical security of inventory through the employment of alarms, locks, closed-circuit television monitoring, and guards. No measures were taken to determine when, how, or why thefts occurred. Unfortunately, this dictated a reactive approach that did nothing to identify fundamental weaknesses within the existing system of internal controls.

The questions confronting management were essentially these: Given the extent and rapid growth of inventory shortages, could this trend be reversed? How quickly would it take? How much would it cost?

In spite of the recent losses, the retail operations and marketing departments did not want any countermeasures adopted that would interfere with their achievement of robust sales. And though the finance department wanted to reduce losses, the expenditures required to hire additional security personnel and purchase more.equipment made these unattractive alternatives. Even so, could the security department reasonably be expected to secure over $41 million in inventory of which 30% was in transit on any given day? If not, would it be forced to secure some products while ignoring others? Any strategy that attempted to require security to achieve control of the entire inventory, given the then current budgetary constraints, held out little hope of success. On the other hand, selective prevention posed the risk of merely displacing losses to other products thereby effectively "institutionalizing" shrinkage for the company. .

Zero-shrinkage Targeting

Emphasis was shifted to improving internal controls that would create audit trails and facilitate tracking the flow of goods from the point of receipt to the point of sale. The intention of this shift, however, was not to abandon the use of physical security assets: It was designed to introduce a much needed perspective and orientation to the department's security approach that enhanced its ability to detect and, thereby, more effectively counter theft. The subsequent creation of an audit division assisted management in developing a historical sense of what products were most frequently stolen and analyzed, in conjunction with its newly formed investigative counterpart, how inventory theft was executed.

Several products were identified as "high-shrinkage" merchandise, and a variety of loss scenarios were identified. Internal thefts were perpetrated by employees acting alone, using fraudulent documentation, or effective stealth techniques, as well as in consort with other co-workers. Often large quantities were stolen at one time, and, in most cases, there was a pronounced breakdown in operational procedures.

The exposure of specific theft trails assisted in securing their closure, but it was evident that a more intensive method of intervention had to be found if the runaway losses were to be stopped. Inherent in the problem of theft was the persistent popularity of electronics for resale on the street, the sheer volume of the inventory that required protection, the numerous opportunities for theft that still remained, and the limited resources that were available to achieve success.

Prior to the implementation of these new controls, not only was theft easily perpetrated, it was also readily concealed. For example, one minute, 50 camcorders were in stock; the next, only 45, with no discernible clues left behind to explain their disappearance or to pinpoint the time frame of their loss.

To accommodate all concerns (the need to merchandise, the need to control costs, and the fear of displacing losses from one product to another), a rational choice approach was embraced (Gottfredson and Hirschi, 1990). Implicit in this theory is the idea that perception of control was equivalent to control. If dishonest employees could be successfully influenced to perceive that risk of detection and capture was high, they could be successfully discouraged from committing theft.

Since all the merchandise could not be secured all the time, a strategy was adopted that targeted two product categories for intensive control. Selection was based upon average cost, contribution to profit margin, loss history, and frequency of turnover. This led to camcorders and VCRs being chosen. The short-term objective was the reduction of losses in both categories to zero within 3 months. It was believed that the employment of a selective zero-shrinkage intervention strategy would remove the preexisting opportunities for employees to steal and increase the ability of the security department to identify when theft occurred, thereby enabling investigators to conduct a more productive inquiry.

By implementing this aggressive strategy, security management hoped to regain control over inventory and reverse the upward spiral of losses. If successful, its achievement of the reduction of shrinkage in a few products was expected to foster an increase in the perception of risk, detection, and apprehension among all groups of employees that would transfer positive gains to other types of shrinkage-sensitive merchandise.

Initial resistance to the approach flowed from three negative assumptions:

- Internal thieves would target other products, i.e., "displace" to other goods.
- A reduction in shortage to zero in some products would not appreciably offset other losses.
- The security department's emphasis on preventing losses in specific categories would imply a reduced sense of its commitment to reversing losses in general.

In spite of these objections, management believed a priori in the merits of the strategy.

PREVENTIVE AUDIT SURVEY

The field procedure used to target on camcorders and VCRs was the preventive audit survey (PAS). It was, in actuality, a minicycle count conducted chainwide on a daily basis.

The intervention objectives were

- To discover and correct inventory discrepancies.
- To expose system weaknesses with receiving, transfers, and distribution.
- To detect theft.
- To reduce opportunities for theft by increasing frequencies of physical inspection.

Beginning January 1, 1991, security personnel entered the locked storage areas where high-shrinkage merchandise was secured to make daily counts of the stock of camcorders and VCRs. The physical counts were then compared to computerized perpetual records. Initially, this was a time-consuming process given the quantities involved. It did, however, ensure an accuracy and timeliness never before attained.

Windows of opportunity were closed, discrepancies (e.g. goods still in transit or sales credits issued for goods not received) were reconciled immediately, and unaccounted for shortages were attributed to internal theft. The PAS enabled investigators to associate losses with employees known to be present, and, since intervention was daily, prevented inventory theft from accumulating over a succession of work shifts, involving numerous employees, resulting in unfathomable problems.

Even so, could this method of intervention realistically be expected to reduce pilferage overall?

Results

The impact of conducting preventive audit surveys was immediate: Discrepancies were reconciled instantly, losses resulting from theft were detected, and guilty employees were confronted. Even the prospect of recovery began to emerge. Consequently, investigators were able to cycle through each loss incident more rapidly (i.e., acquire knowledge of a theft, select suspects, plan, implement the plan, obtain a result) and destabilize the confidence of dishonest employees, who, heretofore, enjoyed both the advantages of confusion and anonymity. Table 3 reflects the decreases achieved in shrinkage.

Management's initial objective of reaching zero shrinkage in 3 months for targeted products was realized in addition to a decline in losses for nontargeted categories. Not only was zero shrinkage achieved for camcorders and VCRs, but also for radar detectors, portable CDs and car stereos. Of the categories reported in Table 2, only big screen TVs and movie video tapes continued to sustain losses, though the loss of big screen TVs was markedly reduced. The contribution of videos to shrinkage was immaterial due to the negligible investment in inventory of this product. Moreover, video tapes, highly vulnerable to external theft, had little chance of benefiting from the preventive audit survey — a strategy strictly designed to thwart internal losses.

Of major significance, in terms of evaluating the effectiveness of the intervening methodology and its overall success, was the trade-off in costs, of which there was none. Identical resources had been merely redeployed and assigned more productive tasks.

Conclusions

The terms "displacement" and "diffusion of benefits" represent two adversarial points of view. Displacement theory suggests that if a criminal is frustrated from perpetrating a crime against target A then the criminal will transfer his or her attack to target B (Clarke *et al.,* 1991). The residential alarm industry's profitability, for example, is dependent upon society's continued acceptance of this simple premise. The concept of diffusion of benefits, on the other hand, implies that a concentration of effort and resources in one area will inevitably spill over to similarly affect another, resulting in a coincidental windfall of "benefits." For retail loss prevention executives (or, for that matter, public law enforcement officials), the advantages to be gained from the successful exploitation of such a phenomenon are economic: Limited resources can be stretched to achieve traditionally costly objectives.

TABLE 3
POST-INTERVENTION CYCLE COUNTS FOR TARGETED AND
NON-TARGETED MERCHANDISE

Count Date	Merchandise Category	Unit Shrinkage	$ Shrinkage in %	Previous Shrinkage in %
Targeted merchandise				
02/02/91	Camcorder/VCRs	46	0.6	6.1
03/09/91	Camcorder/VCRs	6	0.1	0.6
04/16/91	Camcorder/VCRs	0	0	0.1
Non-targeted merchandise				
03/02/91	Big screen TVs	12	1.8	1.9
04/20/91	Radar detectors	0	0	2.7
05/23/91	Portable CDs	0	0	9.8
08/08/91	Movie video tapes	197	1.8	2.1
08/10/91	Car stereos	0	0	9.0
12/28/91	Big screen TVs	2	0.3	1.8

In the case of our electronics and appliance retailer, two observations can be made. First, dishonest employees did not displace to other goods. Second, the efforts of a focused and coordinated security program did appear to extend the "diffusion of benefits" to nontargeted product categories resulting in the significant reduction of overall losses. It is also noteworthy that these results have remained constant over time.

The simple elimination of the opportunity for employees to commit theft was not the sole objective of the strategy adopted. Follow up investigations, terminations, and prosecutions were important ingredients in the rational choice approach that anticipated reductions in losses through selective prevention enhanced by the increased perception of risk. It is impossible to state with certainty, however, that minus these perceptions displacement would have inevitably occurred. A possible explanation for the "diffusion of benefits" may be that once all the dishonest employees were identified and expelled from within the limited confines of the company, the probability of future losses was reduced, de facto, to zero. This presumes that no more dishonest employees were hired, and, of those remaining, none were predisposed to steal. Regardless of the fact that policing a single closed environment of 1,500 employees is much less complex than having to police the entire community at large, any individual's needs, wants, and resistance to temptation are always evolving, creating changes in his or her perception of risk and thus in the ultimate consequences.

It is highly unlikely that the pervasive reductions in shrinkage were due to the achievement of a utopia. (The author can attest to the contrary.) What is likely, is that in smaller environments the potential for displacement can be arguably reduced while conditions for diffusion can be enhanced.

Attempts to generalize the results achieved in a controlled environment to a broader societal level, however, must proceed with caution. Larger environments contain greater numbers of factors that are considerably beyond the control of crime prevention tinkerers. Nevertheless, the accumulation of empirical data derived from any setting will help to validate in absolute terms intervention methods designed to decrease criminal opportunity.

Note

1. Calculation of shrinkage: The measurement of true shrinkage (i.e. the loss of physical inventory due to theft or destruction) is often clouded by the inventory valuation accounting method selected by management. The retail method is frequently used by retailers but it corrupts the true calculation of shrinkage because it assumes that all markdowns and markups are captured and reflected in the final numbers. Because shrinkage is reported in terms of dollars, a significant contribution to shrinkage can be attributed to the failure of this method to accurately reflect the true cost of goods sold. In the case under review, inventory valuation is calculated by average cost. This method avoids the pitfalls of employee carelessness and offers management a clearer picture of its true losses. The dollar values of the shrinkage reported in Table 2 are, therefore, a reflection of problems related to theft and not to some other cause. It is important for administrators to make this distinction so that further drains on revenue are prevented by the misallocation of resources.

14. Preventing Convenience Store Robbery Through Environmental Design

Ronald D. Hunter and C. Ray Jeffery

EDITOR'S NOTE: As explained in the Introduction, the development of situational prevention in Britain was assisted by the parallel development of Crime Prevention through Environmental Design, or CPTED, in the United States. The term was coined by C. Ray Jeffery, one of the authors of this case study. In fact, the prevention of convenience store robbery represents the most sustained CPTED effort, with work on the topic being conducted by Jeffery or his students from the mid-1970s until the present time. This case study, written for this collection, reviews the many CPTED studies undertaken of convenience store robbery, including those commissioned by the police and the convenience store industry. "7-Eleven" in particular has been a pioneer through support of the early research by Crow and Bull (1975). A variety of methodologies has been employed including site surveys, interviews with robbers and victims, and experiments in which robbery rates have been compared between stores with and without new preventive measures. The measures endorsed by the greatest number of studies are: (1) having two or more clerks on duty, especially at night (a form of employee surveillance); (2) cash handling techniques (target removal), (3) access control and (4) natural surveillance. The evidence about two clerks has been criticized by Sherman (1991) and, in a more recent review of the convenience store literature,

Bellamy (1996) has suggested that having two or more clerks on duty may bring greatest benefits for stores that have been the victims of repeated robberies — another indication of the need to study repeat victimization.

Convenience Store Robbery

RECORDED INCIDENTS of robbery ("the taking or attempted taking of anything of value from the care, custody, or control of a person or persons by force or threat of force or violence and/or putting the victim in fear," Sessions, 1990:17), occurred at convenience stores within the United States on 36,434 occasions during 1989. This represented a 28 percent increase in convenience store robberies since 1985, the most rapid growth within all categories of robbery during that period (Sessions, 1990:21).

The dramatic increase in convenience store robberies is of major concern to public officials and the convenience store industry, not only because of the financial losses, but also due to the physical and mental harm to employees and customers which often occurs as a result of this violent offense. Aggravated assaults, abductions, rapes, and homicides have too frequently been the product of the convenience store industry's inability to protect itself, its employees and its customers from robberies.

The average value of property stolen during the commission of convenience store robberies in 1989 was $364. Yet, these losses are minimal when compared to the loss of business from customers who are afraid to shop in the stores, the loss of qualified employees who are afraid to work in them and successful litigation by individuals harmed because of convenience store robberies. In addition, the costs to local governments as a result of these robberies are high due, not only to criminal justice activities (preventive patrols, surveillance, emergency responses, investigations, apprehension and incarceration of offenders, judicial proceedings), but also to the adverse impact upon the quality of life of their citizenry.

The detrimental effects of convenience store robberies are felt not only by victims and their families, but by all residents and visitors whose shopping behavior is restricted due to fear of victimization.

Research

A number of studies have been conducted during the past twenty years to examine the relationship between environmental factors and vulnerability to robbery at convenience stores. The findings from these research projects have led to significant changes in the strategies utilized to prevent convenience store robberies. Some of the more important studies are summarized below.

Crow and Bull. The study which has had the most impact upon subsequent attempts to prevent convenience store robbery was that of Crow and Bull (1975). It began with an examination of 349 convenience stores owned by the Southland Corporation on the basis of which a scale was developed by which stores were ranked as to target attractiveness by former armed robbers. Those stores ranked as highly attractive were found to have been robbed more frequently. Based upon the robbers' input, Crow and Bull developed several robbery prevention strategies which they used in a field experiment involving 120 "24-hour" convenience stores in five Southern California counties. The prevention strategies included: cash handling procedures which limited available cash; signs indicating limited cash; enhanced visibility inside and out; elimination of escape routes; use of security devices; encouraging visits from police and cab drivers; enhancing employee alertness; and, keeping the stores clean. These were implemented in sixty experimental stores, which were closely matched with sixty control stores. The robbery experience of both groups was followed for eight months.

Crow and Bull found that the experimental stores experienced significantly fewer robberies than did the control stores. They concluded that: "The results support the concept that robbers select their targets and that physical and behavioral changes at the site can significantly reduce robberies" (Crow and Bull, 1975: ii).

Crow and Bull's study was perhaps the first application of crime prevention through environmental design (Jeffery, 1971) to the crime of robbery. While limited to a specific convenience store chain (7-11) in Southern California, their findings have influenced the entire convenience store industry. In fact, many of the prevention procedures found within the National Association of Convenience Store's Robbery Deterrence Manual (NACS, 1987) may be traced directly to Crow and Bull's work.

Duffala. Another well-known study which examined convenience store robberies from an opportunity perspective was conducted by Duffala (1976), who sought to test whether or not the vulnerability of convenience stores to armed robbery is associated with certain environmental characteristics. Thirty-nine convenience stores in Tallahassee, Florida, were included in the study. Since the stores in the sample were similar in physical design, Duffala focused upon features of their location as being determinants of vulnerability to robbery. He believed that stores which were more readily accessible to robbers would have a greater likelihood of being robbed.

Duffala hypothesized that stores would be more vulnerable when they were located: (1) within two blocks of a major street, (2) on streets with light amounts of traffic, (3) in a residential and/or vacant land use area, and, (4) in an area with few surrounding commercial activities. His hypotheses relating to a store's location near a major street and in residential areas were not supported and those regarding light traffic and few surrounding commercial activities received only limited support. However, while no one environmental variable was very important in relationship to vulnerability to robbery, all four were significant when viewed in interaction with one another (Duffala, 1976:244).

Scott, Crow and Erickson. In 1985, Scott *et al.* attempted to study the effectiveness of the robbery prevention strategies advocated by Crow and Bull (1975) as well as certain other strategies which had been proposed by various local governments. They supplemented data from an earlier study by the Athena Research Corporation (1981) which had interviewed sixty armed robbers who were inmates at the Texas State Prison at Huntsville, with interviews from 181 robbers confined in prisons in California, Illinois, Louisiana and New Jersey. The robbers were questioned about the deterrent effect of target characteristics, which stores they would be more likely to rob and how much money they would want in order to make a robbery worthwhile.

Based upon the inmates' responses, Scott *et al.* (1985) recommended that Southland Corporation continue in its efforts to improve cash handling procedures which would limit the take from 7-ll Store robberies to less than $100. They further concluded that having two clerks in a store, and closing between 11 p.m. and 6 a.m., were not effective robbery prevention measures. The sex of the clerk was also felt to have little impact upon robberies.

Unfortunately, in the Scott *et al.* study, as well as in the earlier Athena study which it incorporated, the robbers' ratings were not supported by empirical analysis of the actual experience of robberies in convenience stores. As a result, the study may be considered more of an index of inmate attitudes rather than a valid test of environmental crime prevention strategies.

Degner, Comer, Kepner and Olexia. A study which produced contradictory results regarding the influence of environmental factors upon convenience store robberies was conducted by researchers at the Florida Agricultural Market Research Center (Degner *et al.*, 1983). They found that: (1) "The peak robbery period for convenience stores occurred between 9:00 and 11:00 p.m. when nearly one-fourth were committed..." (Degner *et al.*, 1983: 26); and (2) "Surprisingly, the robbery success rate does not appear to decrease as the number of victims increases" (Degner *et al*, 1983:18). These findings may be used to challenge requirements that convenience stores close from 11 a.m. to 6 a.m., and/or utilize more than one clerk. However, other findings of the study reveal that: (1) 94.5 percent of all convenience store robberies had only one victim (Degner *et al.*, 1983:19) and (2) nearly 35 percent of all convenience store robberies in Florida in 1981 occurred between 11 p.m. and 6 a.m. (Degner *et al.*, 1983:27).

The Gainesville Studies. In 1986 the Gainesville Police Department contracted with James White to conduct an analysis of convenience store robberies within the Gainesville area. White (1986) evaluated seventy-two convenience stores within the Gainesville area based upon: lighting of the store and premises; visual obstructions to cashiers; and the number of clerks on duty. He concluded that the number of clerks working was the strongest predictor of convenience store robbery. The store environment was not found to be a statistically significant factor.

In a second study sponsored by the Gainesville Police Department, Swanson (1986) conducted a three-tiered analysis of convenience store robbery. He first interviewed sixty-five convenience store robbers incarcerated at three Florida facilities and asked them to rank order the most desirable characteristics in selecting a store to rob. He then interviewed twenty-four individuals who had been victims of convenience store robberies and asked them to rate the same characteristics. Based upon the responses of robbers and victims, Swanson then constructed a list of thirty-two store characteristics which he correlated with robbery data for forty Gainesville convenience stores.

Analysis of the relationships between store characteristics and number of robberies led him to conclude that having two clerks on duty seemed to be the primary element in deterring convenience store robbery in Gainesville. The use of security cameras and time release safes, the presence of other 24-hour businesses, and closing stores at midnight were also found to reduce the potential for robbery.

The Tallahassee Studies. Jeffery *et al.* (1987) studied thirty-four convenience stores which had been continuously operating within the City of Tallahassee from January 1, 1981, to July 1, 1985. Each site was visited by the researchers and assessed on a series of environmental characteristics thought to be related to robbery. The number of robberies occurring at each site from January 1, 1981, through July 1, 1985, was then obtained from the Tallahassee Police Department.

It was found that convenience stores were less likely to be robbed if: the cashier was located in the center; more than one clerk was on duty; there was clear visibility within the store; there was clear visibility from outside the store; stores were located near commercial property; they were located near residential property (better than near vacant lots or woods); they were near other evening commercial activities; concealed access/escape was eliminated; gasoline pumps were operational on the property; and good cash handling policies were followed which limited available cash.

Jeffery *et al.* (1987:69) concluded that "convenience store robberies were highly responsive to both internal and external physical and geographical features which involve the design of the store and the external environment." Their findings were utilized in justifying an ordinance restricting convenience store operations in Gainesville, Florida, and served as a partial basis for a later statewide analysis of convenience store robbery (Hunter, 1988).

Hunter (1990) re-examined the Tallahassee stores some four years later to determine what changes might have occurred. He found that the number of significant variables had declined from those identified in the earlier study. In 1990, Tallahassee convenience stores were less likely to be robbed if: the cashier was located in the center of the store; more than one clerk was on duty; concealed access/escape was eliminated; the stores were near other evening commercial activities; and, gasoline pumps were operational on the property.

In addition to finding that fewer variables seemed to play a significant part in robbery, Hunter also found that their influence was not permanent. There was a general decline in robberies of 24 percent from June 1985 through December 1989, with robberies of some stores decreasing by as much as 86 percent, whereas other stores experienced increases of up to 50 percent. Stores which had implemented new robbery prevention strategies had fewer robberies, while those that had failed to develop new techniques experienced increased robberies. These findings demonstrated that the influence of environmental factors varies over time. Therefore, robbery prevention strategies must constantly be upgraded and improved.

The Florida Study. In a study funded by the Florida Department of Legal Affairs, Hunter (1988) undertook a statewide survey of convenience store robberies in order to test the application of CPTED principles derived from the local area analysis in Tallahassee to a state-wide area. The sample surveyed consisted of 200 stores selected at random from the population of convenience stores operating within the State of Florida. Seventy-four stores were eliminated from the sample due to not having operated continuously from January 1, 1984, through December 31, 1986, or having changed ownership (an exception was made for Little General Stores purchased by Circle K in that design and marketing strategies were not affected by the transfer). One hundred and twenty-six stores remained within the sample.

A list of pertinent characteristics thought to impact upon a store's vulnerability to robbery, as measured by the number of actual robberies, was selected from those analyzed in earlier studies by Crow and Bull (1975), Duffala (1976), and Jeffery *et al.* (1987). This list incorporated the characteristics found to have significant positive relationships with the number of store robberies within those studies. During the Fall of 1987, each store site was evaluated as to the environmental characteristics inside, immediately outside, and in the surrounding area. An additional sixteen stores were eliminated during the on-site evaluation process as a result of substantial store alterations since 1984. Information about robberies and attempted robberies at each store was then obtained from the law enforcement agencies in whose jurisdictions the stores were located. Data were obtained on 107 stores indicating that 212 robberies had occurred (accurate robbery information was not available for three stores). Data analyses were then conducted using a variety of statistical techniques at the state, regional and local levels.

Based upon his findings, Hunter (1988) recommended the following measures: eliminate concealed access; utilize more than one clerk; enhance visibility from outside the store; close stores between midnight and 6 a.m.; enhance visibility within the store; locate the cashier in the center of the store; install gasoline pumps to increase customer activity; locate the store on a busy street; locate the store in commercial or residential areas; locate the store near other evening commercial activities; and use good cash handling procedures.

The last recommendation, utilizing good cash handling procedures, was made despite a negative finding regarding its usefulness as a deterrent. Hunter explained this negative finding as the result of three factors: over-dependence on cash handling as a prevention technique while neglecting other environmental factors; failure of store management and employees to adhere to cash handling policies; and disbelief on the part of offenders that the amount of cash was actually limited. Hunter (1988) argued that, when used in conjunction with other prevention techniques, cash handling would have a positive effect.

Summary

The studies reviewed herein, clearly demonstrate a linkage between convenience store robbery and environmental influences and, based upon the findings, a variety of robbery prevention strategies have been developed for convenience stores. Among these strategies, having two or more clerks on duty has received the most support, followed closely by: good cash handling practices; elimination of concealed access; and location in areas with evening commercial activities. The results are summarized in Table 1 (next page).

Some strategies may require clarification. Good cash handling includes: limiting the amount of cash available; posting signs indicating limited cash; utilizing time release or drop safes; and training employees to adhere to strict cash-control policies. Eliminating concealed access/escape includes: enhanced lighting at the rear and sides of the store; erection of fencing and walls to prevent or slow the escape of robbers; and removal of sight obstacles which robbers might use for concealment. Enhanced exterior visibility includes: removing obstructions that inhibit seeing into or out of the stores; and ensuring visibility within the parking lots by removing obstacles and increasing available lighting. Security devices include: robbery alarms; camera or video systems; controlled access safes; mirrors; and other prevention devices. Training in robbery prevention includes: compliance with cash-control policies; encouraging visits from police and others; alertness to potential danger; store cleanliness; utilization of prevention devices; and safety procedures in case of robbery.

Findings from Clifton and Callahan (1987) and Butterworth (1991), which will be discussed in the following section, are also included within Table 1. In addition, recent studies on the benefits of multiple staffing and bullet-resistant enclosures (Vogel, 1990; Wilson *et al.,* 1990) are included.

Results of Prevention Programs in Florida

The City of Gainesville provides perhaps the most notable example of the impact of environmental prevention strategies upon convenience store robberies. Based upon the research findings of White (1986) and Swanson (1986), the Gainesville Police Department proposed an ordinance to the Gainesville City Council to regulate the operation of

TABLE 1
ENVIRONMENTAL FACTORS WHICH HAVE BEEN FOUND TO REDUCE THE
POTENTIAL FOR ROBBERY AT CONVENIENCE STORES

	Supporting Research
Two or more clerks	E, F, G, H, I, J, K, L, M,N
Good cash handling	A, C, D, F, H, J, M,N
Concealed access eliminated	A, D, H, I, J, M
Store near evening commercial activity	B, F, H, I, J
Exterior visibility enhanced	A, H, J, M, N
Store closed from 10 p.m. to 6 a.m.	E, F, J, M, N
Security devices in use	A, F, J, M, N
Cashier located in security enclosure	C, K,L, M
Employees trained in prevention	A, J, M, N
Interior visibility enhanced	A, H, J
Store in commercial or residential areas	B, H, J
Gasoline pumps present in front of store	H, I, J
Cashier located in store center	H, I, J
Store on busy street with heavy traffic	B, J
Security guard on premises	C, M

A = Crow and Bull, 1975; B = Duffala, 1976; C = Athena, 1981; D = Scott, Crow and Erickson, 1985; E = Degner, Comer, Kepner and Olexia, 1983; F = Swanson, 1986; G = White, 1986; H = Jeffery, Hunter and Griswold, 1987; I = Hunter, 1990; J = Hunter, 1988; K = Wilson, Rivero and Demings, 1990; L = Vogel, 1990; M = Butterworth, 1991; N = Clifton and Callahan, 1987.

convenience stores. The original ordinance required: limitation of cash; a security safe; parking lot lighting; removal of visual obstructions; robbery detection cameras; and training of clerks.

Following the implementation of the original ordinance in July 1986, convenience store robberies continued at an alarming rate. After efforts by the convenience store industry to reduce the rate failed, the City of Gainesville implemented a second element of the ordinance requiring that stores either utilize two clerks during the hours of 8 p.m. to 4 a.m. or that they close between these hours. Following implementation of the ordinance in April 1987, the Gainesville Police Department reported a dramatic decline in convenience store robberies during that year (Table 2) which has continued each year (Clifton and Callahan, 1987).

Another example of success in deterring convenience store robberies may be found in Jacksonville, Florida, where convenience store robberies increased dramatically during 1987. In lieu of an ordinance, voluntary compliance was sought in limiting cash handling, enhancing lighting, removing visual obstructions and training of clerks. By 1989, robberies had declined by 35%. In 1990 (during which time an ordinance requiring adherence to state-mandated prevention strategies was enacted) robberies declined another 26%.

TABLE 2
CONVENIENCE STORE ROBBERIES IN GAINESVILLE, JACKSONVILLE, AND
THROUGHOUT THE STATE OF FLORIDA, 1986-1990

	Gainesville	Jacksonville	Florida
1986	97	478	5, 288
1987	39	863	5, 222
1988*	—	—	—
1989	29	567	5, 548
1990	18	422	4, 909

Source: Florida Department of Law Enforcement.
* FDLE did not compile UCR data for 1988.

The Florida Department of Legal Affairs began investigating the alarming increase in convenience store robberies within the State of Florida during the 1980s. Utilizing data from Hunter (1988), Clifton and Callahan (1987) and prior studies, the Department of Legal Affairs produced videos on crime prevention through environmental design and preventing convenience store robbery which were provided to every city and county government within the State of Florida. Their recommendations (see Table 3) were enacted by many city and county governments during 1988 and 1989.

TABLE 3
PREVENTION TECHNIQUES RECOMMENDED BY THE FLORIDA
DEPARTMENT OF LEGAL AFFAIRS

Silent robbery alarms.
Security cameras capable of identifying robbery suspects.
Drop safe or other cash management devices.
Well lighted parking lots.
Posted signs indicating less than $50 cash on hand.
Clear and unobstructed windows.
Height markers at entrances.
No concealed access/escape.
Cash handling policies to limit available cash.
Employees trained in robbery deterrence and safety.
Two clerks during night hours.

Source: Butterworth, 1991.

In 1990, the Florida Legislature enacted Florida Statute 90-346, the Convenience Store Security Act. This legislation requires local governments in which a death, serious injury or sexual battery has occurred during a convenience store robbery to develop an ordinance mandating the recommendations listed in Table 3 (with the exception of concealed access and two clerks). At the time of this writing, 45 municipalities and 24 counties had enacted such ordinances (FDLA, 1991). Many of those passed prior to September 30, 1990, also mandate two clerks, security enclosures or closing during night hours. Based upon data provided by the Department of Legal Affairs (Butterworth, 1991), the Florida Legislature is considering supplementing Statute 90-346 by requiring one of the following between the hours of 10 p.m. to 6 a.m.: (1) close the store; (2) provide two clerks; (3) install safety enclosures; or (4) provide a security guard.

The results of Florida's robbery prevention efforts are being felt immediately. Convenience store robberies in Florida declined from 5,548 in 1989 to 4,904 in 1990 (Table 2) despite an overall increase in violent crimes (from 145,473 to 160,544) during the same period. While the rest of the nation is experiencing an increase in convenience store robberies, mandated prevention strategies are working in Florida.

Implications for the Future

It is clear from the research reviewed above and from the experience in Florida that crime prevention through environmental design deters convenience store robbery. Nevertheless, the measures developed in Florida may not be as beneficial in other parts of the nation. Indeed, it is doubtful, that many states will enact such stringent legislation. Therefore, the success of future robbery prevention efforts may well depend upon voluntary compliance by the convenience store industry.

The National Association of Convenience Stores (NACS) is now playing an important part in the development of robbery prevention strategies. In addition to the publication of the Robbery Deterrence Manual, NACS provides seminars on robbery prevention and commissions research to develop new prevention strategies. NACS has been both an advocate and an opponent of the establishment of industry-wide standards for robbery deterrence. This contradiction is a result of the industry's need to provide protection while holding operating costs to a minimum.

Current prevention strategies endorsed by NACS rely upon: signs indicating limited funds; good cash handling procedures; enhanced visibility within and without the stores; alteration of escape routes; use of security devices; encouraging activity in or near the store; employee alertness; and store cleanliness. NACS argues that if these strategies are followed, additional actions are unnecessary and that multiple staffing of stores, security enclosures, or closing at midnight are needless expenses.

As prevention research provides additional support for more stringent robbery prevention policies (including provisions specifically designed to protect clerks during the hours of darkness), it is anticipated that the National Association of Convenience Stores will begin encouraging its members to implement these policies. Such policies are "good business" in that they will protect employees and customers and improve public relations. Implementing them may also prevent mandatory legislation which might limit corporate discretion, and avoid costly lawsuits from injured parties.

15. Biting Back: Preventing Repeat Burglary and Car Crime in Huddersfield

David Anderson and Ken Pease

EDITOR'S NOTE: The title of this case study, written for this volume, makes reference to the earlier seminal paper "Once Bitten, Twice Bitten" by Graham Farrell and Ken Pease (1993) which drew attention to the generality of the phenomenon of repeat victimization and its considerable importance for crime prevention. Apart from demonstrating that police responses "graded" to increase in intensity with the number of repeats (the "Olympic" system of bronze, silver and gold responses) is an effective means for delivering crime prevention in a resource-conscious manner, the study makes some other important contributions. First, it provides evidence lacking to-date that much repeat victimization is the work of offenders returning to the same victims. Second, it suggests that these offenders are often the ones most established in criminal careers. Third, it holds out the intriguing possibility that by concentrating on repeat victims, police might detect more of these hardened offenders than they might with other methods. If so, repeat victimization has as much significance for police detection work as it has for crime prevention. This underlines the importance of using reductions in repeat victimization as a police performance measure. This has been consistently advocated by the Home Office Police Research Group which has supported the research on repeat victimization by Ken Pease and his colleagues.

Introduction

A growing body of criminological literature suggests that past victimization is a good predictor of future victimization (see Farrell and Pease, 1993; Farrell, 1995). This appears to be true of a variety of crime types. It is further clear that the extent of repeat victimization tends to be understated by official data, that when crime against the same victim recurs, it does so swiftly, and that repeat victimization is a characteristic of high crime areas. In fact, high crime areas are such in large part because of the rates of repetition in those areas (Trickett *et al.* 1992).

Recognition of the extent, and time course of repeat victimization has direct implications for criminological theory and crime measurement (Tseloni and Pease, 1997). It means that alongside the conventional measures of prevalence (proportion of those eligible to be victimized who are) and incidence (number of victimization events as a proportion of the number of those eligible to be victimized) should be added concentration (the number of victimizations per victim). Concentration is conspicuous by its absence from conventional crime counts, and frustrating in its difficulty of calculation from extant data.

Repeat victimization also has immediate implications for crime prevention practice. If recent victims are soon likely to become victims again, crime prevention resourcing is most appropriately concentrated on recent victims. Repeat victimization and crime hot spots are separable but closely linked phenomena. Research in progress by Alex Hirschfield show that hot spots are characterized by high levels of repeat victimization. Put another way, repeat victimization makes spots hot. The danger is that police will see these approaches being in competition. They are not. Repeat victims may be helped by addressing area characteristics. Attending to repeat victimization may be a good first move when a hot spot is identified but one does not know what to do next. The optimal form of analysis depends on circumstances, and both methods should be available wherever possible.

The attempt to prevent crime by preventing repeats began in earnest with the Kirkholt Project, designed to reduce levels of domestic burglary in a high crime area of Rochdale, Lancashire. Domestic burglary did fall to less than 40% of its pre-project level, the reduction being characterized by a virtual elimination of repeats (Forrester *et al.*, 1988; Pease, 1991). Replications of varying degrees of faithfulness to the Kirkholt approach yielded results which were in varying degrees successful (Tilley, 1993a). The most recent local burglary reduction initiatives featuring repeat victimization formed part of a series of projects funded by the Direct Line insurance company, and achieved high levels of success (Webb, 1997).

The logic of crime prevention by prevention of repeats seems unassailable, whatever its practical problems. Its local successes are sufficient to justify optimism. The next step concerns its translation to a wider scale, and associated questions about its most efficient implementation.

The Huddersfield Project: Biting Back

This project sought to determine whether the principles of repeat victimization could be translated from an enterprise covering a small area to become a standard approach to crime prevention across an entire police division. Because of the problems of routinization of practice and difficulties of implementation, the dramatic reductions demonstrated in smaller areas were not anticipated. The Huddersfield division of the West Yorkshire Police force covers an area of 83,000 households and a population of 205,000 people, living in settings from the very rural to the inner urban. It is served by a complement of some three hundred police officers. The target offenses were burglary (domestic and other), and theft from or of motor vehicles. Research in the pre-implementation phase of the work showed that all these offenses were characterized by repetition, and that the time course of repetition, whereby repeats happen quickly, were a feature of the Huddersfield situation as they had been elsewhere. In short, repeat victimization was worthy of prevention in Huddersfield. "Biting Back" started in October 1994, but December 1994 is when it began to be implemented in a meaningful way. The graphs below are indexed to January 1994, to give an idea of immediate pre-implementation trends.

The approach in Huddersfield comprised graded responses to victims according to the number of prior victimizations (reported and unreported) about which they told the police officer attending. These responses were termed bronze, silver and gold, which led to

TABLE 1
SUMMARY OF OUTCOMES FROM THE HUDDERSFIELD STUDY

Measure	Effect
Survey of Huddersfield Police Officers	Of responding officers: *97% understood project rationale * 82% thought project successful * 85% thought commitment to project was steady, 7% thought it increasing.
Survey of W.Yorks domestic burglary victims	Of responding victims: *Huddersfield victims advised to take a greater level and range of crime prevention than the average W.Yorks victim. *Levels of repeat victimization during Biting Back were lower in Huddersfield than remainder of force. *Levels of satisfaction among repeat victims higher in Huddersfield than in W.Yorks generally.
Count of numbers of bronze, silver and gold responses deployed	*Reduction over time in the number of silver and gold responses for burglary victims, suggesting a reduction in repeats.
Changes in recorded repeats	*Greater decrease in Huddersfield than elsewhere.
Changes in recorded crime	*Domestic burglary declined to 70% of its pre-project level. *Theft from motor vehicles declined by 20%.
Interview with repeat victims	*Suggests incomplete implementation a factor in continuing repeats.
Examination of displacement	*Evidence suggests displacement not a major factor in declines.

correspondents dubbing it the "Olympic Model of Crime Prevention." A bronze response was made after a first event, silver after a second, and gold after a third or subsequent experience. For example, a silent alarm[1] was to be installed for six weeks in homes subject to a gold response as one component of that response. A Crime Prevention Officer would visit burgled premises as part of a silver response. Bronze victims received crime prevention information. Cocoon Watch, whereby the immediately surrounding homes were alerted after a burglary, was included (see Forrester *et al.*, 1988; Pease, 1991), as was police patrolling which incorporated regular visits to places of recent victimization. The complete list of measures envisaged as part of the three responses is included in the first project report (Anderson *et al.*, 1994) and the revised list in the final project report (Sholan *et al.*, 1997). The resources and implementation which characterized the Huddersfield project are also to be found in Sholan *et al.* (1997). They changed throughout. The packages as delivered at the end of the project were better designed than those at its outset.

The outcomes of the Huddersfield project are provided in full in Sholan *et al.* (1997) and are summarized as Table 1.

Did Targeted Crime Go Down?

Figure 1 illustrates the decline of rates of domestic burglary. It contrasts the month by month change in that offence relative to an indexed rate of 100 in January 1994. The more marked divergence of Huddersfield from force trends from January 1996 onwards (month 25) is interpreted by those who administered the scheme as reflecting a devolution of

FIGURE 1
DOMESTIC BURGLARY IN HUDDERSFIELD AND REST OF FORCE

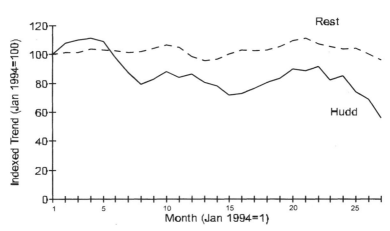

responsibility for the scheme (and equipment to support it) to officers in outlying police stations, which improved its implementation there. It must be acknowledged that disproportionate attention was given by the project team to domestic burglary. One senior officer said of the other burglary component of the scheme that it went into the 'too difficult' drawer, and indeed burglaries of schools in particular were virtually unchanged by the scheme. Thefts from motor vehicles also did not decline significantly relative to the rest of the force as shown in Figure 2 (next page).

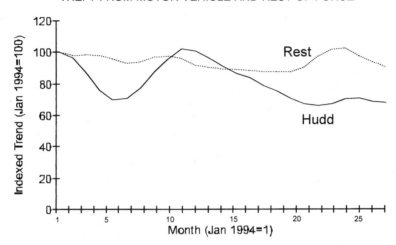

FIGURE 2
THEFT FROM MOTOR VEHICLE AND REST OF FORCE

Analysis of the number of *repeats* by a variety of means all showed a decline. The proportion of households victimized (prevalence) also showed a modest decline. Although the primary focus of the work was upon the reduction of number of victimizations per victim, a reduction in prevalence is unsurprising, since the strategy directs police resources and attention to areas of higher crime prevalence. The failure of prevalence to rise reflects the absence of very local, intra-Divisional, forms of displacement.

Crime Reduction or Displacement?

Whenever crime prevention is claimed, displacement is proposed as a post hoc explanation. Crime, the proponents of displacement claim, has merely been moved, typically to a place outside the area covered by the study. Thus, in the present context, it would be argued that domestic burglary in Huddersfield has not been prevented, merely relocated.

Displacement is a cause for frustration among those seeking to prevent crime, for four reasons:

1. In practice it is impossible to show that displacement has not taken place. A burglary moved from Huddersfield may become a similar crime in an adjacent division. If it does not take place there, it may have moved outside the force boundary or been transmuted to another crime type. If all Huddersfield burglars move out of the country, each to a different destination, modest rises in burglary in each of their destinations will not be measurable against a constantly changing background. Total displacement, however implausible, can never be shown not to have occurred.

2. All reviews of crime displacement *suggest* that crime reductions are never entirely offset by crime increases elsewhere (for example, see Hesseling 1994), and that, not infrequently, the opposite to displacement occurs, whereby a crime reduction effect spills over into adjoining areas and times following an initiative.

This is known as diffusion of benefits.

3. When displacement is claimed to have occurred, the claim is always made after the fact, i.e. when displacement is indistinguishable from crime increases caused by something else. The place to which crime will be displaced is never predicted, always inferred with hindsight.

4. The commonsense answer to the displacement claimant is "We've prevented crime on our patch. Some of it may have been displaced to yours. Now you prevent it rather than complain that the total is non-reducible." This argument makes few friends.

While acknowledging that partial displacement is often a problem, the focus of criminological work has moved to a consideration of the circumstances under which displacement may be expected, and where to (see, for example, Eck, 1993, and Bouloukos and Farrell, 1997, which deals specifically with repeat victimization and displacement). In the Huddersfield study, domestic burglary, if displaced, may be moved elsewhere within the Division or elsewhere outside it. Given what is known of the short travel-to-crime distances characteristic of most burglars in places as diverse as Rochdale and Riyadh (Forrester *et al.*, 1988; Al-Kahtani, 1996), substantial displacement outside the Division seems implausible in the extreme. It makes no sense. A burglar returns to a Huddersfield home he has burgled before. He finds things changed, and decides not to repeat his crime. Why would such a burglar travel fifteen or more miles to commit crimes outside the Divisional boundary when there remain many unprotected homes closer to hand? Eck's (1993) analysis also suggests that displacement is most likely against most similar targets, which will include geographically similar targets.

TABLE 2
1994/5 DOMESTIC BURGLARIES COMMITTED BY THOSE KNOWN TO HAVE
COMMITTED AT LEAST ONE HUDDERSFIELD DOMESTIC BURGLARY
IN JANUARY 1995.

	Huddersfield	Elsewhere
Pre-Scheme	15	0
Scheme	40	0

N.B. The numbers are of offenses, except that offenses by co-offenders both in the sample were counted as single offences. The index offense and other January 1995 offenses are excluded.

Despite these theoretical points that made cross-Divisional displacement unlikely, we have chosen to address the possibility by looking at a sample of those admitting (or found to have committed) domestic burglaries in Huddersfield just after the start of the scheme. The logic behind this is that displacement would require such burglars to locate their crimes outside Huddersfield more in the year following the start of the scheme than in the year before the scheme started. The West Yorkshire Offender Information System yielded details of twenty-four people who had committed a domestic burglary in Huddersfield in January 1995. It was then a simple matter to count the number of *other* domestic burglaries cleared to the same offenders in the West Yorkshire force area in 1994 (hereafter Pre-scheme), and in 1995 (hereafter Scheme). Displacement would suggest an increased number of burglaries outside Huddersfield in 1995 compared with 1994. Table 2 shows this not to be the case.

The way in which the data had to be accessed means that some offenses which could have been domestic burglary in 1994 were excluded. Extending the argument to all offenses cleared to those in the January 95 sample yields Table 3. Again, there is no indication that those who were active burglars around the start of the scheme offended elsewhere in West Yorkshire to a greater extent in the year following the start of the scheme than in the year preceding it.[2]

TABLE 3
1994/5 CRIMES COMMITTED BY THOSE KNOWN TO HAVE COMMITTED AT
LEAST ONE HUDDERSFIELD DOMESTIC BURGLARY IN JANUARY 1995

	Huddersfield	Elsewhere
Pre-Scheme	54	13
Scheme	96	16

N.B. The numbers are of offenses, except that offenses by co-offenders both in the sample were counted as single offenses. The index offense and other January 1995 offenses are excluded.

Since cross-Divisional displacement requires the movement of offenders across Divisional boundaries, it is felt that this analysis, modest though it is, strongly suggests that any such displacement was trivial or absent. Other analyses, contrasting Huddersfield with contiguous Divisions and with non-contiguous Divisions, shows that the trend in contiguous divisions is not in the opposite direction to that in Huddersfield. Lagging crime trends produces no evidence of spatial displacement or crime type displacement. In short, we found no evidence of displacement.

Failures, and Serendipitous Success

Towards the end of the project, when implementation was as good as it was going to get within the project period, the project team routinely interviewed those victimized who had also been victimized earlier during the project. This was important because, if repeats occurred after proper preventive measures had been put in place, the packages were deficient. If proper preventive measures had not been put in place, this was evidence of implementation failure. Overwhelmingly, it turned out that where repeats occurred, the original preventive package had not been put in place. The problem in Huddersfield seems to have been one of incomplete implementation, rather than failure in principle.

One feature of the progression from bronze to gold response was that it represented an increasing emphasis on detection. The temporary installation of silent alarms was one element in the gold response to burglary which reflects this. Such alarms are often installed temporarily on the basis of police "intelligence" activities. Data on the outcome of the installation of temporary alarms provides an interesting serendipitous result. The value of emphasis on repeat victimization is held to be that it focuses attention on places at highest risk within areas of high risk. Insofar as prior victimization is a better predictor of future offenses than "intelligence," the number of arrests and genuine misses from alarms installed as part of a gold response should be higher than those installed for more conventional reasons. Table 4 below makes the crucial comparison between Huddersfield's experience and that of the remainder of the force. The rows refer to the number of installations of temporary alarms, the number of arrests which resulted, and the number of genuine misses, i.e. occasions when an offense occurred but the offenders were not found.

The Huddersfield figures do include some temporary alarms installed other than through the repeat victimization initiative. The bulk of project installations (119/171) formed part of the gold response, however, and arrests and genuine misses from the non-gold installations in Huddersfield occurred at a much lower rate than from gold installations, so the effect of including non-gold installations is to make Table 4 less dramatic than it otherwise would be. In the pre-project period in Huddersfield, outcomes (arrests plus genuine misses) ran at 6% of installations, compared with 12% in the rest of the force. In the project period, outcomes were 21% of installations in Huddersfield, and 7% in the remainder of the force. This analysis provides a neat illustration of the predictive power of prior victimization. The allocation of temporary alarms in the remainder of the force is itself intelligence-driven, so what is demonstrated is performance superior to an allocation system which is already intelligent.

TABLE 4
RESULT OF TEMPORARY ALARM INSTALLATION, BEFORE AND DURING PROJECT

| | Pre-Scheme (Oct.93-Jun.94) | | Scheme (Oct.94-Jun.95) | |
	Huddersfield	Rest of Force	Huddersfield	Rest of Force
Installations	104	616	171	713
Arrests	4 (3.8%)	50 (8.1%)	24 (14%)	31 (4.3%)
True Misses	2 (1.9%)	21 (3.4%)	12 (7%)	19 (2.7%)

Conclusions

The possibility of preventing burglary by the prevention of repeats had already been demonstrated before the Biting Back project in Huddersfield. The results of that project encourage the belief that the prevention of repeats can be routinely incorporated into the strategy of a large police division. That it was not fully implemented is unsurprising. The package of measure improved over time, as did the organizational arrangements to put it in place. The degree of reduction observed is, frankly, gratifying given the scale and difficulty of the operation.

As noted earlier, the emphasis as one moves from bronze to gold response also moves from prevention by deflection to prevention by detection. This was based on what was at the time an unsubstantiated view that the same offenders returned to commit crime against the same victims. As yet unpublished research by the author in collaboration with Steve Everson of West Yorkshire Police using criminal records, and with Julie Ashton and Barbara Senior of West Yorkshire Probation Service using interviews with offenders, show not only that repeats are the work of the same perpetrators, but also that those offenders who repeatedly offend against the same victim are those most established in criminal careers. This not only retrospectively justifies the emphasis on detection in the gold response, but also raises the intriguing possibility that offender targeting may be achieved simply by detecting repeated offenses against the same household or person, since those offenses are committed by the offenders whom one would in any case wish to target. This kind of offender targeting would avoid all the aspects of such an approach deriving from the harassment of known offenders, since it would focus, not on people, but on the subset of acts which prolific offenders habitually commit.

The interviews with offenders also revealed the degree to which burglary and theft repetition is rational, indeed market-driven. This is because repeats:

1. Involve less risk, since the place is known, including escape routes;

2. Will capture new, insurance-replaced goods, which will attract a better price;

3. The value of goods known to remain available can be established during the period between offenses.

Finally, the interviews vindicated another aspect of the theory on which repeat prevention is based, namely that substantial change (or suspected substantial change) in somewhere previously targeted will mean it will not be targeted again by the same offenders.

The imperfections of "Biting Back" should be addressed in implementation of similar schemes. The next phase for advance is the elaboration of the intersection between repeat prevention and offender targeting. In the next demonstration project, we should assess the proportion of an effect attributable to the incapacitation or deterrence of offenders detected in repeat crime against the same people or place.

ACKNOWLEDGMENT. Thanks are due to Sylvia Chenery and Graham Farrell for their help and advice during the preparation of this paper. Those who made the Huddersfield experience into an exciting and successful time are too numerous to mention, but are acknowledged in Sholan *et al.* (1997) and remembered with affection and admiration by the writers.

Notes

1. These alarms give no indication at the offense location that they have been activated, but do so at the police station, thus increasing the chances that perpetrators will still be on site when the police arrive.
2. Tables 2 and 3 give the impression that these offenders were more active in 1995 than in 1994. This is an artefact. Most of the events are linked to the offenders as a result of their admission during official processing in 1995 and later. Thus memory and other factors will reduce the number of offenses more distant in time which are captured. This means that 1994-1995 absolute differences are not interpretable. The point relevant to the displacement issue concerns whether the proportion of events outside Huddersfield changes.

16. The Crime Reducing Effect of Improved Street Lighting: The Dudley Project

Kate Painter and David P. Farrington

EDITOR'S NOTE: Until recently, the received wisdom on improved street lighting was that it might reduce fear, but it has little effect on crime (Tien et al., 1979). This view is now changing, largely due to the work of Kate Painter in Britain. In the face of much skepticism (cf. Atkins et al., 1991; Ramsay and Newton, 1991), she has produced a series of studies suggesting that the crime prevention benefits of street lighting have been underestimated. Each of her studies has sought to improve on the methodology of earlier ones. In this latest study, written for this volume with David Farrington, she avoids the pitfalls of using official crime data by conducting victimization surveys in carefully matched experimental and control areas — two adjacent public housing estates in the town of Dudley. The study produces clear evidence that crime of all kinds decreased significantly in the re-lit estate compared with the control. Moreover, there was little sign of displacement of crime to the control estate. Young people who might have been responsible for much crime on the estates were not displaced to the control estate by the re-lighting. Rather, the improved lighting attracted more young people at night to the experimental area. This might have been expected to produce more crime except that the improved lighting probably increased the fear of apprehension. It is common to criticize situational measures for their harmful social effects, but this study shows, once again, how situational measures can reduce crime and improve the quality of life — in this case by facilitating the congregation of young people.

Previous Research on Street Lighting and Crime

The main aim of this project is to investigate the effects of improved street lighting as a crime prevention technique. Modern interest in the relationship between street lighting and crime began in North America amidst the dramatic rise in crime which took place in the 1960s. Many towns and cities embarked upon major street lighting programs as a means of reducing crime and initial results were encouraging (Wright *et al.*, 1974). A review by Berla (1965) claimed that street lighting improvements caused a substantial reduction in crime in six cities, and other research in New York (Wheeler, 1967) and Newark (Tyrpak, 1975) found that improvements were particularly effective when introduced alongside an increase in police patrols. Following a major relighting program in Kansas City, night-time robbery and assaults decreased by half and property offenses also decreased, but non-significantly (Wright *et al.* 1974). Also, a study of four high crime areas in the District of Columbia reported that night-time crime reduced between 30% to 54% following street lighting improvements (Hartley, 1974).

The proliferation of positive results across North America led to a detailed review of the effect of street lighting on crime by Tien *et al.* (1979) funded by the Law Enforcement Assistance Agency (LEAA). The final report describes how the 103 street lighting projects originally identified were eventually reduced to a final sample of only 15 that were considered by the review team to contain sufficiently rigorous evaluative information. With regard to the impact of street lighting on crime, the authors found that as many projects reported an increase or no change as a reduction in crime. However, each project was considered to be seriously flawed because of such problems as: weak project designs; misuse or complete absence of sound analytic techniques; inadequate measures of street lighting; poor measures of crime (all were based on police records); insufficient appreciation of the impact of lighting on different types of crime; and inadequate measures of public attitudes and behavior.

The Tien *et al.* (1979) review was undeniably painstaking but it may have been too negative and dismissive of the available evidence. Among the 15 projects studied in detail, it did not distinguish between those that were more rigorous methodologically and the remainder. The report concluded (Tien *et al.*, 1979:93) that "... the paucity of reliable and uniform data and the inadequacy of available evaluation studies preclude a definitive statement regarding the relationship between street lighting and crime." However, it is interesting that the most rigorous project, the only one with before and after measures of crime in experimental and control areas (Wright *et al.*, 1974, in Kansas City), found a significant reduction in violent crime. Perhaps the most important point made by Tien *et al.* (1979) was that improved street lighting could lead to increased reporting of crime to the police, and hence that the effects of improved street lighting should *not* be measured using police-recorded crime.

Logically, the Tien *et al.* (1979) review should have led to attempts to measure the effects of improved street lighting using alternative measures of crime, such as victim surveys, self-reports or systematic observation. Unfortunately, it was interpreted as showing that street lighting had no effect on crime, and it basically consigned the issue to the wilderness in North America.

In the United Kingdom, very little research was carried out on street lighting and crime until the late 1980s, and two brief literature reviews bemoaned the "scant and elusive" nature of street lighting research (Mayhew *et al.*, 1976; Fleming and Burrows 1986). There was a resurgence of interest in the issue between 1988 and 1990, when three small scale street lighting projects were implemented and evaluated in different areas of London (in Edmonton, Tower Hamlets and Hammersmith/Fulham). Each project was focused on a poorly lit, essential street or walkway leading from residential accommodation to transport, leisure and shopping facilities. Pedestrians were interviewed about their experiences of crime and disorder six weeks before and six weeks after street lighting improvements were made and pedestrian street use was also monitored. In each location crime, disorder and fear of crime declined and pedestrian street use increased dramatically after the improvements (Painter, 1994). The third project (in Hammersmith and Fulham) also included a follow-up survey twelve months later with elderly people which found that the reduction in crime and disorder had been sustained (Painter, 1991a).

Similar results were obtained in a project using surveys twelve months before and twelve months after street lighting improvements on a local authority estate in the North West of England. Both survey-reported crime and police-recorded night-time crime reduced (Painter, 1991b). More mixed results were obtained when street lighting was upgraded across an inner city area of Birmingham. Survey-reported crime against households reduced but there was no discernible change in crime against pedestrians or commercial premises. Night-time pedestrian street use increased substantially (Bainbridge and Painter, 1993).

In contrast to these generally positive results, a major Home Office-funded evaluation in Wandsworth (Atkins *et al.*, 1991) concluded that improved street lighting had no effect on crime, and a Home Office review, published simultaneously, also asserted that "better lighting by itself has very little effect on crime" (Ramsay and Newton, 1991). The Atkins *et al.* (1991) evaluation appeared to be well designed, since it was based on before and after measures of police statistics and victimization reports in relit (experimental) and control areas. However, in analyzing police statistics, crimes were dubiously classified into those likely or unlikely to be affected by street lighting. Robbery and violence, which decreased significantly in the Wright *et al.* (1974) project, were thought *unlikely* to be affected by street lighting (Atkins *et al.*, 1991: 7). Interestingly, while the "likely" crimes decreased by only 3% after the improved lighting, the "unlikely" crimes decreased by 24% (Atkins *et al.*1991:10). Unfortunately, the response rates in the victimization surveys were very low (37% before and 29% after). Only 39 crimes were reported in the before survey in the experimental area and only 13 in the control area, suggesting that the research had insufficient power to detect changes.

Other British evaluations of the effect of improved street lighting on crime have been carried out in Cardiff (Herbert and Moore, 1991), Hull (Davidson and Goodey, 1991), Leeds (Burden and Murphy, 1991) and Strathclyde (Ditton *et al.* 1993). These evaluations produced mixed results; for example, the number of crimes increased after relighting in the Cardiff study but decreased in the Strathclyde study. Unfortunately, these projects, along with all other published British street lighting evaluations except Atkins *et al.* (1991), involved simple before-after comparisons in a relit area, and lacked a control area. This simple one-group pre-test/post-test design has been described as "the least sophisticated approach to evaluation" (Lurigio and Rosenbaum 1986:34) because of the numerous threats to internal validity which make it impossible unambiguously to attribute changes in an outcome measure (e.g. crime) to the effects of an intervention program (e.g. improved street lighting).

A control area is required to rule out the following major threats to internal validity (Cook and Campbell, 1979):

   a. *History*: changes in crime after lighting improvements might be attributable to events other than the improvements;

   b. *Maturation*: changes in crime after lighting improvements might be attributable to a continuation of pre-existing trends;

   c. *Testing*: changes in measured crime after lighting improvements may be attributable to the effects of the "before" measurement;

   d. *Instrumentation*: changes in crime after lighting improvements may be attributable to changes in methods of measurement;

   e. *Regression*: especially if lighting improvements are implemented in a high-crime area, decreases in crime after the improvements may reflect regression to the mean as a result of natural fluctuations over time; and

   f. *Mortality*: changes in reported crime after lighting improvements may be attributable to non-comparable samples caused by dropping out of respondents.

The main aim of the present research is to assess the effect of improved street lighting on crime, using before and after victimization surveys in experimental and control areas, with samples that are sufficiently large to detect likely effects of the intervention. To the extent that the areas are comparable, selection effects (changes in crime attributable to pre-existing differences between the samples) are controlled. Also, the study resembles a "double-blind" clinical trial, since neither respondents nor interviewers knew about its purpose. Also, it permits the investigation of displacement of crime from the experimental to the control area.

Theoretical Relationships between Street Lighting and Crime

There is no specific body of theory that relates street lighting to crime. Nonetheless, explanations of the way street lighting improvements could prevent crime can be found in "situational" approaches which focus on reducing opportunity and increasing perceived risk through modification of the physical environment (Clarke, 1992); and in perspectives which have stressed the importance of strengthening informal social control and community cohesion through more effective street use (Jacobs, 1961; Angel, 1968) and investment in neighborhood conditions (Taub *et al.*, 1984; Fowler and Mangione, 1986; Lavrakas and Kushmuk, 1986; Taylor and Gottfredson, 1986).

Situational crime prevention suggests that crime can be prevented by environmental measures which directly affect offenders' perceptions of increased risks and decreased opportunities. Street lighting is likely to increase the visibility of offenders at night and hence to increase their perceived risks of being seen, recognized, reported, interrupted or caught. Certainly, the deterrent effect of visibility and potential surveillance has been a consistent theme to emerge when offenders have been interviewed about their motives, methods and target selection (Bennett and Wright, 1984; Feeney, 1986; Nee and Taylor, 1988; Nugent *et al.*, 1989; Cromwell *et al.*, 1991; Light *et al.*, 1993), although there is no direct evidence that offenders are less willing to define a well-lit street as a criminal opportunity than a dark street. It might be thought that improved lighting might possibly increase criminal opportunities if it encourages more potential victims to go out at night. Against this, however, is the deterrent effect of having more people on the street.

Jane Jacobs drew attention to the role of good visibility combined with natural surveillance as a deterrent to crime. In particular, she emphasized the association between levels of crime and public street use and suggested that less crime would be committed in areas with an abundance of potential witnesses (Jacobs, 1961). Similarly, Angel (1968) observed that opportunities for street robbery were high on streets used by few people: a sufficient number to provide targets without too much waiting around, but not enough to operate as a deterrent. As pedestrian street use increased, streets became safer because of the proximity of potential guardians, an effect also stressed by routine activity theorists (Cohen and Felson, 1979). In a British context, Hillier (1987) found that areas with the highest public use experienced low burglary rates in comparison to areas with low pedestrian use. Hence, if good street lighting encourages more effective use of neighborhood streets at night, opportunities for natural surveillance and informal social control will be enhanced.

Street lighting improvements may also reduce crime and fear by eliminating areas where offenders can hide prior to committing an offense. Areas of concealment have been identified as a design characteristic affecting public surveillance and defensibility of space (Newman, 1972; Merry, 1981) and they have been shown to influence an offender's choice of crime locations (Phelan, 1977; Bennett and Wright, 1984). In addition, increased illumination and visibility could reduce crime if an increased range of vision alerts pedestrians to potential offenders sufficiently in advance to allow them to take evasive action. Feeney (1986) noted that a substantial number of robbery victims were aware that they were about to be robbed when they saw the aggressor approach, wait or pass them on the street. In turn, fears for personal safety, which dramatically undermine the quality of life in a neighborhood (Skogan, 1990), might reduce if the perceived risk of a surprise attack diminishes.

Other theoretical perspectives have emphasized the importance of investment to improve neighborhood conditions as a means of strengthening resident confidence, cohesion and social control (Wilson and Kelling, 1982; Taub *et al.*, 1984; Taylor and Gottfredson, 1986; Skogan, 1990; Foster and Hope, 1993). As a highly visible sign of positive investment, improved street lighting might reduce crime if it physically improves the environment and signals to residents that efforts are being made to invest in and restore their neighborhood. In turn, this may lead them to have a more positive image of their area and increased community pride, optimism and cohesion. It should be noted that this theoretical perspective predicts a reduction in both day-time and night-time crime. Consequently, attempts to measure the effects of improved lighting should not concentrate purely on night-time crime.

In addition to leading to a positive change in resident opinions and physically creating a brighter and safer environment, street lighting might also send a non-verbal message to offenders that the reputation of the area is improving, that there is more social control, order and surveillance and hence that crime at that location is riskier than elsewhere. Crime could further reduce because offenders living in the area will be deterred from committing offenses there and potential offenders from outside the area will be dissuaded from entering it. Crime and fear in the area should diminish as perceived risks and personal knowledge of crime reduce. Furthermore, street lighting may also prevent crime by discouraging disorderly behavior, thereby preventing trivial offences from escalating into more serious crime (Wilson and Kelling, 1982).

In summary, the relationship between visibility, social surveillance and criminal opportunities is a consistently strong theme to emerge from the literature. A core assumption of both opportunity and informal social control models of prevention is that criminal opportunities and risks are influenced by environmental conditions in interaction with resident and offender characteristics. While street lighting is not a direct solution to crime, it can act as a catalyst to stimulate crime reduction through a change in the perceptions, attitudes and behavior of residents and offenders.

The Present Research

RESEARCH DESIGN

This evaluation employed a non-equivalent control group design with before and after measures of crime in experimental (relit) and control areas. Using a victim survey, the prevalence and incidence of crime were measured twelve months before and twelve months after the installation of improved street lighting in the experimental area and at the same times in a control area where the street lighting remained unchanged. The questions on crime were identical in all surveys. An adjacent area was selected as the control area because it was envisaged that the people living there would be similar in many respects to those in the experimental area, and also to facilitate the investigation of spatial and temporal displacement. Hence, demographic factors which might influence crime rates should be equivalent at the outset. It becomes more plausible, therefore, that any change in crime between the relit and non-relit areas can be attributed to the street lighting program rather than to pre-existing differences between the samples. This design controls for the major threats to internal validity outlined above.

RESEARCH HYPOTHESES

The primary hypothesis guiding the evaluation was that street lighting improvements would reduce crime in the relit area. A subsidiary hypothesis was that, if effective, street lighting might displace crime to the adjacent non-relit area. In order to investigate theoretical links between street lighting and crime prevention, other predictions concerning intervening causal mechanisms were tested. It was hypothesized that any decrease in crime would be mediated by measurable changes in attitudes, perceptions and behavior. Additional subsidiary hypotheses were that street lighting improvements might:

    a. reduce fear for personal safety after dark;

    b. reduce vicarious victimization (knowing someone who has been victimized);

    c. alleviate perceptions of neighborhood problems;

    d. enhance the perceived quality of neighborhood life;

    e. increase night-time pedestrian street use.

SELECTION AND DESCRIPTION OF THE PROJECT AREAS

The research was carried out in Dudley, West Midlands. The experimental area was selected for re-lighting by local authority engineers on the basis of need. The street lighting was in a bad state of repair and had been the subject of complaints from tenants. The adjacent control area was similar to the experimental area on basic demographic and design characteristics. Both areas were local authority housing estates which had been built at approximately the same time (mid-1930s) and had similar architectural design (semi-detached and terraced rows of four, low-rise dwellings with gardens front and back); a similar number of dwellings (approximately 1,200-1,300 on each estate); the same housing authority and similar housing allocation policies; and clear geographic boundaries (both backed on to a nature reserve and were separated and bounded by main arterial roads). The design and layout of the estates, and the type of dwellings, facilitated natural surveillance, which was potentially important for street lighting to be effective as a crime prevention strategy.

DESCRIPTION OF THE STREET LIGHTING PROGRAM

In a four-week period during February-March 1992, 129 high-pressure sodium (white) street lights were installed over 1,500 meters of roadway in the experimental area. The new lighting replaced the older type mercury lamps. The improvements were made only to residential roads; footpaths between the houses were not relit. The area was illuminated in accordance with category 3/2 of BS 5489, which gives an average illuminance of 6 lux and a minimum of 2.5 lux. The British Standard (BS 5489, Part 3) lists three categories of lighting levels corresponding to low, medium and high crime risk areas and levels of traffic and pedestrian usage. Given the improved technology and required lighting level, column spacing decreased from 40 meters before to 33 meters after. The new lighting scheme resulted in savings in energy and maintenance costs and the amount of useful light more than doubled. The pre-existing street lighting in the experimental area did not achieve the minimum standard of 3/3 laid down in British Standards. Consequently, the lighting upgrade constituted a noticeable alteration of the night-time environment.

THE BEFORE AND AFTER VICTIMIZATION SURVEYS

The timing of data collection was the same in both survey areas. The before survey was completed between February and the end of the first week in March 1992. The after survey was completed during the four week period mid-February to mid-March 1993. Both surveys enquired about events in the previous twelve months. Thus, the before survey period covered January 1991-January 1992 and the after survey period covered February 1992-February 1993, including the street lighting installation period which began in the third week of February 1992. Care was taken to ensure that nobody in the before survey was interviewed after the lights were improved.

The before and after surveys measured household victimization and respondents' perceptions, attitudes and behavior. The majority of questions on victimization, fear of crime and quality of life were similar to those used in successive British Crime Surveys (e.g. Mayhew *et al.*, 1993). Respondents were only asked about crimes which had occurred *on their estate* during the previous twelve months, and supplementary questions ensured that the same criminal event did not generate reports of two categories of crime. Additional questions on public reactions to the new lighting and travel behavior after dark were included at the end of the after survey as part of a process evaluation of program implementation. Other crime prevention, strategies, such as Neighborhood Watch and policing strategies, were monitored through closed and open-ended questions and interviewer fieldwork sheets, as were other possible extraneous historical influences which might have caused a change in outcomes within and between the survey areas.

SAMPLING PROCEDURES

The sampling frame was the electoral register which contained 2,560 addresses in the two areas. This was supplemented by field enumeration to identify missing properties. Statistical power analysis (Cohen, 1988) was carried out to estimate the minimum sample sizes needed to detect an effect of the intervention on crime in the experimental area. The analysis was based on the likely prevalence of victimization, which was assumed to be about 50%; any sample sizes that were sufficient to detect differences in prevalence would be likely also to detect differences in incidence (the number of crimes), since incidence is the more sensitive measure.

It was assumed that the sample sizes should be sufficient to detect a 10% decrease in the prevalence of victimization, from 50% to 40%. Setting the probability of a Type I error or alpha (the probability of falsely rejecting the null hypothesis) to the conventional level of .05, two-tailed, and the statistical power, or 1 minus beta (where beta is the probability of falsely accepting the null hypothesis) to the conventional level of .80 (Cohen, 1988:56), yielded a required sample size of 407 per group (Fleiss, 1981:273). Relaxing alpha to .05, one-tailed, reduced the required sample size to 325 per group; relaxing power to .75 reduced it to 362; and assuming a decrease in prevalence from 40% to 30% reduced it to 376. These sensitivity analyses suggested that samples of about 325-400 people before and after in both areas were required.

In the 1992 British Crime Survey, 10,059 interviews were achieved from 14,890 issued addresses (Mayhew *et al.*, 1993:154). Assuming the same success rate in the present survey suggested that about 600 addresses should be issued in each area in order to achieve about 400 interviews. Exactly 600 addresses were issued to interviewers in each area (essentially a 50% random sample drawn from the electoral register); 431 interviews were achieved in the experimental area and 448 in the control area. Excluding void properties (6% experimental, 3% control), the before response rate was 77% in each area, exactly the same as in the 1992 British Crime Survey. This response rate is likely to be an underestimate, because there was a high rate of non-contact (14% experimental, 16% control) and some of these properties should probably have been classified as void (empty or ineligible); 12% of issued addresses were classified as void in the 1992 British Crime Survey.

Only the addresses interviewed in the before survey were issued to interviewers for the after survey. The number of households re-interviewed was 372 (86% of the before sample) in the experimental area and 371 (83%) in the control area. Of those re-interviewed, 90% were the same respondent as in the before survey, 7% were the same household but a different respondent, and 3% were a different household at the same address. Unfortunately, it was not possible to link up before addresses with after addresses in order to carry out longitudinal analyses with each address acting as its own control. Hence, the before and after surveys had to be treated as repeated cross-sectional surveys.

The household face-to-face interviews took between 45 and 90 minutes depending on the extent of victimization. Prior to an interviewer calling, households were sent a leaflet which explained that a crime survey was taking place, but no mention was made of the proposed street lighting initiative. To minimize any unwitting interviewer bias, interviewers were *not* told about the true purpose of the survey and were, therefore, unaware of the lighting improvements that were to take place. They were also unaware that there were experimental and control areas. The same interviewing team, consisting of 17 interviewers, were employed in each of the study areas, before and after. For the after survey, every effort was made to match interviewers to their before respondents. The research was carried out by a company which had previous experience of undertaking community surveys. A 20% quality control check was undertaken. Each week the fieldwork supervisor visited 10% of respondents, and a further 10% were mailed a self-completion questionnaire which asked whether the interview had been conducted in a satisfactory manner.

The type of local authority dwelling ensured that only one household lived at each address. A "household" was defined as "people who are catered for by the same adult(s) and share the same meals." An individual over the age of 18 years was selected for interview by a random procedure, which involved the interviewer listing, in alphabetical order, the first names of household members. The individual for interview was selected on the basis of a pre-assigned random number between one and nine, depending on the number of persons living in the household. The initial cross-sectional target samples can therefore be considered as representative of people living in the areas.

In the before survey, interviewers were instructed to make unlimited call-backs to contact the selected individual and no substitution was allowed. In the after survey, interviewers were instructed to contact the same individual from the same household. After six call-backs, another member of the household could be selected for interview, using the same randomized procedures described above. New tenants who had moved in were interviewed in the after survey, but no attempt was made to trace individuals who had moved from one address on the estate to another.

Victimization surveys have many limitations. Respondents may experience memory decay, especially in relation to less important events which have occurred within the previous twelve months. "Telescoping" is also a possible distorting factor, in that respondents may recall events from outside the twelve-month period as occurring within it. However, the comparison of experimental and control areas, and before and after surveys, largely controls for these kinds of measurement limitations, which should be similar in all surveys.

Results

COMPARABILITY OF EXPERIMENTAL AND CONTROL AREAS IN THE BEFORE SURVEYS

Table 1 shows the extent to which the experimental and control areas were comparable in the before surveys. For example, 64.0% of experimental respondents were female, compared with 65.6% of control respondents, a non-significant difference on the 2x2 chi-squared test. Experimental and control respondents were overwhelmingly white, and most had lived on their estate for 20 or more years. However, more of the control respondents were aged 60 or over.

TABLE 1
COMPARABILITY OF EXPERIMENTAL AND CONTROL AREAS BEFORE

Variable	Experimental %(N=431)	Control %(N=448)	Chi-Squared
Demographics			
Female respondent	64.0	65.6	ns
White respondent	97.4	97.8	ns
Age 18-44 respondent	47.8	45.3	ns
Age 60+ respondent	25.3	35.0	**9.45
Age 13-17 in house	18.1	15.4	ns
Age over 60 in house	31.1	39.5	*6.45
On estate 20+ years	55.2	56.0	ns
Not employed	70.7	67.2	ns
Vehicle owner	43.2	46.6	ns
Area Cohesion			
Satisfied with estate	63.3	68.5	ns
Estate is friendly	88.7	90.9	ns
Know most neighbours	76.5	80.3	ns
Neighbours keep watch	60.7	65.2	ns
Area Lighting			
Estate well lit	51.4	55.0	ns
Lighting adequate	49.9	50.6	ns
Lighting bright	46.9	43.8	ns
Fear of Crime			
Crime is a problem	78.4	75.8	ns
Lot of crime on estate	70.5	63.8	*4.16
Estate safe after dark	45.2	45.2	ns
Won't go out alone if dark	43.2	46.6	ns
Risks for women after dark	69.6	68.3	ns
Risks for men after dark	29.7	36.8	*4.64
Feel unsafe in own home	28.6	34.8	ns
Experimental estate crime worse	17.9	48.4	**90.87
Control estate crime worse	9.7	2.7	**17.82
Crime Prevalence			
Burglary	11.6	8.3	ns
Outside theft/vandalism	20.9	19.4	ns
Vehicle crime	15.1	13.6	ns
Property crime	37.8	34.6	ns
Personal crime	13.5	8.9	*4.10
All crime	42.0	39.1	ns
% Committed in dark	69.2	73.1	ns
% Reported to police	49.7	51.6	ns
Saw police on estate last month	17.4	27.5	*12.04

Notes: * $p<.05$, ** $p<.01$ (two-tailed). ns = not significant.
For committed in dark, N=250 crimes (experimental), 193 crimes (control).
For reported to police, N=300 crimes (experimental), 246 crimes (control).

Experimental and control respondents were equally likely to say that they were satisfied with their estate, and about 90% thought that their estate was friendly. They did not differ in their opinion of the street lighting on their estate. More experimental respondents thought that there was a lot or a fair amount of crime on their estate, but more control respondents thought that there were risks for men after dark on their estate. However, experimental and control respondents were equally likely to say that crime was a problem on their estate, that their estate was safe after dark, or that they would not go out alone after dark. Control respondents thought that crime was worse on the experimental estate, while experimental respondents were significantly more likely to say that crime was worse on the control estate.

Crimes were divided into four types:

a. burglary (including attempts);

b. theft outside the home, vandalism of the home or bicycle theft;

c. theft of or from vehicles or damage to vehicles; and

d. personal crime: robbery, snatch theft, assault, threatening behavior, sexual assault or sexual pestering.

Categories (a), (b) and (c) together constitute property crime. Table 1 shows that the experimental and control estates were comparable on the prevalence of property crime, but there was a marginally significant (p=.043) tendency for the prevalence of personal crime to be higher on the experimental estate. About 70% of crimes on both estates were committed in the dark, and about half were reported to the police according to victims. One significant difference between the estates was that the control respondents were more likely to say that they had seen a police officer on the estate in the previous month.

On most variables, the experimental and control areas seemed closely comparable. If anything, however, the experimental area seemed slightly worse on crime.

FIGURE 1
PREVALENCE OF ALL CRIME

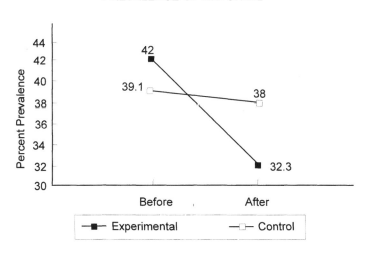

CHANGES IN THE PREVALENCE OF CRIME

Figure 1 shows that for all crime in the experimental area, prevalence decreased by 23% after the improved street lighting compared with before (from 42.0% victimized to 32.3%). In the control area, prevalence decreased by only 3% (39.1% victimized to 38.0%).[1] The changes in the experimental area were significantly greater than the changes in the control area for burglary, personal crime and all crime.

One problem of interpretation centers on the non-equivalence of the experimental and control areas before the intervention. The most important differences were that more of the control sample were aged 60 or over and more of the control sample said that they had seen a police officer on their estate in the previous month. Combining experimental and control samples before and after, persons aged 60 or over were significantly less likely than others to be victimized (for all crime, the prevalence was 23.5% of those aged 60 or over and 44.4% of the remainder: chi-squared = 63.02, p<.0001). However, seeing a police officer on the estate in the previous month was not significantly related to the prevalence of victimization (39.6% as opposed to 37.3%: chi-squared = 0.64, not significant).

To investigate whether these differences between experimental and control samples before the intervention might have influenced the results, the logistic regression for all crimes was repeated, entering age and seeing a police officer in the equation first and the interaction term last. However, the interaction term was unchanged (likelihood ratio chi-squared = 3.29, p=.035). Hence, the greater decrease in prevalence in the experimental area held independently of the prior non-equivalence of the experimental and control samples.

CHANGES IN THE INCIDENCE OF CRIME

Figure 2 shows changes in the incidence of crime (the average number of victimizations per 100 households, allowing a maximum of 10 per household) in the experimental and control areas. For all crime in the experimental area, incidence decreased by 41% after

FIGURE 2
INCIDENCE OF ALL CRIME

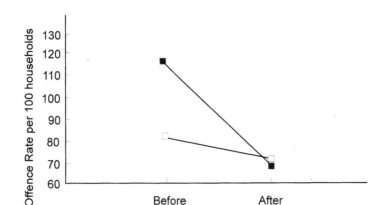

the improved street lighting compared with before (from 114.8 crimes per 100 households to 68.0). In the control area, incidence decreased by 15% (from 82.1 crimes per 100 households to 69.8). There was a highly significant decrease in the incidence of all crime in the experimental area after the improved lighting compared with before (t=3.73, p=.0001). The decrease in the experimental area was significantly greater than in the control area, both according to an Ordinary Least Squares (OLS) multiple regression analysis (F change = 4.69, p=.015) and according to a Poisson regression (likelihood ratio chi-squared = 10.42, p=.001).

In the experimental area, there was a substantial and significant decrease in the incidence of all categories of crime after the improved street lighting. There were no significant changes in the control area. The changes in the experimental area were significantly greater than the changes in the control area for vehicle crime, property crime, personal crime and all crime.

In order to investigate the effect of prior non-equivalence of the experimental and control samples on the results, the OLS multiple regression equation for all crime was repeated, entering age and seeing a police officer first and the interaction term last. The interaction term was still significant (F change = 4.28, p=.019), showing that the greater decrease in incidence in the experimental area held independently of this prior non-equivalence.

CHANGES IN THE PREVALENCE OF KNOWN VICTIMS

An additional, indirect measure of crime is a resident's personal knowledge of the victimization of other residents living on the estate (Foster and Hope, 1993). Hence, respondents were asked whether they, personally, knew anyone else from their estate who had experienced a number of specified crimes in the previous twelve months. Figure 3 shows changes in the prevalence of known victimization in the experimental and control

FIGURE 3
PREVALENCE OF KNOWN VICTIMS

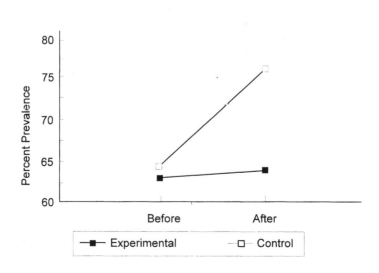

areas. For all crime in the experimental area, there was no change in the percentage of respondents who said that they personally knew a victim (62.9% before, 63.7% after). However, in the control area, significantly more respondents said that they knew a victim after compared with before (76.0% compared with 64.3%; Z=3.70, p=.0001). The change in the control area was significantly different from the change in the experimental area (Z=2.34, p=.010).

With only one exception (personal crime), the prevalence of respondents who personally knew a victim significantly increased for all types of crimes in the control area. Similarly, with only one exception (vandalism of the home, which decreased), the prevalence of respondents did not change significantly for all types of crimes in the experimental area. With the exception of all crime, prevalence decreased in the experimental area and increased in the control area. As before, the changes in the experimental area were in a significantly more desirable direction than in the control area, even though changes in the prevalence of known victims were somewhat different from changes in the prevalence and incidence of crime.

OTHER CHANGES ON THE ESTATES

Table 2, modeled on Table 1, shows differences between the estates after the improved street lighting in the experimental estate. The experimental sample were somewhat more satisfied with their estate after the intervention (65.6% versus 59.6%), but not significantly so. However, they had been somewhat less satisfied with their estate before the intervention (63.3% versus 68.5%; see Table 1). On the difference of difference of proportions test, the change in the experimental sample was significantly more favorable than the change in the control sample (Z=2.35, p=.009). Therefore, it can be concluded that, compared with the control sample, the experimental sample became significantly more happy with their estate after the improved street lighting. The vast majority of the experimental sample clearly noticed the improved street lighting. For example, just over 80% said that their estate was well lit.

On some measures, fear of crime was less in the experimental area than in the control area. The experimental sample were significantly less likely to say that crime was a problem or that there were risks for women going out after dark, and significantly more likely to say that their estate was safe after dark and that the quality of life had improved.

The crimes that were committed were just as likely to be committed after dark in the experimental area as in the control area, both before and after the improved street lighting. There was some tendency for the probability of reporting crimes to the police to be higher in the experimental area after the improved street lighting than in the control area, but none of the statistical tests were significant. Respondents on the experimental estate were significantly more likely to say that they had seen a police officer on the estate in the previous four weeks after the improved street lighting than those on the control estate, reversing the result shown in Table 1. However, as already explained, this difference did not affect the major results. Finally, control respondents were significantly more likely to say that burglary, vandalism and vehicle crime had got worse on their estate during the previous twelve months.

Statements from respondents in the experimental area suggested that they thought that the improved street lighting had decreased crime rates and improved their quality of life, especially because the improved illumination led to increased surveillance:

TABLE 2
DIFFERENCES BETWEEN EXPERIMENTAL AND CONTROL AREAS AFTER

Variable	Experimental %(N=372)	Control %(N=371)	Chi-squared
Area Cohesion			
Satisfied with estate	65.6	59.6	ns
Estate is friendly	88.5	87.6	ns
Area Lighting			
Estate well lit	83.2	44.7	**117.18
Lighting worse	9.9	48.8	**133.30
Lighting better	65.1	2.4	**322.89
Fear of Crime			
Crime is a problem	73.7	85.2	**14.38
Lot of crime on estate	62.1	66.0	ns
Estate safe after dark	45.9	35.1	**8.40
Won't go out alone if dark	54.3	60.4	ns
Risks for women after dark	66.9	76.0	**7.06
Risks for men after dark	28.0	34.2	ns
Feel unsafe in own home	24.5	26.1	ns
Experimental estate crime worse	17.7	39.6	**42.42
Control estate crime worse	12.4	6.2	**7.67
Crime			
% Committed in dark	68.8	70.8	ns
% Reported to police	50.6	46.4	ns
Saw police on estate last month	38.2	30.7	*4.23
Burglary worse	40.9	56.9	**18.43
Vandalism worse	40.1	49.1	*5.74
Vehicle crime worse	41.9	50.4	*5.03

* $p<.05$, ** $p<.01$ (two-tailed).
ns = not significant.
For committed in dark, N=144 crimes (experimental), 154 crimes (control).
For reported to police, N=164 crimes (experimental), 179 crimes (control).

Last year I told you [the interviewer] that my greenhouse [at the side, towards the back of the house] had been smashed twice at night and I was really frightened because the kids used to come into the garden and knock on my door and windows. I sleep on the ground floor since my husband died last year and I was scared to death in case they came in. It's all stopped now. They know they can be seen and my neighbor across the road has been out to them when they've got noisy.

The lighting is so much better. It's champion up here now. We never feel frightened here at all now. We've got one just outside our window. It's great. There are no shadows or dark patches.

The street lighting has improved. It's 100% better. Bound to feel safer because you can see who's about. It's lighter on the roads and in the gardens. These lights spread the light all around. Feel so much better.

The villains have gone. They don't like lights when they're up to no good. Everything is brighter and quieter. There are less places for people to hide with it being so light.

You can see things so much more clearly. It puts the villains off. You can recognize people in the street now. Before you could not. There are a lot less burglaries.

Things have really improved on this estate with regard to crime since the lights were put in. You can't half see a long way with this new lighting.

The lighting has brought more people on to the streets at night. Especially young girls. It's so much brighter and you can see people. Before you could not see people at all. It's cut out all the shadows in the street. It even shows up the gardens and you can see better in previously dark alleyways.

Pedestrian street use increased in the experimental area after the improved street lighting. The number of pedestrians was counted in two streets in each area on Thursday and Saturday evenings between 7:00 p.m. and 10:00 p.m. during the first week of March in 1992 and 1993. In both years the weather conditions were similar (cold but dry). The number of male pedestrians increased by 22.1% (from 515 to 629) in the experimental area and by 15.0% (from 347 to 399) in the control area, a non-significant difference (chi-squared = 0.35, not significant). However, the number of female pedestrians increased by 27.7% (from 386 to 493) in the experimental area but decreased by 21.2% (from 312 to 246) in the control area, a highly significant difference (chi-squared = 19.20, p<.0001). Hence, it is plausible that the improved street lighting encouraged more women to use the streets after dark.

Unfortunately, it was not possible to compare changes in police-recorded crimes in the experimental and control areas before and after, because of changes in recording procedures and inadequacies of available data.

Summary and Conclusions

In the Dudley project, improved street lighting was followed by significant decreases in the prevalence and incidence of crime in the experimental area compared with the control area. The experimental sample noticed that the lighting had improved, became more satisfied with their estate, and had less fear of crime. After the improved lighting, the experimental sample were less likely to say that there were risks for women after dark, and there was a significant increase in the number of female pedestrians on the street after dark in the experimental area. However, crimes were no less likely to be committed after dark compared with during the daylight and no more likely to be reported to the police after the improved street lighting.

Most threats to internal validity are controlled by the experimental-control, before-after design. For example, mortality (the loss of subjects from the pre-test to the post-test) was the same in the experimental and control areas and therefore could not account for differential changes in reported crime between the areas. The major uncontrolled threats were selection (the control sample were older) and history (apparently, police were seen more on the control estate before the intervention and more on the experimental estate after). However, the greater decrease in the prevalence and incidence of crime in the experimental estate held after controlling statistically for both these factors.

Extensive monitoring of other factors which might have contributed to the decreases in crime was undertaken through the questionnaire, interviewer fieldwork sheets and liaison with other agencies including the police and housing personnel. There were no changes to policing strategies or to Neighborhood Watch or to the history of the survey areas in any way which might account for the differential changes in crime.

The evaluation was designed to look for evidence of spatial, temporal and target displacement. The study found no evidence that any of these types of displacement occurred. Crime decreased in both estates, but decreased significantly more in the experimental estate. Also there was no evidence of displacement of crime from night to day. Of course, it is not possible to state conclusively that displacement did not take place because the phenomenon is so complex and can take so many different forms that no single research study can adequately encompass all possibilities (Barr and Pease, 1990; Ekblom and Pease, 1995). Notwithstanding this caveat, the findings from this study are entirely consistent with a growing body of research which shows that displacement is only a possible, not inevitable, outcome of effective crime prevention strategies. A collection of 22 studies presented by Clarke (1992) provided many examples of genuine reductions in crime with little or no displacement. Similarly, a review of 55 crime prevention projects, which specifically looked for evidence of displacement, found that in 22 cases no displacement occurred and that in 6 of these studies there was evidence of diffusion of benefits. Of the remaining 33 studies, some displacement was observed but it was limited in amount and scope (Hesseling, 1994).

An understanding as to why displacement did not occur in this study can be gleaned from a parallel, pre-post test household survey of 350 young people, aged 11-17 years carried out in the experimental and control areas. Results revealed that one reason crime was not displaced was because young people were not deflected from the re-lit area by the improved street lighting. On the contrary, they preferred to remain in the relit area; on both the adult and young people's surveys, respondents reported a highly significant increase in the number of young people in the relit area after dark (p<.0001). In theory, this could have led to an increase in crime, in practice it did not — presumably because the improved lighting not only made the relit areas more attractive to young people, but also increased the perceived risks of offending through enhanced natural surveillance of the streets.

The most plausible conclusion from this research is that the improved street lighting was responsible for the decrease in crime. Further research is needed to investigate how far these results can be replicated in different types of areas (external validity); it may be that improved lighting works better within certain contexts or "boundary conditions." Another key issue is the "dose-response" curve relating street lighting and crime; it may be that improved street lighting decreased crime in Dudley because the improvement was so dramatic. Further research is also needed to advance knowledge about the intervening processes, and interviews with potential offenders may be especially informative.

Our hypothesis is that more eyes and ears on the street and community improvements led residents to be more confident and optimistic and less afraid of crime. In turn, the increased community pride tended to exert increased informal social control on potential offenders, inhibiting them from committing crimes both day and night. Hence, improved street lighting was the catalyst which physically altered the built environment and brought about changes in resident and offender behavior which reduced crime and improved the quality of life on the experimental estate.

It is not impossible that alternative physical interventions, for example closed circuit television or increased locks and bolts, might have achieved a similar effect on crime as did street lighting improvements. However, street lighting has some advantages over other situational measures which have been associated with the creeping privatization of public space, the exclusion of sections of the population and the move towards a "fortress" society (Bottoms, 1990). Street lighting benefits the whole neighborhood rather than particular individuals or households. It is not a physical barrier to crime, it has no adverse civil liberties implications and, as has been demonstrated, it can increase public safety and effective use of neighborhood streets at night. In short, improved street lighting has no negative effects and has demonstrated benefits for law-abiding citizens.

ACKNOWLEDGMENTS.This research formed part of Kate Painter's Ph.D. thesis, supervised by Dr. Trevor Bennett. The authors are grateful to Patrick Baldrey, Managing Director of Urbis Lighting, for funding the research, to Wyn Cridland for fieldwork supervision, to Jacqueline Pate for presentation of results, to Ian Golton for data entry and initial analyses, and to Pat Altham for statistical advice.

Note

1. The difference of proportions test was used to investigate whether changes in prevalence were significant. For example, there was a significant decrease in the prevalence of all crime in the experimental area after the improved lighting compared with before ($Z=2.87$, $p=.002$). Two methods were used to contrast the change in prevalence of the experimental sample with the change in prevalence of the control sample. The difference of difference of proportions test produced a significant Z value for all crime of 1.80 ($p=.036$). The interaction term in a logistic regression equation produced a likelihood ratio chi-squared value of 3.29 ($p=.035$). Hence, both tests showed that the decrease in all crime in the experimental area was significantly greater than in the control area.

17. Operation Identification, or the Power of Publicity?

Gloria K. Laycock

EDITOR'S NOTE: This case study, first published as a Security Journal *article (Laycock, 1991), reports a successful property marking project (Operation Identification) undertaken in a rural community in Wales. Burglary rates in three discrete but adjacent areas had declined by about 50 percent by the second year of the project. The reasons for the success of OI in this case, when it has frequently failed before, are spelled out clearly by Gloria Laycock in classic Home Office style, and barely require comment here. However, the case study has one important lesson, supporting the conclusion reached by Poyner (1988) in his study of CCTV on buses: Local publicity can exert a powerful effect in maximizing the impact of situational measures. In both instances, the local publicity comprised not just TV and newspaper coverage, but also more direct communication with the offenders concerned. The video bus in Poyner's study, which visited local schools to explain the problems of graffiti and vandalism and to demonstrate the cameras, no doubt succeeded in frightening some of the offending children. In this project, undertaken in a relatively isolated rural community, many of the burglars are likely to have been residents of Graig-y-Rhacca, the area of public housing with a "rough" reputation. "It is almost certainly the case that the police, in calling at almost every door as they did, were also calling at the doors of burglars." As Laycock concludes, it may therefore be worth considering in the course of every situational project how best to communicate to offenders that serious crime prevention efforts are being made.*

227

THE MARKING of property as a means of identification is hardly new. There is a long-established belief that the branding or labeling of property with a personalized symbol will in some way protect it from theft or ensure its return should it be lost. In recent years, the practice has been given fresh impetus because, in the United Kingdom, we now have the "post code." The post code is rather different from the ZIP code used in the United States; it covers a very much smaller area, and in combination with the house name or number, uniquely identifies the household to which goods belong.

The development of the post code, together with the commitment of the police to search recovered property for signs of marking, led, in the mid-1980s, to widespread publicity in the United Kingdom aimed at encouraging the marking of property as a crime prevention device.

Earlier research studies of the efficacy of "operation identification" (OI) as it is known in the United States, were inconclusive. Work in the United States (Heller *et al.*, 1975) suggested that OI participants had significantly lower burglary rates than those not in the scheme, although there was no city-wide reduction. There was no evidence that goods were more likely to be returned after marking, nor was there any suggestion that the apprehension of burglars increased.

In 1984, Knutsson reported the results of a comprehensive study of OI in Sweden. This initiative covered a residential area about 20 miles from Stockholm and included about 3,500 houses. Over a four-year period, the participation rate in the scheme rose from about 13% to just under 30%. The results failed to demonstrate a reduction in burglary even for those participating in the scheme (Knutsson, 1984).

Despite the mixed empirical results, the British police were enthusiastic proponents of OI. For example, the Metropolitan Police, who are responsible for policing London, spent almost £250,000 on advertising OI during 1983/84 with a further £90,000 on equipment. Partly in response to this expenditure, the Home Office Crime Prevention Unit set up a "demonstration project" on OI, the results of which were first published in 1985 (Laycock, 1985).

The background to and some of the results of this scheme were fairly complex and are summarized below. The main purpose of the present paper, however, is to describe the effect of the OI program on burglary in the second year following implementation.

The South Wales Program

The primary aim of the South Wales initiative, where the Home Office demonstration project was set, was to determine the effect on domestic burglary rates for those participating in the program. In view of this, it was felt that, although the marking of goods might be important, the extent to which this was *advertised* was even more so. It was stressed to those participating that the use of the door or window decal was of crucial importance to the success of the scheme. It was assumed that the decal would convey not only the message that goods are marked and disposal may be difficult, but, also, and in practice more significantly, that the residents in this house are concerned about burglary and that the risks to the potential offender may thereby be increased. Displaying the decal was taken by the researchers as the only indication of participation.

A high take-up rate by residents in the target area was regarded as crucial. This was in order to make statistical analysis possible and to reduce the pool of unprotected homes, thus, hopefully, limiting the opportunity for the displacement of burglary. Three methods were employed to achieve this — the program was launched with as much publicity as possible, door-to-door visits were made by the police or special constables,[1] and free marking equipment and door or window decals were provided for the residents.

One week following the initial visit, all those participating were revisited by the police or special constables. A questionnaire was completed recording that goods were marked, whether any difficulties were encountered (help was offered if necessary), and whether, and if so where, the "property marked" label had been placed (e.g. front door, back window).

After three months had elapsed, a further letter was sent to residents from the chief constable reinforcing the aims of the program and enclosing another window/door decal. Finally, in order to check on the extent to which interest continued to be maintained, a further visit to those participating was carried out approximately six months after the initial launch. A record was made of the number of houses still displaying the decal and an extract from *Crime Prevention News,*[2] which ran a feature on the property marking scheme, was provided to each home.

The Target Area

The area chosen covered a part of the Caerphilly subdivision of the South Wales Constabulary. Three fairly distinct "villages" were included that covered the floor of a valley. Low-lying and largely uninhabited hills defined the area, which limited the opportunity for displacement. Burglaries were not uniformly distributed throughout the villages. They were concentrated on a group of local authority homes that fell more or less in the middle of the valley. Thus, any displacement of burglary from the initially higher-risk area would be likely to fall on one of the other two villages within the program.

The three villages, Trethomas, Graig-y-Rhacca, and Machen, can be described as follows:

> *Trethomas:* a mixed area of detached, owner-occupied accommodation together with an area of older "mining" houses once owned by the coal board but now either local authority owned or owner-occupied. These houses are mainly back-to-back row houses. Approximately 800 dwellings are located in this area.
>
> *Graig-y-Rhacca*: an area of public housing arranged as condominiums or row houses. The estate is rather untidy in places, although some houses are well cared for and of good decorative order. Approximately 700 homes exist on this estate.
>
> *Machen:* an area of largely privately owned accommodation with gardens, garages, etc. Some houses are local authority owned but are less "estate-like" than those in Graig-y-Rhacca. Some of the outlying houses back onto picturesque woodland. Approximately 700 houses are found in this area.

Criteria Employed in the Evaluation

A *dwelling* was considered in the target area if it appeared on the electoral register and was part of the subdivision area. A total of 2,234 houses were thus included in the target sample. A *house* was considered to have been burglarized if it appeared in the police list of "reported burglaries." A *household* was regarded as *in* the program if, following the second police visit, a "property marked" decal was on display on any outside door or window. Otherwise, it was regarded as a nonparticipating household.

Results

The Take-up Rate

The participation rate for households in the three areas is shown in Table 1. Those excluded from the scheme include households in which there was nobody at home or which were unoccupied at the time of the visit; those who declined to join; and those who, although agreeing to join the scheme, declined to display the decal.

Of the nonparticipants, 185 had joined the scheme, in the sense that they had claimed to mark their property, but had declined to use the window decal and were thus counted as nonparticipants. In almost all cases, their reluctance was because they felt that they would be more likely to attract a burglar if they did so.

Interestingly, the incidence of the nonuse of decals appeared in small clusters in the data; i.e., it seemed as though neighbors had discussed whether or not to place the decals in the window and had decided as a group not to do so. Thus, there might be a small street or group of houses where the decals were not displayed, but where the response to the program was otherwise positive.

TABLE 1
PARTICIPATION RATE BY AREA

Area	In Program	Not in Program	Total	Take-up Rate*
Trethomas	618	203	821	75%
Graig-y-Rhacca	499	209	708	70%
Machen	497	208	705	70%
Total	1614	620	2234	72%

* Indicates display of decal, signifying participation in the program

Burglaries Before And After The Launch

In the 12-month period before the launch of the program, 128 burglaries were reported to the police. In the 12-month period after the launch, 74 burglaries were reported — a reduction of 40%. The effect of the scheme on the rate at which homes were victimized appears, of course, rather less dramatic. Allowing for the fact that some houses were burglarized more than once, the burglary rate before the launch was 5.1% and after it was 3.0%.

To determine whether the property marking scheme was relevant to these reductions in burglary rate, comparisons were made between those participating and those not participating. The results of these comparisons are shown in Table 2. The table records incidents of burglary rather than houses burglarized: that is, if a house was burglarized on more than one occasion, it is counted more than once.

Table 2 shows a reduction in the number of burglary incidents for those participating. While there was no reduction for the nonparticipants, there was also no significant increase in incidents; i.e., there was no displacement of burglary from one group to another.

TABLE 2
BURGLARY INCIDENTS FOR PARTICIPANTS AND
NONPARTICIPANTS BEFORE AND AFTER THE LAUNCH
OF THE PROGRAM

	Before	After	
Participants	91	35	(probability <.001)
Nonparticipants	37	39	(no significant change)

The total number of 74 burglaries for the first year following the launch *fell* further in the second year, to 66. This was felt to be quite a surprising result. Analysis by month is shown in Figure 1. As can be seen, the drop in the number of burglaries is particularly

FIGURE 1
BURGLARIES BY MONTH, 1 AND 2 YEARS AFTER IMPLEMENTATION

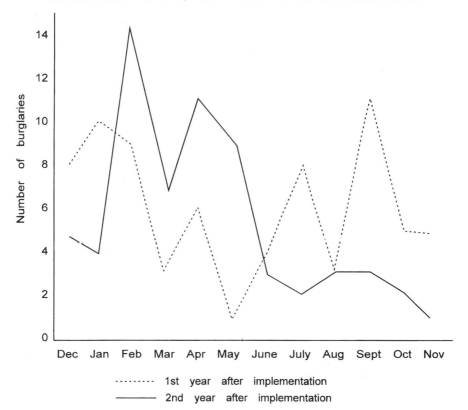

noticeable from June to November. This drop, from 49 in the first half of the period to 14 in the second, is statistically significant. Comparison with figures for the previous year does not lead to an explanation in terms of seasonal variation. Comparable half-year figures for the previous year were 37, dropping to 36 — an insignificant change. The probable reasons for this are discussed below.

Discussion

A number of unexpected results from this study emerge that require some explanation. First, the high take-up rate; second, the reduction in burglary itself; and last, the greater drop in the second year. Each of these points is discussed in turn below, and this is followed by a consideration of the implications for prevention.

THE TAKE-UP RATE

The take-up rate of this program was almost twice as high as that achieved elsewhere. There are three factors of immediate significance. First, the considerable advance publicity given to the program in the locality; second, the door-to-door approach by the police; and, finally, the provision of free marking equipment. It is not possible to determine which of these three factors was of most importance, but the fact that the police were prepared to visit every home and to follow-up this with a further visit one week later must have played an important part in convincing the public of the worth of the exercise.

A more general point in relation to the high take-up rate is that whatever the public were being asked to do in protecting themselves against burglary had to be made as effortless as possible on their part; this was a guiding principle in the design of this program. It was helped greatly by the existence of the post code and the efforts by the post office to extend its use. In other OI schemes that have been launched, particularly in the United States, householders have been urged to register their personal code with the police or lodge with them a list of items marked with the appropriate marking recorded. This clearly requires far more effort on the part of the individual members of the public. In this respect, the existence of a nationally available post code in the United Kingdom is a considerable advantage.

Looking in detail at the take-up rate along the valley, and bearing in mind that the householders are from different social classes and live in remarkably different property, there was a notable similarity in take-up rate in the three "villages." It is particularly remarkable that a high participation rate was achieved on the public housing estate, the area that had the highest rate of burglary. The police were themselves surprised at the positive reception that they received in this area because it has a rather "rough" reputation and, they felt, housed some so-called problem families. Indeed, a few police officers were reluctant to include their homes in the door-to-door canvass. In retrospect, however, it is obvious that nobody likes to be the victim of a burglary, not even a burglar.

REDUCED BURGLARY

One of the major differences between the results reported here and those from other studies is that there was no apparent displacement in burglary from participants to nonparticipants. The most plausible explanation for this seems to relate to the exceptionally high take-up achieved by police. Of the approximately 30% "unprotected" houses, a number would perhaps be less likely to be burglarized for other reasons; for example, they may have a burglar alarm or be particularly visible from the surrounding area. This would have the effect of reducing the pool of potential targets still further. Although it remains an empirical question to determine at what level of participation displacement ceases to occur, it seems to be that in the case of the present initiative that level was surpassed. This lack of displacement, combined with the high take-up rate, probably accounts for the area wide reduction in crime.

In other studies, it has never been as clear that in persuading the public to mark their property the police were at the same time persuading the potential burglars that the scheme would be effective. Bearing in mind the original distribution of burglary throughout the valley, it is almost certainly the case that the police, in calling at almost every door as they did, were also calling at the doors of the burglars. It seems plausible that this contributed to the impact of the scheme.

THE SECOND-YEAR DROP

The additional drop in the second year was quite contrary to expectation. The monthly figures that show when the fall occurred go a long way in offering an explanation of why it happened. The results of the first-year evaluation were *published* in June of the second year and resulted in an enormous amount of local publicity showing the effect of property marking. This report (Laycock, 1985) received some national publicity, but was very widely reported at the local level to the extent that the area was visited by the local TV company and a series of interviews was held with the chief constable and residents of the research area. While the burglary rate had been in the process of returning to its former relatively high level, at least on the central estate, this process was slowed dramatically following the considerable amount of publicity.

Interestingly, the published research report had not argued that OI reduced crime. Although crime levels had certainly been reduced, it was far from clear that the process underlying that reduction was as simplistic as marking property. The subtleties of the arguments that the researcher had liked to think were made were certainly lost, however, in the media presentation of the message, which came out along the lines of "crime crashes as a result of marking property."

Practical Implications

There are a number of practical points that may be drawn from the experience in South Wales. These are summarized below:

1. Areas with high crime rates, including burglary, may welcome the launch of crime prevention initiatives even if the areas have a reputation for poor relations with the police.

2. The easier it is for the public to participate in crime prevention schemes the more likely they will be to do so.

3. It is probably as important to tell the burglars about the scheme as it is to tell the general public. It may be worth giving some thought as to how this can be achieved.

4. The evidence suggests that the use of a window or door label, indicating marked property, is effective in reducing burglary. The public can be reassured, therefore, that any anxieties that decals increase the chances of victimization are unfounded.

The increased reduction in crime during the second year suggests, in addition:

1. The positive effect of the initial reduction in burglary from the property marking scheme was transitory.

2. A dramatic illustration of the power of positive local advertising on the burglary rate in a small, clearly defined area. This probably rests on the fact that the offenders, certainly in the central area of the research study, were also the residents. With the benefit of hindsight, in the light of the second-year follow-up, the importance of local publicity at all stages of the implementation of this project is worth highlighting.

3. On a methodological point, the results bear testimony to the importance of detailed analysis. At first sight, there might have been a temptation to claim an increased reduction in burglary on the basis of the annual figures: Total pre-program burglaries were 128, first-year post-program were 74, and second-year post-program were 66. It is only the month-by-month figures which show that the drop was concentrated in the second period and only the local knowledge that leads to the explanation in terms of publicity.

ACKNOWLEDGMENTS. I am grateful to the chief constable of the South Wales Constabulary and his officers for their support in carrying out this study. Particular thanks are due to Superintendent M. Bowden and the crime prevention staff. I am also grateful to the head of the Home Office Crime Prevention Unit, Kevin Heal, for his unfailing support and good advice.

Notes

1. Special constables, who wear uniforms similar to that of police officers themselves, are volunteer members of the public who help the police in certain areas of their work.
2. *Crime Prevention News* is a bulletin published and distributed by the Home Office that reports on crime prevention initiatives around the country; it is circulated to police crime prevention officers among others.

18. Housing Allowances in a Welfare Society: Reducing the Temptation to Cheat

Eckart Kuhlhorn

EDITOR'S NOTE: Resentment of those "getting a free ride" on welfare is close to the surface in any society and frequently erupts in witch hunts for welfare cheats or "social security scroungers." This resentment has been exploited in a recent British government campaign, "Beat-A-Cheat," to encourage members of the public to turn in people whom they think are making fraudulent welfare claims. The campaign was dubbed a "snoopers' charter" by the government's opponents, one of whom angrily said in Parliament: "Encouraging your next-door neighbor to snoop on you is the sort of community values we now expect in Britain" (New York Times, *October 29, 1996, p.A10). That there is a better way to reduce welfare fraud is shown by this pioneering case study first published by the Swedish National Council for Crime Prevention (Kuhlhorn, 1982). When statements made about personal income to obtain housing allowances could be cross-checked by computer with other statements of income to determine sickness payments, this reduced the temptation for claimants to cheat by understating their incomes in order to obtain higher housing allowances. A survey of the public revealed that nearly 90 percent of the recipients of housing allowances approved of these computer checks. Most had nothing to fear, of course, but some may have been relieved that the temptation for them to cheat as well had been removed.*

Housing Allowances

In a modern welfare society the state and the local authorities have an important role as redistributors of economic resources. People who have high incomes and/or are at the peak of their productive career have to pay higher taxes, which are then distributed to low-income earners and persons in unproductive phases. This redistribution function creates a tempting opportunity structure for white collar crime; a person who conceals his financial assets avoids payment of taxes and can benefit by various allowances provided by the Welfare State. This paper will deal with one such crime against the Welfare State, namely cheating on housing allowances in Sweden and the effects of preventive measures.

The Swedish system of housing allowances covers 472,000 households, i.e. 14 per cent of all households.[1] The intention is that housing allowances shall provide support especially for families with children having low incomes and high housing costs. There are accordingly three significant criteria for obtaining a housing allowance:
- high housing costs
- large household, particularly with children
- low income.

The housing allowance differs for small and large households. The National Housing Board publishes catalogs about housing allowances which present standard figures for the various household sizes.[2] The table for single, childless persons is reproduced as Table 1. The income of a single person may not be above 43,000 Swedish Crowns if he or she is to receive a housing allowance, even if the rent is very high. For a family with two children the situation is different as shown by the extract from the official table reproduced in Table 2.

TABLE 1
HOUSING ALLOWANCES PER MONTH FOR SINGLE, CHILDLESS PERSONS,
SWEDEN 1980.

Qualifying annual income (Swedish Crowns)	Rent/housing cost (Swedish Crowns per month)					
	525-549	575-599	625-649	675-699	725-749	750 & over
29,000	20	60	100	140	180	200
31,000		35	75	115	155	175
33,000			50	90	130	150
35,000			25	65	105	125
37,000				40	80	100
39,000					55	75
41,000					30	50
43,000						25

Source: National Housing Board

TABLE 2

HOUSING ALLOWANCE PER MONTH FOR COUPLES WITH TWO CHILDREN, SWEDEN 1980

Qualifying annual income (Swedish Crowns)	Rent/housing cost (Swedish Crowns per month)					
	0-524	625-649	775-799	875-899	1025-1049	1205 & over
0 - 38,000	310	410	530	610	730	910
42,000	260	360	480	560	680	860
46,000	210	310	430	510	630	810
50,000	160	260	380	460	580	760
54,000	110	210	330	410	530	710
58,000	60	160	280	360	480	660
62,000		88	208	288	408	588
66,000			128	208	328	508
70,000			48	128	248	428
74,000				48	168	348
78,000					88	268
82,000						188
86,000						108
90,000						28

Source: National Housing Board.

The housing allowance system thus has a fairly limited significance for single persons and childless households, but extends to more than one-third of families with children. Table 3 shows the extent to which different types of household received housing allowances in May 1980.[3]

It is also of interest to see the economic significance of housing allowances for the recipients. Table 4 shows for households which received housing allowances both the mean housing cost (e.g. rent) and the mean allowance. In total, housing allowances covered a good third of the housing cost.

TABLE 3

HOUSING ALLOWANCES BY HOUSEHOLD COMPOSITION, SWEDEN 1980

Type of household	Number of households with housing allowance	In relation to all households in Sweden
Households with one person	65,153	6 %
Households without children	73,475	3 %
Households with children of which:	394,853	34 %
with 1 child	103,024	25 %
with 2 children	168,933	37 %
with >3 children	95,896	54 %
All households	472,009	14 %

TABLE 4
AVERAGE RENT/HOUSING COSTS AND HOUSING ALLOWANCE, SWEDEN,
MAY 1980 (SWEDISH CROWNS).

Type of household	Rent/housing costs (mean)	Housing allowance (mean)	Allowance in relation to costs
Households without children	850	146	17 %
Households with children	1,299	483	37 %
All households	1,229	430	35 %

The Temptation

Housing allowances are calculated on the basis of the applicant's statement of taxable income in the calendar year for which an allowance is requested. This means that the applicant must make a forecast. The recipient of an allowance must also submit a statement of property as recorded in his or her last income tax return, and of the size and type of household. A pessimistic forecast thus has certain beneficial effects for the applicant - *low income gives a high housing allowance.*

A similar statement of income and of changes in income must, in addition, be submitted to the social insurance offices by practically all income-earners in Sweden, since all must be registered with them. Here, however, the situation is the reverse of that for housing allowances - *high income gives a high sickness allowance.*

Consequently, there is a great temptation for a person to be considerably more pessimistic when estimating income as the basis for calculation of a housing allowance than as basis for sickness insurance. As these two income statements are based on somewhat different time frames - for housing allowances on income during a calendar year, and for sickness insurance on income during a twelve-month period - some people will consciously or unconsciously succumb to the temptation to report too low an income when applying for a housing allowance. They are also more likely to forget to report an *increase* than a *decrease* of income for adjustment of their housing allowance.

Control and its Legitimacy

Since statements of income both for housing allowance and sickness benefits are data-processed, a crime prevention eldorado exists. By linked processing of the data for housing allowances and for sickness insurance it is possible to identify households which have reported different incomes. But no eldorado is without limit. In the first place there is an administrative limitation. Whereas the income statements for sickness insurance are collected centrally for all citizens at the National Social Insurance Board, the housing allowances are administered by the local authorities. Each of Sweden's 277 local author-ities thus has its own file with data of incomes for housing allowances. The second limitation is legal. To prevent the use of computers encroaching upon citizens' personal privacy, Sweden has fairly rigorous data legislation. Linked processing of files containing data submitted by citizens to different authorities for different purposes is therefore a delicate matter. On the other hand, it may be considered legitimate that authorities make checks on economically important data submitted by citizens and the Government consequently gave permission for a trial of linked processing of data for this purpose. Of importance for crime prevention, however, is not only the particular methods used but also how citizens appraise the legitimacy of such measures. In 1979, therefore, the National Housing Board commissioned a public opinion poll of a nationally representative sample of 1000 persons aged 16 - 69 years. The responses were as follows:

1. 94 per cent thought it proper that local authorities should make these checks on statements of income.
2. 87 per cent of the recipients of household allowances (24 per cent of the sample were recipients of household allowances) thought it wholly or partly proper that such checks should be made.
3. 91 per cent thought that such checks had at least a fairly great significance for the scrupulousness with which people report changes of income to the local authorities.

The first year in which linked processing of the relevant data took place was 1979. These operations were extensively discussed in the press and other mass media. Consequently, many people had the opportunity to notify local authorities of any mistakes in their statements of income. Linked processing operations continued in 1980. The criterion adopted was that all households whose statement of annual income for housing allowances exceeded the statement made to the Social Insurance Office by at least 1000 Swedish Crowns were selected by the computer. These households than received a letter and were asked to state the reasons for the difference. (It should be mentioned that the probability of reporting too high an income to the Social Insurance Office is fairly low, since these statements of income are later compared with and corrected with respect to the annual income tax return).

Results of the Check

A large number of local authorities employ the services of a company, Kommun Data AB, which performs computer runs for them and which also performed the linked processing operations. As it appears from Table 5, a large majority of local authorities using Kommun Data AB's Computer Service System made such checks.[4] Practically all households with housing allowance have been checked, usually once in each year. The local authorities spread these checks over several points of time during the year, i.e. the first check comprised certain households selected at random, the second other households, until

TABLE 5
THE SCOPE OF THE CHECK

Local authorities (Swedish 'kommun')	1979	1980
Number of Swedish local authorities	277	277
Local authorities using the Computer Service System*	248	251
Local authorities which check their housing allowances by means of the Computer Service System	218	225
Percentage of checking local authorities in relation to all local authorities using the Computer Service System	88 %	90 %

* Kommun Data AB

all households had been checked. The results are shown in Table 6.

Before discussing the results, is should be noted that the authorities had undertaken important preventive action without at the same time instituting a rigorous evaluation. The evaluation reported here was retrospective and was based on available data. However, the results are so striking that in all probability they would hold good even after thorough examination of the primary material. The tragedy of this type of subsequent analysis of secondary material lies rather in the losses of precision. For example, the preventive effect cannot be precisely defined, the costs of control in relation to the gain cannot be calculated and, in particular, the effect of the data control on the local authorities' administrative routines cannot be determined. This missed opportunity for a more rigorous evaluation of results of great interest for preventive theory must, however, not be allowed to detract from the importance of the results actually obtained. These can be summarized as follows:

1. *The extent of this type of welfare criminality — 2.7 per cent in the first year and 1.2 per cent in the second — is considerably less than asserted in debates about economic crime or the extent of demoralization in Swedish society.* Some protagonists are unlikely to accept a basic assumption of a law-abiding society with limited mass economic criminality. They will undoubtedly maintain that most recipients of housing allowances are not so stupid as to get caught in the data controls. They would instead under-report their income to all the relevant bodies, i.e. they would be consistent in their errors.

2. *As far as can be judged, a preventive effect exists.* The frequency of fraud fell from 2.7 per cent in the first year to 1.2 per cent in the second. The real preventive effect may be rather higher as the check in the first year was discussed in the mass media and thus gave recipients of housing allowances a chance to notify wrong or out-dated statements of income before the check was made.

3. *After the opportunity structure was changed, the compliance among recipients of allowances increased.* The number of spontaneous reports of changed income increased considerably from the first to the second year. This lends support to the Marxist thesis that changes of attitude are conditional upon changes of realities, and contradicts the socio-psychological thesis that the attitude to crime must change before criminality can be reduced. But it should be emphasized that this result was obtained in a sphere where a large majority of recipients of allowances considered the controls to be legitimate. It is by no means certain that the same results would be obtained when the legitimacy of control was questioned.

4. *The number of persons with legitimate differences of income is much greater than the number with illegitimate.* During 1979 and 1980, 19 per cent of the households were found to have a difference of income in their statement of at least 1000 Swedish Crowns. Some of them had notified differences of income before the check, some had *de facto* differences which entitled them to housing allowance or sickness benefit, and only a minority (14 per cent in 1979 and 6 per cent in 1980) had reported wrong income figures. From the calculation made by some local authorities of reduction in housing allowances after the check, it is apparent that the local authorities make quite considerable gains through their improved administrative routines for dealing with housing allowances.

To sum up, it may be said that the linked processing of data files opens up substantial and interesting probabilities of crime prevention. In this concrete case it is apparent that the great gains to be made lie in a direct change of the crime opportunity structure— namely that, on the basis of a common income concept for sickness insurance and housing allowances, people submit a single statement and so avoid making mistakes or being subjected to too much pressure of temptation.

TABLE 6
RESULTS OF THE CHECKS IN 1979 AND 1980

	1979	1980
Households with housing allowance	512,644	472,009
Such households in local authorities using the Computer Service System*	496,040	462,000
Households checked	340,577	314,683
Checked households as percentage of households registered in the Computer Service System	69 %	68 %
Households which reported an income at least 1,000 crowns a year too low	64,710	58,487
As a percent of checked households	19 %	19 %
Households which lost their allowance or received a reduced allowance because of the check	9,179	3,649
Percentage of such households in relation to checked households	2.7 %	1.2 %
Households registered in the Computer Service System which lost their allowance or received a reduced allowance because of spontaneously reported changes in income (June-December)	30,238	52,753
Percentage of such households in relation to all households registered in the Computer Service System	6.1%	11.4%

* Kommun Data AB

Notes

1. Bostadsbidrag for December 1980 (Housing allowances for December 1980). National Housing Board, No 1981: 22. June 16, 1981.
2. Information published by the National Housing Board: Housing allowances 1981.
3. The figures of households with housing allowance are taken from a statistical investigation entitled 'Hushåll med bostadsbidrag for maj 1980' (Households with housing allowance, May 1980), National Housing Board, Dec. 23, 1980. The figures for households, households with children, etc., have been estimated on the basis of the 1975 population and housing census and on changes in population since then.
4. Some of the figures are taken from "Utvärdering av samkörning av kommunernas bostadsbidragsregister under bidragsåret 1979 med riksförsäkringsverkets register över sjukpenninggrundande inkomst" (Evaluation of linked processing of local authorities' housing allowance files for 1979 with the National Social Insurance Board's file of sick-benefitcarrying income), National Housing Board (Dnr 99-1691 u) May 29, 1980; some directly from the National Housing Board and Kommun Data AB.

19. Subway Graffiti in New York City: "Gettin' up" vs. "Meanin' it and Cleanin' it"

Maryalice Sloan-Howitt and George L. Kelling

EDITOR'S NOTE: This case study, first published as a Security Journal *article (Sloan-Howitt and Kelling, 1990), is one of the most remarkable in the collection. It documents the process by which the graffiti-ridden trains of the New York City subway were finally made clean, after years of failed initiatives involving a variety of law enforcement and target hardening measures. The successful idea adopted by management was a simple one: once a car had been cleansed of graffiti it would never again be allowed to enter service with graffiti. Underlying this principle was the notion that "getting up," seeing one's handiwork on public display, was the offender's main motivation and that the rewards of this behavior had to be denied. Implementing the policy involved formidable political and logistical problems (how the latter were solved will repay close study by other managers confronted with implementation difficulties), but the results are plain for anyone to see. The subway cars in New York are now no longer the disgrace they once were. This classic study represents only one of many important contributions to criminal policy made by George Kelling, who is now at Rutgers. He directed the Police Foundation's Kansas City Preventive Patrol Experiment which prompted a re-evaluation of the concept of preventive patrol and, together with James Q. Wilson, authored the famous* Atlantic Monthly *"Broken Windows" piece (Wilson and Kelling, 1982), which advocated intervention at the first sign of persistent "incivilities" to prevent a*

*community's decline into serious crime. The successful application of this principle on
a wide scale in New York City is documented in his recent book,* Fixing Broken
Windows *(Kelling and Coles, 1996).*

━━━━━━━━━━━━━━━━━

THE IMPULSE toward graffiti writing — that furtive defacement of public property
through the inscription of messages typically rich in political humor or sexual innuendo,
or simple distress calls — can be found in all societies and is generally tolerated or even
enjoyed when wittily or attractively executed. During the 1970s and early 1980s in New
York City, however, the problem of graffiti writing on subway trains developed into a
serious public policy problem. The phenomenon of random scratching of names on transit
property blossomed until a well-defined subculture that included hundreds of youths were
emblazoning subway cars with murals that covered entire trains, obscuring windows and
subway maps. These young people not only developed the genre, but also transformed
graffiti writing into a way of life — "getting up" — drawing their self-esteem from their
ability to keep their names and other creative designs in constant circulation on the transit
lines. The New York City government's and the New York City Transit Authority's (NYCTA)
striking attempts — and failures — to outwit these youths and deter their spectacular
defacement of public property only served to embolden the graffitists (Castelman, 1982).

Apologists such as Norman Mailer (1974) perceived the graffitists' work as vibrant
folk art — the colorful self-expression of creative adolescents. Others, however, decried
the graffitists' work as the criminal defacement of public property that created a climate of
fear in the city's transit system. Giving voice to the majority opinion, Nathan Glazer (1979)
argued persuasively that subway riders made an unconscious connection between the
visual assault of graffiti and the more serious crimes of robbery, rape, assault, and murder.
Riders also associated the chaotic graffiti with other maintenance problems — the shattered
glass, broken doors, and vandalized maps — that diminished the quality of public
transportation. Furthermore, and perhaps most compelling, the graffiti could be construed
as hard evidence that authorities were incapable of controlling the environment and
securing it against offenders.

Additional observations lent credence to Glazer's argument. Increased fear of the
subway resulted in diminished ridership, which, in turn, led to increased danger to those
riders who braved traveling at off-peak hours. As significantly, a connection was demonstrated between a youth's career as a graffitist and subsequent adult criminal behavior,
suggesting that the subculture of graffiti vandalism served as a training ground for future
adult offenders. Internal studies by the NYCTA Police, for example, indicated that a
substantial proportion of those arrested for graffiti writing (40%) went on to commit
robberies and burglaries (Glazer, 1979:6). Moreover, graffiti writers typically stole the
enormous quantities of paint required for their craft.

Myriad policies failed. Police knew who the graffitists were: They had detailed
records about and profiles of the some 500 individuals who were responsible for the train
graffiti — after all, the whole purpose of subway graffiti was to get one's "tag up" and be
renowned. Yet, when police arrested graffitists, they were merely released by a juvenile
justice system overwhelmed by more serious youthful offenders (Glazer, 1979:6). Major
antigraffiti efforts were launched by both Mayors Lindsay and Koch. The briefly popular
program of punishment by detention of offenders, with the requirement of cleaning up

graffiti-marred trains, failed for two reasons. First, the supervision proved too expensive. Second, the program furnished offenders with superior technical knowledge that then permitted them to create more durable graffiti on their release — for every technological "fix," there was a counter-technological response (Castleman, 1982). "Target hardening" of the train yards likewise failed to deter graffitists because of the vastness of the areas needing to be secured and the youths' ability to cut through those wire fences that were erected. Police urged that group and social work be targeted at graffitists to channel their talents, but few such efforts were initiated (Glazer, 1979). Various (and expensive) experiments with graffiti-resistant train paints failed. Media pressure caused the NYCTA to abandon plans to use attack dogs (Castleman, 1982).

After more than half a decade of failed policies, Glazer (1979:10-11) summarized the problem as follows:

> Graffiti raise the odd problem of a crime that is, compared to others, relatively trivial but whose aggregate effects on the environment of millions of people are massive. In the New York situation especially, it contributes to a prevailing sense of the incapacity of government, and the uncontrollability of youthful criminal behavior, and a resultant uneasiness and fear. Minor infractions aggregate into something that reaches and affects every subway passenger. But six years of efforts have seen no solution.

The problem of graffiti must be seen within the context of the NYCTA during the late 1970s and early 1980s. The neglect of New York City's infrastructure, which had arisen from New York's 1970s fiscal crisis, was calamitous in the subway: Fires were epidemic; subway trains derailed on the average of one every 18 days; in 400 places in the system, track conditions were so bad that train speeds had to be reduced 75%; and on any given day, a third of the subway fleet was out of service during the morning rush hour. Moreover, as a consequence of liberalized pension laws, skilled and managerial personnel had been leaving the NYCTA in droves: When Robert Kiley, the current Chairman of the Board of the Metropolitan Transportation Authority (MTA), was appointed in 1983, 50,000 workers were directed by 300 managers (Kiley, 1989). As Kiley noted: "[T]he organization was in utter chaos, its spirit broken, its sense of purpose and effectiveness long since lost" (Kiley, 1988). The subway system was on the verge of collapse.

In April 1984, David Gunn, the new president of the NYCTA, announced the Authority's Clean Car Program (CCP). All new and overhauled cars would be placed in the program. Once placed in the CCP, no car would remain in service if it was vandalized. To implement and maintain the CCP, Gunn created the Car Appearance and Security Task Force (CAST), which represented 15 separate NYCTA departments.

At its initiation in May 1984, two trains were placed into the CCP: One train was composed of new R62 Kawasaki cars on the #4 line, and another, of 20-year-old reconditioned and repainted R36 St. Louis cars on the #7 line. On May 12, 1989, 5 years later, the last graffiti-covered car was removed from service and cleaned. Now, subway trains in New York City are not only graffiti-free, they are among the cleanest subway cars in the world.

The "Clean Car Program"

David Gunn had worked as Kiley's director of operations in the Massachusetts Bay Transit Authority during the 1970s, gone on to direct Philadelphia's transportation system, and rejoined Kiley as president of the NYCTA in 1983. The NYCTA was one of three major units of the MTA, the other two being the Long Island Rail Road and the Metro North Rail Road. Each operates with considerable autonomy.

The transportation infrastructure Gunn inherited is massive. Not counting the bus system, he is responsible for a network of 230 route miles, having 26 transit lines that serve 468 stations. Trains are operated throughout the system 24 hours a day, with headways between trains as frequent as two minutes during peak periods and as long as 20 minutes during off-peak hours. Over 5,000 cars are used every day during the peak period, and the Transit Authority has an inventory of approximately 6,000 train cars. When out of use, trains are stored in 25 yards and 45 layup sites. Over 3,700,000 riders are carried on the average workday.

Gunn also inherited "the financial means and... the political will" (Kiley, 1988) to improve the system. Richard Ravitch, Kiley's predecessor as chairman of the MTA, was responsible for the first 5-year $8 billion capital program that was initiated in 1982. Kiley extended the capital program and provided the administrative mandate to improve the system. Gunn was responsible for administering the renovation of the system.

Gunn, who holds a master's degree in business administration, is both deeply committed to public transportation and a self-confessed train "buff." In a very real sense, the NYCTA is "his." He identifies with the system, uses it regularly,[1] suffers as a result of its problems and incivilities, and was personally aggrieved by graffiti. Not daunted by the failures of earlier attempts to alleviate graffiti, indeed learning from them, he put out the word early in his administration: Ending graffiti was one of his highest priorities — kids were no longer going to make canvases out of Gunn's trains.

The NYCTA's CCP was based on a relatively simple idea: Once a car was cleaned and entered into the program, it would never again leave a storage, maintenance, or lay-up area with graffiti. Its implementation was difficult and included risks: If it meant keeping a car out of service, even during rush hours (as it did 10 times during the program's 5 years), so be it. No one would "get up" again on cars entered into the program.

The first step was to "chunk" the problem (Peters and Waterman, 1982:136-144). Two trains, a manageable number, were entered into the program. Crews, composed of supervisory and cleaning personnel, were set up at the end of each line (numbers 4 and 7) to immediately clean cars entered into the program if they had been "tagged" by vandals. All graffiti was to be removed within two hours or the car would be pulled from service. Police were assigned to ride these trains full-time while they were in service. When out of service, clean trains were stored in yards specially protected by the NYCTA's Property Protection Department. In these yards, lighting was upgraded, cleaning personnel worked 24 hours a day, fences were checked daily and mended within 24 hours if damaged, and police worked undercover as cleaners.

The CAST was created by President Gunn at the initiation of the CCP. Its goals were:

- To heighten the awareness of each NYCTA department about NYCTA goals;

- To focus on problems that have an impact on meeting those goals;

- To indicate the course of action required to resolve any problems;

- To monitor the progress of the CCP;

- To encourage an active role and participation in the program by each department; and

- To familiarize committee members, and through them their respective departments, with their duties and responsibilities to enhance the effort. (Transit Authority Police Department, 1988).

CAST met biweekly during the period 1984-1987; in 1988, its meeting schedule was reduced to once a month. Administrative authority and overall direction for the CCP was lodged with the chief mechanical officer of the Car Equipment Department.

Yearly goals were established for the CCP. By May 1985, 1720 cars were to be cleaned; by 1986, 3434; by 1987, 4707; and by 1988, 5946. The entire fleet was to be graffiti-free in 1989.

As the program expanded to more trains, and as a result of learning from the past experience with cleaning technologies, the Car Equipment Department tested and approved new cleaning commodities (40 new products were developed) and tools (14 were developed) to ensure swift and sure removal of graffiti. Although total hourly personnel declined in the Car Equipment Department during this period (from 5231 to 5201), cleaning personnel increased from 691 to 1622 (from 13% to 31% of the personnel) (Transit Authority, 1989).

Police tactics changed over time. As more clean cars entered the program, police switched from riding all clean trains to a random approach: ride a clean train for several stops, get off, and then ride another clean train in another direction. They concentrated on times and locations when students and youths tended to ride trains. No longer were summonses to be issued; if action was to be taken against a graffitist, it would be formal arrest. Police focused on repeat offenders by identifying their "tags," contacting their parents, threatening civil action for restitution, and requesting special prosecutorial and judicial responses. Undercover officers were placed on especially difficult lines. When the number of clean cars exceeded the capacity of secured lay-up areas, the police created the Anti-Graffiti Unit for two purposes: to consult about methods of improving security in lay-up areas and to safeguard the trains in unsecured or loosely secured yards until their security could be upgraded (Transit Authority Police Department,1988:2-3).

TABLE 1
CLEAN CAR PROGRAM, GOALS, AND ACHIEVEMENTS, 1984-1989

	Clean Cars	
	Goal	Actual
1984		400
1985	1720	1915
1986	3434	3454
1987	4707	4839
1988	5946	6077
1989	6221	6245

Source: "Clean Car Program," Car Equipment Department, NYCTA, May 1989.

Other departments of the NYCTA Police contributed their efforts to the program. Property Protection increased their patrol and improved security in yard and lay-up areas. Public Affairs developed programs to educate high-school and other youths about the effects and consequences of graffiti. Other departments contributed as well.

By May 1989, the trains were graffiti-free. The CCP not only achieved its overall goal, as Table 1 indicates it exceeded its annual goals every year.

Discussion

What is to be said about the success of the Kiley-Gunn administration in eradicating graffiti in the light of past failures and a resultant growing consensus that perhaps train graffiti was just one more element in "the complex of apparently unmanageable problems amidst which New Yorkers live" (Glazer, 1979:11)? Three basic factors appear to be responsible:

- A management philosophy of "meaning it" — graffiti was going to be eradicated on subway trains — and an administration that delineated responsibility clearly, broke the problem into manageable portions, established attainable and challenging goals, and provided the resources necessary to attain those goals.

- A "problem-oriented" (Goldstein, 1979) approach that looked at the nature of the problem and crafted tactics based on understandings gained through such a diagnosis.

- The creation of a management matrix that coordinated and monitored the activities of responsible units, especially the Car Equipment, Rapid Transit Operations, Transit Authority Police, Property Protection, Station, and Track and Structures Departments.

We will briefly examine each one of these factors.

Meaning It

Gunn established early in his administration that graffiti eradication would be a priority. He lodged authority for achieving that goal with the department responsible for car maintenance, the Car Equipment Department. The plan included on-site supervision of cleaning activities and clear subgoals: Each car in the program, if tagged by graffitists, would be cleaned in two hours or removed from service. The program was initiated modestly, with two trains, and expanded as the organization gained unpretentious but real successes — at first protecting those two trains and later expanding the base of clean cars. Removing cars from service — a drastic measure in a transportation service that was plagued with quality-of-service problems at that time — was meant: Cars were removed from service during rush hour at least 10 times during the 5-year life of the program. Authority to remove those cars from service was lodged with the program's leader, the head of the Car Equipment Department. Moreover, internal transfer of resources within the lead department both emphasized the high priority of the effort and the willingness to commit additional resources to problem solution.

Problem Orientation

The CCP redefined the problem of train graffiti as a maintenance rather than a law enforcement or police problem. Reading Glazer's paper, "On Subway Graffiti in New York," from the contemporary perspective, one is impressed by two things. First, the paper is prescient of the current concern about the impact of disorder and incivility on the quality of urban life, citizen fear, and, arguably, the level of crime in cities. One is also impressed by how strongly Glazer and others believed that the solution to the problem of graffiti was to be found in police or other criminal justice agencies. The focus of almost all early efforts was on arrest or deterrence through the action of criminal justice agencies.

The genius of the CCP, apart from its implementation and administration, was that by focusing efforts on immediate removal of graffiti, it attacked graffiti directly at the heart of its motivation: "getting up" — that is, getting one's work up on the sides of trains and having it seen citywide. This drive for recognition was so strong, and the penalties for getting caught so trivial, that it drove an entire subculture.

The CCP simply deprived youths of the satisfaction of having their work seen. Certainly not immediately, but slowly, however, graffitists learned that tagging trains entered into the program was hopeless — the work would be in vain, it would never be seen. In fact, the NYCTA got its first taste of ultimate victory when graffitists who broke into yards in which both program and nonprogram cars were stored, painted on previously marred rather than on clean cars. Moreover, the ante had been raised. Not only would not one's work be seen, but police and other agencies would go to extraordinary lengths to ensure punishment of those who marred newly cleaned or purchased cars. For a while, there were plenty of trains to paint that were unsecured and without police or other protection. But gradually the graffiti-marred stock was reduced.

TABLE 2
ARRESTS FOR GRAFFITI/VANDALISM, 1984-1988

	Felonies	Misdemeanors
1984	237	2681
1985	147	2560
1986	114	1984
1987	87	1063
1988	114	974

The role of the police, formerly the lead agency in the fight against graffiti, changed to one of support and assistance. The previous focus on the number of arrests as an indicator of success in dealing with graffiti was replaced by meeting the yearly goals of clean cars. Interestingly, as the various departments involved in the project worked toward achieving those goals, arrests plummeted (Table 2). When arrests were made, as noted above, they were targeted on particular offenders and offenses (against clean trains) and then processed with vigor.

Coordination

The creation of CAST and its empowerment was an attempt to ensure coordination among the responsible departments. The NYCTA, like almost all large organizations, had been characterized by limited levels of interdepartmental cooperation. In fact, the atmosphere of disorganization, failure, and collapse that had dominated the NYCTA during its neglect worsened the problem. Fingerpointing (it's somebody else's responsibility or fault) and boundary maintenance activities ("tell 'em what we can't do, not what we can") were rife in the organization.

CAST, in contrast, emphasized accountability and coordination of activities. Accountability was obtained by closely linking CAST with Gunn. Rather than push the problem off to some committee for deliberation, Gunn developed a vision of the subway and specific goals, set goals for CAST, met regularly with it or its leaders, and monitored both its long- and short-term wins and losses. Coordination was achieved by regular meetings, working under a strong mandate, linking CAST's activities to achievement of goals, and by noteworthy early successes.

In sum, by thwarting graffitists' delight with "getting up" through an effective maintenance program backed up by police, property protection, and public relations efforts, the NYCTA achieved a spectacular success over a seemingly insoluble problem — train graffiti. In retrospect, the solution now seems relatively obvious and attainable. The fact that train graffiti was so intractable a problem is a powerful example of the consequences that occur when unchallenged conventional thinking about the nature of problems and their solution dominates.

Authors' Postscript

Since this case was first published some have questioned whether the amount of "tagging" really declined or whether graffiti is merely being cleaned more efficiently. As noted above, massive increases in cleaning were required, both routine in the train yards and at the end of each train route during the 5 years of the Clean Car Program. By the end of the third year, however, tagging had declined to the extent that it was no longer necessary to have crews at the end of each line and they were removed. If "tagging" behavior had continued at earlier levels, it would follow that as the program progressed more crews would have been required to clean cars at the end of the lines rather than fewer because many more cars were clean. (In May of 1985 only 1720 cars had been entered into the program. By 1987, when the crews at the end of the line were removed, 4707 cars were clean.) Yet, exactly the opposite was true. As David Gunn noted in a newspaper interview: "The initial battle was that you spent an awful lot of time actually cleaning graffiti. But by the time the trains were all clean, the incidence of new graffiti had dropped to almost nothing" (*New York Times*, March 21, 1996:B1). Obviously, this does not suggest that officials can be any less vigilant. However, the dimensions of the problem, as is apparent to anyone riding the subway currently, are quite different than in the mid-1980s.

Note

1. Gunn is the first NYCTA president in recent history who has forgone his car and driver in preference to using the subway for all personal and professional local transportation.

20. Refund Fraud in Retail Stores

Dennis Challinger

EDITOR'S NOTE: Reference was made in the editor's note to Case Study #8 to the difficulty that can arise in publishing evaluations of business crime prevention — publication may reveal commercially sensitive data. One solution is illustrated by Figures 1 and 2 in this article, first published in Security Journal *(Challinger, 1996), neither of which have values attached to the vertical axis. Instead, the graphs illustrate only the relative magnitude of fraud losses before and after new rules were introduced for the stores concerned about giving refunds to customers. Supplementary information in the text permits the reader to estimate the magnitude of the effect. This satisfies both scientific and commercial requirements in that detailed proof of the effect of the new rules is provided without revealing current losses. It may be no coincidence that the author of the study, a senior security officer for Australia's largest retailer, was once a university teacher. He therefore well understands the needs of both the business and academic worlds.*

ALLOWING CUSTOMERS to return merchandise for a refund is one of the major ways in which retailers increase customer satisfaction. However, it also provides considerable opportunities for the dishonest to take advantage of the retailer by fraudulently claiming such refunds. One commentator describes that practice as involving "unscrupulous people ... (who) take advantage of a company's zeal for customer service" (Dacy, 1994:27).

This paper explores the refund fraud phenomenon in retailing and looks at the way in which Australia's leading retail company, Coles Myer Ltd, has been addressing it. The company has more than 1700 retail outlets and sales of almost $17 billion last financial year. Like many retailers around the world, Coles Myer has been exposed to the activities of refund fraudsters in recent years.

Fraud and Advantage Taking

The commission of fraud is seldom spontaneous. It generally requires some thought and planning, so fraudsters can be confidently described as reasoning criminals who can be seen as exercising "rational choice" in determining where, when and how they will commit their offenses. In turn, that means that situational crime prevention techniques are appropriate to reduce the opportunities for fraud as previous research has shown to be true. For instance, Smith and Burrows (1986) showed that "inexpensive revisions of administrative procedures were able to reduce fraud" in two distinct environments. Such action falls into the category of what Clarke (1992) refers to as "rule setting," an important strand of situational crime prevention that reduces the rewards from offending.

In fact, refund fraud is no different from the variety of other frauds that are perpetrated precisely by people taking advantage of the generosity or loopholes provided by facilities which provide convenient or streamlined facilities to consumers. Typical of these are fraudulent applications for telephone services or provision of utilities where the identity of customers is not verified, or fraudulent insurance claims where detailed documentation relating to stolen goods may not be required.

Such frauds also include the careless provision of credit cards without thorough vetting of applicants, a procedure that has led to a new variation of credit card fraud called true name fraud. It occurs when a fraudster obtains the personal details of a real person and uses them to acquire house brand credit cards in that name which the fraudster then uses to purchase expensive items. It has been suggested that true name fraud arises because "in their frenzy to get consumers to spend more money, retailers will give virtually anybody who applies approval to start buying on credit immediately provided they have what appears to be legitimate identification and their past payment history is okay" (Perry, 1995:38).

This broad generalization is precisely that. Most credit providers not only have in place procedures to ensure that they do not leave themselves vulnerable to true name fraud, but also keep tightening procedures to guard against other frauds involving credit cards. Nevertheless, outside observers such as Perry can continue to be critical mainly because of the success of those seeking to circumvent procedures, for instance, by engaging in true name fraud instead of attempting to use stolen credit cards. Such successes invariably lead to revision of the procedures that allowed the offender an opportunity and sometimes also occasion public criticism.

Public Criticism of the Victim

Public criticism of the refund policies of Australian retailers started to appear early in 1993 when the Chief Magistrate of the State of Western Australia was reported in the business press as "fining people who have stolen goods and then claimed cash refunds, but has refused to order them to give the money back. The magistrate says the refund policy proudly advertised and encouraged people in difficult financial circumstances to steal" (*Business Review Weekly*, February 5, 1993, p.12). That report describes "trouble-free refunds" as a "key sales pitch" which the retailers might find too expensive and, therefore, might have to drop.

In the State of Victoria another Magistrate was similarly critical in January 1993 when he heard the case of a 19-year-old woman who had pleaded guilty to 97 charges of obtaining property by deception, 59 charges of theft, and eight counts of handling stolen goods. She was sentenced to 12 months imprisonment but the Magistrate refused to order that she repay the $7,000 involved to the department store victim. He claimed the store had to "wear the consequences" of its negligence in letting the woman repeatedly get refunds for stolen merchandise. He said the store made it "far too simple for people to go into the store, steal property and ask for a refund ... It doesn't say too much for the system in place in the store ... I think the store needs to learn a lesson as well as the accused" (*Truth*, January 13, 1993, p.11).

Another Magistrate dealt with a 17-year-old girl reported as having obtained $1,282 in cash by visiting a department store and taking goods direct from the shelves to cashiers for refunds on 17 separate occasions. "I am amazed that she could get away with these types of offenses so many times" he said, adding that "department stores made it too easy for people to return goods" (*The Age*, February 6, 1993, p.18).

In a 1993 retail industry publication, police in the State of Victoria criticized a discount department store for promoting cash refunds to customers unable to supply a receipt with goods they returned. A senior police officer claimed that the promotion contravened an agreement between police and major retailers that the latter would insist on seeing receipts before giving cash refunds. He further suggested that retailers not doing so was a key factor in escalating theft from shops and claimed that the customer-friendly policies of some retailers were promoting a culture of dishonesty among young people. (*Inside Retailing*, February 8, 1993, p.7).

A Commercial Decision

It could be suggested that these critical police and judicial officers themselves were, like the majority of customers, happy enough to be able to return goods to stores. They may even have expected that facility to be extended to them. However, the commercial reality is that the provision of any facility to customers has to be seen in a financial context. Thus, only if it can be shown to produce more negative effects than positive, will it be discontinued. In this context negative effects include not only real financial losses, but also loss of sales and public patronage through, for instance, adverse publicity such as that above.

In this case, the above publicity arose precisely because the courts were faced with an increasing number of fraudulent offenders; in turn, those offenders were causing increased losses for the Company. In addition, feedback from the Company's focus groups of customers found that there was actually support for a tightening of the refund policy and no sympathy at all for those who were ripping off the Company. Taken together, these factors enabled a commercial decision to be made to tighten the refund procedures across the country.

Such a decision needs the active co-operation of staff and the experience of the American retailer J.C. Penney provides an interesting illustration of this point. When Penney's introduced a "no questions asked" return policy under which customers received refunds "even if the merchandise was not purchased at the store or was clearly used improperly" (Levy and Weitz, 1992:619), some loyal Penney staff refused to give such refunds. They did so because they saw some customers taking advantage of the company by cashing in goods they had not bought. However, they apparently followed the new policy when the commercial reality was explained to them; that is, the policy generated more sales than the losses due to customer abuse of it.

Despite that, it is hard not to see staff morale declining if the staff can still see that what they are asked to do will directly cause losses for their employer. This is particularly important because low staff morale is known to be related to a store's overall shrink or losses (Hollinger and Dabney, 1994). However, the level of losses is what is crucial here, and the assumption that those losses can be accurately measured is by no means certain.

The Extent of Losses from Refund Fraud

The effects of refund fraud are effectively hidden in the financial records compiled by retailers. There is no single place in a store's accounts where retail fraud losses appear, although depending on the accounting systems used, such losses may insidiously reduce sales figures (since they constitute negative sales), or cause increased expenses, both of which impact upon gross margins and profit.

The difficulty in providing a clear measure of the problem explains why it is generally not included in research on retailers' losses such as the British Retail Consortium's Cost of Crime Survey or the University of Florida's annual National Retail Security Survey, even though detected cases indicate that losses through refund fraud are considerable. The virtual invisibility of these losses also helps explain why some retailers appear to remain unconcerned about refund fraud as a major source of loss and in the only published study of refund fraud, Bickerton and Hodge (1992) note that "most retailers believe that refund fraud has historically been under-reported."

Those authors report an American study that revealed annual refund fraud losses of $472 million from 11 million separate fraudulent returns for a sample of 17 retail companies with stores having sales of $233 billion and some 5 billion transactions annually. That study also cites American retailer Dayton Hudson reporting in 1992 that their refunds without receipts amounted to 36% of the total number of refunds, and that 9% of them were conservatively estimated to be fraudulent, leading to losses at that time of close on $4 million.

The level of refund fraud activity is indicated by the number of fraudulent refund incidents that are actually detected in the stores. There is a direct parallel here with statistics related to detected customer thieves (or shoplifters). In neither case are the detected incidents any more than indicators of the actual activity and pretty poor indicators at that. For instance, the value of goods discovered in the possession of customer thieves detected in a year is often around 1% of the annual unexplained losses or shrinkage.

Another important comparison of these two offense types is provided by the average loss for each. Within the company, the average value of goods stolen by customer thieves in 1993/94 was less than a third of the average loss from a detected refund fraud. In the 1994/95 year that ratio was closer to a fifth. The main reason for detected refund fraud cases involving larger sums of money is that they are often only identified after multiple offending. The consequences of that offending is that losses are considerable. Not untypical is the 19-year-old woman with no prior criminal history who pleaded guilty to 132 counts of theft from department stores, 115 of obtaining property by deception and six of possessing an article to steal (a plastic shopping bag in which stolen goods were presented at the counter for refund), having caused the company losses of $11,700.

A further way to gain an indication of the extent of the problem is to measure the proportion of all refunds sought that are fraudulent. As noted above, Dayton Hudson's estimate of its refunds that are fraudulent is substantial. Over 20 years ago, when refund fraud was arguably far less of an issue than it is today, Zabriskie (1972) undertook a small study of 134 complaints taken to a customer service department in an American store. He found that ten of them could be described as provable fraud, six as suspected fraud, and 14 reflected unrealistic expectations about the product being returned. In turn, the ten provable frauds involved only two that he called criminal, the other eight being called "household cheating," (which is discussed below). Conversely, it is plain, and should not be forgotten, that the vast majority of requests for refunds in retail stores are quite legitimate and a source of no aggravation.

All these indicators suggest that refund fraud is a considerable problem for retailers, but possibly the most convincing reflection of the gravity of the problem is demonstrated by the increase in sales that is recorded in retail companies after they have succeeded in reducing the activity in their stores, of which more will be discussed later.

Types of Offenders

It is useful to consider the more common types of refund fraudsters before considering the strategies to prevent the offense. The following crude typology of refund fraudsters is necessarily based on the characteristics of those people who have been detected making fraudulent refunds, as is the case with most criminological typologies of offenders.

Professional shop thieves are those who steal goods from shops and then return them for cash refund at any obliging store. From their point of view, their financial returns were far greater from this practice — realizing 100% of the value of the stolen goods — than through their previous practice of getting 20 or 30% of the goods' value from a receiver (a fence) or a customer in a pub or bar. These thieves have not actually changed their past stealing behavior but are simply using the laxity of some refund procedures to increase their revenue flow from their stealing — a good example of the reasoning criminal in action.

The prevalence of this practice is supported by business consultants Ernst and Young who in the USA in 1993 found that "a growing number of shoplifters are taking advantage of liberal return policies to elicit refunds for stolen merchandise" (Dacy, 1994:27). And the shift from shop thief to fraudster is not a giant step for some, as reflected in a study reporting similarities in the psychodynamics of women who steal from shops and women who commit fraud (Women Who Shoplift, 1986). However, that study is based on only a small group of offenders who were referred for some sort of psychiatric assessment, so by definition they could all expect to be described as suffering some form of neurosis or character disorder, though not generally an acute psychiatric disorder.

In no way does this mean that refund fraudsters are different from the normal population. Their very ordinariness allows them to ply their trade in a concerted way as indicated by Western Australian Police who reported uncovering 114 teams involved in the "no-receipt refund" racket in Perth stores in the 12 months up to April 1993.

Staff thieves who engage in processing fraudulent refunds for their own benefit are also taking advantage of a different opportunity to steal. They may retain a receipt from a previous sale and later process a refund with it, or depending on the in-store procedure may be able to process a false refund even without a receipt. Mostly, they take cash for the refund although it is possible to credit their own or another's credit card. The latter might be offered as a service to third parties for a lesser cash payment to the staff member outside the store.

Drug-related offenders are offenders who are active in order to finance their drug habits. Some admit to having been functionally displaced from their previous money-raising activities of armed robberies or house burglaries owing to increased security in those areas. Others have simply learned of the opportunities provided by generous refund procedures.

Check fraudsters are those who regularly pass stolen or forged checks to "buy" goods from stores. Like the professional thief they can improve their revenue by then refunding those goods for full price instead of taking what they can get from receivers.

Opportunistic fraudsters buy goods at sale prices or at cheaper prices in some other store, and obtain full refunds for them at a later time. Bickerton and Hodge (1992) relate the example of a retired American who relied upon this practice to supplement his retirement income.

Manipulative thieves are amateur or occasional offenders who wish to acquire goods that are too well protected to steal directly. They, therefore, steal other more accessible goods and obtain refunds for them. They also are happy with gift or credit vouchers and exchange those vouchers for the goods they actually wanted.

Temporary thieves actually buy some product, use it, and then subsequently claim a refund for it. In his 1972 work, Zabriskie refers to these sorts of activities as "household cheating" although he is somewhat generous in his use of that description. He included the traditional instance of young women buying ball gowns, and returning them after the ball with "makeup, perspiration and lipstick stains" on them. This practice known as "wardrobing" would appear to be common. Cole (1989) reports two random surveys of shoppers reporting 22% and 24% participation in the activity.

Zabriskie also included as household cheating the man who bought five sports coats of the same colour and pattern, but different sizes, for members of a band. Four days later he returned them for refund because they didn't fit (anybody!). "By chance a man from the store's security department was a photography fan and had taken a picture at a trade show with the men using the jackets in one of the exhibit booths" (Zabriskie, 1972:26). It was the day after the trade show that the refund was sought, however, on seeing the photograph, the exhibitor company involved apologized and paid for the coats. By today's standards that event would certainly be seen as constituting a fraudulent offense.

Some Australian retailers have responded to that sort of activity by adopting no-refund policies and displaying signs to this effect. However, those are actually illegal actions as there are circumstances in which the law requires refunds be made. Specifically, retailers cannot deny refunds: where the purchased goods were unsuitable for the purpose for which they were bought and this purpose had been made known to the retailer; where the goods are defective; where goods differed from the sample goods that were shown to the customer; or where the customer has described to the retailer what it is they wanted, but when received by the customer the goods do not conform to that description.

Responses

The above typology indicates the sorts of ways in which offenders are able to take advantage of retailers' refund procedures. It, therefore, also allows the development of changes to the procedures that will reduce opportunities for frauds. In the last two years retailers around the world have been tightening their procedures to do just that and these are reflected in the cash refunds policy developed by the Retailers Council of Australia in May 1993, for the guidance of their members. It comprises the following requirements:

1. Inform customers that proof of purchase is required for later refund (by signage or warning printed on register docket).

2. Require presentation of proof of purchase when refund requested.

3. If no proof of purchase is provided when refund is requested — (a) proof of identity must be seen; (b) the customer should provide a signed statement in their own handwriting detailing their identity, address, and details of the purchase; (c) a cash refund should not exceed a specified value set by the retailer and greater amounts should be paid by check; and (d) if the purchase had been made with a check, a refund should not be processed until the check is cleared.

This policy plainly constitutes "rule setting" in the situational crime prevention context as it categorically sets requirements which, if faithfully followed, remove some of the opportunities for offenders. After consideration of its own commercial considerations, the Company promulgated its own refund policy to be implemented in all stores from 1 March 1994. It was not as extensive as the above; for instance, it says nothing of payment by check or maximum value of cash refunds, but it does set clear rules. It reads:

> Coles Myer is committed to excellence in retailing. Customer satisfaction is an integral part of that commitment. In the event that a customer is not entirely satisfied with goods purchased from any Company business those goods will be cheerfully exchanged or a credit voucher provided. A customer who produces a valid receipt and does not wish to accept an exchange or credit voucher may be provided with a refund. Where the original purchase was made in cash, a cash refund may be given. Cash refunds will not be given for credit card sales.

It will be observed that the requirements of the policy addressed all the offender types described above but without introducing any burdensome requirement for legitimate refunders. Indeed the policy actually streamlined the refund procedures for the legitimate customer as proof of purchase led to a less complicated refund procedure than before. In that way, customer satisfaction was actually increased.

Notwithstanding that the commercial realities of retailing require flexibility and commonsense, there are obviously occasions when rigid application of the policy is inappropriate. For instance, a known regular customer who happens not to have proof of purchase would not be refused a refund from a salesperson who remembers the purchase the day before. So it is necessary for store management to have and to exercise some flexibility with the policy, especially insofar as it relates to cash refunds.

Impact of the New Policy

When viewed as a crime prevention initiative to reduce the opportunities for fraudulent refunders, the policy would be successful if detected fraudulent refunds did decrease in number and value after its introduction.

To assess this, data were collected from the Company's 500 supermarkets, 391 discount stores, and 70 department stores as they were the types of stores in which refund frauds had been most problematic. Those data are presented in Figures 1 and 2 and clearly show a marked reduction in fraudulent refund activity after the introduction of the policy. Specifically, the number of fraudulent refunds for all these stores fell from an indexed base of 100 to 17, and the dollar value of all those refunds dropped from an indexed base of 100 to 37. The actual quantum of the fraudulent refunds and their values are not able to be specified as they are commercially sensitive data. What can be said is that in the peak months around 600 fraudsters were detected and associated monthly losses ran to six figure sums. The relatively low statistics for supermarkets reflects the fact that only some of them sell apparel and general merchandise products which are those more likely to be the subject of fraudulent refund claims.

Apart from showing reductions in fraudulent refund activity following the crime prevention initiative, the figures also show that some such activity continues. But the data

FIGURE 1
NUMBER OF DETECTED REFUND FRAUDS 1993-1995
(3 MONTH MOVING AVERAGES)

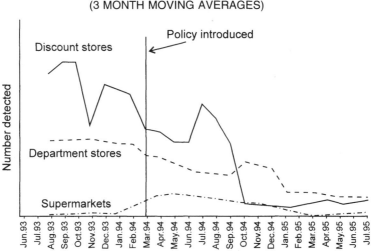

cannot show whether those continuing offenses are committed by new offenders or by previous offenders who may have changed their methods of offending to counter the new procedural requirements of the policy. This latter adaptation by offenders, often called tactical displacement, was to be expected as refund fraud had become a lucrative activity for many offenders, and as Clarke points out "where the stakes are high, criminals are likely to test the limits of the new defences, and in due course may succeed in identifying vulnerabilities" (Clarke, 1992:33).

Adaptations Following the Policy

The ways that refund fraudsters have adapted to beat the new policy have been, and continue being, identified and addressed. They are summarized below in the context of the elements of the policy.

The requirement for *proof of purchase* is fundamental to the success of the policy and has been widely publicized to customers. It has also produced a variety of activities by offenders. One frequent practice is what is referred to as double-docketing, described by one American retail loss prevention director as when "shoplifters will come into a store, pick up two of the same items, and buy only one of them. Then they will come back with the receipt and return the stolen item for cash. We end up buying back stolen merchandise" (Dacy, 1994:27).

The more common practice in Australia is for the offender to buy an item, then re-enter the store, steal another of the same item, and present it with the quite legitimate receipt for a cash refund, although if the offender had been seen stealing the second item they could, of course, be charged with theft. If the original receipt is returned unmarked to the offender, they can then also get a cash refund on the first item, and they can then continue stealing and returning items, usually to different company stores until the receipt is retained, marked or defaced in some fashion by one of the stores.

At its simplest, offenders can simply collect legitimate receipts left in shopping

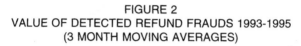

FIGURE 2
VALUE OF DETECTED REFUND FRAUDS 1993-1995
(3 MONTH MOVING AVERAGES)

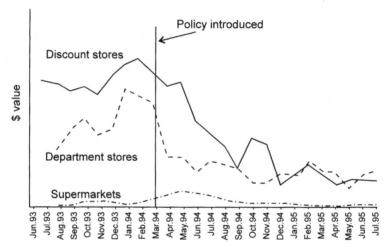

trolleys or dropped outside the store, return to the store and steal the item described on the receipt, and claim a cash refund. Some offenders deliberately deface receipts they may have obtained by using a bad check so that it is not clear whether a cash sale and, therefore, a cash refund is involved, but there has also been more direct forgery of receipts.

To date those forgeries have not reached the extraordinary proportions of the professional offender described by Berlin (1993) as active through Canada, New York, and Massachusetts in 1993. That offender was alleged to travel around and send details of local store names and product information (stock codes, prices, and other information) to an unknown location via overnight mail. He would then receive forged printed cash and/or charge receipts back via express mail at designated locations the next day, steal the described goods at the specified stores, and use the forged receipts to obtain cash refunds or credit to a credit card in one of five different names. It is unlikely that the unknown supplier of these detailed forged receipts was supplying only this one detected offender, suggesting that this operation may have generated considerable losses for retailers.

Giving a *cash refund* only if the refunder can prove that cash was originally paid for the goods is the crucial part of the crime prevention thrust of reducing the rewards for the offense. However, some offenders have discovered that they can sometimes effect a refund without a receipt and have the refund credited to a credit card which they claim was used to make the original purchase. They then contact the credit card provider pointing out their card is in credit, requesting and receiving a reimbursement.

The company's preference is for refund applicants to accept gift or exchange *vouchers* in preference to cash. This is a most unattractive proposition for a fraudster, as it means that without proof of purchase they would only get vouchers not the cash that is their real aim. In some stores, customers are provided with green exchange vouchers if they have a cash receipt for the merchandise they have returned, and a red voucher if they do not. The green voucher can be used as cash in the store, the red can only be used to purchase goods and if those goods cost less than the red voucher's value, they will not be given cash as change but are given a lower value red voucher. This has led to some legitimate customers in the stores being offered red vouchers at a discount, presumably by thwarted refund fraudsters.

The greater problem has been the emergence of a secondary market in ordinary gift vouchers which are sold at a discounted price in other locations like pubs and bars to customers who are openly solicited in the stores, and to some pawnbrokers or cash converters. The policy has thus reduced the rate of return for offenders. On the other hand, the increased use of such vouchers in the stores does open the way for the successful use of forged vouchers which are less likely to draw attention than previously, when they were used sparingly.

An associated issue that has come to light is the tendency for some staff to fail to view gift vouchers as equivalent to cash. In practice, some staff appear quite ready to happily give vouchers to a person seeking a refund with no receipt, where they would never consider passing them cash of the same value. This is sometimes especially so if the person's demeanor is aggressive.

Customer satisfaction is the major thrust of the company's refund policy — a fact of which refund fraudsters are well aware. They also know that store managers have some discretion with the policy and are very concerned about the ambiance of their stores. Accordingly, some fraudsters are often unashamedly loud and aggressive, hoping to harass store staff into giving them a cash refund when they have no proof of purchase. There is some indication that the tactic works more often than it should, although it is easy to be critical from afar. The reality is that some of these offenders can be extraordinarily aggressive and disruptive, and if sales to legitimate customers are lost because they go elsewhere to avoid the unpleasant environment, then the commercial value of a hard line can be negative.

It should not be thought that the offender necessarily enjoys creating a scene in a store. Indeed, offenders are likely to avoid returning to a store where it has been a hassle. The greater problem is that if a professional refund fraudster finds a weak manager who will quickly cave in to them, they will visit that store often. That such managers exist is supported by the existence of two Company discount stores geographically close to each other with roughly the same refund rates before the introduction of the policy, but one of which now has a greatly increased rate, while the other's rate has similarly decreased. Local knowledge is that the manager at one of those stores is an easy touch.

Tightening up Further

The adaptations outlined in the previous section indicate that further action is necessary to counter the determined offender who has worked out ways around the policy. There is nothing novel about this; the continuing battle between credit card fraudsters and credit providers is another illustration of offenders adapting their activities to continue gaining rewards from their offending. Smith and Burrows (1986:21) put it well. They say that given "the intractable nature of crime, and the scope that exists to exploit opportunities for crime in even the tightest administrative arrangements, it would of course be foolhardy to assume that reductions can be maintained without constant review."

Precisely because retailers are aware of the above adaptations, various responses have been taken around the world to push refund fraudsters out of stores. They include the following.

An on-line *refund authorization program* is a particularly powerful tool. It effectively tracks all sales, can verify them as genuine, and note any refunds claimed against them. Such a program exists in the Target chain of stores in America, where each sales transaction is given a unique identifier, the purpose of which is "to deter the use of duplicated or counterfeit receipts that can be used by shop thieves to obtain cash refunds" (Robins, 1994: 48). However, the program has further merit as it can supply valuable information on product returns for company buyers and it streamlines the refund process for the legitimate customer.

A *refunders' database* highlights frequent refunders to allow legitimate customers to be fast-tracked but also causes suspect refunders to be identified. At present, the Company is using only negative refunders' databases, which could be said to be incomplete as they depend upon somebody deciding that a particular refund is suspect and should, therefore, be entered onto the database. Nevertheless, the databases do provide valuable information, not only for other stores through bulletins identifying possible and proven fraudsters, but also for use by police in interviewing suspects concerning their documented unusual refunding patterns.

A typical example of a suspect fraudster identified through the refunders' database is the woman who in an 8-week period early in 1995 visited three different Company discount stores close to her home, on ten different occasions seeking no-receipt refunds for computer games and toys. This professional refund fraudster succeeded in getting $2,849 in cash refund for those goods. Accompanying those details, which were given to police, were details from the stores' merchandise records which showed that no copies of the particular computer games she was returning had actually been sold in any of the three stores in the period in question. (It was later discovered the goods were actually stolen from her husband's small retail business!)

There are a number of *in-store changes* that would make life harder for fraudulent refunders, and hopefully drive them away. They include: changes to store layout to ensure that the point at which refunds are processed does not allow easy access to stock on the selling floor; introducing gift refund cards that can be provided to purchasers of gifts instead of receipts and allow the recipients of those gifts to effect a no-receipt exchange without delay; and upgrading receipts to make their forgery very difficult, perhaps by including some form of electronic branding like an infra-red trace.

An in-store change that specifically targets the previously mentioned "wardrobing" is the use of special labels which are prominently placed on garments sold in the store. Printed on these labels is a message thanking the customer for shopping in the store, and explaining that a refund is only available if the garment is returned with the label intact. The label of course cannot be removed in one piece and the garment would not be worn with it intact.

Staff adherence to policy is a particularly powerful weapon against the fraudulent refunder (and the computer game refund case cited above would not have reached the proportions it did if staff vigilance had been greater). As noted earlier, such refunders look for stores where they have a greater chance of getting a refund and will return to those which provide them with a service. If all stores were resolute in their use of the policy, even allowing for discretion to be used, then only the most brazen fraudster would continue.

It has been argued that staff adherence could be improved if refunds were somehow linked to staff compensation. This occurs at Nordstrom, the American retailer, where sales staff are paid by commission on sales that they make. It means that they have a personal "stake in making every sale the final sale" as any merchandise that is returned for refund brings a loss of income for the original salesperson (Levy and Weitz, 1992:651). This lack of staff application could in part be explained by the general difficulty in *getting fraudulent refunds taken seriously* in the community. If those who commit the offense, those who are the victims of it, those who should enforce the law against it, and those who should punish it, all see it as minor, then it will be difficult to get rid of it.

But do those groups think that way? Strutton *et al.* (1995) suggest "the consequences of being found out for unethically returning a product are probably perceived to be less serious than the consequences of being caught stealing an item." So a fraudulent refunder might feel that the consequences of being charged with obtaining a financial advantage or property by deception will not be viewed by others — store staff, police, and even the courts — as seriously as theft from stores, which is an offense more readily recognized as wrong but still not itself seen as particularly bad.

This is a fine state of affairs for the fraudulent refunder who sees that the risks involved in the offense are low precisely because the offense itself is not seen as serious. It is, therefore, important that store staff in the first instance are made well aware that fraudulent refunds are a major source of loss for retailers and must be handled courteously but rigorously.

The Value of Tackling Refund Fraud

The dynamic nature of retailing makes it difficult to state unequivocally that the introduction of a stricter policy is responsible for positive changes in a store's financial performance. Changes in selling strategies, store display, product range, consumer sentiment, and merchandising methods occur all the time and their effects too cannot be easily isolated. Nevertheless, the American retail company Dayton Hudson Corporation, which through its Target stores has to be seen as the world's leader in tackling refund fraud, has no doubts about the contribution of their approach. As indicated above, they have in place a sophisticated refund authorization program which they claim has produced an increase in sales of two percentage points for them (Gantenbein and Rogers, 1995). That is a remarkable result and even if only half of that increase resulted from preventing refund fraud, it emphasizes that the offense does in fact cost retailers dearly.

A further success of Target's crime prevention approach to refund fraud is a diffusion of benefits in that there has been "a reduction in crimes not directly addressed by the preventive measure" (Clarke, 1992:25). In particular, theft of stock has decreased apparently because there were a number of offenders who were stealing from stores simply so they could then effect a fraudulent refund. With the refund option cut off, theft became pointless (or insufficiently rewarding) for them.

From a retailer's point of view, there are further positive results from clamping down on refund fraud. The Company's statistics show that since the policy was introduced there has been a considerable drop in the value of soiled and damaged stock that is written off or marked down. That would appear to result from customers no longer bringing back damaged goods for refund as they could when the refund practice was so open.

These are considerable and positive results of the crime prevention approach to refund fraud. And the approach itself indicates how far retailers have moved from their suggested stance 20 years ago when Zabriskie extraordinarily wrote: "famous retailers have been known to say that it is the privilege of a good customer to take advantage of the store a couple of times a year" (Zabriskie, 1972:22).

Good customers today do not view fraud as a privilege but they do expect professional service and a satisfying shopping experience. In that sort of environment they are happy to assist retailers reduce their losses. This is evidenced by the way that customers have readily adopted the practice of retaining their receipts until the possibility of a refund has passed. By doing that, they have assisted in reducing refund fraud by making it more difficult, and helped prevent many offenses from occurring.

21. Preventing Drunkenness and Violence around Nightclubs in a Tourist Resort

Ross Homel, Marg Hauritz, Gillian McIlwain, Richard Wortley and Russell Carvolth

EDITOR'S NOTE: In the days when opportunity reduction meant target hardening and access control, a distinction was commonly made between these "physical" prevention measures and "social" prevention measures designed to reduce criminal and delinquent dispositions. "Physical" has been replaced by "situational" in recognition of the fact that many opportunity-reducing measures achieve their ends by manipulating not just the physical but also the social and psychological setting for crime. However, the contrast continues to be made with "social" prevention (e.g. O'Malley and Sutton, 1997), with the erroneous implication that situational measures are in some ways unsocial. These points have been noted by Homel (1997), who directed the present case study, a shortened version of one published in Crime Prevention Studies *(Homel et al., 1997). Indeed, the points are exemplified by the study, which shows that a substantial reduction was achieved in violence and drunkenness around nightclubs in Surfers Paradise, a large tourist resort in Queensland, by modifying management practices and by eliminating numerous risky features of the immediate social and physical environments. The study also illustrates how intensely political can be the introduction of situational measures. By chance, I happened to be present when the Surfers Paradise licensees met with those from the Westend Forum, a similar consortium of licensees in Melbourne who had implemented changes to reduce the likelihood of violence associated with their establishments. I can attest to the powerful effect of the Melbourne contingent's arguments about the compatibility of responsibility and profitability in persuading the licensees of Surfers Paradise to follow their example.*

THIS PAPER reports the manner of implementation and results of a community-based intervention designed to reduce alcohol-related crime, violence, and disorder in and around licensed premises in a major tourist location. The project, carried out between March and December 1993, involved a partnership of a university research team, police, health, and other government agencies, and community and business groups, and was extremely successful in the short-term in reducing violence and other offenses. The absence of a formal control group and the difficulties involved in measuring displacement prevent precise quantification of the causal impact of the intervention. However, the project was less successful in the long-term, for reasons that are reasonably well understood but are difficult to control. The paper therefore reflects on the lessons arising from the project for effective long-term regulation of licensed premises.

Paradise Lost: the Context and the Problem

Surfers Paradise, located at the center of the Gold Coast region of southern Queensland, is an international tourist resort not dissimilar to Miami in style and climate. Given the large and diverse population of more than a quarter of a million permanent residents and millions of visitors each year, a sophisticated hospitality industry is required to provide the entertainment and leisure services that can satisfy both formal government regulations and the informal standards sought by the community.

While a vibrant entertainment industry brings considerable economic benefits, it can also create major problems, especially when entertainment is equated with alcohol consumption and licensed venues are concentrated in a small area. The physical transformation of Surfers Paradise in the 1960s and 1970s from a quiet seaside town to an area of high-rise apartment blocks and international hotels was accompanied by an explosive growth in the number of bars, nightclubs, restaurants, and registered clubs. There are approximately 187 licensed premises in the immediate area, and by late 1992 there were 22 nightclubs (not counting a number of cafes and restaurants) in the small central business district (CBD), within a few hundred meters of each other.

The incidence of violence and disorder in Surfers Paradise had become a matter of major community concern by the time of the present study and a security company was employed by the Chamber of Commerce with instructions to patrol the CBD and help keep the peace, especially at the times when hundreds of drunken revelers emerged from the nightclubs in the early hours of the morning. Two years previously, agitation from residents and from the Gold Coast City Council had resulted in the construction by the State Government of a police booth in the CBD, helping to give police a public presence and facilitating occasional "sweeps" of the area to crack down on drunkenness and disorder. Despite these initiatives, many retailers had fled Surfers creating vacant commercial accommodation, there was an obvious decline in business profitability, and the media were increasingly referring to the area using terms like "Slurpers Paradise" and "Surfers Sleaze."

Practices adopted by the nightclubs did nothing to improve Surfers' image. Encouraged by a political environment that rejected "paternalistic" regulation and embraced a "free enterprise liquor system" to promote tourism (*Queensland Legislative Assembly Hansard*, May 7, 1992, p. 5178), licensees engaged in extensive price discounting, extending to free drinks for several hours on some nights and free cocktails all night for women. The reputation of Surfers for cheap booze, sex, and drugs helped to ensure a large turnover of patrons but less certain profits for the nightclubs. Indeed, many were in financial difficulties, with managers blaming a quiescent Liquor Licensing Division, which was operating under a new Liquor Act that transformed proactive "inspectors" into reactive "investigators," for allowing too many licenses in a very small area and for not cracking down on "cowboy operators."

A clear finding of previous research is that inappropriate drinks promotions that encourage mass intoxication are a major risk factor for violence, although subtle interactions involving several factors, including groups of young males, crowding, lack of comfort, aggressive bar staff and security personnel, and inept methods for dealing with drunken patrons, are also of critical importance (Graham *et al.*, 1980; Homel *et al.*, 1992). All these factors were present in abundance in Surfers Paradise, and so it is not surprising that surveys conducted between March and June 1993 involving 701 residents of surrounding areas and 81 business people working in the immediate neighborhood revealed that a large number of people had had some experience with violence. Nearly three quarters (71.0%) of these groups considered that it was unsafe to be on the streets of Surfers Paradise at night, and 72.6% agreed that there were too many intoxicated people in Surfers Paradise at night. The groundswell of community and business concern, combined with the constant media attention, ensured that the proposal for a broadly based community response to the problem was warmly received.

Community Action Directed at Licensed Venues

A common way of attempting to minimize alcohol-related harm in licensed premises is through responsible beverage service programs (Carvolth, 1991; Saltz, 1987; Wagenaar and Holder, 1991), and it would therefore seem desirable to incorporate their principles into any community intervention that has licensed venues as a target. In addition, there is an emerging literature, that suggests that community regulation of alcohol-related disorder and violence must utilize other strategies as well, including safety audits of the immediate area (where teams of observers walk around, especially at night, identifying and recording unsafe features of the physical environment) and the introduction of procedures that empower residents to resolve problems with licensed establishments (Alcohol Advisory Council of Western Australia, 1989; Gilling, 1993; Lakeland and Durham, 1993; Parkdale Focus Community, 1995). These additional strategies are of particular importance in Australia, partly because civil law suits are very seldom used against licensees, thus removing one of the major incentives for licensees to introduce server training programs, and partly because liquor licensing laws are not very effectively enforced on a routine basis (Homel and Clark, 1994; Stockwell, 1994).

Perhaps as a response to the vacuum created by an inadequate regime of legal regulation, action projects targeting licensed premises have proliferated in recent years in Australia. One of the most important, the Melbourne Westend Forum (Melbourne City Council, 1991), arose from a recommendation of the Victorian Community Council Against Violence, that was funded through the Ministry for Police. No quantitative evaluation was carried out, so it is not possible to determine the impact of the project, although qualitative evidence suggests a substantial short-term effect. Despite the lack of formal evidence of long-term effectiveness, the Westend Forum is important for the vigor with which it was implemented and for the level of inter-agency cooperation and community involvement achieved.

Other "safety action projects" that have emerged recently in Australia include the Eastside Sydney Project (Lander, 1995) the "Geelong Accord" in Victoria (Felson *et al.*, In press), the "Freo Respects You" project in Fremantle, Western Australia (Stockwell *et al.*, 1993), and several in South Australia (Fisher, 1993; Walsh, 1993). Specialists are also emerging in the staging of major events such as New Year's Eve, so that they are promoted as positive celebrations rather than as dysfunctional events characterized by high levels of disorder and violence (The Magnificent Events Company, 1996). Significantly, the methods developed by these specialists rely explicitly on situational crime prevention concepts as well as on theories of ritual and community (Dunstan and McDonald, 1996).

From the literature, features that characterize successful community interventions include: strong directive leadership during the establishment period; the mobilization of community groups concerned about violence and disorder; the implementation of a multi-agency approach involving licensees, local government, police, health and other groups; the use of safety audits to engage the local community and identify risks; a focus on the way licensed venues are managed (particularly those that cater to large numbers of young people); the "re-education" of patrons concerning their role as consumers of "quality hospitality;" and attention to situational factors, including serving practices, that promote intoxication and violent confrontations. Attempts were made to learn from these lessons in the design and implementation of the Surfers Paradise Safety Action Project.

Project Design

The major aims of the project were to reduce alcohol-related violence and disorder in and around Cavill Mall, the major nightclub and entertainment area in the CBD, and as a result to improve the image of Surfers as a tourist destination and to reduce fear of crime victimization by patrons, residents, tourists, and local businesses. The senior author (Homel) obtained federal funds in late 1992 for a demonstration project in Surfers Paradise, with funding to be directed through the Gold Coast City Council. Major stakeholders were the Council, the Queensland Health Department (who had as a major policy objective the reduction of alcohol-related violence), and the university research team (as designers and evaluators).

The project design was based on three major strategies:

- The creation of a *Community Forum*, and the consequent development of community-based *Task Groups* and the implementation of a safety audit;

- The development and implementation of *risk assessments* and *Model House Policies* in licensed premises by the Project Officer and the Queensland Health Department, and the consequent development and implementation of a *Code of Practice* by nightclub managers;

- Improvements in the *external regulation* of licensed premises by police and liquor licensing inspectors, with a particular emphasis on preventive rather than reactive strategies and a focus on the prevention of assaults by bouncers, and compliance with provisions of the Liquor Act prohibiting the serving of intoxicated persons.

Evaluation Design

The project commenced in March 1993 and concluded, for evaluation purposes, in December 1993. Year 1 (1992) was the Pre-Implementation Year. It was conceived as a baseline year when no community activity to reduce alcohol-related violence was undertaken, other than reactive policing of venues and immediate environs. Year 2 (1993), the Implementation Year, consisted of three periods:

Period 1:   January - March 1993 .... Pre-Project
Period 2:   April - July 1993 .... Development of Code of Practice
Period 3:   August - December 1993 .... Code of Practice operational

The design was based on a comparison of baseline or pre-implementation measures of violence and other problems with the same measures taken after the project had been operating for nine months (April to December 1993). Multiple databases were used, including community surveys, interviews with licensees, direct observation of premises, incidents recorded by security companies, and official police records.

When the project was planned, considerable thought was given to the possibility of a control area or areas. Propinquity ruled out other areas on the Gold Coast, but coastal resorts to the north remained as possibilities. However, the realities of funding were such that in the end the idea of even one control area had to be abandoned.

Given the unique place of Surfers Paradise as a national and international tourist destination it is doubtful that a true "control" could in fact have been found. In addition, there is the more general problem that in any "N = 1" community study the concept of a control area is problematic. How can one establish comparability, and how are differences in outcome measures between single "experimental" and "control" areas to be interpreted? In our view, it is more appropriate in an evaluation of an intervention in one community to base inferences about the causal impact of the project on "internal linkages," on variations over time in "input" and "output" variables, and on experience with replications in other communities (replications are currently being conducted in three cities in Queensland).

With respect to "internal linkages," previous research (Homel and Clark, 1994) has shown that, amongst other factors, levels of intoxication and the way intoxication is managed are strong predictors of aggression and violence in licensed premises. If it can be shown not only that aggression and violence declined after the project, but that levels of intoxication declined and that methods of handling the problem in nightclubs improved, then there are good grounds for concluding that the project may well have been at least partially responsible for the observed reductions in aggression. This is particularly the case if the project can be demonstrated to have influenced in a positive way the management of licensed premises.

Monitoring variations over time in a community, particularly if a "treatment" is introduced and then withdrawn, is analogous to experimentation with a single subject using something like an ABA design. In the case of Surfers Paradise, baseline levels of violence and many other factors were established, the intervention was carried out, further measures were taken, and then, as we shall see, critical elements of the intervention started to decay. The decay was reflected in a third set of measures, that showed a return to pre-project management practices and an increase in violence. Although unfortunate for the community, this pattern increases one's confidence that the project itself, and not some unknown exogenous factors, caused the initial decline in violence.

Implementation

An initial meeting convened by the Surfers Paradise Civic Committee was held in January 1993, inviting those members of the community who wished to express their concerns about issues related to violence and safety in their area. A Steering Committee, composed of representatives of the City Council, Queensland Health, Police, Liquor Licensing Division, Gold Coast Tourism, Griffith University and the Chamber of Commerce, was elected and made responsible for directing the jointly proposed community project.

The Steering Committee elected a Project Officer (McIlwain) whose responsibilities were to:

- provide coordination of all elements of the project;

- facilitate development of the Community Forum;

- liaise with Liquor Licensing investigators and the Police Service to develop programs of awareness, surveillance and compliance with the Liquor Act;

- incorporate the use of the Risk Assessment Policy Checklist in assessing how responsibly licensees manage their venues, and work cooperatively with them to develop responsible hospitality practices; and

- coordinate any training required from Patron Care (a Health Department host responsibility training program) or other sources.

COMMUNITY FORUM

Drawing on the results of the resident survey described previously, a major Community Forum was conducted on May 14th, 1993. Its main purpose was to offer the people of Surfers Paradise the opportunity to take ownership of, and responsibility for their own problems. Of paramount importance was that this Forum had to conclude with outlined strategies for *problem resolution*, rather than conclude with yet another agreement on the extent of the problem.

From this Community Forum, four Task Groups were formed, concerned with safety of public spaces, security and policing, community monitoring and venue management.

SAFETY OF PUBLIC SPACES TASK GROUP

The purpose of this task group was to examine the physical environment within public spaces, and examine the role each environmental factor played either individually or interactively in preventing Surfers Paradise being a safe recreational area for a broad cross section of people. This examination was undertaken using a Safety Audit of the CBD area of Surfers Paradise. Surfers is a 24-hour town and for this reason the audit was conducted over that entire time in two-hour blocks by eleven teams of people. Auditors were drawn from the community through extensive advertising and television coverage. No particular age group was targeted and a broad cross-section of residents and non-resident workers responded. Auditors were each able to choose the area and time most suitable and with an allocated leader set off with a questionnaire for guidance, a cue sheet, flashlights, pens and paper.

Innovative testing strategies, such as walking onto the unlit beach of Surfers Paradise at night and screaming to see if anyone on the nearest footpath could hear, and children trying to reach telephones in the event of emergency calls, evolved as the auditors progressed through the week. The emphasis was on the subjective feelings and perceptions of participants. At the completion of each team's audit an hour was spent collating the results, putting them in order of priority, and recommending solutions. Final results were grouped into areas related to the Gold Coast City Council, private organizations, and the police.

SECURITY AND POLICING TASK GROUP

The Security and Policing Task Group was concerned with the "around licensed premises" aspect of the problem of violence and disorder. This task group, whose members were drawn mainly from the police, security firms, and managers of nearby shopping and office complexes, aimed to provide a forum for exchange of ideas and information between police, the commercial sector of Surfers Paradise, security personnel, and representatives of public transport bodies. The group utilized its resources to:

- Implement and monitor the concept of Neighborhood Watch in the commercial sector of the Surfers Paradise CBD.

- Pilot an appropriately recognized registration and training program for security personnel, giving consideration to the Queensland Security Providers Act which at that time had been proposed but not enacted.

- Ensure, through coordination with all licensees and the commercial sector, that only trained security personnel were employed in the Surfers Paradise CBD.

- Implement a trial program of shuttle bus services to ensure safe transport for patrons out of the nightclub area (and to reduce the incidence of drinking and driving).

Probably the most important achievements of the group were in the areas of training and in improved relationships between police and security personnel. The Project Officer chaired meetings of the task group that resulted in agreement that the streets of Surfers be jointly patrolled by police and by police-approved security firms. Separate meetings restricted to security personnel helped to create a sense of group identity and contributed to a process whereby they negotiated a degree of "professional legitimacy" with police and the business community. These protracted, and at times heated, meetings led to the adoption in September 1993 of full crowd control and security training for all bouncers. This was quickly followed by security management training for licensees and some police. The training, provided by a professional security training organization, included ethics and good practice, management skills, staff recruitment, conflict resolution, venue security, civil and criminal law related to the operation of public venues, licensing law, the (proposed) Security Providers Bill, major incidents and emergencies, and incident reporting (Advanced Techniques, 1994; McIlwain, 1994).

The major problem unresolved by the task group concerned strategies for policing Cavill Mall and the venues themselves. Local police were committed to "Operation Cleanout," which involved periodic sweeps of the streets in the early hours of the morning to arrest drunken or disorderly patrons. The attention of police was drawn to the success of strategies in England that involved friendly visits with venue managers by uniformed police at random times. This strategy, in contrast to Operation Cleanout, focused on compliance by managers with the Liquor Act, rather than on patron peccadilloes, and relied on general deterrence through a visible but unpredictable police presence rather than on arrests (Jeffs and Saunders, 1983). Although the police agreed in principle with the proposal, in practice little preventive policing along the lines suggested appears to have taken place during the implementation period.

COMMUNITY MONITORING TASK GROUP

The primary aim of this task group was to develop a positive image of Surfers Paradise and to disseminate information about the achievements of the Safety Action Project. However, the workload entailed in the other task groups meant that this group soon ceased to function, and the role of media liaison devolved to the Project Officer. Fortunately, the perceived success of the project from its earliest stages meant that the media beat a path to her door, and many newspaper and television reports about the "new-look Surfers" appeared. The positive media coverage gave project participants a great boost, and was a key factor in generating great commitment and enthusiasm — critical elements in community action projects.

VENUE MANAGEMENT TASK GROUP

The Venue Management Task Group consisted of the Project Officer and representatives of the Police Service, the Liquor Licensing Division, and licensees. Its aims were to develop ways of delivering alcohol in a responsible manner, and to establish positive working relationships between the Surfers Paradise Licensees, the Surfers Paradise Police, and the Queensland Liquor Licensing Division. A further aim was to encourage the involvement of licensees in decision-making which affected the regulation of their liquor licenses.

The regulation of liquor licenses has always been a particularly difficult issue for the licensees. Like liquor acts in other states, the Queensland Liquor Act 1992 is a powerful piece of legislation, yet the policy of the Queensland Liquor Licensing Division to abandon a "paternalistic" role, to de-regulate, and to allow the market to find its own level of operation, had undermined the licensees' confidence in the Division's regulatory powers. The Division is also hampered by limited resources; it has about 14 investigators to cover an area larger than Western Europe. Almost all licensees knew they were able to "get away" with irresponsible practices and had done so for quite some time in order to survive competition during an economic recession. The role of the project was to engender in the licensees an acceptance of responsibility for the control of their own behavior within a community context, regardless of the extent of external enforcement.

The shift from alcohol to entertainment was achieved in part through the administration of the Risk Assessment Policy Checklist and through the Model House Policies developed from them. The risk assessments offered licensees the opportunity to focus on those areas of their businesses that could be optimized for profit and where the standards of serving practices could be raised.

The risk assessments were conducted by the Project Officer in April 1993 with the manager, one bar staff employee, and one security employee from each of eight licensed venues. The assessments were repeated in November. The instrument was adapted from work of Stockwell *et al.* (1993), and involved separate structured interviews with management and staff, as well as observations of the venue layout, signage, promotions and other

TABLE 1
ITEMS COMPRISING THE RISK ASSESSMENT POLICY CHECKLIST

Item	Description
Discounting	Happy hours and other binge drinking incentives vs. Discounting low or non-alcohol drinks, snacks and so on.
Pricing	Differential pricing on low vs. Standard alcohol beer.
Information for staff	House policies: From verbal instruction to admit/serve underage and intoxicated patrons, through to written responsible policies.
Information for customers	Signage: From promotions for binge drinking, through to responsible promotions and legal requirements.
Under age policies	Instructions regarding admitting and serving under age persons.
Low and non-alcohol	Availability of a range of low or non-alcohol drinks.
Intoxication	Drunkenness. Instructions regarding entry and serving.
Food	Times and range of snacks/meals available.
Entertainment	Promoting all-male, heavy drinking crowd, through to varied and attracting mixed clientele, responsible atmosphere.
Transport policies	Nature and extent of the transport strategy.
Serve size	Degree of restriction on size of glasses, on jugs and on drink strength.
Staff drink	Policy on staff drinking at the venue, during and outside their rostered hours.
Problem patron	Strategy for dealing with problem drinking customer.
Community relations	Extent of involvement, perceived involvement and likelihood of support from community and stakeholder groups.
Personnel	Preferred staff style, recruitment, communication, management and support.
Security	Preferred security style, recruitment and training.

operational features of the venue (Carvolth, 1993; 1995). Inter-rater reliability (94%) of the 16 items was established through concurrent ratings taken across three reviews by an independent rater. A brief description of the 5-point items comprising the checklist is given in Table 1.

Customized reports from the risk assessments led to the development of individual Model House Policies for each licensee. However, although individual reports and House Policies were prepared, the issues that arose from the risk assessments were dealt with in a *group* setting (the task group). The most pervasive factor in the irresponsible practices of Surfers Paradise licensees was competition, and to have introduced further suggestions as to how each club could "better" itself and increase its profit over others would only have fueled and perpetuated that competitive environment. Individual suggestions regarding changes to premises or practices were verbally fed back in informal meetings with licensees. In essence the individual Model House Policies became the property of the licensees as a group.

To complement the strategies of risk assessments, Model House Policies, and democratic problem solving, ongoing training was provided in the areas of responsible hospitality practices, management of personnel, care of patrons, crowd control techniques, and harm minimization principles. The negotiation in a group setting of the outcomes of the risk assessments and the discussion and resolution of the agreed problems of running licensed venues, together with the training, provided the framework and the impetus for the formulation of a Code of Practice. This process was further boosted by the visit in July 1993 of a group of nightclub managers from Melbourne who had been heavily involved in the Westend Forum. Those licensees had extensive experience with self-regulation in a competitive environment and were able to convey the message, in a credible fashion, that responsibility and profitability are compatible. By August 2nd, 1993, all but one licensee had put into place Codes of Practice which were prominently displayed.

MONITORING COMMITTEE

Compliance with the Code of Practice was overseen by a Monitoring Committee, chaired by the Project Officer, with members drawn from the Australian Hotels Association, the nightclub licensees, the Health Department, the Chamber of Commerce, the Gold Coast City Council, representatives of local five-star hotels, the Restaurant and Caterers Association, and the Gold Coast Tourism Bureau.

Non-compliance by any licensee was immediately brought to the attention of the Chairperson of the Monitoring Committee. Examples of incidents referred to the committee included free drinks, the advertising of "specials" on alcohol, and overcrowding. Within days of notification, the Monitoring Committee would meet and the issue opened for discussion with the licensee involved present. The purpose of this discussion was to produce a workable solution which would reduce the likelihood of the event recurring. It was also clearly understood that should the problem not be addressed by the licensee, the Monitoring Committee would be required to brief police and Liquor Licensing on the problem (who were not represented on the Committee).

Notwithstanding the success of the committee, it became clear during the implementation year that although the informal community control that it exercised was an essential feature of a system of self-regulation, formal action by police and/or Liquor Licensing investigators would be required on some occasions. Although the Monitoring Committee could greatly enhance the role of these official agencies if they chose to act, in retrospect it is apparent that a satisfactory model of cooperation at local and headquarters levels between the committee, police, and Liquor Licensing that could be sustained over time and would keep violence at low levels had not been developed.

Results: Paradise Regained

RISK ASSESSMENTS

In order to complete the Risk Assessment Policy Checklist interviews were conducted with the manager, one bar staff employee, and one security employee in each of eight venues at the beginning of the implementation period (April 1993) and following the introduction of the Code of Practice in November 1993. In Table 2, a positive score indicates responsible practices, and a negative score irresponsible practices (the theoretical minima and maxima are -2 and +2).

There were significant changes on all but two items (Staff Drinking and Personnel). Because the risk assessments were not conducted under operational conditions, it is not

TABLE 2
MEAN SCORES ACROSS EIGHT VENUES ON THE
RISK ASSESSMENT POLICY CHECKLIST

Risk assessment items	April 1993	November 1993	p [a]
Discounting	-1.9	+1.5	.018
Pricing	-1.8	-0.9	.018
Information for staff	-0.3	+1.6	.043
Information for customers	+0.1	+1.9	.018
Under age policies	+0.6	+1.6	.028
Non or low alcohol	-0.5	+0.8	.043
Intoxication	-1.1	+1.4	.012
Food	0.0	+1.6	.043
Entertainment	-0.4	+1.1	.018
Transport policies	-1.9	+0.6	.018
Serve size	+0.3	+1.8	.043
Staff drinking	+0.1	0.0	.317
Problem patron	+0.1	+1.6	.028
Community relations	-0.3	+0.1	.018
Personnel	+0.8	+1.8	.094
Security	-0.4	+1.6	.018
Total	-6.6	+18.1	

[a] Wilcoxon Signed-Rank Test

possible to assess from these results whether policy was fully implemented. For this, direct observation is required.

VENUE OBSERVATIONS

Activities in 16 nightclubs in the central area of Surfers Paradise were observed by teams of students during January and February 1993 (before the project) and January and February 1994 (after the main features of the project had been implemented).

A structured, systematic observation technique was employed, based on an observation schedule of some 20 pages consisting of hundreds of items. These items covered details of the physical and social environments, patron characteristics, bar staff and security staff, drinking patterns, serving practices and aggression and violence. The schedule was almost identical with the instrument developed in Sydney by Homel and his students (Homel and Clark, 1994).

A group of 22 university students acted as patron-observers within the selected venues. About half of the students observed in both years but were sent to different venues in 1994. Students observed in mixed sex groups of three or four to ensure their safety when leaving in the early hours of the morning. Several training sessions were conducted to ensure that students were thoroughly familiar with the aims of the project and the observation schedule. It was emphasized during training that observers were there for scientific purposes, and that although they should act as normal patrons, their job was not to have a good time but to observe as comprehensively and as accurately as possible. A limit of one alcoholic drink per hour was imposed for each observer. Observers' responses to items in the observation schedule were calibrated for consistency within and across groups. Each observer completed the survey form in isolation as soon as possible after the visit, and then at a subsequent meeting, inconsistencies between observers were checked and agreement established.

All observation sessions were of about two hours duration and were unobtrusive. Fifty-six visits were conducted in January 1993 and 43 in January 1994. Thus there were 99 visits in all, a total of about 200 hours of observation. The same clubs were visited in each year. All visits were on Thursday, Friday or Saturday nights, and the days of visits were comparable in the two years. Times of visits were also comparable, except that in 1994 there was a slight unintended bias toward pre-midnight starts.

Differences in observer ratings in the two years were tested for statistical significance. Not unexpectedly, relatively few aspects of the physical environment of venues changed. Lighting, seating capacity, seating styles, appearance, decor, and ventilation remained more or less constant. What did improve was cleanliness, bar access, and the availability of public transport, consistent with the activities of the Venue Management Task Group.

A major response of venue managers was to employ many more private security officers. Interestingly, this coincided with a marked decline in a visible police presence. The effect of training was also apparent in the greater friendliness of bouncers, the more rigorous enforcement of age identification checks at the door, and a reduced level of non-directed patrolling or aimless "roaming about" by bouncers.

Many changes were apparent in the social environment. Bar crowding reduced, consistent with the observation that bar access was easier, although overall crowding levels appeared to remain the same. The musical style moved from thrash, heavy metal or acid to more "mainstream" genres, with greater use of Top 40 hits and popular "classics." Patrons seemed to be friendlier and more relaxed, with less blatant sexual activity and competition and less hostility, rowdiness, and swearing. The only negative change appeared to be that the women were less cheerful! Apart from this, the extent to which patrons appeared to be entertained did not change. Significantly, food was available in the great majority of visits in 1994.

Perhaps the greatest changes occurred in the appearance of patrons. Dressing up, particularly in business suits, was far more common in 1994 than 1993. This could mean that an entirely new type of patron was attracted to more "upmarket" venues, or that the same patrons responded to the project initiatives by improving their dress standards. Discussions with venue managers lead us to conclude, tentatively, that both processes occurred simultaneously. That is, some patrons, such as those observed in 1993 in manual working gear or those seeking to "pick up" a sexual partner, moved to other venues, while others kept coming but altered their dress and behavior. The age and gender profile did not alter, nor did the size or gender composition of groups.

The appearance of bar staff and the way they related to patrons did not alter, except that there were apparently no Pacific Islander staff during the second round of visits. This may reflect a deliberate strategy of management, given the reputation of Islanders for violence

(Homel and Clark, 1994). There was, however, a dramatic decline in male drinking rates and male drunkenness, with more consumption of low-alcohol beer and less obvious round shouting (i.e., the obligation to share in drinking as a group activity, with each person taking turns to buy a round of drinks for all). Rates of heavy male drinking (more than four standard drinks per hour) dropped by 76.0%, and responsible host practices, such as publicity to patrons and fewer drinks promotions, were strongly in evidence in 1994, presumably reflecting implementation of the Code of Practice.

Significantly, cover charges and prices of drinks did not appear to change, consistent with licensee and press reports that business was very good in the summer of 1994 (McIlwain, 1994). Since the overall numbers of patrons appeared to be as high or higher in 1994 as in the same period in 1993, it is possible to conclude, tentatively, that at least in the initial post-implementation period the project achieved the objective of maintaining or improving profitability.

Corresponding to all these changes, levels of observed aggression and violence declined markedly in 1994. Aggressive and violent incidents occurred disproportionately in a small number of venues, with as many as four assaults being observed within one venue in a 1993 visit. Total incidents (physical and non-physical) dropped from a mean of .63 per visit in 1993 to .18 per visit in 1994, while non-physical incidents dropped from .43 to .09. The drop for physical assaults was from .20 per visit (11 incidents) to .09 (4 incidents), but this decline was not statistically significant given the small numbers of incidents. Expressed as a rate per 100 hours of observation, physical assaults declined by 52.0%, from a rate of 9.8 to 4.7. The 1993 figure was close to the rate observed by Homel and Clark (1994) in some of the worst establishments in Sydney. Verbal abuse declined by 81.6%, from 12.5 to 2.3 per 100 hours, and arguments by 67.6%, from 7.1 to 2.3 per 100 hours.

SECURITY DATA

The security companies contracted by the business community provided security personnel five nights per week (Wednesday to Sunday: 9 p.m. to 5 a.m.). Written reports of incidents were supplied. The most common types of incidents encountered were drunk and disorderly behavior, urinating in public places, minor assaults, and general brawling. These incidents were observed mainly in streets around only a few of the venues, especially where hot-dog stands were located.

TABLE 3
INCIDENTS RECORDED BY SECURITY COMPANIES FOR 1992 AND 1993

Period	Incidents	
	1992	1993
1. Jan-Mar	235	192
2. Apr-July	215	115
3. Aug-Nov	141	50

Data for 1990 and 1991 were sparse and not considered reliable. In addition, data for December 1993 could not be included as the security company only collected data for the first week. Consequently, the data available for comparison are for the periods January - November 1992 and January - November 1993. These periods have been divided, for analytical purposes, into the three time periods described in the project design: pre-project

(January - March), development of the Code of Practice (April - July), and post-Code of Practice (August - November).

It can be seen from Table 3 that there was a decline in recorded incidents in each of the time periods between 1992 and 1993. The decline in Period 1 was 18.3% but increased to 46.5% for Period 2 and 64.5% for Period 3 (all changes were statistically significant). This suggests that although there was a downward trend in incidents recorded by security staff before the project began, the project may have contributed to an acceleration of the trend.

POLICE DATA

Police occurrence sheets at Surfers Paradise CBD for the period 1 January 1992 to 31 December 1993 were coded and analyzed. These sheets relate to events not offenders, so one brawl involving five people was listed as one occurrence. Incidents (occurrences) were used as the unit of analysis regardless of whether an arrest took place, and were grouped into the offense categories listed in Table 4.

The same logic and time periods were used as in the analysis of security data. In this case there was not the problem of incomplete December data, so the last period represents

TABLE 4
POLICE RECORDED INCIDENTS BY OFFENSE CATEGORY
FOR 1992 AND 1993

Period	Assault		Indecent Act		Stealing	
	1992	1993	1992	1993	1992	1993
1. Jan-Mar	12	32	4	27	6	19
2. Apr-Jul	22	24	12	8	29	34
3. Aug-Dec	50	33	30	16	37	17
Period	Disturbances		Drunkenness		All Others	
	1992	1993	1992	1993	1992	1993
1. Jan-Mar	36	71	149	243	17	42
2. Apr-Jul	28	92	181	188	85	112
3. Aug-Dec	66	94	258	146	21	40

data for August to December inclusive for both years. Interpretation of the police data was problematic because of mass arrests arising from Operation Cleanout. An attempt was made to omit all incidents resulting from an Operation Cleanout sweep, but this was only partially successful.

Table 4 shows occurrences broken down by offense categories. For assault there was a significant increase in 1993 for Period 1 (chi-square = 9.09, 1 d.f., p=.003), and no significant difference for Periods 2 and 3. However, the decline for Period 3 was very close to statistical significance, with a chi-square of 3.48 (p = .062). The actual decline in assaults in Period 3 was 34% which in real terms is quite substantial, especially in comparison with the 167% increase in Period 1 (before the project began). This pattern of an increase in Period 1 in 1993 compared with the same period in 1992, a static pattern in Period 2, and a substantial decline in Period 3 characterized all the offense categories analyzed except for street disturbances, which were largely generated by Operation Cleanout.

If serious assaults are separated from less serious assaults, there was a statistically significant decline for Period 3. Serious assaults occurring in Period 1 were 0 in 1992 and 2 in 1993; 1 in Period 2 in both years; but 10 in Period 3 in 1992 and 2 in the same period in 1993. The numbers in Periods 1 and 2 are too small for statistical analysis, but the decline in Period 3 is statistically significant, with a chi-square of 5.30 (p=.021).

Overall, results of the analysis of police data are consistent with the other findings of the study. The number of recorded incidents was higher across the board at the beginning of 1993 than for the same period in 1992, but the gap between 1992 and 1993 began to narrow after the appointment of the Project Officer. After the introduction of the Code of Practice, there was an overall drop in occurrences, including stealing and indecent acts. The outcome for stealing may reflect the fact that there were fewer drunks on the streets to victimize, while the result for indecent acts may have been caused partly by the improvements in standards of entertainment. Perhaps most significantly, given that reducing rates of intoxication was one of the main aims of the project, there was a large drop in the number of incidents of drunk and disorderly behavior after the introduction of the Code of Practice.

Of central importance to the evaluation, the decline in Period 3 in the number of assaults was 34%, which was marginally statistically significant. The decline in serious assaults, although the numbers involved are very small, was significant for Period 3.

DISPLACEMENT

The evidence from the four data sets, taken together, strongly supports the contention that there was a real reduction in violence, crime, and disorder in the Surfers Paradise CBD, especially after the Code of Practice was introduced. A key question, however, is the extent of displacement to neighboring areas.

Evidence from the venue observations suggests that to some extent a new, better dressed and better behaved group of patrons was attracted to the "new look" nightclubs. On the other hand, licensees observed that many of the old patrons were still around, but were better behaved. In addition, there are indications from the observational data that "marginal patrons" increased in number (i.e., people who looked "down and out"), so the hypothesis of a complete transformation to an up-market clientele is not fully supported.

Further research will involve detailed analyses of police data to assess the extent of displacement to adjoining areas.

Recent Trends: Paradise Lost Again?

The intensive intervention ceased in December 1993 as the Project Officer eased herself out of the many roles that she had assumed during the implementation period. As indicated earlier, it was intended that maintenance of change in licensed venues become process dependent rather than person dependent, with the Monitoring Committee playing a crucial role in maintaining compliance with the Code of Practice.

In order to assess the effectiveness of the processes put in place for the ongoing maintenance period, a third wave of observational data was collected during January and February 1996 (two years after the second wave of data collection). Forty-eight visits were made to 17 venues in the Surfers CBD, using exactly the same procedures as previously. Most students involved in the data collection had not been involved in the earlier studies. Data on aggression and violence are summarized in Table 5.

TABLE 5
VENUE OBSERVATIONS: RATES OF AGGRESSION AND VIOLENCE PER 100
HOURS OBSERVATIONS, 1993, 1994 AND 1996

Type of aggression	1993 (n=56)	1994 (n=34)	1996 (n=48)
Verbal abuse	12.50	2.33	9.34
Arguments	7.15	2.33	13.54
Challenges/Threats	1.79	0.00	9.38
Physical assaults	9.82	4.65	8.34

It is apparent that all forms of aggression had increased between 1994 and 1996, with the 1996 assault rate being comparable with, although not quite as high as, the pre-project rate. Arguments, challenges, and threats appeared to be at record levels. These data are consistent with the statistics on male drunkenness and hostility, which also show a return to the levels of early 1993. As noted earlier, these depressing results do at least strengthen confidence that the initial decline in violence was directly caused by the Code of Practice and other aspects of the intervention.

When presented with these figures at a meeting in mid-1996, several licensees agreed that the figures reflected reality. They argued that adherence to the Code of Practice was now an economic liability since so many licensees were flaunting its provisions in order to secure short-term profits. The licensees we spoke to were unanimous that the Liquor Licensing Division had still failed to discipline the errant operators, although they also pointed to an increased drug problem associated particularly with "rave parties." On the positive side, however, our observation is that the community itself is in a much better position to respond to the problem of increased drunkenness and violence than was the case in 1992 (Blazevic, 1996).

Towards a Permanent Solution

At one level the Surfers Paradise Safety Action Project succeeded, at least for a period, because it changed a number of situational factors like intoxicated patrons and aggressive bouncers. The real question is how to carry out these changes in a community setting where people are intent on drinking and making merry and where licensees want to make money. A number of lessons can be learned from the Surfers project in this respect.

One important lesson is that the community sought the change, and a strong sense of militancy could be channeled for creative action. In particular, everyone was aware that businesses were losing money because of the area's poor reputation, and there is nothing quite as effective as a shared economic incentive to promote cooperative action for change!

A second lesson is that licensees need to be empowered and motivated as primary decision-makers in the process of change. Historically in Australia they have not been accountable to the community and have not, in fact, been seen generally as responsible business people who typically would be members of the local Chamber of Commerce. Yet when the Gold Coast licensees were persuaded that responsible hospitality practices could be economically viable, and they were provided with a framework for change, they quickly demonstrated that they had known all along what the problems were and how they could be fixed.

A third lesson is that the media can be used as a positive force for change. Initially parts of the local press portrayed the moves to responsible hospitality practices as bad news for patrons, which naturally provoked a negative reaction toward licensees. However, when the goals of the project were explained to the journalists, and the beneficial results started to become apparent, this negative portrayal was reversed.

A fourth, somewhat unexpected, conclusion from the project was that the gender of the Project Officer was a crucial factor in gaining licensees' confidence and commitment. The reality in Australia is that the majority of licensees are male and the "drinking culture" is driven by male values and standards, with an emphasis on control and dominance within drinking environments. Practices that encourage excessive drinking and aberrant behavior are encouraged and often seen as a rite of passage for young men entering adulthood. In this context, it seems that the female Project Officer was not perceived as posing a challenge or a threat to the male licensees, and was less likely than a man to encounter resistance when attempting to persuade them to adopt more responsible alcohol policies.

A final, perhaps most important lesson from the Surfers Project, is that a community-based Monitoring Committee is essential to underpin the attempts at self-regulation by licensees, especially when some irresponsible practices (such as heavy price discounting) are not actually illegal. The licensees must have a forum in which non-compliance with the Code of Practice can be addressed and dealt with. *This forum should not include representatives of the formal agencies of control if it is to retain the trust, confidence, and cooperation of the licensees, but the formal control agencies — especially the liquor licensing authority - must be willing to act against errant operators, based on information provided, when they breach a regulation and fail to heed the directives of the community forum.* Nothing will undermine self-regulation more quickly and more effectively than the sight of "cowboys" who exploit their industry peers with impunity. On the other hand, if licensees can see that others are "playing the game," they will be prepared to make considerable efforts, and even financial sacrifices, to comply with the Code of Practice.

IMPLEMENTATION FOR SUSTAINABLE CHANGE

Our conclusions with respect to the role and composition of the Monitoring Committee are relevant not only to the question of how to achieve an initial reduction in violence in and around licensed venues, but also to the question of how a reduction in violence can be sustained. The experience in Surfers Paradise during the maintenance phase (post-1993) is instructive.

Due to funding exigencies, an unsworn police officer became project co-ordinator for the first 18 months of the maintenance period. Although not apparent at first, it became obvious some months into the maintenance phase that the licensees were complying, if at all, because of the pressure of the law. Their working relationships with police remained positive, but with an unsworn police officer as the project co-ordinator they felt there was no arena in which informal arrangements could safely be made. The Monitoring Committee, which had previously struck a crucial balance between formal and informal regulation, lost its neutrality by inviting police and licensing inspectors to become members. As a result the licensees may have become reluctant to discuss inappropriate practices for fear of retribution. This is not a criticism of the relationship that police attempted to build with the licensees, but simply an observation that it was clearly too early in the project to expect two groups that had traditionally been in conflict to be comfortable working together in an informal regulatory environment.

These difficulties were compounded by a perceived unwillingness of the Liquor Licensing Division to act on breaches by licensees of the Liquor Act. Although police generally maintained their vigilance with licensed premises, their attempts to enforce the Act were, as the licensees saw it, constantly being undermined by the Liquor Licensing Division's lack of support. For their part, licensing investigators complained that the evidence that the police collected would not stand up in court. Whatever the truth of the matter, the licensees' perception appears to have contributed directly to the breakdown in compliance with the Code of Practice.

The problems encountered in getting the Monitoring Committee "right" underline the importance of strong project management. In principle, the Steering Committee should take a leadership role in ensuring that conflicts between agencies are resolved and that appropriate structures are put in place. In practice, of course, members are engaged in a process of rapid learning, particularly in the early stages of a project, and the Committee typically does not have the expertise, cohesion, or political muscle required to understand and act on these kinds of difficulties. Nevertheless, our conclusion from the Surfers project is that these qualities can be developed within a few months with input from the Project Officer, and that the Steering Committee can play a pivotal role. Indeed, our perception is that a cohesive Steering Committee, regularly briefed on project developments, is essential for the long-term success of a community intervention in two crucial respects: *managing the transition between stages of the project, and political advocacy for the community change process.*

It appears that the actual sequencing of events is imperative in the implementation of various strategies. If licensees are not able to engage in the process of problem identification from their perspective at an early stage of the project, they are very difficult to "recapture" later in the project. Equally important is the timing of problem identification and the development of solutions.

Of further interest is the patterning that became apparent at a deeper level throughout the different phases of the Surfers project. During the Implementation Year, when most of the key stakeholders are focusing on their positions within the project, and each task group is establishing its boundaries and terms of reference, much is being achieved. With strategies being implemented at a fairly hectic pace, and with change occurring regularly, community action projects are dynamic: hopes are raised, licensees enjoy their increased status in the community, and generally, as the project nears the end of the Implementation Phase, there is an increase in business confidence.

It is at this key transition point, and also at later points of transition, that the Steering Committee must be aware of the need to move the project from dependency on personnel, such as the Project Officer, to dependency on a process. A certain loss of momentum is probably inevitable at these times and should not be taken as a sign of failure, provided the key decisions are made to move the project to the next stage.

Part of the business of "moving the project on" is political advocacy. It is the responsibility of the Steering Committee to lobby politically for formalization of the processes of the project into government legislation or policy (for example, through amendments to the Liquor Act), or into the routine procedures of government agencies. The initial role of the Steering Committee is to be a high profile support to the Project Officer, but eventually it must become the vehicle for the "normalizing" of the processes of community change.

The Future of Safety Action Projects

In a recent paper, Lang and Rumbold (1996) argue that the Melbourne Westend project and the Surfers Paradise Safety Action project have both failed, and that a new approach is required, emphasizing the changing of cultural attitudes to alcohol and violence through community involvement and public education. They maintain that alcohol-related violence cannot be prevented by simple opportunity reduction strategies and enforcement measures alone, methods that they see as the basis of the Melbourne and Surfers projects.

One purpose of this paper has been to describe in detail the complexities of the processes of community change, and to demonstrate that there is nothing "simple" about the implementation of effective opportunity reduction strategies or regulatory procedures. However, can one describe as anything other than a failure a project that has Table 5 as an outcome, with its depressing V-shape for the rates of violence?

In response to this challenge, several points can be made. First, and most obviously, few community projects anywhere in the world have succeeded in demonstrating any reduction in violence or other forms of alcohol-related harm, even for a short period.

Secondly, the fact that the project - and other similar projects elsewhere - came into being in the first place indicates the failure of traditional modes of regulation. The decline in effectiveness during the maintenance period simply underlines the continuing failure of the formal regulatory mechanisms, and demonstrates the inability of the responsible agencies, operating within a political environment of deregulation, to adopt new, more effective approaches even when a virtual blueprint for implementation is provided. In a real sense it was not the project that failed but a political process that falsely pits strong state regulation against deregulation, without recognizing that public and private orderings are interdependent and that some kind of symbiosis between them is inevitable (Ayres and Braithwaite, 1992).

Thirdly, it needs to be recalled that community projects are dynamic and pass through many phases, but that the lessons learned in earlier phases are seldom completely forgotten. Success, even if tasted briefly, is a heady brew that generates its own impetus for further change.

Safety action projects will, in our judgment, survive and thrive because they do, at heart, seek to empower groups and individuals that have hitherto been largely ignored in the formulation of laws and policies concerning licensed venues. They facilitate the development of what Ayres and Braithwaite (1992) call tripartism - the empowering of citizen associations -- thereby promoting cooperation and self-regulation, while helping to avoid harmful forms of regulatory capture. Safety action projects also fit nicely into "Safe City" strategies being developed at the local government level in some places throughout the world (Wekerle and Whitzman, 1995), and indeed have already begun to evolve into more general urban crime prevention programs in several cities in Queensland. The combination of a problem-specific situational focus and a dynamic, community-based framework for change guarantees, in our view, that safety action projects will make an important contribution to the prevention of alcohol-related crime in the years ahead.

ACKNOWLEDGMENTS.The research reported in this chapter was funded by a National Education Grant under the National Campaign Against Drug Abuse (now the National Drug Strategy), administered by the Commonwealth Department of Health, Housing, and Community Services; and by the Criminology Research Council. We should like to acknowledge the assistance of Dick Roebuck with project management, and Jeff Clark and Michael Townsley with data collection and analysis, as well as numerous Griffith University students who acted as patron-observers. The assistance of the Gold Coast City Council, Old Department of Health, Old Police Service, Surfers Paradise Chamber of Commerce, and the Old Liquor Licensing Division is also gratefully acknowledged.

Editor's Postscript

The Surfers Paradise Safety Action Project was replicated in 1995/96 in three cities in North Queensland: Cairns (population 204,000), Townsville (population 125,000), and Mackay (population 72,000). Based on 164 hours of venue observations in 1994 and 230 hours in 1996, there was a 75% drop in assaults and a 49% drop in all forms of verbal aggression within the venues of the three cities (Hauritz et al., In press). The evidence is that the intervention model is robust and will produce positive results in diverse communities, although not all components that were considered important in the Surfers project (such as the establishment of an independent community monitoring committee to oversee self-regulation) emerged as essential in all replication sites.

22. Security by Design on the Washington Metro

Nancy G. La Vigne

EDITOR'S NOTE: Any business or public facility catering to large numbers of the public — airports, department stores, leisure complexes, transit systems — must make deliberate use of mangement and design to minimize the risks of their clients becoming offenders or victims. Sometimes the measures adopted can be intrusive and irksome. In other cases, exemplified by Disney World in case study #23, they can be unobjectionable or largely unnoticed. When incorporated at the design stage these measures can be difficult to evaluate as before-and-after comparisons of crime rates cannot be made. This was the situation confronting Nancy La Vigne in this case study, first published in Crime Prevention Studies *(La Vigne, 1996a), when she set out to evaluate the effectiveness of the crime prevention measures incorporated in the design of the Washington Metro. By using a variety of research methods and data, however, she succeeds in demonstrating that the Metro's crime rates are lower than those of other subway systems and also lower than above-ground crime rates in the city. That situational measures can help to make riding the subway a tranquil experience in one of the nation's most crime-ridden cities, provides powerful evidence that they can work even in unpromising settings. This lesson has not been lost on the designers of new subway systems in other parts of the world (cf. Lopez, 1996; Myhre and Rosso, 1996).*

SINCE IT BEGAN operating in 1976, "Metro," Washington, DC's subway system, has been recognized as one of the safest, relatively "crime free" subway systems in the world. Metro officials explain the success of the system as stemming from a combination of three factors: (1) architectural design, which employed crime prevention principles; (2) vigilant maintenance policies; and (3) stringent enforcement of rules and laws. While Metro authorities did not intentionally apply a specific theory or group of theories to the philosophy behind Metro's design and the way in which it is managed and maintained, the philosophy employed is nonetheless compatible with situational crime prevention (Clarke, 1992) and the earlier Crime Prevention Through Environmental Design (CPTED) model (Jeffery, 1977). In addition, because crime prevention techniques were built into Metro's original design, Metro presents an example of a comprehensive design that avoids the pitfalls of measures that are implemented after a crime problem has already presented itself to officials. These characteristics make Metro an excellent setting for which to test the comprehensive application of crime prevention principles in a "built-in" design. Thus, this paper poses two research questions: (1) Is Metro safer than one would expect, given the incidence and prevalence of crime on other subway systems and crime occurring in communities that Metro serves? and (2) Is Metro's unusually low crime rate explained by its environment[1]—the way the system is designed, managed, and maintained?

Demonstrating that Metro's environment explains its unusually low crime rates, or even demonstrating that Metro's crime rates are unusually low, is not an easy task. Metro's design is highly uniform from station to station, a characteristic of the system that Metro's architects deliberately planned to ensure that riders could recognize and use the system with ease, wherever their travels took them. The only differences among stations that do exist— such as whether the station is elevated, the length of the escalators, and whether the station connects two or more lines—are characteristics that are either unavoidable due to construction restrictions, or necessary to serve the needs of Metro's ridership. Likewise, the maintenance of Metro's stations is stringent throughout: graffiti and litter are removed within hours; lights are replaced promptly; and structures damaged by vandalism or wear and tear are removed or repaired immediately.

Metro's uniformity in design and maintenance, while exemplary, nonetheless makes it difficult to test the impact that design might have on crime within Metro, as the lack of variation in design and maintenance variables would yield little in the way of statistically significant results. Because Metro's design has remained uniform from its inception in 1976, and because there was no subway system in place before that time, this topic does not lend itself to an interrupted time series design, as there is no appropriate "before" or "after." Nor are other traditional forms of quasi-experimental designs suitable for this study; due to the vast differences between subway systems, the use of a "control" subway system is inappropriate. Given these design limitations, this study requires a series of tests that build upon one another.

The results of no single test within this study can prove or disprove a causal relationship between Metro's environment and crime, and it should be noted that the claim to have "proven" a causal relationship in the social sciences is a highly suspect achievement, no matter how rigorous the research design. The argument for this research design is that, in combination, these tests will make a strong case that a relationship between Metro's environment and crime does or does not exist.

Methodology

The first step was to determine whether there is good reason to think that Metro's characteristics would prevent crime. If this cannot be established, there is little use in proceeding with the remaining analyses, as we would be unable to tie crime rates to prevention in any meaningful way. Further, Metro's success (if indeed it is demonstrated) could hardly be explained by preventive characteristics that do not exist. Thus, the first test is to review the history behind Metro's design and assess Metro's environment to determine the extent to which it embodies characteristics of crime prevention that theory suggests would be successful.

Given that Metro's environment scores high on preventive characteristics, this paper moves to the question of whether Metro's crime rates are unusually low. This question is explored by comparing Metro's crime rates to those of three comparable subway systems through an ANOVA and a series of significance tests to determine if Metro's crime rates are significantly lower than those of the comparison systems.

The finding that Metro's crime rates are significantly lower than other subway systems' would suggest that Metro's environment is to be credited for this difference. Additional tests of Metro's environment, however, should explore the extent to which Metro has been able to insulate itself from hot spots, variations, and trends occurring in the areas above ground that Metro serves. This question is explored with three tests. First, Pearson correlation coefficients measuring the degree of association between Metro crime rates to those above ground in census tracts where Metro stations are located are assessed. The argument here is that if Metro's environment explains its low crime rates, then one would expect no significant correlations in crime rates between Metro stations and the areas directly above the stations. One would also expect Metro's variation in crime rates across subway stations to be low relative to that of the above-ground areas served by Metro, and this is examined through F-tests comparing coefficients of relative variation for Metro crimes versus those occurring above ground in census tracts where Metro stations are located. Finally, a comparison of trends over time for Metro crime rates versus crime rates above ground in Washington, DC, is conducted to determine the extent to which crime rates covary over time.

Findings

METRO'S CRIME PREVENTION DESIGN

Many have cited Metro's low crime rate as an example of the successful application of CPTED principles (Nation's Cities, 1977; Welke, 1981; Hyde, 1993). Indeed, the planning stages of Metro coincided with Jeffery's (1971, 1977) publication which coined the phrase "CPTED" and introduced the concept of preventing crime through manipulation of the physical environment, rather than the social environment. However, Metro's planners and architects were not operating under any pre-existing theory of the relationship between design and crime. Telephone interviews with both the original Metro Transit Police Chief Angus MacLean and his Deputy Chief John Hyde verify that Metro's design was not theory-based, but rather based on their years of experience with security (Hyde, 1995; MacLean, 1995). In addition to their reliance on prior experience in security issues, Metro's team of planners visited the world's major mass transit systems to compile the best aspects of these systems (New York State Senate Committee on Transportation, 1980).

Thus, Metro's architects and planners deliberately created a design to deter criminals and make riders feel comfortable and secure (Siegel, 1995; Bochner, 1995; Hyde, 1995). They were blessed by the fortunate coincidence that many of their efforts to create good architectural form—one that was structurally sound as well as free of embellishments—also promoted a secure environment. Instead of the tension between aesthetics and security that is often observed with target hardening and other design measures (see Weidner, 1996), these two factors were considered to make a "good marriage" (Siegel, 1995). For example, Metro's high arched ceilings resolve some structural requirements (the 600-foot platform requires high ceilings) while also providing passengers with a feeling of openness, thus reducing levels of fear (see Illustration 1).

ILLUSTRATION 1
EXAMPLE OF METRO'S HIGH ARCHED CEILINGS AT METRO CENTER

Source: WMATA photograph by Larry Levine, February 28, 1992.

Today, Metro consists of a route of 89 miles and 74 stations, with 9 more stations under construction; by early 2001, the total system should consist of 83 stations serving 103.06 miles. It operates from 5:30 a.m. to midnight on weekdays, and 8:00 a.m. to midnight on weekends and holidays to reduce operating costs when Metro services are less likely to be used. Fares on Metro are distance-based, ranging from $1.10 to $3.15, and dependent on the hours of travel, with rush-hour fares slightly more expensive than fares during off-peak times.

Besides serving the District proper, Metro's five lines also extend into the surrounding communities in Maryland and Virginia. Within the District, some lines share railways, enabling Metro to provide more service to within-city travelers and tourists; trains of different lines diverge at various points after leaving the District. The following discussion outlines how the specific design and management characteristics of Metro's environment were created to discourage criminals and ensure the safety of its riders.

PLATFORMS

Metro's platforms are a uniform 600 feet long, designed to accommodate a train of eight, 75-foot-long cars. The platforms are spacious, with the vaults extending as wide as 60 feet, to increase riders' perceptions of safety by ensuring an uncrowded environment.

The platforms have a minimal number of supporting columns, which can provide cover for criminals. A high, free-standing vaulted ceiling arches above the tracks, giving the appearance of a wide-open design. As MacLean noted, "... from a security standpoint [the uniformity of stations] is very handy because you can look down and see 600 feet straight and no place to hide." As added measures, "[e]very one of those stations has at least eight Closed-Circuit Television Cameras" and "[e]very mezzanine has a uniformed station attendant" (New York State Senate Committee on Transportation, 1980:9).

To ensure safety on the platforms during off-peak hours, trains are shortened from their maximum size of eight cars to four cars at around 8:00 p.m.. Shorter trains keep people close together, and safety in numbers is a theory subscribed to by Metro officials (New York State Senate Committee on Transportation, 1980).

ENTRANCES, EXITS, AND PATHWAYS

DC Metro has the second-longest escalator in the world, surpassed only by one in Leningrad (Means,1995). Planners designed lengthy escalators and stairs, used as pathways to and from the train railways, as an alternative to the winding pathways with curves and corners found in many older subway systems. Such corners were deliberately avoided because of planners' beliefs that they create shadows in which potential criminals can hide and approach their victims suddenly, and also can serve as nooks that panhandlers and homeless people like to occupy (Deiter, 1990).

Planners designed overhead crossovers at the mezzanine level of the station to serve as pathways to connecting lines and trains traveling in the opposite direction, as opposed to dark and confining tunnels below the tracks. The absence of long passageways discourages people from lingering in the station after they have disembarked from the train, reducing opportunities for crime.

LIGHTING AND MAINTENANCE

Lighting within the subway system is a minimum of one foot-candle[2] and all new lighting is a minimum of two foot-candles. Lighting is recessed so as not to cast shadows, which can cause fear in riders and serve as cover for potential criminals. In addition, walls are indented to provide greater reflection of the light.

Metro's planners chose concrete, brick, granite, and bronze as the primary materials for the system because of their durability, their fire-resistance, and their easy maintenance (Falanga, 1988). Walls are recessed and bars were installed in front of the walls in order to discourage graffiti (Deiter, 1990; Mooney, 1976). Litter bins were situated along the platform and *Washington Post* donated newspaper recycling bins that were installed at each station. Metro's policy is to clean graffiti and repair damages from vandalism within 24-hours.[3] Maintaining the public restrooms is not an issue, as such facilities are not available to the public in order to keep undesirable activity out of the station (Falanga, 1988).

SECURITY DEVICES

Closed circuit television cameras (CCTVs) are located on the end of each platform and on ceilings at entrances and exits, and are strategically placed in the few areas that could potentially offer concealment. Elevators, designed with large glass side panels to ensure greater visibility from the outside to deter potential criminals, are also equipped with CCTVs. Cameras are purposefully visible to riders to bolster their feelings of safety, as well as to alert potential criminals that they are being monitored.

Attendants are positioned at kiosks at the entrances to the platforms to provide assistance to riders, keep an eye on potential fare evaders, and monitor the CCTV screens located inside the kiosk. In addition to CCTVs, surveillance is enhanced by the high, domed ceilings in the station, which allow for greater visibility to the railway below.

Another key component of Metro's security design is its communications system. All Metro employees—including maintenance personnel—are equipped with two-way radios so that they can be located or alerted at any time (MacLean, 1995). In addition, passenger-to-operator intercoms exist on each rail car to enable passengers to alert drivers of dangerous situations or crimes in progress. Blue light boxes with emergency phones and Power Take Down buttons are located every 600 feet along the right of way.

ILLUSTRATION 2
EXAMPLE OF CCTV SURVEILLANCE AT ANACOSTIA,
ONE OF METRO'S NEWER STATIONS

Source: WMATA photography by Larry Levine, January 8, 1992.

SIGNAGE

The original design of Metro's stations called for a minimum of signage on the station platforms. However, economic considerations revived the architect's idea of placing backlit panels in spaced intervals along the platform for advertising purposes. These panels also display system maps, which were originally intended to appear only at mezzanine level. Station names and directions of system lines are listed vertically on pylons, and also duplicated at eye level on walls. Signage is probably the weakest element of Metro's system, and even today Metro's signage is criticized by riders despite repeated efforts to improve visibility (McGhee, 1995; Silver, 1995; Le Cam, 1995).

MONEY HANDLING POLICIES

Metro's farecards limit cash transactions and prevent fare evasion. Unlike token systems, which are susceptible to the use of slugs and require a separate token for each ride, the farecard system allows passengers to buy cards of any dollar amount, which can be used for multiple trips and enable passengers to reduce the frequency with which they must exchange cash for fares (and expose their wallets to pickpocketers). Metro encourages riders to buy high-dollar farecards by providing a 10 percent bonus on all farecards of twenty dollars or more.

ILLUSTRATION 3
JUDICIARY SQUARE'S STATION ATTENDANT KIOSK, WITH FARECARD
VENDING MACHINES IN FOREGROUND

Source: WMATA photography by Larry Levine, August 14, 1992.

Farecards have magnetic strips encoded with the dollar value of the card. Riders insert cards in a reader at the entry gate, which encodes the card with the boarding station and ejects it at the other end of the gate. When riders exit at the destination station, they again insert the farecard, which calculates and deducts the fare amount from origin to destination, and emits the card at the other end of the gate if it has a positive balance, or retains it if the dollar value is equal to the fare. Because Metro's distance-based fares require use of the farecard at both entry and exit, the risk of being detected evading a fare is double that of a traditional token system.

With the exception of farecard and newspaper vending machines, Metro planners allowed no other commercial activity in the stations in order to deter criminal activity (Deiter, 1990).

Metro Transit Police and Personnel

Metro's transit police force (MTP), approximately 278 sworn officers and officials, are trained to be vigilant and take immediate action toward "quality of life" violations by making arrests and issuing citations (Morrow, 1994). Riders are prohibited from eating, drinking, smoking, playing radios, transporting animals, or moving from one rail car to another. These rules are clearly posted at the entrance and exit to the station platforms, as well as on the rail cars themselves, and they are stringently enforced by Metro police. In fact, in Metro's early years, there was a great deal of criticism by the media that transit police were too aggressive in enforcing the rules against prohibited behaviors, but the transit police continued their zero-tolerance approach (New York State Senate Committee on Transportation, 1980).[4]

In addition to formal surveillance of the system, station attendants have an important role in contributing to Metro's safe environment. They are trained to intervene, usually through the use of the public address system, and notify riders if they are committing violations. Despite what some consider to be an unpleasant "Big Brother" mentality of kiosk attendants, this approach is an important component of Metro's security philosophy.

Summary of Environmental Characteristics

To summarize, Metro's environment has most of the 16 opportunity-reducing characteristics described by Clarke and Homel (1997). While an itemization of each design characteristic and how it relates to individual crime prevention techniques is beyond the scope of this paper, a few are summarized here. Metro scores high on visibility, and this open environment is assisted by CCTV cameras, which optimize formal, employee, and natural surveillance capabilities. Second, the environment is well-lit and well-maintained, contributing to the overall feeling of safety of Metro's users. Metro's rigorous maintenance policies also reduce the rewards of vandalism and graffiti to offenders—they are deprived of the pleasure of enjoying their work because it is repaired or removed within hours. Further, rule and law enforcement on the system is stringent, inducing guilt and shame among rule violators and sending a message to would-be criminals that even the most minor of violations will be observed and even the most petty of offenders apprehended. In conclusion, Metro's careful plan to create an attractive, comfortable, and safe environment for its riders appears, at least in theory, to be a success.

Comparison of Crime Rates on Subway Systems

The most obvious means of determining whether Metro's crime rates are lower than one would expect is to compare them to rates of other subway systems. While this may appear a simple task, differences in reporting and record-keeping practices of transit systems present difficulties in making accurate comparisons across subway systems. Much of the serious crime on subway systems occurs outside of subway stations, particularly in and around commuter parking lots, so a comparison of crime on different systems could be misleading; one system could appear to have much higher crime rates than another, when in fact it may have twice as many commuter parking lots. Thus, a truly thorough comparison of crime rates among a number of subway systems requires data that disaggregate above-ground crimes from those occurring below ground or within the subway station. These detailed data are not always collected by transit police and when such data exist, they tend to be difficult to obtain from authorities.

Because of the difficulties in obtaining crime data that disaggregates above- and below-ground crimes, this comparison of crime rates examines just four subway systems: Metro, Atlanta (MARTA), Boston (MBTA), and Chicago (CTA). It should be acknowledged that these systems are far from identical in terms of important factors such as ridership demographics, number of riders, number of stations, or route miles. However, this sample is not strictly one of convenience, as care was taken to choose systems that are similar in size and service area, but varied in design characteristics.

Table 1 outlines the differences and similarities among the systems chosen for this analysis. Metro, MBTA, and CTA are similar in terms of daily ridership, but differ in terms of route miles and number of stations. MARTA is much smaller than the other systems in

TABLE 1
COMPARISON OF CHARACTERISTICS FOR WASHINGTON, BOSTON, ATLANTA, AND CHICAGO SUBWAY SYSTEMS

Subway System	Daily Ridership	Route Miles	Stations	Year Established
Metro	500,000	89	74	1976
Boston (MBTA)	562,000	80	101	1897
Atlanta (MARTA)	219,000	40	33	1979
Chicago (CTA)	424,000	191	117	1943

Sources: Washington Metropolitan Area Transit Authority, Metropolitan Boston Transit Authority, Metropolitan Atlanta Rapid Transit Authority; Chicago Transit Authority.

terms of riders, mileage, and stations, and is the newest of the systems, beginning operations in 1979 — just three years after Metro. This makes it a good comparison for Metro due to the fact that MARTA's planners, like Metro's, were able to benefit from the successes and failures of other systems, as well as from a greater knowledge of crime prevention tactics. Like Boston, CTA is an old system; its first elevated line was constructed in 1892, and its first subways began running in 1943. CTA is the only system that operates 24-hours per day, with Metro, MARTA, and MBTA opening between 5:00 a.m. and 6:00 a.m., and closing between midnight and 1:30 a.m. For comparison purposes, those crimes occurring on CTA between 1:00 a.m. and 6:00 a.m. were subtracted from total crime counts before rates per 1 million riders were calculated.

F-tests of ANOVA results reveal that Metro's mean crime rate, at just 1.7 per million riders, is significantly lower than those of the other three systems ($F = 8.45$, $p < .001$), and that Boston's and Atlanta's rates, at 7.81 and 8.85 respectively, do not differ significantly. Chicago's mean rate of 12.05 is significantly higher than Metro's, Boston's and Atlanta's (see Table 2).[5] While the sample of subway systems is very small, this finding of much lower Part I rates on Metro supports the hypothesis that Metro's crime rates are unusually low compared to other subway systems.

Correlations between Metro and Above-ground Crime

An examination of Metro's independence in crime rates from crime rates in the neighborhoods served by Metro is another means of testing Metro's security. With the

TABLE 2

ANALYSIS OF DIFFERENCES OF MEAN PART I CRIME RATES (PER 1 MILLION RIDERS) ON FOUR SUBWAY SYSTEMS

Groups	No. of Stations	Mean	Standard Dev.	Standard Error	F
A. Metro	74	1.70	1.72	.20	8.45*
B. MARTA	33	8.85	6.07	1.06	
C. MBTA	68	7.81	12.03	1.46	
D. CTA	79	12.05	19.68	2.21	
Contrasts	Coefficient	Standard Error	t-Value	Significance	
1. X_A-X_B	7.15	2.69	2.66	.008	
2. X_A-X_C	6.10	2.16	2.83	.005	
3. X_A-X_D	10.35	2.08	4.98	.000	
4. X_B-X_C	1.04	2.73	.38	.702	
5. X_B-X_D	3.20	3.16	1.01	.310	
6. X_C-X_D	4.24	2.12	1.99	.047	

*$p < .001$.

Sources: Washington Area Metropolitan Transit Authority Transit Police, Metropolitan Atlanta Rapid Transit Authority Transit Police, Metropolitan Boston Transit Authority Transit Police, and Chicago Police Department.

exception of Clarke *et al.* (1996), prior research suggests that subway stations with the highest crime rates are located in high-crime areas (Shellow *et al.*, 1974a,b; Richards and Hoel, 1980; Falanga, 1988). If Metro's underground environment deters criminals even when they are perpetrating crimes directly overhead, one would expect a departure from prior research findings: Metro's crime rates should not be significantly positively correlated with those above ground.

A Pearson Correlation matrix of crime on Metro versus that above ground by census tract[6] for the crimes of robbery, aggravated assault, and total Part I crimes,[7] indicates no significant correlations between the two data sets (see Table 3). An examination of scatterplots indicates that, with the exception of aggravated assault, outliers are not driving the coefficients. After excluding two outliers that appeared to be wielding undue influence on the correlations, however, the relationship between above-ground assaults by census tract and below-ground assaults by Metro station is positive and significant, at .46 (p=.000). This unexpected finding raises a question as to whether Metro is not as successful in insulating itself from some above-ground crimes as it is from others, a question that is explored in the following section.

TABLE 3
CORRELATION COEFFICIENTS FOR METRO VERSUS
ABOVE-GROUND CRIME RATES (N=74)

Metro crime	Above-ground crime		
	Assault	Robbery	Part I
Assault	.184	.089	.073
	p = .117	p = .451	p = .535
Robbery	-.104	-.102	-.107
	p = .378	p = .388	p = .365
Part I	.165	.077	.076
	p = .159	p = .515	p = .517

Variation in Metro versus Above-Ground Crime

A different means of determining the extent to which Metro's crime rates are influenced by those occurring above ground involves an analysis of coefficients of relative variation for crime rates for the two data sets. This test is based on the premise that, if Metro's environment is structured in such a way as to reduce criminal opportunities, one would expect little variation from station to station, compared to that occurring above ground. Washington, DC, has great variations in crime rates above ground, with most of northwest DC being quite safe, and pockets of high-crime areas existing in the northeast, southeast, and southwest quadrants of the District (Gebhardt, 1996). The argument put forth here is that if Metro is doing its job, the underground environment should reflect little of this above-ground variation.

For this test, variations are measured by calculating each variable's coefficient of relative variation, which is simply the variable's standard deviation divided by its mean. Comparing coefficients of variation allows one to assess the *relative* difference in variation between variables that may have dramatically different ranges (Weisberg, 1992).

TABLE 4
COMPARISON OF COEFFICIENTS OF RELATIVE VARIATION
METRO VERSUS ABOVE-GROUND CRIME RATES

	Assault	Robbery	Part I Crimes
Metro Crime Rates (including car parks, bus bays, and other above-ground Metro property) N=74	2.45	1.96	1.49
Above-Ground Crime Rates by Census Tract N=74	2.56	2.82	3.19
F value	F = 1.09	F = 2.07	F = 4.58
Significance:	p > .25	p < .01	P < .001

Coefficients were calculated for both data sets for the crimes of robbery, aggravated assault, and total Part I crimes. As Table 4 indicates, variations are significantly smaller on Metro for Part I crimes and robberies, but for assaults, Metro's coefficients are smaller than those for above-ground rates, yet they do not differ significantly.[8] Again, the crime of assault is not behaving as one would expect; it appears that Metro is not successful in insulating itself against assaults occurring above-ground in the immediate area that Metro serves.

These unexpected findings for assault may be explained by the nature of the act itself. The genesis for an assault may commence underground, but actually take place above, or vice versa. Thus, it is possible that, because assaults are less likely to begin and end in the same location, the difference between crime settings is less distinct to such offenders, and therefore the preventive capabilities of Metro are less likely to influence offending behavior.

Comparison of Crime Trends

The tests above, while not entirely supportive, nonetheless build an argument that Metro is indeed safer than one would expect, and that its environment has been successful in insulating itself against crime, even when it occurs directly overhead. Another means of testing this hypothesis is to determine the degree to which Metro crime rates and above-ground crime rates covary over time. Prior research indicates that crime in the New York subway varies in the same way as crime in the rest of New York over time (Del Castillo, 1992), and the same has been found for the London Underground (Department of Transport, 1986). Thus, the logic behind this test is that, if Metro's environment has been successful in insulating itself against crime—regardless of crime above ground—one would expect to see little or no similarity in variations over time for Metro *vis a vis* variations in crime above ground.[9]

The first iteration of this test is to compare crime rates over time. Figure 1 depicts total crime rates for the District of Columbia versus Metro. The Washington crimes are per 100,000 inhabitants, while Metro crimes are per 1,000,000 riders; to make the two data sets suitable for graphical comparison purposes, the Metro data was multiplied by 5 for total crimes. Visually, it appears that these two trend lines do not covary consistently, although

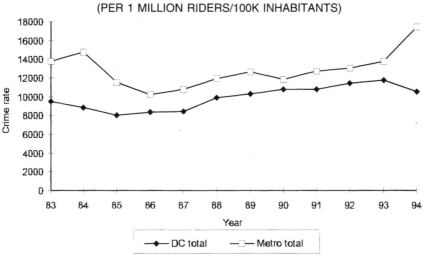

FIGURE 1
COMPARISON OF METRO AND DC TOTAL CRIME RATES, 1983-1994
(PER 1 MILLION RIDERS/100K INHABITANTS)

Source: Washington Metropolitan Area Transit Association and FBI Uniform Crime Report.
*Metro Crime rates multiplied by five for comparison purposes.

the two trends for the years of 1986 to 1989, and 1991 to 1993, look similar.

An alternative to comparing trend lines, which offer a somewhat skewed visual depiction because the two data sets have different denominators and are scaled differently, is to compare rates after they are standardized as Z-scores. Figure 2 depicts the changes in Z-scores for the total crime rates of each data set over time.

In comparing changes in Z-scores over time, half of the pairs changed in the same direction, and the other half changed in opposite directions. It appears, then, that changes in crime rates over time for Washington above ground are not mirrored by Metro crimes below.

FIGURE 2
COMPARISON OF CRIME RATES FOR METRO VERSUS DC, 1983-1994
STANDARDIZED TOTAL RATES (PER RIDER/INHABITANT)
REPRESENTED AS Z-SCORES

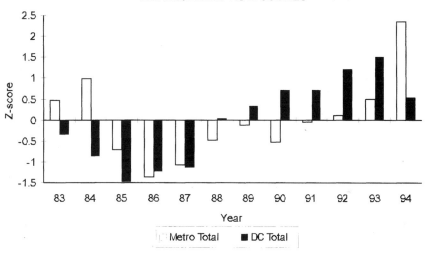

Source: Washington Metropolitan Area Transit Association and FBI Uniform Crime Report.

Rival Hypotheses

The apparent weakness of this study's research design is that other rival explanations exist that might explain Metro's unusually low crime rates. Some may argue, for example, that Metro has such low crime rates because riders do not represent a cross-section of DC's population; rather, they are predominantly white, middle- to upper middle-class working people. An analysis of a 1991 Metro ridership survey conducted in a previous study indicates that Metro riders are more advantaged than the general population (measured as those residing in the DC SMSA) in terms of employment, income, and education, but they are roughly representative of the population in terms of racial representation, and, on average, they are much younger than the general population (La Vigne, 1996b).

These findings provide some support for the argument that Metro riders are more advantaged than the overall DC SMSA population. However, the survey did not include all those riders living in areas that Metro currently serves, because it does not capture riders using Metro's green line stations, which did not begin operating until mid-1991, and which were expanded up through 1993. These green line stations are located in areas with lower income levels and higher unemployment than most other Metro station locations. In addition, the survey did not capture two important Metro rider subpopulations: tourists, and persons under the age of eighteen, such as college and high school students who ride Metro to and from school. While one would guess that tourists are much more likely to be victims than offenders, students and youths in general are more prone to offending than working people.

Another way of exploring this hypothesis is to examine changes in crime rates as Metro expanded its service area. Some believe that Metro's unusually low crime rates are explained by the fact that Metro serves a very small area, and that the area it serves is predominantly white and middle- to upper-class. This argument became significantly less valid in 1991, when Metro's new green line began operating to some high-crime inner city points and southeast to Anacostia, adding six stations; by the end of 1993, the green line was further extended northwest to Greenbelt, adding another four new stations. However, a prior analysis of crime rate trends before and after this additional construction does not indicate a significant increase in crime rates for total crimes, Part I property crimes, nor Part I violent crimes (La Vigne, 1996b). Looking more specifically at crime types, auto theft, pick pocketing, and assault declined from 1989 to 1995, while robbery increased slightly and grand larceny increased more markedly (La Vigne, 1996b). These trends do not suggest a dramatic change in crime following the addition of the green line, which can be interpreted as further supporting the hypothesis that Metro has been relatively successful in insulating itself against crime occurring above ground.

Given the information at hand, the argument that Metro riders are more advantaged than the general population can be neither refuted nor supported on statistical grounds. The ridership and service area arguments are, in themselves, troublesome because their assumptions have little or no support in prior research. The ridership argument implies that regular subway riders are the same people who are perpetrating crimes, rather than the occasional, opportunistic rider, or the potential offender who loiters above ground without paying a fare and using the system. There is no basis in prior research or theory to support or refute this hypothesis. The service area argument suggests that the type of people who offend are those who are in a racial minority, poor, uneducated, and unemployed. One does not have to search far in the literature to refute such an argument (see Gabor's (1994) *"Everybody Does It!": Crime by the Public*). Suffice it to say that the answer cannot be gleaned from the data at hand, but that there is no convincing support for these rival hypotheses.

Summary

The impetus for this paper stemmed from the need to explore and document the purported success of Metro as an application of crime prevention measures in a mass transit system that were built in at the creation of the system, rather than retrofitted. While Metro authorities did not intentionally apply a specific theory to the philosophy behind the planning of Metro's environment, this philosophy is nonetheless compatible with theories of crime prevention, making this study a means of testing the comprehensive application of crime prevention principles in a built-in design.

Is Metro Safer Than One Would Expect?

Tests of Metro's crime rates compared to three other systems for which detailed data were available provides evidence of Metro's success, as Metro experiences significantly fewer serious crimes per rider than comparison systems. While data access difficulties precluded a comparison between Metro and a larger range of subway systems, the systems examined here are similar to Metro in size and service area, and, despite the age or design of the comparison system, Metro's crime rates are only a small fraction of the other systems.

Is Metro's Safety Explained by Its Environment?

The second question, is Metro's safety explained by its environment, was assessed through an examination of the crime prevention characteristics built into Metro, and a series of tests to determine the extent to which Metro has succeeded in insulating itself from crime occurring outside the system. An assessment of Metro's environment suggests that it has the majority of opportunity-reducing characteristics recommended by both theory and practice. The system is clean, well-lighted, has excellent opportunities for natural and employee surveillance, and both rules and laws are strictly enforced. Judging from Metro's environmental characteristics alone, one would expect Metro to have low crime rates and be relatively crime neutral, rather than attracting or generating crime.

Metro also experiences less crime than one would expect given the distribution of crime above ground in communities that Metro serves. With the exception of assaults, Metro crime rates by station do not covary with crime rates for the census tracts in which Metro stations are located. However, the relationship between above-ground assaults by census tract and below-ground assaults by Metro is positive and significant, suggesting that assaults may not be as situationally influenced as other crime types.

The idea that offenders are less willing to perpetrate crimes on Metro property than in the areas around Metro is also supported by the fact that Metro demonstrates less variation in crime rates from station to station as compared to census tract variations, indicating that Metro does not reflect crime occurring above ground. In addition, a comparison of crime rates over time for Metro versus Washington, DC, indicates that these trends do not covary, again supporting the notion that Metro crime rates are independent of those occurring above-ground.

Implications for Theory and Practice

The tests conducted above, when considered in combination, support the position that Metro is unusually safe and that there is something unique about Metro's environment that explains its low crime rates. The fact that Metro's design characteristics and maintenance and management policies reflect well-established crime prevention principles supports the hypothesis that what is special about Metro's environment is that it reduces criminal opportunities. Metro's success suggests that it is indeed possible to manipulate environments to reduce criminal opportunities. Further, it implies that offenders *do* consider the costs and benefits of their actions, weighing the risks of apprehension versus the effort and expected payoff, and considering the presence of capable guardians when weighing those risks.

Characteristics of Metro's environment, from design elements to enforcement strategies, can be applied to new or existing systems in an effort to reduce crime. While prior research indicates that the base rates of subway crime are quite low, and that individuals have a greater risk of victimization above ground than below (Del Castillo, 1992; Kenney,

1987), increasing security on subway systems is an important public policy objective. Fear of victimization has been found to be greater underground than above (Wekerle and Whitzman, 1995; Levy, 1994; Kenney, 1987; Schnell *et al.*, 1973), and levels of passenger fear have an impact on ridership and therefore have widespread implications for urban policy, including issues of traffic congestion and pollution created by alternative modes of transportation, such as taxicabs, buses, and private automobiles. These indirect costs not only affect the system itself, but are ultimately translated into higher sales taxes and cutbacks on governmental services. Thus, the benefits of implementing crime prevention tactics on subways are far-reaching; reducing subway crime saves money and increases revenues at the same time, as riders will be more willing to use the system. In an urban area, the well-being of its subway system, in terms of low crime rates and ample ridership, can affect the well-being of the entire metropolitan area.

Further Research

The fact that this study's hypotheses were supported with the tests detailed above has important implications for crime prevention. The majority of evaluations of crime prevention efforts focus on interventions to address pre-existing crime problems, and these evaluations tend to study the impact of an intervention over a relatively short time period (see Felson *et al.*,1996; Bichler and Clarke, 1996;Weidner, 1996; and Barclay *et al.*, 1996). Counter to this typical approach to crime prevention evaluation, this study enables us not only to determine the impact of a comprehensive preventive effort created before a crime problem occurred, but also to assess the impact of these measures over a period of almost 20 years. Metro has had plenty of time to fail, and yet it remains as relatively crime-free as the day it began operating in 1976. This is particularly impressive considering that Washington, DC, still ranks high in crime rates among cities of comparable size.[10]

Quite often in crime prevention studies, evaluations are criticized because of the difficulties in disentangling preventive measures to determine which specific tactics are having an impact on crime. Indeed, scholars have rendered evaluations of what have been termed "modification blitzes" as unhelpful from both a theoretical and policy perspective (Rubenstein *et al.,* 1980). It is important to remember, however, that researchers are rarely involved in the intervention stage of a preventive effort, and therefore have little control over the measures implemented. In the real world, it is extremely rare for a crime problem to be addressed with a single preventive tactic; this should not render these preventive efforts as unworthy of evaluation, as there is a great deal to learn from evaluations such as the one conducted in this study. Further efforts to evaluate a mix of preventive measures should be encouraged, rather than dismissed as fruitless. In addition, studies of subway offenders, in terms of who they are, where they live, where they commit their crimes, and what kinds of crime they commit, are sorely needed if researchers are to truly understand the nature and distribution of subway crime and how it can be prevented.

Notes

1. "Environment" will be used hereafter to refer to this combination of factors (design, management, and maintenance).
2. A foot-candle is a measure of illumination for which one foot-candle equals illumination on a surface of one square foot in area on which is uniformly distributed one lumen of light (Fennelly, 1989).

3. These stringent maintenance practices are supported by the author's countless site visits to various Metro stations, including observations during her daily commute on Metro. It should be noted, however, that Metro's high standard of maintenance below-ground is not always practiced on Metro's above-ground properties, which may have implications for crimes occurring in Metro's bus bays and parking lots.

4. When Metro was first in operation, with only five stations and five miles of track, Metro transit police saturated the system with 100 police officers, both uniformed and plain clothes (Hyde, 1995). As former Chief Angus MacLean relates, "The first pickpocket there, the victim was an Assistant United States Attorney, and the two detectives down there almost had a fist fight over who was going to book the first pickpocket" (New York State Senate Committee on Transportation, 1980).

5. Because this analysis involves multiple comparisons, the Scheffé correction was used to produce wider confidence intervals with which to conduct t-tests.

6. Crime statistics were obtained from each of the eight jurisdictions Metro serves: the District of Columbia, Montgomery County, MD, Prince George's County, MD, Arlington County, VA, Fairfax County, VA, and the cities of Alexandria, Fairfax, and Falls Church, VA. In some cases statistics were already collected by census tract; in other cases, patrol areas were overlaid on a map of census tract boundaries and apportioned accordingly. Because Metro crimes are reported by transit police to the police department in the above-ground jurisdiction, Metro crimes were subtracted from census tract totals prior to analysis.

7. Crime types were selected to test correlations of comparable crimes, and to avoid reliability problems associated with differences in reporting by jurisdiction; Part I crimes tend to be documented in a more uniform manner across jurisdictions than less serious crime types (Gove *et al.*, 1985). Robbery and aggravated assault were selected in an attempt to compare like crimes. In addition, prior research indicates that crimes against persons have high correlations between rates that are calculated with number of inhabitants as the denominator, and those with more meaningful denominators, such as those based on opportunity (Boggs, 1966; Harries, 1980).

8. Calculated by dividing the coefficients of variation (large over small), and squaring (SD/mean)^2.

9. Originally, it was hoped that annual crime statistics could be obtained for the greater Washington metropolitan area. However, changes in the Bureau of Census definition of the metropolitan area over the years under study were such that an examination of trends would paint an inaccurate picture of crime patterns over time. Instead, crime statistics for the District of Columbia were used for this analysis.

10. In fact, in a comparison of mean homicide rates from 1985 to 1994 for U.S. cities with populations exceeding 200,000, Washington ranked the highest at an average of 60.42 homicides per 100,000 residents (National Institute of Justice, 1995).

ACKNOWLEDGMENTS. This paper would not have been possible without the assistance of countless individuals, the list of whom is too long to mention here but can be found in La Vigne (1996b). In particular, I would like to thank George McConnell, Deputy Chief Barry McDevitt, and Officer J.D. Smith, of the Transit Police, for their patience in responding to my countless requests for data and information. Larry Levine of WMATA's Office of Marketing allowed me to select and use the photographs that appear in this paper. Stephanie Bourque of the National Institute of Justice and Martha J. Smith of Rutgers' Center for Crime Prevention Studies were kind enough to provide comments on an earlier version of this manuscript. I would especially like to thank Ronald Clarke for his guidance, encouragement, and comments throughout this research process.

23. From the Panopticon to Disney World: the Development of Discipline

Clifford D. Shearing and Phillip C. Stenning

EDITOR'S NOTE: Though it contains no evaluative data, this case study was too good to omit. First published in a book of edited readings (Shearing and Stenning, 1984), it describes the way that consensual control is incorporated into the design and management of Disney World, in ways not too different from the Washington Metro. The broader societal implications have been discussed in the Introduction and little more needs to be said here. However, I cannot resist paraphrasing the title under which the study was last reprinted (Shearing and Stenning, 1987): the Disney order may not be so Mickey Mouse!

ONE OF THE most distinctive features of that quintessentially American playground known as Disney World is the way it seeks to combine a sense of comfortable — even nostalgic — familiarity with an air of innovative technological advance. Mingled with the fantasies of one's childhood are the dreams of a better future. Next to the Magic Kingdom is the Epcot Center. As well as providing for a great escape, Disney World claims also to be a design for better living. And what impresses most about this place is that it seems to run like clockwork.

Yet the Disney order is no accidental by-product. Rather, it is a designed-in feature that provides — to the eye that is looking for it, but not to the casual visitor — an exemplar of modern private corporate policing. Along with the rest of the scenery of which it forms a discreet part, it too is recognizable as a design for the future.

We invite you to come with us on a guided tour of this modern police facility in which discipline and control are, like many of the characters one sees about, in costume.

The fun begins the moment the visitor enters Disney World. As one arrives by car one is greeted by a series of smiling young people who, with the aid of clearly visible road markings, direct one to one's parking spot, remind one to lock one's car and to remember its location and then direct one to await the rubber-wheeled train that will convey visitors away from the parking lot. At the boarding location one is directed to stand safely behind guard rails and to board the train in an orderly fashion. While climbing on board one is reminded to remember the name of the parking area and the row number in which one is parked (for instance, "Donald Duck, 1"). Once on the train one is encouraged to protect oneself from injury by keeping one's body within the bounds of the carriage and to do the same for children in one's care. Before disembarking one is told how to get from the train back to the monorail platform and where to wait for the train to the parking lot on one's return. At each transition from one stage of one's journey to the next, one is wished a happy day and a "good time" at Disney World (this begins as one drives in and is directed by road signs to tune one's car radio to the Disney radio network).

As one moves towards the monorail platform the directions one has just received are reinforced by physical barriers (that make it difficult to take a wrong turn), pavement markings, signs and more cheerful Disney employees who, like their counterparts in other locations, convey the message that Disney World is a "fun place" designed for one's comfort and pleasure. On approaching the monorail platform one is met by enthusiastic attendants who quickly and efficiently organize the mass of people moving onto it into corrals designed to accommodate enough people to fill one compartment on the monorail. In assigning people to these corrals the attendants ensure that groups visiting Disney World together remain together. Access to the edge of the platform is prevented by a gate which is opened once the monorail has arrived and disembarked the arriving passengers on the other side of the platform. If there is a delay of more than a minute or two in waiting for the next monorail one is kept informed of the reason for the delay and the progress the expected train is making towards the station.

Once aboard and the automatic doors of the monorail have closed, one is welcomed aboard, told to remain seated and "for one's own safety" to stay away from open windows. The monorail takes a circuitous route to one of the two Disney locations (the Epcot Center or the Magic Kingdom) during which time a friendly disembodied voice introduces one briefly to the pleasures of the world one is about to enter and the methods of transport available between its various locations. As the monorail slows towards its destination one is told how to disembark once the automatic doors open and how to move from the station to the entrance gates, and reminded to take one's possessions with one and to take care of oneself, and children in one's care, on disembarking. Once again these instructions are reinforced, in a variety of ways, as one moves towards the gates.

It will be apparent from the above that Disney Productions is able to handle large crowds of visitors in a most orderly fashion. Potential trouble is anticipated and prevented. Opportunities for disorder are minimized by constant instruction, by physical barriers which severely limit the choice of action available and by the surveillance of omnipresent employees who detect and rectify the slightest deviation.

The vehicles that carry people between locations are an important component of the system of physical barriers. Throughout Disney World vehicles are used as barriers. This is particularly apparent in the Epcot Center, the newest Disney facility, where many exhibits are accessible only via special vehicles which automatically secure one once they begin moving.

Control strategies are embedded in both environmental features and structural relations. In both cases control structures and activities have other functions which are highlighted so that the control function is overshadowed. Nonetheless, control is pervasive. For example, virtually every pool, fountain, and flower garden serves both as an aesthetic object and to direct visitors away from, or towards, particular locations. Similarly, every Disney Productions employee, while visibly and primarily engaged in other functions, is also engaged in the maintenance of order. This integration of functions is real and not simply an appearance: beauty *is* created, safety *is* protected, employees *are* helpful. The effect is, however, to embed the control function into the "woodwork" where its presence is unnoticed but its effects are ever present.

A critical consequence of this process of embedding control in other structures is that control becomes consensual. It is effected with the willing cooperation of those being controlled so that the controlled become, as Foucault (1977) has observed, the source of their own control. Thus, for example, the batching that keeps families together provides for family unity while at the same time ensuring that parents will be available to control their children. By seeking a definition of order within Disney World that can convincingly be presented as being in the interest of visitors, order maintenance is established as a voluntary activity which allows coercion to be reduced to a minimum. Thus, adult visitors willingly submit to a variety of devices that increase the flow of consumers through Disney World, such as being corralled on the monorail platform, so as to ensure the safety of their children. Furthermore, while doing so they gratefully acknowledge the concern Disney Productions has for their family, thereby legitimating its authority, not only in the particular situation in question, but in others as well. Thus, while profit ultimately underlies the order Disney Productions seeks to maintain, it is pursued in conjunction with other objectives that will encourage the willing compliance of visitors in maintaining Disney profits. This approach to profit making, which seeks a coincidence of corporate and individual interests (employee and consumer alike), extends beyond the control function and reflects a business philosophy to be applied to all corporate operations (Peters and Waterman, 1982).

The coercive edge of Disney's control system is seldom far from the surface, however, and becomes visible the moment the Disney-visitor consensus breaks down, that is, when a visitor attempts to exercise a choice that is incompatible with the Disney order. It is apparent in the physical barriers that forcefully prevent certain activities as well as in the action of employees who detect breaches of order. This can be illustrated by an incident that occurred during a visit to Disney World by Shearing and his daughter, during the course of which she developed a blister on her heel. To avoid further irritation she removed her shoes and proceeded to walk barefooted. They had not progressed ten yards before they were approached by a very personable security guard dressed as a Bahamian police officer, with white pith helmet and white gloves that perfectly suited the theme of the area they were moving through (so that he, at first, appeared more like a scenic prop than a security person), who informed them that walking barefoot was, "for the safety of visitors," not permitted. When informed that, given the blister, the safety of this visitor was likely to be better secured by remaining barefooted, at least on the walkways, they were informed that their safety and how best to protect it was a matter for Disney Productions to determine while they were on Disney property and that unless they complied he would be compelled to escort them out of Disney World. Shearing's daughter, on learning that failure to comply with the security guard's instruction would deprive her of the pleasures of Disney World, quickly decided that she would prefer to further injure her heel and remain on Disney property. As this example illustrates, the source of Disney Productions' power rests both in the physical coercion it can bring to bear and in its capacity to induce cooperation by depriving visitors of a resource that they value.

The effectiveness of the power that control of a "fun place" has is vividly illustrated by the incredible queues of visitors who patiently wait, sometimes for hours, for admission to exhibits. These queues not only call into question the common knowledge that queueing is a quintessentially English pastime (if Disney World is any indication Americans are at least as good, if not better, at it), but provide evidence of the considerable inconvenience that people can be persuaded to tolerate so long as they believe that their best interests require it. While the source of this perception is the image of Disney World that the visitor brings to it, it is, interestingly, reinforced through the queueing process itself. In many exhibits queues are structured so that one is brought close to the entrance at several points, thus periodically giving one a glimpse of the fun to come while at the same time encouraging one that the wait will soon be over.

Visitor participation in the production of order within Disney World goes beyond the more obvious control examples we have noted so far. An important aspect of the order Disney Productions attempts to maintain is a particular image of Disney World and the American industrialists who sponsor its exhibits (General Electric, Kodak, Kraft Foods, etc.). Considerable care is taken to ensure that every feature of Disney World reflects a positive view of the American Way, especially its use of, and reliance on, technology. Visitors are, for example, exposed to an almost constant stream of directions by employees, robots in human form and disembodied recorded voices (the use of recorded messages and robots permits precise control over the content and tone of the directions given) that convey the desired message. Disney World acts as a giant magnet attracting millions of Americans and visitors from other lands who pay to learn of the wonders of American capitalism.

Visitors are encouraged to participate in the production of the Disney image while they are in Disney World and to take it home with them so that they can reproduce it for their families and friends. One way this is done is through the "Picture Spots," marked with signposts, to be found throughout Disney World, that provide direction with respect to the images to capture on film (with cameras that one can borrow free of charge) for the slide shows and photo albums to be prepared "back home." Each spot provides views which exclude anything unsightly (such as garbage containers) so as to ensure that the visual images visitors take away of Disney World will properly capture Disney's order. A related technique is the Disney characters who wander through the complex to provide "photo opportunities" for young children. These characters apparently never talk to visitors, and the reason for this is presumably so that their media-based images will not be spoiled.

As we have hinted throughout this discussion, training is a pervasive feature of the control system of Disney Productions. It is not, however, the redemptive soul-training of the carceral project but an ever-present flow of directions for, and definitions of, order directed at every visitor. Unlike carceral training, these messages do not require detailed knowledge of the individual. They are, on the contrary, for anyone and everyone. Messages are, nonetheless, often conveyed to single individuals or small groups of friends and relatives. For example, in some of the newer exhibits, the vehicles that take one through swivel and turn so that one's gaze can be precisely directed. Similarly, each seat is fitted with individual sets of speakers that talk directly to one, thus permitting a seductive sense of intimacy while simultaneously imparting a uniform message.

In summary, within Disney World control is embedded, preventative, subtle, co-operative and apparently non-coercive and consensual. It focuses on categories, requires no knowledge of the individual and employs pervasive surveillance. Thus, although disciplinary, it is distinctively non-carceral. Its order is instrumental and determined by the interests of Disney Productions rather than moral and absolute. As anyone who has visited Disney World knows, it is extraordinarily effective.

While this new instrumental discipline is rapidly becoming a dominant force in social control it is as different from the Orwellian totalitarian nightmare as it is from the carceral regime. Surveillance is pervasive but it is the antithesis of the blatant control of the Orwellian State: its source is not government and its vehicle is not Big Brother. The order of instrumental discipline is not the unitary order of a central State but diffuse and separate orders defined by private authorities responsible for the feudal-like domains of Disney World, condominium estates, commercial complexes and the like. Within contemporary discipline, control is as fine-grained as Orwell imagined but its features are very different. It is thus, paradoxically, not to Orwell's socialist-inspired Utopia that we must look for a picture of contemporary control but to the capitalist-inspired disciplinary model conceived of by Huxley, who, in his *Brave New World*, painted a picture of consensually based control that bears a striking resemblance to the disciplinary control of Disney World and other corporate control systems. Within Huxley's imaginary world people are seduced into conformity by the pleasures offered by the drug "soma" rather than coerced into compliance by threat of Big Brother, just as people are today seduced to conform by the pleasures of consuming the goods that corporate power has to offer.

The contrasts between morally based justice and instrumental control, carceral punishment and corporate control, the Panopticon and Disney World and Orwell's and Huxley's visions are succinctly captured by the novelist Beryl Bainbridge's (1984) observations about a recent journey she made retracing J.B. Priestley's (1934) celebrated trip around Britain. She notes how during his travels in 1933 the center of the cities and towns he visited were defined by either a church or a center of government (depicting the coalition between Church and State in the production of order that characterizes morally based regimes).

During her more recent trip one of the changes that struck her most forcibly was the transformation that had taken place in the center of cities and towns. These were now identified not by churches or town halls, but by shopping centers; often vaulted glass-roofed structures that she found reminiscent of the cathedrals they had replaced both in their awe-inspiring architecture and in the hush that she found they sometimes created. What was worshipped in these contemporary cathedrals, she noted, was not an absolute moral order but something much more mundane: people were "worshipping shopping" and through it, we would add, the private authorities, the order and corporate power their worship makes possible.

References

Advanced Techniques. 1994. Crowd control training manual. In G. McIlwain (ed.), *Report on the Surfers Paradise Safety Action Project,* March-December, 1993. Gold Coast, Queensland: Surfers Paradise Safety Action Project.

Alcohol Advisory Council of Western Australia 1989. *Licensed Premises: Your Right to Object.* Perth, AUS: Author.

Aldridge, J. 1994. *CCTV Operational Requirements Manual Version 3.0.* Publication number 17/94, Sandridge Hertfordshire: Home Office Police Scientific Development Branch

Al-Kahtani S. 1996. *Travel to Crime Distances of Burglars in Saudi Arabia,* Unpublished Ph.D. Thesis, University of Manchester.

Allatt, P. 1984. Residential security: Containment and displacement of burglary. *Howard Journal of Criminal Justice* 23:99-116.

Anderson D., Chenery, S. and Pease, K. 1994. *Tackling Repeat Burglary and Car Crime.* Crime Detection and Prevention Paper 58. London: Home Office.

Anderson, D., Chenery S. and Pease, K. 1995. *Preventing Repeat Victimization: A Report on Progress in Huddersfield.* Police Research Group Briefing Note 4/95. London: Home Office.

Angel, S. 1968. *Discouraging Crime Through City Planning.* Berkeley, CA: Institute of Urban and Regional Development.

Ardrey, R. 1966. *The Territorial Imperative.* New York: Dell Publishing Co.

Athena Research Corporation. 1981. Robber interview report. Presented to the Crime Committee of the Southland Corporation, June 9, 1991. Dallas, TX.

Atkins, S., Husain, S. and Storey, A. 1991. *The Influence of Street Lighting on Crime and Fear of Crime.* Crime Prevention Unit Paper 28. London: Home Office.

Atlas, R. and LeBlanc, W.G. 1994. The impact on crime of street closures and barricades. *Security Journal* 5: 140-145

Ayres, I. and Braithwaite, J. 1992. *Responsive Regulation: Transcending the Deregulation Debate.* New York: Oxford University Press.

Ayres, I. and Levitt, S.D. 1996. Measuring positive externalities from unobservable victim precaution: An empirical analysis of Lojack. Unpublished manuscript, Yale Law School.

Baehr, G.T. 1992. P.A. rescues bus terminal phones from clutches of overseas hustlers. *The Star*

Ledger, August 6, p.20.

Bainbridge, B. 1984. Television interview with Robert Fulford on "Realities" Global Television, Toronto, October.

Bainbridge, D.I. and Painter, K. 1993. *The Impact of Public Lighting on Crime, Fear of Crime and Quality of Life : A Study in the Moseley and Showell Green Areas of Birmingham*. Birmingham: Aston Business School and University of Cambridge: Institute of Criminology.

Bamfield, J. 1994. Electronic article surveillance: Management learning in curbing theft. In M. Gill (ed.), *Crime at Work*. Leicester, UK: Perpetuity Press.

Bandura, A. 1976. Social learning analysis of aggression. In E. Ribes-Inesta and A. Bandura (eds.), *Analysis of Delinquency and Aggression*. Hillsdale, NJ: Lawrence Erlbaum Associates, Publishers.

Barclay, P., Buckley, J., Brantingham, P. J., Brantingham,P.L. and Whin-Yates, T. 1996. Preventing auto theft in suburban Vancouver: Effects of a bike patrol. In R.V. Clarke (ed.), *Preventing Mass Transit Crime. Crime Prevention Studies*, vol. 6. Monsey, NY: Criminal Justice Press.

Barr, R. and Pease, K. 1990. Crime placement, displacement and deflection. In M. Tonry and N. Morris (eds.), *Crime and Justice: A Review of Research* vol. 12. Chicago: University of Chicago Press.

Bauer, Y. 1990. The evolution of Nazi Jewish policy, 1933-38. In F. Chalk and K. Jonassohn (eds.), *The History and Sociology of Genocide: Analysis and Case Studies*. New Haven: Yale University Press.

Becker, G.S. 1968. Crime and punishment: An economic approach. *Journal of Political Economy* 76:169-217.

Bell, J. and Burke, J. 1989. Cruising Cooper Street. *Police Chief*, January:26-29.

Bellamy, L. 1996. Situational crime prevention and convenience store robbery. *Security Journal* 7: 41-52.

Belson, W.A. 1978. *Television Violence and the Adolescent Boy*. Westmead, UK: Saxon House.

Bennett, T. 1990. *Evaluating Neighbourhood Watch*. Aldershot, Hants: Gower.

Bennett, T. and Wright, R. 1984. *Burglars on Burglary*. Farnborough, Hants: Gower.

Berkowitz, L. and LePage, A. 1967. Weapons as aggression-eliciting stimuli. *Journal of Personality and Social Psychology* 7:202-227.

Berla, N. 1965. *The Impact of Street Lighting on Crime and Traffic Accidents*. Education and Public Welfare Division, Library of Congress Legislative Reference Service, 4 October.

Berlin, P. 1993. New scam detected using counterfeit sales and charge receipts. *The Peter Berlin Report on Shrinkage Control* (executive ed.), June 2.

Bichler, G. and Clarke, R.V. 1996. Eliminating pay phone toll fraud at the Port Authority Bus Terminal in Manhattan. In R.V. Clarke (ed.), *Preventing Mass Transit Crime. Crime Prevention Studies*, vol. 6. Monsey, NY: Criminal Justice Press.

Bickerton, D. and Hodge, G.T. 1992. Refund fraud. *Retail Business Review* 60:26-28.

Biron, L.L. and Ladouceur, C. 1991. The boy next door: Local teen-age burglars in Montreal. *Security Journal* 2:200-204.

Bjor, T., Knutsson, J. and Kuhlhorn, E. 1992. The celebration of midsummer eve in Sweden — a study in the art of preventing collective disorder. *Security Journal* 3:169-174.

Blagg, H., Pearson, G., Sampson, A., Smith, D. and Stubbs, P. 1988. Inter-agency co-ordination: Rhetoric and reality. In T. Hope and M. Shaw (eds.), *Communities and Crime Reduction*. London: H.M. Stationery Office.

Blazevic, G.R. 1996. *Creating a Culture of Collaboration for Addressing Alcohol-Related Violence*. Qld. Police Service, South East Region.

Block, C.R. 1990. Hot spots and isocrimes in law enforcement decision making. Paper presented at conference on Police and Community Responses to Drugs, University of Illinois at Chicago.

Bochner, R.J. 1995. Personal interview with Richard J. Bochner, Supervisor, Facilities and Planning Section, Office of Planning, Washington Metropolitan Area Transit Authority, May 21, 1995,

Washington, DC.

Boggs, S. 1966. Urban crime patterns. *American Sociological Review* 306:899-908.

Boss, R.W. 1980. The library security myth. *Library Journal* 105:683.

Bottomley, A.K. 1986. Blue-prints for criminal justice: Reflections on a policy plan for The Netherlands. *Howard Journal of Criminal Justice* 25:199-215.

Bottoms, A.E. 1990. Crime prevention facing the 1990s. *Policing and Society* 1:3-22.

Bouloukos, A. and Farrell, G. 1997. On the displacement of repeat victimization. In G. Newman, R.V. Clarke and S.G. Shoham (eds.), *Rational Choice and Situational Crime Prevention: Theoretical Foundations.* Aldershot, UK: Dartmouth Publishing Company.

Bourne, M.G. and Cooke, R.C. 1993. Victoria's speed camera program. In R.V. Clarke (ed.), *Crime Prevention Studies*, vol. 1. Monsey, NY: Criminal Justice Press.

Braga, A. and Clarke, R.V. 1994. Improved radios and more stripped cars in Germany: A routine activities analysis. *Security Journal* 5: 154-159.

Brantingham, P.J. and Brantingham, P. L. 1975. The spatial patterning of burglary. *Howard Journal of Criminal Justice* 14:11-23.

Brantingham, P.J. and Brantingham, P.L. 1981. *Environmental Criminology.* Beverly Hills, CA: Sage.

Brantingham, P.J. and Brantingham, P.L. 1984. *Patterns in Crime.* New York: MacMillan.

Brantingham, P.J. and Brantingham, P.L. 1991. *Environmental Criminology.* (2nd ed.) Prospect Heights, IL: Waveland Press.

Brantingham, P.J. and Faust, F.L. 1976 A conceptual model of crime prevention. *Crime and Delinquency*, 22:130-46.

Brantingham, P.L. and Brantingham, P.J. 1981. Mobility, notoriety, and crime: A study in the crime patterns of urban nodal points. *Journal of Environmental Systems* 11:89-99.

Brantingham, P.L. and Brantingham, P.J. 1984. Burglar mobility and crime prevention planning. In: R. Clarke and T. Hope (eds.), *Coping with Burglary.* Boston: Kluwer-Nijhoff.

Brantingham, P.L. and Brantingham, P.J. 1991. Niches and predators: Theoretical departures in the ecology of crime. Paper read at the Western Society of Criminology annual meetings, Berkeley.

Brantingham, P.L. and Brantingham, P.J. 1993a. Environment, routine and situation: Toward a pattern theory of crime. In: R.V. Clarke and M. Felson (eds.), *Routine Activity and Rational Choice,* Advances in criminological theory, Vol. 5: New Brunswick, NJ: Transaction Press.

Brantingham, P.L. and Brantingham, P. J. 1993b. Nodes, paths and edges: Considerations on environmental criminology. *Journal of Environmental Psychology* 13:91-95.

Brantingham, P.L. and Brantingham, P.J. 1995. Criminality of place: Crime generators and crime attractors. *European Journal on Criminal Policy and Research* 3:5-26.

Brantingham, P.L., Brantingham, P.J. and Wong P.S. 1991. How public transit feeds private crime: Notes on the Vancouver SkyTrain experience. *Security Journal* 2:91-95.

Briar, S. and Piliavin, I.M. 1965. Delinquency, situational inducements and commitment to conformity, *Social Problems* 13:35-45.

Bridgeman, C. 1997. Preventing pay phone damage. In M. Felson and R.V. Clarke (eds.), *Business and Crime Prevention.* Monsey, NY: Criminal Justice Press.

Bright, J. 1992. *Crime Prevention in America: A British Perspective.* Chicago, IL: Office of International Criminal Justice, The University of Illinois at Chicago.

Brody, S.R. 1976. *The Effectiveness of Sentencing.* Home Office Research Study No. 35. London: H.M. Stationery Office.

Brown, B. 1996. *CCTV in Town Centres: Three Case Studies.* Police Research Group Crime Detection and Prevention Series Paper 68. London: Home Office.

Buck, W., Chatterton, M. and Pease, K.. 1995. *Obscene, Threatening and Other Troublesome Telephone Calls to Women In England and Wales: 1982-1992.* Research and Planning Unit Paper 92. London: Home Office.

Burden, T. and Murphy, L. 1991. *Street Lighting, Community Safety and the Local Environment.* The

Leeds Project, Leeds, UK:Leeds Polytechnic.

Burrows, J. 1991. *Making Crime Prevention Pay: Initiatives from Business*. Crime Prevention Unit Paper 27. London: Home Office.

Burrows, J. 1997. Criminology and business crime: Building the bridge. In M. Felson and R.V. Clarke (eds.), *Business and Crime Prevention*. Monsey, NY: Criminal Justice Press.

Burrows, J. and Tarling, R. 1985. Clearing up crime. In K. Heal *et al.* (eds.), *Policing Today*. London: H.M. Stationery Office.

Burt, C. 1925. *The Young Delinquent*. London: University of London Press (reprinted 1969).

Butterworth, R.A. 1991. *Study of Safety and Security Requirements for 'At Risk Businesses.'* Tallahassee, FL: Florida Department of Legal Affairs.

Carr, K. and Spring, G. 1993. Public transport safety: A community right and a communal responsibility. In R.V. Clarke (ed.), *Crime Prevention Studies*, vol. 1. Monsey, NY: Criminal Justice Press.

Carroll, J. and Weaver, F. 1986. Shoplifter's perceptions of crime opportunities: A process-tracing study. In D.B. Cornish and R.V. Clarke (eds.), *The Reasoning Criminal*. New York: Springer-Verlag.

Carvolth, R. 1991. Does responsible hospitality work? A Synopsis of research findings. In T. Stockwell, E. Lang & P. Rydon (eds.), *The Licensed Drinking Environment: Current Research in Australia and New Zealand* pp. 134-141. Perth, WA: National Centre for Research into the Prevention of Drug Abuse.

Carvolth, R. 1993. Surfers — sunny, safe and secure: Responsible hospitality finds a new home. Paper delivered to the Perspectives for Change Conference, Rotorua, New Zealand, February 1993.

Carvolth, R. 1995. The contribution of risk assessment to harm reduction through the Queensland safety action approach. In *Proceedings of the Second Window of Opportunity Congress* pp. 63-72. Brisbane, AUS: Alcohol and Drug Foundation.

Casey, S. and Lund, A. 1993. The effects of mobile roadside speedometers on traffic speeds. *Accident Analysis and Prevention* 24:507-520.

Cassels, J. 1985. Prostitution and public nuisance: Desperate measures and the limits of civil adjudication. *Canadian Bar Review* 53:764-787.

Castleman, C. 1982. *Getting Up: Subway Graffiti in New York*. Cambridge, MA: MIT Press.

Cavallo, A. and Drummond, A. 1994. Evaluation of the Victorian random breath testing initiative. In D. South and A. Cavallo (eds.), *Australasian Drink-Drive Conference 1993, Conference Proceedings*. Melbourne, AUS: VicRoads.

Chaiken, J., Lawless, M. and Stevenson, K. 1974. *The Impact of Police Activity on Crime: Robberies on the New York City Subway System*. Report No. R-1424-N.Y.C. Santa Monica, CA: Rand Corporation.

Challinger, D. 1991. Less telephone vandalism: How did it happen? *Security Journal* 2:111-119.

Challinger, D. 1996. Refund fraud in retail stores. *Security Journal* 7: 27-35.

Challinger, D. 1997. Will crime prevention ever be a business priority? In M. Felson and R.V. Clarke (eds.), *Business and Crime Prevention*. Monsey, NY: Criminal Justice Press.

Chatterton, M.R. and Frenz, S.J. 1994. Closed-circuit television: Its role in reducing burglaries and the fear of crime in sheltered accommodation for the elderly. *Security Journal* 5:133-139.

Clarke, M. 1994. Blind eye on the street. *Police Review* August 5, pp. 28-29.

Clarke, R.V. 1977. Psychology and crime. *Bulletin of the British Psychological Society* 30:280-3.

Clarke, R.V. 1980. Situational crime prevention: Theory and practice. *British Journal of Criminology* 20:136-147.

Clarke, R.V. 1983. Situational crime prevention: Its theoretical basis and practical scope. In M.Tonry and N. Morris (eds.), *Crime and Justice: An Annual Review of Research*, vol. 4. Chicago: University of Chicago Press.

Clarke, R.V. 1984. Opportunity-based crime rates. *British Journal of Criminology* 24:74-83.

Clarke, R.V. 1990. Deterring obscene phone callers: Preliminary results of the New Jersey experience. *Security Journal* 1:143-148.

Clarke, R.V. (ed.) 1992. *Situational Crime Prevention: Successful Case Studies*. Albany, NY: Harrow and Heston.

Clarke, R.V. 1993. Fare evasion and automatic ticket collection on the London Underground. In R.V. Clarke (ed.), *Crime Prevention Studies*, vol. 2. Monsey, NY: Criminal Justice Press.

Clarke, R.V. 1995. Situational crime prevention. In M. Tonry and D. Farrington (eds.), *Building a Safer Society. Strategic Approaches to Crime Prevention. Crime and Justice: A Review of Research*, vol. 19. Chicago: University of Chicago Press.

Clarke, R.V. 1997. Problem-oriented policing and the potential contribution of criminology. Report to the National Institute of Justice. Grant # 95IJCX0021.

Clarke, R.V., Belanger, M. and Eastman, J.A. 1996. Where angels fear to tread: A test in the New York City subway of the robbery/density hypothesis. In R.V.Clarke (ed.), *Crime Prevention Studies*, vol.6. Monsey, NJ: Criminal Justice Press.

Clarke, R.V., Cody, R. and Natarajan, M. 1994. Subway slugs: Tracking displacement on the London Underground. *British Journal of Criminology* 34:122-138.

Clarke, R.V. and Cornish, D.B. 1972. *The Controlled Trial in Institutional Research: Paradigm or Pitfall*. Home Office Research Study No. 12. London: H.M. Stationery Office.

Clarke, R.V. and Cornish, D.B. 1983. *Crime Control in Britain: A Review of Policy Research*. Albany, NY: State University of New York Press.

Clarke, R.V. and Cornish, D.B. 1985. Modeling offenders' decisions: A framework for policy and research. In M. Tonry and N. Morris (eds.), *Crime and Justice: An Annual Review of Research*, vol. 6. Chicago: University of Chicago Press.

Clarke, R.V. and Felson, M. (eds.), 1993. *Routine Activity and Rational Choice. Advances in Criminological Theory*, vol. 5. New Brunswick, NJ: Transaction Publishers.

Clarke, R.V., Field, S. and McGrath, G. 1991. Target hardening of banks in Australia and displacement of robberies. *Security Journal* 2:84-90.

Clarke, R.V. and Harris, P.M. 1992a. Autotheft and its prevention. In M.Tonry (ed.), *Crime and Justice: A Review of Research*, vol. 16. Chicago: University of Chicago Press.

Clarke, R.V. and Harris, P.M. 1992b. A rational choice perspective on the targets of auto theft. *Criminal Behaviour and Mental Health* 2:25-42.

Clarke, R.V. and Homel, R. 1997. A revised classification of situational crime prevention techniques. In Lab, S.P. (ed.), *Crime Prevention at a Crossroads*. Cincinnati, OH: Anderson

Clarke, R.V., and Lester, D. 1987. Toxicity of car exhausts and opportunity for suicide: Comparison between Britain and the United States. *Journal of Epidemiology and Community Health* 41:114-120.

Clarke, R.V. and Mayhew, P.M. 1980. *Designing out Crime*. London: H.M. Stationery Office.

Clarke, R.V. and Mayhew, P. 1988. The British gas suicide story and its criminological implications. In M.Tonry and N. Morris (eds.), *Crime and Justice*, vol. 10. Chicago: University of Chicago Press.

Clarke, R.V. and McGrath, G. 1990. Cash reduction and robbery prevention in Australian betting shops. *Security Journal* 1:160-163.

Clarke, R.V. and Weisburd, D. 1994. Diffusion of crime control benefits: Observations on the reverse of displacement. In R.V. Clarke (ed.), *Crime Prevention Studies*, vol. 2. Monsey, NY: Criminal Justice Press.

Clifton, W., Jr. and Callahan, P.T. 1987. *Convenience Store Robberies in Gainesville, Florida: An Intervention Strategy by the Gainesville Police Department*. Gainesville: Gainesville Police Department.

Cohen, J. 1988. *Statistical Power Analysis for the Behavioural Sciences,* 2nd ed. Hillsdale, N.J. : Erlbaum.

Cohen, L.E. and Felson, M. 1979. Social change and crime rate trends: A routine activity approach.

American Sociological Review 44:588-608.

Cohen, L.E., Felson, M. and Land, K.C. 1980. Property crime rates in the United States: A macrodynamic analysis, 1947-1977; with ex ante forecasts for the mid-1980s. *American Journal of Sociology* 86:90-118.

Cole, C.A. 1989. Deterrence and consumer fraud. *Journal of Retailing* 65:107-120.

Coleman, A. 1985. *Utopia on Trial: Vision and Reality in Planned Housing.* London: Hilary Shipman.

Connell, J.P., Kubisch, A.C., Schorr, L.B. and Weiss, C.H. (eds.), 1995. *New Approaches to Evaluating Community Intiatives.* Washington, DC: The Aspen Institute.

Cook, T.D. and Campbell, D.T. 1979. *Quasi-Experimentation: Design and Analysis Issues for Field Settings.* Chicago: Rand McNally.

Cooper, B. 1989. Preventing break-ins to pre-payment fuel meters. *Research Bulletin* No. 26. Home Office Research and Planning Unit. London: Home Office.

Cornish, D.B. 1993. Theories of action in criminology: Learning theory and rational choice approaches. In R.V. Clarke and M. Felson (eds.), *Routine Activity and Rational Choice.* Advances in Criminological Theory, vol. 5. New Brunswick, NJ: Transaction Publishers.

Cornish, D. 1994. The procedural analysis of offending and its relevance for situational prevention. In: R.V. Clarke (ed.), *Crime Prevention Studies,* vol. 3. Monsey, NY: Criminal Justice Press.

Cornish, D.B. and Clarke, R.V. (eds.). 1986. *The Reasoning Criminal. Rational Choice Perspectives on Offending.* New York: Springer-Verlag.

Cornish, D.B. and Clarke, R.V. 1987. Understanding crime displacement: An application of rational choice theory. *Criminology* 25:933-947.

Cornish, D.B. and Clarke, R.V. 1988. Crime specialisation, crime displacement and rational choice theory. In H. Wegener, F. Losel and J. Haisch (eds.), *Criminal Behavior and the Justice System.* Berlin: Springer-Verlag.

Cromwell, P. (ed.) 1996. *In Their Own Words: Criminals on Crime.* Los Angeles, CA: Roxbury Publishing Co.

Cromwell, P.F., Olson, J.N. and Avary, D.W. 1991. *Breaking and Entering: An Ethnographic Analysis of Burglary.* Newbury Park, CA: Sage.

Crow, W.J. and Bull, J.L. 1975. *Robbery Deterrence: An Applied Behavioral Science Demonstration—Final Report.* La Jolla, CA: Western Behavioral Sciences Institute.

Crowe, T.D. 1991. *Crime Prevention through Environmental Design: Applications of Architectural Design and Space Management Concepts.* Boston: Butterworth-Heinemann.

Crowe, T.D. and Zahm, D. 1994. Crime Prevention through Environmental Design. *Land Development* 7: 22-27.

Curtis, R. and Sviridoff, M. 1994. The social organization of street-level drug markets and its impact on the displacement effect. In R.P. McNamara (ed.), *Crime Displacement: The Other Side of Prevention.* East Rockway, NY: Cummings and Hathaway.

Cusson, M. 1986. L'analyse strategique et quelques developpements recente en Criminologie. *Criminologie* XIX:51-72.

Cusson, M. 1993. Situational deterrence: Fear during the criminal event. In R.V. Clarke (ed.), *Crime Prevention Studies,* vol. 1. Monsey, NY: Criminal Justice Press.

Dacy, J. 1994. When shoplifters ask for refunds. *Nation's Business* 82: 27.

Dalby, J.T. 1988. Is telephone scatalogia a variant of exhibitionism? *International Journal of Offender Therapy and Comparative Criminology* 32:45-50.

Davidson, N. and Goodey, J. 1991. *Street Lighting and Crime.* The Hull Project, Hull University.

Davies, S. 1996a. *Big Brother: Britain's Web of Surveillance and the New Technological Order.* London: Pan Books.

Davies, S.G. 1996b. The case against: CCTV should not be introduced. *International Journal of Risk, Security and Crime Prevention* 1:327-331.

Davis, M. 1990. *City of Quartz. Excavating the Future in Los Angeles.* London: Verso.

Decker, J.F. 1972. Curbside deterrence: An analysis of the effect of a slug rejectory device, coin view window and warning labels on slug usage in New York City parking meters. *Criminology* August: 127-142.

Degner, R.L., Comer, D.A., Kepner, K.W. and Olexia, M.T. 1983. *Food Store Robberies in Florida: Detailed Crime Statistics.* Gainesville, FL: Florida Agricultural Market Research Center.

Deiter, R.H. 1990. *The Story of Metro: Transportation and Politics in the Nation's Capital.* Glendale, CA: Interurban Press.

Del Castillo, V. 1992. *Fear of Crime in the New York City Subway.* Doctoral dissertation, Fordham University, Department of Sociology, New York.

Department of Environment. 1977. *Housing Management and Design.* (Lambeth Inner Area Study). IAS/IA/18. London: Department of Environment.

Department of Transport 1986. *Crime on the London Underground.* London: H.M. Stationery Office.

DesChamps, S., Brantingham, P.L. and Brantingham, P.J. 1991. The British Columbia transit fare evasion audit: A description of a situational prevention process. *Security Journal* 2:211-218.

DiLonardo, R.L. 1985. *Profits through merchandise preservation.* Deerfield Beach, FL: Electronics corporation.

DiLonardo, R.L. 1996. Defining and measuring the economic benefit of electronic article surveillance. *Security Journal* 7:3-9.

DiLonardo, R. L. and Clarke, R.V. 1996. Reducing the rewards of shoplifting: An evaluation of ink tags. *Security Journal* 7:11-14.

Ditton, J., Nair, G. and Phillips, S. 1993. Crime in the dark: A case study of the relationship between street lighting and crime. In H. Jones (ed.), *Crime and the Urban Environment.* Aldershot, UK: Avebury.

Downes, D. and Rock, P. 1982. *Understanding Deviance.* Oxford: Clarendon Press.

Duffala, D.C. 1976. Convenience stores, armed robbery and physical environmental features. *American Behavioral Scientist* 20:227-246.

Dunn, V. 1984. *A Study of Prostitution in Finsbury Park.* Research Thesis submitted to North London Polytechnic.

Dunstan, G. and McDonald, R. 1996. Situational Crime Prevention and the Art of Celebration. Paper presented at the Last Night First Light Conference, Byron Bay, NSW, September 1996.

Durham, P. 1995. Villains in the Frame. *Police Review*, January 20, pp. 20-21.

Dwyer, J. 1991. *Subway Lives.* New York: Crown.

Eck, J.E. 1993. The threat of crime displacement. *Criminal Justice Abstracts* 25: 527-546.

Eck, J.E. 1995. A general model of the geography of illicit retail marketplaces. In D. Weisburd and J. Eck (eds.), *Crime and Place. Crime Prevention Studies*, vol. 4. Monsey, NY: Criminal Justice Press.

Eck, J. and Spelman, W. 1992. Thefts from vehicles in shipyard parking lots. In R.V. Clarke (ed.), *Situational Crime Prevention: Successful Case Studies.* Albany, NY: Harrow and Heston.

Eck, J. and Weisburd, D. (eds.). 1996. *Crime and Place. Crime Prevention Studies*, Vol. 4. Monsey, NY: Criminal Justice Press.

Edwards, P. and Tilley, N. 1994. *Closed Circuit Television: Looking out for You.* London: Home Office Police Department.

Ekblom, P. 1987a. Crime prevention in England: Themes and issues. Unpublished paper presented at Australian Institute of Criminology, November 24, 1987. London: Home Office Crime Prevention Unit.

Ekblom, P. 1987b. *Preventing Robbery at Sub-Post Offices: An Evaluation of a Security Initiative.* Crime Prevention Unit Paper 9. London: Home Office.

Ekblom, P. 1988a. *Getting the Best out of Crime Analysis.* Crime Prevention Unit Paper 10. London: Home Office Prevention Unit.

Ekblom, P. 1988b. Preventing post office robberies in London: Effects and side effects. *Journal of*

Security Administration 11:36-43.

Ekblom, P. 1991. Talking to offenders: Practical lessons for local crime prevention. In O. Nel-lo (ed.), *Urban Crime: Statistical Approaches and Analyses.* Barcelona, Spain: Institut d'Estudis Metropolitans de Barcelona.

Ekblom, P. 1994. Proximal circumstances: A mechanism-based classification of crime prevention. In R.V. Clarke (ed.), *Crime Prevention Studies*, vol. 2. Monsey, NY: Criminal Justice Press.

Ekblom, P. and Heal, K. 1982. *The Police Response to Calls from the Public.* Home Office Research and Planning Unit Paper No. 9. London: H.M. Stationery Office.

Ekblom, P. and Pease, K. 1995. Evaluating crime prevention. In M. Tonry and D.P. Farrington (eds.), *Building a Safer Society: Strategic Approaches to Crime Prevention. Crime and Justice: A Review of Research*, vol. 19. Chicago: University of Chicago Press.

Ellul, J. 1965. *Propaganda: The Formation of Men's Attitudes.* New York: Vintage Books.

Engstad, P. 1975. Environmental opportunities and the ecology of crime. In R.A. Silverman and J.J. Teevan, Jr. (eds.), *Crime in Canadian Society.* Toronto: Butterworth.

Engstad, P. and Evans, J.L. 1980. Responsibility, competence and police effectiveness in crime control. In R.V. Clarke and J.M. Hough (eds). *The Effectiveness of Policing.* Farnborough, Hants: Gower.

Falanga, M. 1988. *Reducing Crime Through Design in the Chicago Subway System.* Doctoral Dissertation, The University of Michigan, Department of Urban, Technological, and Environmental Planning, Ann Arbor, Michigan.

Farrell G. 1995. Predicting and preventing revictimization. In M.Tonry and D.P.Farrington (eds.), *Building a Safer Society* Chicago: University of Chicago Press.

Farrell, G. and Pease, K. 1993. *Once Bitten, Twice Bitten: Repeat Victimisation and its Implications for Crime Prevention.* Crime Prevention Unit Paper 46. London: Home Office.

Farrington, D.P. 1983. Randomized experiments on crime and justice. In M. Tonry and N. Morris (eds.), *Crime and Justice: An Annual Review of Research*, vol. 4. Chicago: University of Chicago Press.

Farrington, D.P., Bowen, S., Buckle, A., Burns-Howell, T., Burrows, J. and Speed, M. 1993. An experiment on the prevention of shoplifting. In R.V. Clarke (ed.), *Crime Prevention Studies*, vol. 1. Monsey, NY: Criminal Justice Press.

Fattah, E.A. 1993. The rational choice/opportunity perspectives as a vehicle for integrating criminological and victimological theories. In R.V. Clarke and M. Felson (eds.), *Routine Activity and Rational Choice, Advances in Criminological Theory*, vol. 5. New Brunswick, NJ: Transaction Publishers.

Federal Bureau of Investigation. 1975. Motor vehicle thefts — A uniform crime reporting survey. *FBI Law Enforcement Bulletin*, August 10th.

Feeney, F. 1986. Robbers as decision-makers In D.B. Cornish and R.V. Clarke (eds.), *The Reasoning Criminal: Rational Choice Perspectives on Offending.* New York: Springer-Verlag.

Felson, M. 1986. Linking criminal choices, routine activities, informal control, and criminal outcomes. In D.B. Cornish and R.V. Clarke (eds.), *The Reasoning Criminal.* New York: Springer Verlag.

Felson, M. 1992. Routine activities and crime prevention: Armchair concepts and practical action. *Studies on Crime and Crime Prevention* 1:31-34.

Felson, M. 1994a. *Crime and Everyday Life: Insight and Implications for Society.* Thousand Oaks, CA: Pine Forge Press.

Felson, M. 1994b. A crime prevention extension service. In R.V. Clarke (ed.), *Crime Prevention Studies*, vol. 3. Monsey, NY: Criminal Justice Press.

Felson, M. 1995. Those who discourage crime. In D. Weisburd and J. Eck (eds.), *Crime and Place. Crime Prevention Studies*, vol. 4. Monsey, NY: Criminal Justice Press.

Felson, M., Belanger, M.E., Bichler, G., Bruzinski, C., Campbell, G.S., Fried, C.L., Grofik, K.C., Mazur, I.S., O'Regan, A., Sweeney, P.J., Ullman, A.L., and Williams, L.M. 1996. Redesigning hell: Preventing crime and disorder at the Port Authority Bus Terminal. In R.V. Clarke (ed.), *Preventing Mass Transit Crime. Crime Prevention Studies*, vol. 6. Monsey, NY: Criminal Justice Press.

Felson, M. and Clarke, R.V. 1995. Routine precautions, criminology, and crime prevention. In H. D. Barlow (ed.), *Crime and Public Policy.* Boulder, CO: Westview Press.

Felson, M. and Clarke, R.V. (eds.). 1997a. *Business and Crime Prevention.* Monsey, NY: Criminal Justice Press.

Felson, M. and Clarke, R.V. 1997b. The ethics of situational crime prevention. In G. Newman, R.V. Clarke and S.G. Shoham (eds.), *Rational Choice and Situational Crime Prevention: Theoretical Foundations.* Aldershot, UK: Dartmouth Publishing Company.

Fennelly, L.J. 1989. *Handbook of Loss Prevention and Crime Prevention.* 2nd Ed. Stoneham, MA: Butterworth-Heinemann.

Ferreira, B. 1995. Situational crime prevention and displacement: The implications for business, industrial and private security management, *Security Journal.* 6: 155-162.

Field, S. 1993. Crime prevention and the costs of auto theft: An economic analysis. In R.V. Clarke (ed.), *Crime Prevention Studies*, vol. 1. Monsey, NY: Criminal Justice Press.

Fisher, J. 1993. Partnership for personal safety: Preventing violent crime in and around licensed premises. A paper presented at the National Conference on Crime Prevention, School of Justice Administration, Griffith University, Brisbane.

Fleiss, J.L. 1981. *Statistical Methods for Rates and Proportions,* 2nd ed. New York: Wiley.

Fleming, R. and Burrows, J. 1986. The case for lighting as a means of preventing crime. *Home Office Research Bulletin* 22:14-17.

Fleming, Z. 1993. British Columbia Association of Chiefs of Police auto theft study and recommendations — Summary report. Vancouver: British Columbia Association of Chiefs of Police.

Fleming, Z., Brantingham, P.L. and Brantingham, P.J. 1994. Exploring auto theft in British Columbia. In R.V. Clarke (ed.), *Crime Prevention Studies,* vol. 3. Monsey, NY: Criminal Justice Press.

Florida Department of Law Enforcement. 1991. Information provided by Ms. Linda Booz of the Uniform Crime Reporting Section.

Florida Department of Legal Affairs. 1991. Information provided by Mr. Daniel A. Gilmore of the Office of the Attorney General, Bureau of Criminal Justice Programs.

Forrester, D., Chatterton, M. and Pease, K. 1988. *The Kirkholt Burglary Prevention Project, Rochdale.* Crime Prevention Unit Paper 13. London: Home Office.

Foster, J. and Hope, T. 1993. *Housing, Community and Crime: The Impact of the Priority Estates Project.* Home Office Research Study No.131. London: H.M. Stationery Office.

Foucault, M. 1977. *Discipline and Punish: The Birth of the Prison.* New York: Vintage.

Fowler, F.J. and Mangione, T.W. 1986. A three pronged effort to reduce crime and fear of crime: The Hartford Experiment. In D. Rosenbaum (ed.), *Community Crime Prevention: Does it Work?* London: Sage.

Gabor, T. 1981. The crime displacement hypothesis: An empirical examination. *Crime and Delinquency* 26:390-404.

Gabor, T. 1990. Crime displacement and situational prevention: Toward the development of some principles. *Canadian Journal of Criminology* 32:41-74.

Gabor, T. 1994. *Everybody Does It! Crime by the Public.* New York: Macmillan

Gammino, J. 1992a. Payday for private payphone providers and premise owners? *Phone+,* March: 34-35.

Gammino, J. 1992b. *PABT Payphone Fraud Interim Report,* John Richard Associates, Inc. NJ.: Hazelet.

Gantenbein, J.M. and Rogers, E.K. 1995. Return fraud. Presentation at the National Retail Federation's Loss Prevention and Internal Audit Conference, June 25-28. Las Vegas, NV.

Garland, D. 1996. The limits of the sovereign state: Strategies of crime control in contemporary society. *British Journal of Criminology* 36: 445-471.

Geason, S. and Wilson, P.R. 1990. *Preventing Car Theft and Crime in Car Parks*. Canberra: Australian Institute of Criminology.

Gebhardt, C. 1996. Metropolitan police department crime analysis and mapping agenda. Handout from presentation at a meeting of the Department of Justice Geographic Information System Working Group, March 4, 1996.

Gilling, D. 1993. The multi-agency approach to crime prevention: The British experience. A paper presented at the National Conference on Crime Prevention, School of Justice Administration, Griffith University: Brisbane.

Gilling, D. 1996. Problems with the problem-oriented approach. In R. Homel (ed.), *Crime Prevention Studies*, vol. 5. Monsey, NY: Criminal Justice Press.

Gladstone, F.J. 1980. *Co-ordinating Crime Prevention Efforts*. Home Office Research Study No. 47. London: H.M. Stationery Office.

Glazer, N. 1979. On subway graffiti in New York. *Public Interest* (Winter).

Goldberg, R. and Wise, T. (1985). Psychodynamic treatment for telephone scatalogia. *American Journal of Psychoanalysis* 45:291-297.

Goldstein, H. 1979. Improving policing: A problem-oriented approach. *Crime and Delinquency* 25: 236-258 .

Goldstein, H. 1990. *Problem-Oriented Policing*. New York: McGraw Hill.

Gottfredson, M.R. and Hirschi, T. 1990. *A General Theory of Crime*. Stanford, CA: Stanford University Press.

Gove, W.R., Hughes, M. and Geerken, M. 1985. Are uniform crime reports a valid indicator of the index crimes? An affirmative answer with minor qualifications. *Criminology* 233:451-501.

Grabosky, P. 1996. Unintended consequences of crime prevention. In R. Homel (ed.), *Crime Prevention Studies*, vol. 5. Monsey, NY: Criminal Justice Press.

Graham, K., La Roque, I., Yetman, R., Ross, T. and Guistra, E. 1980. Aggression and barroom environments. *Journal of Studies on Alcohol* 41:277.

Grandjean, C. 1990. Bank robberies and physical security in Switzerland: A case study of the escalation and displacement phenomena. *Security Journal* 1:155-159.

Greenwood, L. and McKean, H. 1985. Effective measurement and reduction of book loss in an academic library. *Journal of Academic Librarianship* 11:275-283.

Griswold, D.B. 1984. Crime prevention and commercial burglary: A time series analysis. *Journal of Criminal Justice* 12:493-501.

Guhl, T. 1993. Consultant solves payphone fraud problem at Port Authority Bus Terminal. *Public Communications Magazine*, No.63, May, 24-26.

Hackler, J.C. 1978. *The Prevention of Youth Crime: The Great Stumble Forward*. Toronto: Methuen.

Hakim, S., Gaffney, M.A., Rengert, G., and Shachmurove, J. 1995. Costs and benefits of alarms to the community: Burglary patterns and security measures in Tredyffrin township, Pennsylvania. *Security Journal* 6:197-204.

Hall, J. 1952. *Theft, Law and Society*. New York: Bobbs-Merrill.

Harding, A., Allport, W., Hodges, D. and Davenport, J. 1987. *The Guinness Book of the Car*. London: Guinness Superlatives Ltd.

Harries, K.D. 1980. *Crime and the Environment*. Springfield, IL: Charles C. Thomas.

Harris, P.M. and Clarke, R.V. 1991. Car chopping, parts marking and the Motor Vehicle Theft Law Enforcement Act of 1984. *Sociology and Social Research* 75:228-238.

Hartley, J.E. 1974. *Lighting Reinforces Crime Fight*. Pittsfield: Buttenheim.

Hartshorne, M. and May, M.A. 1928. *Studies in the Nature of Character (Vol. I): Studies in Deceit*. New York: Macmillan.

Hauber, A.R. 1977. *Gedrag van Mensen in Beweging* (The behaviour of people on the move). Krommenie: Rotatie Boekendruk.

Hauritz, M., Homel, R., McIlwain, G., Burrows, T. and Townsley, M. In press. Reducing violence in licensed venues through community safety action projects: The Queensland experience. *Contemporary Drug Problems.*

Hawley, A. 1950. *Human Ecology: A Theory of Community Structure.* New York: Ronald.

Heal, K. and Laycock, G. 1986. *Situational Crime Prevention: From Theory into Practice.* London: H.M. Stationery Office.

Heijden, A.W.M. van der. 1984. Onrustgevoelens in verband met criminaliteit, 1982-1984 (Feelings of disquiet over criminality). *Monthly Statistics of the Police.* Public Prosecutor's Office, 28: 11:8-14 (Central Bureau of Statistics).

Heller, N.B., Stenzel W.W., Gill, A.D., Kolde, R.A. and Schimerman, S.R. 1975. *Operation Identification Projects: Assessment of Effectiveness.* National Evaluation Program, Phase 1, Summary Report. Washington, DC: National Institute for Law Enforcement and Criminal Justice.

Hemenway, D. and Weil, D. 1990. Phasers on stun: The case for less lethal weapons. *Journal of Policy Analysis and Management* 9: 94-98.

Herbert, D. and Moore, L. 1991 *Street Lighting and Crime.* The Cardiff Project, Cardiff University.

Hesseling, R.B.P. 1994. Displacement: A review of the empirical literature. In R.V. Clarke (ed.), *Crime Prevention Studies*, vol. 3. Monsey, NY: Criminal Justice Press.

Hesseling, R.B.P. 1995. Theft from cars: Reduced or displaced? *European Journal of Criminal Policy and Research*, 3:79-92.

Hill, N. 1986. *Prepayment Coin Meters: A Target for Burglary.* Crime Prevention Unit Paper 6. London: Home Office.

Hillier, B. 1987 *Against Enclosure.* Paper presented to the British Criminology Conference.

Hindelang, M.J., Gottfredson, M.R. and Garofalo, J. 1978. *Victims of Personal Crime: An Empirical Foundation for a Theory of Personal Victimization.* Cambridge, MA: Ballinger.

Hirschi, T. 1969. *Causes of Delinquency.* Berkeley and Los Angeles: University of California Press.

Hoey, S. 1992a. P.A. Trying to hang up on thieves. *Staten Island Advance*, June 11.

Hoey, S. 1992b. P.A. Putting brakes on phone fraud at bus terminal. *Staten Island Advance*, Aug. 6.

Hollinger, R. and Dabney, D. 1994. Reducing shrinkage in the retail store: It's not just a job for the loss prevention department. *Security Journal* 5:2-10.

Holloway, L. 1992. Shoulder surfing: Life in phone credit-card theft. *New York Times*, November, 20.

Homel, R. 1993. Drivers who drink and rational choice: Random breath testing and the process of deterrence. In R.V. Clarke and M. Felson (eds.), *Routine Activity and Rational Choice. Advances in Criminological Theory*, vol. 5. New Brunswick, NJ: Transaction Publishers.

Homel, R. (ed.). 1996. Editor's introduction. *Crime Prevention Studies*, vol. 5. Monsey, NY: Criminal Justice Press.

Homel, R. 1997. Preventing alcohol-related injuries. In P. O'Malley and A. Sutton (eds.), *Crime Prevention in Australia.* Sydney: The Federation Press.

Homel, R. and Clark, J. 1994. The prediction and prevention of violence in pubs and clubs. In R.V. Clarke (ed.), *Crime Prevention Studies*, vol. 3. Monsey, NY: Criminal Justice Press.

Homel, R., Hauritz, M., Wortley, R., McIlwain, G. and Carvolth, R. 1997. Preventing alcohol-related crime through community action: The Surfers Paradise Safety Action Project. In R. Homel (ed.), *Policing for Prevention. Crime Prevention Studies*, vol. 7. Monsey, NY: Criminal Justice Press.

Homel, R., Tomsen, S. and Thommeny, J. 1992. Public drinking and violence: Not just an alcohol problem. *The Journal of Drug Issues* 22:679-697.

Honess, T. and Charman, E. 1992. *Closed-Circuit Television in Public Places: Its Acceptability and Perceived Effectiveness.* Crime Prevention Unit Series Paper 35. London: Home Office.

Hope, T. 1985. *Implementing Crime Prevention Measures.* Home Office Research Study No. 86. London: H.M. Stationery Office.

Hope, T. 1991. Crime information in retailing: Prevention through analysis. *Security Journal* 2:240-

245.

Hope, T. 1994. Problem-oriented policing and drug market locations: Three case studies. In R.V. Clarke (ed.), *Crime Prevention Studies*, vol. 2. Monsey, NY: Criminal Justice Press.

Hope, T. and Murphy, D.J.I. 1983. Problems of implementing crime prevention: The experience of a demonstration project. *Howard Journal* 83:38-50.

Horne, C.J. 1996. The case for: CCTV should be introduced. *International Journal of Risk, Security and Crime Prevention* 1:317-326.

Hough, J.M., Clarke, R.V., and Mayhew, P. 1980. Introduction. In R.V. Clarke and P. Mayhew (eds.), *Designing out Crime*. London: H.M. Stationery Office.

Houghton, G. 1992. *Car Theft in England & Wales: The Home Office Car Theft Index*. Crime Prevention Unit Paper No.33. London: Home Office.

Hughes, G. 1996. Strategies of multi-agency crime prevention and community safety in contemporary Britain. *Studies on Crime and Crime Prevention* 5:221-244.

Hunter, R.D. 1988. *The Effects of Environmental Factors upon Convenience Store Robbery in Florida*. Tallahassee, FL: Florida Department of Legal Affairs.

Hunter, R.D. 1990. Convenience store robbery in Tallahassee: A reassessment. *Journal of Security Administration* 13:3-18.

Hunter, R.D. and Jeffery, C.R. 1992. Preventing convenience store robbery through environmental design. In R.V.Clarke (ed.), *Situational Crime Prevention: Successful Case Studies*. Albany, NY: Harrow and Heston.

Hyde, J.F. 1993. CPTED goes underground. Presentation made at the Crime Prevention Through Environmental Design Conference, Washington, D.C., December 10, 1993.

Hyde, J.F. 1995. Telephone interview with John F. Hyde, former Deputy Chief of the Metropolitan Transit Police, Washington Metropolitan Area Transit Authority, September 12, 1995.

Indermaur, D. 1996. Reducing the opportunity for violence in robbery and property crime: The perspectives of offenders and victims. In R. Homel (ed.), *Crime Prevention Studies*, vol. 5. Monsey, NY: Criminal Justice Press.

Insurance Institute for Highway Safety. 1995. Study of light timing is part of larger Institute focus on urban crashes. *The Year's Work* April: 26.

Jacobs, J. 1961. *The Death and Life of Great American Cities*. New York: Random House.

Jannis, P.C., Poedtke, C.H., Jr. and Ziegler, D.R. 1980. *Managing and Accounting for Inventories*. New York: Ronald.

Jeffery, C.R. 1971. *Crime Prevention Through Environmental Design*. Beverly Hills, CA: Sage.

Jeffery, C.R. 1977. *Crime Prevention Through Environmental Design,* 2nd edition. Beverly Hills, CA: Sage.

Jeffery, C.R., Hunter, R.D. and Griswold, J. 1987. Crime prevention and computer analysis of convenience store robberies in Tallahassee, Florida. *Security Systems* August, 1987 and *Florida Police Journal* Spring, 1987.

Jeffs, B.W. and Saunders, W.M. 1983. Minimizing alcohol related offences by enforcement of the existing licensing legislation. *British Journal of Addiction* 78:67-77.

Jones, B. and Wood, N. 1989. Traffic Safety Impact of the 1988 Ignition Interlock Pilot Program. Oregon: Motor Vehicles Division.

Jones, T., MacLean, B. and Young, J. 1986. *The Islington Crime Survey*. Farnborough, Hants.: Gower.

Karmen, A. 1981. Auto theft and corporate irresponsibility. *Contemporary Crises* 5:63-81.

Karmen, A. 1984. *Crime Victims: An Introduction to Victimology*. Monterey, CA: Brooks/Cole Publishing Co.

Kelling, G. and Coles, C. 1996. *Fixing Broken Windows*. New York: Free Press

Kennedy, D.B. 1990. Facility site selection and analysis through environmental criminology. *Journal of Criminal Justice* 18:239-252.

Kenney, D.J. 1987. *Crime, Fear, and the New York City Subways: The Role of Citizen Action*. New

York: Praeger.

Kiley, R.R. 1988. An address to the Police Executive Research Forum, May 17. Washington DC.

Kiley, R.R. 1989. An address at the Celeste Bartos forum. New York: New York Public Library (February 9).

Kinsey, R., Lea, J. and Young, J. 1986. *Losing the Fight Against Crime*. London: Blackwells.

Klepper, S. and Nagin, D. 1987. The anatomy of tax evasion. Annual meeting of the American Society of Criminology, Montreal, November.

Knutsson, J. 1980. *The Charge Card and Credit Card Mess - Cases of Charge Card and Credit Card Fraud Reported to the Police in Stockholm in 1979*. Department of Sociology, University of Stockholm, 1980. Mimeographed and in Swedish.

Knutsson, J. 1984. *Operation Identification — A Way to Prevent Burglaries?* Report No. 14 Stockholm: National Swedish Council for Crime Prevention.

Knutsson, J. and Kuhlhorn, E. 1981. *Macro-measures Against Crime. The Example of Check Forgeries*. Information Bulletin No. 1. Stockholm: National Swedish Council for Crime Prevention.

Kohfeld, C.W. and Sprague, J. 1990. Demography, police behavior, and deterrence. *Criminology* 28:111-136.

Kube, E. 1988. Preventing bank robbery: Lessons from interviewing robbers. *Journal of Security Administration* 11:78-83.

Kuhlhorn, E. 1976. *Deprivation of Freedom and the Police — An Evaluation of the Temporary Custody Act*. Stockholm: National Swedish Council for Crime Prevention.

Kuhlhorn, E. 1982. Juggling with housing allowances: An example of prevention of fraud against the welfare society. In E. Kuhlhorn and Svensson, B. (eds.), *Crime Prevention*. Stockholm: Swedish National Council for Crime Prevention.

La Vigne, N.G. 1994. Rational choice and inmate disputes over phone use on Rikers Island. In R.V. Clarke (ed.), *Crime Prevention Studies*, vol. 3. Monsey, NY: Criminal Justice Press.

La Vigne, N.G. 1996a. Safe transport: Security by design on the Washington Metro. In R.V. Clarke (ed.), *Preventing Mass Transit Crime. Crime Prevention Studies*, vol. 6. Monsey, NY: Criminal Justice Press.

La Vigne, N.G. 1996b. Crime prevention through the design and management of built environment: the case of the DC Metro. Doctoral Dissertation, Rutgers, the State University of New Jersey, School of Criminal Justice, Newark, NJ.

Lakeland, G. and Durham, G. 1993. AHB and community organisation: Building a coalition in preventing alcohol problems. Paper delivered to the Perspectives for Change Conference, Rotorua, New Zealand, February 1993.

Lambert, B. 1995. Croissants? A clam bar? Is this the Port Authority Terminal? *New York Times*, August 6.

Lander, A. 1995. Preventing alcohol-related violence: A community action manual. Darlinghurst, NSW: Eastern Sydney Area Health Service and St. Vincent's Alcohol and Drug Service.

Landes, W.M. 1978. An economic study of U.S. aircraft hijacking, 1961-1976. *Journal of Law and Economics* 21:1-31.

Lang, E. and Rumbold, G. 1996. A critical review of local industry accords in Australia. Paper presented to the International Conference on Intoxication and Aggressive Behavior: Understanding and Preventing Alcohol-Related Violence, Toronto, Canada, October 1996.

Langworthy, R.H. and Le Beau, J. 1992a. The spatial evolution of a sting clientele. *Journal of Criminal Justice* 20:135-146.

Langworthy, R.H. and Le Beau, J. 1992b. The spatial distribution of sting targets. *Journal of Criminal Justice* 20: 541-552.

Lateef, B.A. 1974. Helicopter patrol in law enforcement— An evaluation. *Journal of Police Science and Administration* 2:62-65.

Lavrakas, P.J. and Kushmuk, J. 1986. Evaluating crime prevention through environmental design:

The Portland commercial demonstration project. In D. Rosenbaum (ed.), *Community Crime Prevention: Does it Work?* London: Sage.

Laycock, G.K. 1985. *Property Marking: A Deterrent to Domestic Burglary?* Crime Prevention Unit Paper 3. London: Home Office.

Laycock, G.K. 1991. Operation identification, or the power of publicity? *Security Journal* 2:67-72.

Laycock, G. and Austin, C. 1992. Crime prevention in parking facilities. *Security Journal* 3:154-160.

Le Cam, D. 1995. Quit complaining about metro signs. Letter to the editor. *The Washington Post*, September 12, 1995, p.A18.

Lea, J. *et al.* 1988. *Preventing Crime: The Hilldrop Project.* London: Centre for Criminology, Middlesex Polytechnic.

Lee, B.N.W. and Rikoski, G.P. 1984. *Vehicle Theft Prevention Strategies.* Washington DC: US Department of Justice, National Institute of Justice.

Lejeune, R. 1977. The management of a mugging. *Urban Life* 6:123-148.

Levi, M. 1992. Preventing credit card fraud. *Security Journal* 3:147-153.

Levi, M., Bissell, P. and Richardson, T. 1991. *The Prevention of Cheque and Credit Card Fraud.* Crime Prevention Unit Paper 26. London: Home Office.

Levine, P. 1988. *Prostitution in Florida: A Report Presented to the Gender Bias Study Commission of the Supreme Court of Florida.*

Levy, M. and Weitz, B.A. 1992. *Retailing Management.* Boston, MA: Irwin.

Levy, N.J. 1994. *Crime in New York City's Subways: A Study and Analysis of Issues with Recommendations to Enhance Safety and the Public's Perception of Safety within the Subway System.* New York: Senate Transportation Committee.

Lewin, K. 1947. Group decisions and social change. In T.M. Newcomb and E.L. Hartley (eds.), *Readings in Social Psychology.* New York: Atherton Press.

Liddle, A.M. and Gelsthorpe, L. 1994. *Crime Prevention and Inter-Agency Co-Ordination.* Crime Prevention Unit Series Paper 53. London: Home Office.

Light, R., Nee, C. and Ingham, H. 1993. *Car Theft: The Offender's Perspective.* Home Office Research Study, No. 130. London: H.M. Stationery Office.

Lingenfelter, R.E. 1986. *Death Valley and The Amargosa: A Land of Illusion.* Berkeley: University of California Press.

Lopez, M.J. 1996. *Crime Prevention Guidelines for the Construction and Management of Metro Systems.* The Hague: Result Crime Management.

Lowman, J. 1986. Street prostitution in Vancouver: Some notes on the genesis of a social problem. *Canadian Journal of Criminology* 28:1-16.

Lowman, J. 1992. Street prostitution control: Some Canadian reflections on the Finsbury Park experience. *British Journal of Criminology* 32:1-17

Lurigio, A.J. and Rosenbaum, D.P. 1986. Evaluative research in community crime prevention: A critical look at the field. In D. Rosenbaum (ed.), *Community Crime Prevention: Does it Work?.* London: Sage.

MacLean, A.B. 1994. The Metro Transit Police: Metropolitan Washington's Tri-State Police Force. *The Police Chief* December:29-30.

MacLean, A.B. 1995. Telephone interview with the former chief of the Metro Transit Police, September 13.

Maguire, K. and A.L. Pastore (eds.). 1995. *Sourcebook of Criminal Justice Statistics, 1994.* U.S. Department of Justice, Bureau of Justice Statistics. Washington, DC: U.S. Government Printing Office.

Maguire, M. 1980. Burglary as opportunity. *Research Bulletin* No. 10. Home Office Research Unit. London: Home Office.

Magnificent Events Company, The. 1996. *Concept Plans for Managing Dysfunctional Events at Bondi Beach on Christmas Day and New Year's Day.* Bond University, AUS: The Australian Institute of Dramatic Arts.

Maguire, M. 1982. *Burglary in a Dwelling*. London: Heinemann.

Mailer, N. 1974. *The Faith of Graffiti*. New York: Praeger/Alskog Publishers.

Makris, G. 1996. The myth of a technological solution to television violence: Identifying problems with the V-chip. *Journal of Communication Inquiry* 20:72-91

Mancini, A.N. and Jain, R. 1987. Commuter parking lots — Vandalism and deterrence. *Transportation Quarterly* 41:539-553.

Markus, C.L. 1984. British Telecom experience in payphone management. In C. Levy-Leboyer (ed.), *Vandalism Behaviour and Motivations*. Amsterdam: Elsevier North-Holland.

Martinson, R. 1974. What works? -Questions and answers about prison reform. *The Public Interest* 35(Spring): 22-54.

Marx, G.T. 1986. The iron fist and the velvet glove: Totalitarian potentials within democratic structures. In J. Short, Jr. (ed.), *The Social Fabric: Dimensions and Issues*. Beverly Hills, CA: Sage.

Marx, G.T. 1989. Letter. *New York Times*.

Masuda, B. 1992. Displacement vs. diffusion of benefits and the reduction of losses in a retail environment. *Security Journal* 3: 131-36.

Masuda, B. 1993. Credit card fraud prevention: A successful retail strategy. In R.V. Clarke (ed.), *Crime Prevention Studies*, vol. 1. Monsey, NY: Criminal Justice Press.

Matthews, R. 1986. *Policing Prostitution: A Multi-Agency Approach*. Centre for Criminology Paper No. 1. London: Middlesex Polytechnic.

Matthews, R. 1990. Developing more effective strategies for curbing prostitution. *Security Journal* 1:182-187.

Matthews, R. 1993. *Kerb-Crawling, Prostitution and Multi-Agency Policing*. Crime Prevention Unit Paper 43. London: Home Office

Matza, D. 1964. *Delinquency and Drift*. New York: Wiley.

Mawby, R.I. 1977. Kiosk vandalism: A Sheffield study. *British Journal of Criminology* 17:30-46.

Mayhew, P. 1979. Defensible space: The current status of a crime prevention theory. *The Howard Journal of Penology and Crime Prevention* 18:150-159.

Mayhew, P. 1984. Target hardening: how much of an answer? In R.V. Clarke and T. Hope (eds.), *Coping with Burglary*. Boston: Kluwer-Nijhoff.

Mayhew, P., Clarke, R.V., Burrows, J.N., Hough, J.M. and Winchester, S.W.C. 1979. *Crime in Public View*. Home Office Research Study No. 49. London: H.M. Stationery Office.

Mayhew, P., Clarke, R.V. and Elliott, D. 1989. Motorcycle theft, helmet legislation and displacement. *Howard Journal of Criminal Justice* 28:1-8.

Mayhew, P., Clarke, R.V., Sturman, A. and Hough, J.M. 1976. *Crime as Opportunity*. London: H. M. Stationery Office.

Mayhew, P., Elliott, D., and Dowds, L. 1989. *The 1988 British Crime Survey*. Home Office Research Study No.111. London: H.M. Stationery Office.

Mayhew, P., Maung, N.A. and Mirrlees-Black, C. 1993. *The 1992 British Crime Survey*. Home Office Research Study No.132. London: H. M. Stationery Office.

McCullough, D., Schmidt, T. and Lockhart, B. 1990. *Car Theft in Northern Ireland*. Cirac Paper No. 2. Belfast, UK: The EXTERN Organisation.

McFadden, R. D. 1987. Phone codes: Newest scam on the street. *New York Times*, May 12, p.1.

McGhee, K. 1995. Disoriented around the district. Letter to the editor, *The Washington Post*, September 5, 1995, p. A16.

McIlwain, G. 1994. *Report on the Surfers Paradise Safety Action Project, March - December 1993*. Gold Coast, AUS: Surfers Paradise Safety Action Project.

McNamara, R.P. 1994. Crime displacement and male prostitution in Times Square. In R.P. McNamara (ed.), *Crime Displacement: The Other Side of Prevention*. East Rockway, NY: Cummings and Hathaway.

Means, H. 1995. Why we love Washington. *Washingtonian*. October, 1995:111.

Meier, B. 1992. Speak your phone-card number softly. *New York Times*, August 15.

Melbourne City Council. 1991. Westend forum project — 1990/91. *Final Report.* Melbourne, Victoria: Author.

Meredith, C. and Paquette, C. 1992. Crime prevention in high-rise rental apartments: Findings of a demonstration project. *Security Journal* 3:161-169.

Merry, S.E. 1981. Defensible space undefended: Social factors in crime control through environmental design. *Urban Affairs Quarterly* 16:397-422.

Miethe, T.D. 1991. Citizen-based crime control activity and victimization risks: An examination of displacement and free-rider effects. *Criminology* 29:419-440.

Mischel, W. 1968. *Personality and Assessment.* New York: Wiley.

Mooney, B. 1976. Metro: Building rapid rail transit in the national capital region. Washington, DC: Transcript.

Moore, J. 1987. Safeguarding patient valuables: A case study. *Journal of Security Administration* 10:52-57.

Morris, N. and Hawkins, G. 1970. *The Honest Politician's Guide to Crime Control.* Chicago: University of Chicago Press.

Morrison, S. and O'Donnell, I. 1996. An analysis of the decision making processes of armed robbers. In R. Homel (ed.), *Crime Prevention Studies*, vol. 5. Monsey, NY: Criminal Justice Press.

Morrow, B.E. 1994. Personal interview with the chief of the Metro Transit Police Department, Washington Area Transit Authority, June 14.

Morse, B.J. and Elliott, D.S. 1990. Hamilton County Drinking and Driving Study: 30 Month Report. Institute of Behavioral Science. Boulder, CO: University of Colorado.

Murray, C. 1983. The physical environment and the community control of crime. In J. Wilson (ed.), *Crime and Public Policy.* San Francisco: ICS Press.

Myers, S. L. 1992. New York plans attack on pay-phone abuses. *New York Times*, Aug. 23.

Myhre, M. and Rosso, F. 1996. Designing for security in Meteor: A projected new Metro line in Paris. In R.V. Clarke (ed.), *Preventing Mass Transit Crime. Crime Prevention Studies*, vol. 6. Monsey, NY: Criminal Justice Press.

Nasar, J.L. and Fisher, B. 1992. Design for vulnerability: Cues and reactions to fear of crime. *Sociology and Social Research* 76:48-58.

Nasar, J. L. and Fisher, B. 1993. Hot spots of fear and crime: A multi-method investigation. *Journal of Environmental Psychology* 13:187-206.

Natarajan, M., and Clarke, R.V. 1994. The role of helmet laws in preventing motorcycle theft in Madras, India. *Indian Journal of Criminology* 22:22-26.

Natarajan, M., Clarke, R.V. and Belanger, M. 1996. Drug dealing and pay phones: The scope for intervention. *Security Journal* 7:245-251.

Natarajan, M., Clarke, R.V. and Johnson, B.D. 1995. Telephones as facilitators of drug dealing. *European Journal of Criminal Policy and Research* 33: 137-153.

National Association of Convenience Stores. 1987. *Robbery Deterrence Manual.* Alexandria, VA: National Association of Convenience Stores.

National Institute of Justice. 1995. *Violence in US Cities: A Project of the National Institute of Justice Intramural Research Working Group.* NIJ Intramural Milestone Report 1: Site Selection. September 21, 1995.

Nee, C. and Taylor, M. 1988. Residential burglary in the Republic of Ireland: A situational perspective. *Howard Journal of Criminal Justice* 27:80-95.

Netherlands, Ministry of Justice. 1984. *Interimrapport van de Commissie Kleine Criminaliteit* (Interim report of the committee on petty crime). The Hague: Government Printing Office.

Netherlands, Ministry of Justice. 1985. *Society and Crime: A Policy Plan for the Netherlands.* The Hague: Ministry of Justice.

New Jersey Board of Public Utilities. 1988. Submission by New Jersey Bell. Docket No. TT87070560.

New Jersey Board of Public Utilities. 1989. Submission by New Jersey Bell. Docket No. TT88070825.

New South Wales Bureau of Crime Statistics and Research. 1987. *Robbery*. Sydney: Attorney General's Department.

New York State Senate Committee on Transportation. 1980. *National Conference on Mass Transit Crime and Vandalism: Compendium of Proceedings*. Albany, NY: New York State Senate.

Newman, G. 1997. Introduction: Towards a theory of situational crime prevention. In G. Newman, R.V. Clarke and S.G. Shoham (eds.), *Rational Choice and Situational Crime Prevention: Theoretical Foundations*. Aldershot, UK: Dartmouth Publishing Company.

Newman, Sir K. 1986. *Report of the Commissioner of the Police of the Metropolis*. London: H.M. Stationery Office.

Newman, O. 1972. *Defensible Space: Crime Prevention Through Urban Design*. New York: Macmillan. (Published by Architectural Press, London, in 1973).

Newman, O. 1996. *Creating Defensible Space*. Washington, DC: Office of Policy Development and Research, U.S. Department of Housing and Urban Development.

Normandeau, A. and Gabor, T. 1987. *Armed Robbery: Cops, Robbers and Victims*. Springfield, IL: Charles C. Thomas.

NRMA Insurance Ltd. 1990. *Car Theft in New South Wales*. Sydney: National Roads and Motorists' Association.

Nugent, S., Burnes, D., Wilson, P. and Chappell, D. 1989. *Risks and Rewards in Robbery: Prevention and the Offender's Perspective*. Melbourne: Australian Bankers' Association.

O'Malley, P. 1994. Neo-liberal crime control: Political agendas and the future of crime prevention in Australia. In D. Chappell and P. Wilson (eds.), *The Australian Criminal Justice System: The Mid 1990s*. Sydney, AUS: Butterworths.

O'Malley, P. 1997. The politics of crime prevention. In P. O'Malley and A. Sutton (eds.), *Crime Prevention in Australia*. Sydney: The Federation Press.

O'Malley, P. and Sutton, A. (eds.). 1997. Introduction. *Crime Prevention in Australia*. Sydney: The Federation Press.

Olsson, O. and Wikstrom, P.-O. 1982. Effects of the experimental Saturday closing of liquor retail stores in Sweden. *Contemporary Drug Problems*, Fall: 324-53.

Olsson, O. and Wikstrom, P.-O. 1984. Effects of Saturday closing of liquor retail stores in Sweden. *Alcohol Policy: Journal of Nordic Alcohol Research* 1:95 (English Summary).

Opp, K.-D. 1997. Limited rationality and crime. In G. Newman, R.V. Clarke and S.G. Shoham. (eds.), *Rational Choice and Situational Crime Prevention: Theoretical Foundations*. Aldershot, UK: Dartmouth Publishing Company.

Painter, K. 1991a. *An Evaluation of Public Lighting as a Crime Prevention Strategy with Special Focus on Women and Elderly People*. Manchester: University of Manchester.

Painter, K. 1991b. *The West Park Estate Survey: An Evaluation of Public Lighting as a Crime Prevention Strategy*. Cambridge: University of Cambridge.

Painter, K. 1994. The impact of street lighting on crime, fear and pedestrian use. *Security Journal* 5:116-124.

Parkdale Focus Community. 1995. *Liquor Licensing and the Community: Resolving Problems With Licensed Establishments*. Toronto, Canada: Author.

Pease, K. 1979. Some futures in crime prevention. *Research Bulletin* No. 7. Home Office Research Unit. London: Home Office.

Pease, K. 1985. Obscene telephone calls to women in England and Wales. *The Howard Journal* 24:275-281.

Pease, K. 1988. *Judgements of Crime Seriousness: Evidence from the 1984 British Crime Survey*. Research and Planning Unit Paper 44. London: Home Office.

Pease, K. 1991. The Kirkholt project: Preventing burglary on a British public housing estate. *Security Journal* 2:73-77.

Pease, K. 1994. Crime prevention. In M. Maguire, R. Morgan and R. Reiner (eds.), *The Oxford Handbook of Criminology*. New York: Oxford University Press.

Pease, K. 1997. Predicting the future: The roles of routine activity and rational choice theory. In G. Newman, R.V. Clarke and S.G. Shoham (eds.), *Rational Choice and Situational Crime Prevention: Theoretical Foundations*. Aldershot, UK: Dartmouth Publishing Company.

Perry, N.J. 1995. How to protect yourself from the credit fraud epidemic. *Money* 24:38-42.

Peters, T. J. and Waterman, R.H. 1982. *In Search of Excellence*. New York: Warner Books.

Phelan, G.I. 1977. *Testing 'Academic' Notions of Architectural Design for Burglary Prevention: How Burglars Perceive Cues of Vulnerability in Suburban Apartment Complexes*. Paper presented to the Annual Meeting of the American Society of Criminology, Atlanta.

Pidco, G. 1996. Check print: A discussion of a crime prevention initiative that failed. *Security Journal* 7:37-40.

Police Services Division. 1995. *Summary Statistics—Police—Crime: 1985-1994*. Vancouver: Ministry of Attorney General, Province of British Columbia.

Port Authority of New York and New Jersey. 1994. *Customer Survey Results*, September 1994.

Poyner, B. 1980. *A Study of Street Attacks and their Environmental Settings*. London: The Tavistock Institute of Human Relations (unpublished).

Poyner, B. 1981. Crime prevention and the environment: Street attacks in city centers. *Police Research Bulletin* 37: 10-18.

Poyner, B. 1983. *Design Against Crime: Beyond Defensible Space*. London: Butterworths.

Poyner, B. 1988. Video cameras and bus vandalism. *Journal of Security Administration* 11: 44-51.

Poyner, B. 1991. Situational crime prevention in two parking facilities. *Security Journal* 2:96-101.

Poyner, B. 1993. What works in crime prevention: An overview of evaluations. In R.V. Clarke (ed.), *Crime Prevention Studies*, vol. 1. Monsey, NY: Criminal Justice Press.

Poyner, B. 1994. Lessons from Lisson Green. An evaluation of walkway demolition on a British housing estate. In R.V. Clarke (ed.), *Crime Prevention Studies*, vol. 3. Monsey, NY: Criminal Justice Press.

Poyner, B., Warne, C., Webb, B., Woodall, R. and Meakin, R. 1988. *Preventing Violence to Staff*. London: H.M. Stationery Office.

Poyner, B. and Webb, B. 1987a. *Successful Crime Prevention: Case Studies*. London: The Tavistock Institute of Human Relations.

Poyner, B. and Webb, B. 1987b. Pepys Estate: Intensive policing. In B. Poyner and B. Webb. *Successful Crime Prevention: Case Studies*. London, UK: Tavistock Institute (unpublished).

Poyner, B. and Webb, B. 1991. *Crime Free Housing*. Oxford, UK: Butterworth Architect.

Poyner, B. and Woodall, R. 1987. *Preventing Shoplifting: A Study in Oxford Street*. London, UK: Police Foundation.

Press, S.J. 1971. *Some Effects of an Increase in Police Manpower in the 20th Precinct of New York City*. New York: Rand Institute.

Priestley, J.B. 1934. *English Journey: Being a Rambling but Truthful Account of What One Man Saw and Heard and Felt and Thought During a Journey Through England Autumn of the Year 1933*. London: Heinemann & Gollancz.

Project for Public Spaces, Inc. 1990. *Port Authority Bus Terminal Renovation Program: Telephone Activity*. New York. Author.

Ramsay, M. 1991a. *The Influence of Street Lighting on Crime and Fear of Crime*. Crime Prevention Unit Paper 28. London: Home Office.

Ramsay, M. 1991b. A British experiment in curbing incivilities and fear of crime. *Security Journal* 2:120-125.

Ramsay, M. and Newton, R. 1991. *The Effect of Better Street Lighting on Crime and Fear: A Review*. Crime Prevention Unit Paper 29. London: Home Office.

Rengert, G.F. and Wasilchick, J. 1985. *Suburban Burglary*. Springfield, IL: Chas. C. Thomas.

Reppetto, T.A. 1974. *Residential Crime*. Cambridge, MA: Ballinger.

Reppetto, T.A. 1976. Crime prevention and the displacement phenomenon. *Crime and Delinquency*, 22:166-177.

Richards, L.G. and Hoel, L.A. 1980. *Planning Procedures for Improving Transit Station Security.* Washington, DC: U.S. Department of Transportation.

Richards, P. 1993. *Vehicle Theft: The European Perspective.* London: Home Office.

Robins, G. 1994. Target tests merchandise refund authorisation. *Stores* 48-49, September.

Rosenbaum, D. 1988. A critical eye on neighborhood watch: Does it reduce crime and fear? In T. Hope and M. Shaw (eds.), *Communities and Crime Reduction.* London: H.M. Stationery Office.

Ross, H.L. 1960. Traffic law violation: A folk crime. *Social Problems* 8:231-241.

Ross, H.L. 1973. Law, science and accidents: The British Road Safety Act of 1967. *Journal of Legal Studies* 4:285-310.

Rubenstein, H., Murray, C., Motoyama, T. and Titus, R.M. 1980. *The Link Between Crime and the Built Environment: The Current State of Knowledge.* U.S. Department of Justice, National Institute of Justice, Washington, DC: U.S. Government Printing Office.

Safe Neighbourhood Unit. 1985. *After Entry Phones: Improving Management and Security in Multi-Storey Blocks.* London: National Association for the Care and Resettlement of Offenders.

Saltz, R.F. 1987. The roles of bars and restaurants in preventing alcohol-impaired driving: An evaluation of server education. *Evaluation in Health Professions* 101:5-27.

Samdahl, D. and Christensen, H.H. 1985. Environmental cues and vandalism: An exploratory study of picnic table carving. *Environment and Behavior* 17:445-458.

Sampson, A., Blagg, H., Stubbs, P., and Pearson, G. 1988. Crime localities and the multi-agency approach. *British Journal of Criminology* 28:478-493.

Savitz, L. 1986. Obscene phone calls. In T.F. Hartnagel and R.A. Silverman, (eds.), *Critique and Explanation: Essays in Honor of Gwynne Nettler.* New Brunswick, NJ: Transaction Books.

Scarr, H.A. 1973. *Patterns of Burglary.* 2nd ed. Washington, DC: U.S. Department of Justice, National Institute of Law Enforcement and Criminal Justice.

Scherdin, M.J. 1986. The halo effect: Psychological deterrence of electronic security systems. *Information Technology and Libraries* September: 232-235.

Schnell, J.B., Smith, A.J., Dimsdale, K.R. and Thrasher, E.J. 1973. *Vandalism and Passenger Security: A Study Of Crime and Vandalism on Urban Mass Transit Systems in the United States and Canada.* Washington, DC: Department of Transportation.

Scott, L., Crow, W.J. and Erickson, R. 1985. *Robbery as Robbers See It.* Dallas: Southland Corporation.

Scottish Central Research Unit. 1995. *Running the Red: An Evaluation of the Strathclyde Police Red Light Camera Initiative.* Edinburgh: The Scottish Office.

Scottish Council on Crime. 1975. *Crime and the Prevention of Crime.* Scottish Home and Health Department. Edinburgh: H.M. Stationery Office.

Sessions, W.S. 1990. *Crime in the United States: 1989 Annual Report.* Washington, DC: Federal Bureau of Investigation.

Seve, R. 1997. Philosophical justifications of situational crime prevention. In G. Newman, R.V. Clarke and S.G. Shoham (eds.), *Rational Choice and Situational Crime Prevention: Theoretical Foundations.* Aldershot, UK: Dartmouth Publishing Company.

Shaver, F. 1985. Prostitution: A critical analysis of three policy approaches. *Canadian Public Policy* 2:493-503.

Shaw, S. 1986. Crime prevention: A counsel of despair? In A. Harrison and J. Gretton (eds.), *Crime U.K.: An Economic, Social and Policy Audit.* Hermitage: Policy Journals.

Shearing, C.D. and Stenning, P.C. 1984. From the Panoptican to Disney World: The development of discipline. In A. Doob and E. Greenspen (eds.), *Perspectives in Criminal Law: Essays in Honour of John H. J. Edwards.* Aurora: Canada Law Book.

Shearing, C.D. and Stenning, P.C. (eds.). 1987. *Private Policing.* Beverly Hills, CA: Sage.

Shellow, R., Romualdi, J.P. and Bartel, E.W. 1974a. Crime in rapid transit systems: An analysis and a recommended security and surveillance system. *Crime and Vandalism in Public Transportation.* Washington, DC: Transportation Research Board.

Shellow, R., Romualdi, J.P. and Bartel, E.W. 1974b. Crime in rapid transit systems: An analysis and a recommended security and surveillance system. *Transportation Research Record* 487:1-12.

Shepherd, J. and Brickley, M. 1992. Alchohol-related hand injuries: An unnecessary social and economic cost. *Journal of the Royal College of Surgeons* 75: 69.

Sherman, L.W. 1990. Police crackdowns: Initial and residual deterrence. In M. Tonry and N. Morris (eds.), *Crime and Justice: A Review of Research*, vol. 12. Chicago: University of Chicago Press.

Sherman, L.W. 1991. Review of problem-oriented policing by Herman Goldstein. *Journal of Criminal Law and Criminology* 82:690-707.

Sherman, L.W. 1996. Policing Domestic Violence: The Problem-Solving Paradigm. Paper prepared for the conference on Problem-Solving as Crime Prevention, Swedish National Police College, Stockholm, September 1996.

Sherman, L., Gartin, P. and Buerger, M. 1989. Hot spots of predatory crime: Routine activities and the criminology of place. *Criminology* 27:27-55.

Sholan, S.G., Chenery, C.D., Anderson, D. and Holt, J. 1997. *Biting Back: Preventing Repeat Victimisation in Huddersfield.* Crime Detection and Prevention Paper XX. London: Home Office.

Short, J.F.,Jr. and Strodtbeck, F.L. 1965. *Group Processes and Gang Delinquency.* Chicago: University of Chicago Press.

Siegel, M. 1995. Personal interview with Melvin Siegel, Deputy Director for Architecture, Office of Engineering and Architecture, Washington Metropolitan Area Transit Authority, May 21, 1995, Washington, DC.

Silver, J. 1995. Disoriented Around the District. Letter to the Editor. *The Washington Post*, September 5, 1995, p.A16.

Skogan, W.G. 1990. *Disorder and Decline: Crime and the Spiral of Decay in American Neighborhoods.* New York: Free Press.

Sloan-Howitt, M. and Kelling, G. 1990. Subway graffiti in New York City: "Gettin' up" vs. "meanin' it and cleanin' it." *Security Journal* 1:131-136.

Smith, D.J. 1995. Youth crime and conduct disorders: Trends, patterns, and causal explanations. In M. Rutter and D.J. Smith (eds.), *Psychosocial Disorders in Youth Populations. Time Trends and their Causes.* Chichester, UK: John Wiley and Sons.

Smith, L.J.F. 1987. *Crime in Hospitals: Diagnosis and Prevention.* Crime Prevention Unit Paper 7. London: Home Office.

Smith, L.J.F. and Burrows, J. 1986. Nobbling the fraudsters: Crime prevention through administrative change. *The Howard Journal* 25:13-24.

Smith, M.J. 1996. *Assessing Vandalism Cues in an Experimental Setting: A Factorial Design Involving State of Repair, Presence of Graffiti, Target Vulnerability, and Target Suitability.* Ph.D. Dissertation, School of Criminal Justice, Rutgers, The State University of New Jersey.

Sparrow, M. 1994. *Imposing Duties. Government's Changing Approach to Compliance.* Westport, CT: Praeger.

Speed, M., Burrows, J. and Bamfield, J. 1995. *Retail Crime Costs 1993/94 Survey: The Impact of Crime and the Retail Response.* London: British Retail Consortium.

Spencer, E. 1992. *Car Crime and Young People on a Sunderland Housing Estate.* Crime Prevention Unit Paper 40. London: Home Office.

Spinks, P., Pittman, S., Singh, K., Barclay, P. and Jahn, R. 1995. Criminology 350 Term Project: Evaluating the Impact of a Bicycle Patrol Initiative on Reducing Auto Crime at the Scott Road Park-and-Ride. Burnaby, BC: Unpublished seminar report, School of Criminology, Simon Fraser University.

Stanford Research Institute. 1970. *Reduction of Robbery and Assault of Bus Drivers.* Volume III: Technological and operational methods. Stanford, CA: Author.

Stockwell, T. 1994. *Alcohol Misuse and Violence: An Examination of the Appropriateness and Efficacy of Liquor Licensing Laws Across Australia. Report No.5.* Presented at the National

Symposium on Alcohol Misuse and Violence. Prepared for the Commonwealth Department of Health, Housing, Local Government and Community Services. Canberra: Australian Government Publishing Service.

Stockwell, T., Rydon, P., Lang, E. and Beal, A. 1993. *An Evaluation of the 'Freo Respects You' Responsible Alcohol Service Project.* Perth, AUS: National Centre for Research into the Prevention of Drug Abuse.

Strutton, D., Vitell, S.J. and Pelton, L.R. 1995. Making an impact on the shoplifter. *International Journal of Retail Distribution and Management* 23: xii-xiii.

Sutton, A. 1996. Taking out the interesting bits? Problem-solving and crime prevention. In R. Homel (ed.), *Crime Prevention Studies*, vol. 5. Monsey, NY: Criminal Justice Press.

Swanson, R. 1986. Convenience store robbery analysis: A research study of robbers, victims, and environment. Gainesville, FL: Unpublished report to the Gainesville Police Department.

Sykes, G.M. and Matza, D. 1957. Techniques of neutralization: A theory of delinquency. *American Sociological Review* 22:664-670.

Taub, R.P., Taylor, D.G. and Dunham, J.D. 1984. *Paths of Neighborhood Change: Race and Crime in Urban America.* Chicago: University of Chicago Press.

Taylor, R.B. and Gottfredson, S. 1986. Environmental design, crime and crime prevention: An examination of community dynamics. In A.J. Reiss and M. Tonry (eds.), *Communities and Crime. Crime and Justice: A Review of Research*, vol.8. Chicago: University of Chicago Press.

Tedeschi, J.T. and Felson, R.B. 1994. *Violence, Aggression and Coercive Actions.* Washington, DC: American Psychological Association.

Telecom and Network Security Review. 1995. Telecom toll fraud expected to reach $3.755 Billion in 1995, Vol.3, No.3, March.

Temple, R.K. and Regan, M. 1991. Recent developments relating to Caller-ID. *Western State University Law Review* 18: 549-63.

Tien, J.M., O'Donnell, V.F., Barnett, A. and Mirchandani, P.B. 1979. *Phase I Report: Street Lighting Projects.* Washington, DC: U.S. Government Printing Office.

Tilley N. 1993a. *After Kirkholt: Theory, Method and Results of Replication Evaluations.* Crime Prevention Unit Paper 47. London: Home Office.

Tilley, N. 1993b. Crime prevention and the Safer Cities story. *Howard Journal of Criminal Justice* 32:40-57.

Tilley, N. 1993c. *Understanding Car Parks, Crime and CCTV: Evaluation Lessons from Safer Cities.* Crime Prevention Unit Paper 42. London: Home Office.

Tizard, J., Sinclair, I. and Clarke, R.V. 1975. *Varieties of Residential Experience.* London: Routledge and Kegan Paul.

Transit Authority Police Department. 1988. *The Role of the Transit Police Department in the 'Clean Car' Program.* New York: Transit Authority Police Department (July 1).

Transit Authority. 1989. Clean Car Program. New York: NYCTA Car Equipment Program. New York: Transit Authority Police Department (May).

Travis, J. 1997. Foreword. In M. Felson and R.V. Clarke (eds.), *Business and Crime Prevention.* Monsey, NY: Criminal Justice Press.

Tremblay, P. 1986. Designing crime. *British Journal of Criminology* 26:234-253.

Trickett A., Osborn, D., Seymour, J. and Pease, K. 1992. What is different about high crime areas? *British Journal of Criminology* 32:81-89.

Tseloni A. and Pease, K. 1997. Repeat victimisation and policing: Whose home gets victimised, where and how often? In P.-O. Wikstrom, W. Skogan and L. Sherman (eds.), *Problem-Oriented Policing and Crime Prevention.* New York: Wadsworth.

Tyrpak, S. 1975. *Newark High-Impact Anti-Crime Program: Street Lighting Project Interim Evaluation Report.* Newark, NJ: Office of Criminal Justice Planning.

United States Congress. 1968. House of Representatives. Subcommittee on Communications and Power. *Obscene or Harassing Telephone Calls in Interstate or Foreign Commerce* (H.R. 611,

S375). Hearings, January 30.

URBED Urban and Economic Development Group. 1994. *Vital and Viable Town Centers: Meeting the Challenge*. London: H.M. Stationery Office.

van Andel, H. 1989. Crime prevention that works: The case of public transport in the Netherlands. *British Journal of Criminology* 29:47-56.

van Dijk, J.J.M. 1997. Towards effective public-private partnerships in crime control: Experiences in the Netherlands. In M. Felson and R.V. Clarke (eds.), *Business and Crime Prevention*. Monsey, NY: Criminal Justice Press.

Van Straelen, F.W.M. 1978. Prevention and technology. In J. Brown (ed.), *Cranfield Papers*. London: Peel Press.

Veno, A. and Veno, E. 1993. Situational prevention of public disorder at the Australian Motorcycle Grand Prix. In R.V. Clarke (ed.), *Crime Prevention Studies*, vol. 1. Monsey, NY: Criminal Justice Press.

Vogel, R.L. 1990. *Convenience Store Robbery*. Deland, FL: Volusia County Sheriff's Department.

von Hirsch, A. 1976. *Doing Justice*. New York: Hill and Wang.

Waddington, P.A.J. 1993. *Calling the Police: The Interpretation of, and Response to Calls for Assistance from the Public*. UK: Avebury.

Wagenaar, A.C. and Holder, H.D. 1991. Effects of alcoholic beverage server liability on traffic crash injuries. *Alcoholism; Clinical and Experimental Research* 15:942-947.

Waller, I. and Okihiro, N. 1979. *Burglary: The Victim and the Public*. Toronto: University of Toronto Press.

Walsh, B. 1993. Communities working together side by side to create safe seaside suburbs. A paper presented at the Australian Institute of Criminology Conference: Melbourne, 1993.

Walsh, D. 1978. *Shoplifting: Controlling a Major Crime*. London: Macmillan.

Walsh, D. 1980. *Break-Ins: Burglary from Private Houses*. London: Constable.

Walters, R. 1996. The dream of multi-agency crime prevention: Pitfalls in policy and practice. In R. Homel (ed.), *Crime Prevention Studies*, vol. 5. Monsey, NY: Criminal Justice Press.

Warner, P.K. 1988. Aural assault: Obscene telephone calls. *Qualitative Sociology* 11:302-318.

Webb, B. 1994. Steering column locks and motor vehicle theft: Evaluations from three countries. In R.V. Clarke (ed.), *Crime Prevention Studies*, vol. 2. Monsey, NY: Criminal Justice Press.

Webb, B. 1996. Preventing plastic card fraud in the UK. *Security Journal* 7:23-25.

Webb, B., Brown, B. and Bennett, K. 1992. *Preventing Car Crime in Car Parks*. Crime Prevention Unit, Paper 34. London: Home Office.

Webb, B. and Laycock, G. 1992a. *Tackling Car Crime: The Nature and Extent of the Problem*. Crime Prevention Unit, Paper 32. London: Home Office.

Webb, B. and Laycock, G. 1992b. *Reducing Crime on the London Underground: An Evaluation of Three Pilot Projects*. Crime Prevention Unit Series Paper 30. London: Home Office Police Department.

Webb J. 1997. *Report on The Direct Line Projects*. Swindon, UK: Crime Concern.

Weidner, R.R. 1996. Target hardening at a New York City subway station: Decreased fare evasion —at what price? In R.V. Clarke (ed.), *Preventing Mass Transit Crime. Crime Prevention Studies*, vol. 6. Monsey, NY: Criminal Justice Press.

Weigman, F. and Hu, D. 1992. *An Analysis of Auto Theft in Vancouver Using the Network Capabilities of the Arc Info Geographic Information System*. Burnaby, BC: British Columbia Institute of Technology.

Weisberg, H.F. 1992. *Central Tendency and Variability*. Newbury Park, CA: Sage.

Weisburd, D. 1997. *Reorienting Crime Prevention Research and Policy: From the Causes of Criminality to the Context of Crime*. National Institute of Justice Research Report. Washington DC: U.S. Department of Justice.

Weiss, C. 1995. Nothing as practical as good theory: Exploring theory-based evelution for comprehensive community initiatives for children and families. In J.P. Connell, A.C. Kubisch,

L.B. Schorr and C.H. Weiss (eds.), *New Approaches to Evaluating Community Intiatives.* Washington, DC: The Aspen Institute.

Wekerle, G.R. and Whitzman, C. 1995. *Safer Cities. Guidelines for Planning, Design and Management.* New York: Van Nostrand Reinhold.

Welke, L. 1981. CPTED and mass transit. In B. Galaway and J. Hudson (eds.), *Perspectives on Crime Victims.* St. Louis, MO: C.V. Mosby.

Wheeler, S. 1967. *The Challenge of Crime in a Free Society.* President's Commission on Law Enforcement and Administration of Justice. Washington, DC: U.S. Government Printing Office.

White, D.J. 1986. *Convenience Store Robbery Analysis.* Gainesville, FL: Unpublished report to the Gainesville Police Department.

White, J. and Humeniuk, R. 1994. *Alcohol Misuse and Violence: Exploring the Relationship.* Canberra: Australian Government Publishing Service.

White, R. and Sutton, A. 1995. Crime prevention, urban space and social exclusion. *Australian and New Zealand Journal of Sociology* 3:82-99.

Wiersma, E. 1996. Commercial burglars in The Netherlands: Reasoning decision makers? *International Journal of Risk, Security and Crime Prevention* 1:217-228.

Wilkins, L.T. 1964. *Social Deviance.* London: Tavistock.

Wilkins, L.T. 1990. Retrospect and prospect: Fashions in criminal justice theory and practice. In D. Gottfredson and R.V. Clarke (eds.), *Policy and Theory in Criminal Justice.* Aldershot, UK: Avebury.

Wilkinson, P. 1977. *Terrorism and the Liberal State.* London: Macmillan.

Wilkinson, P. 1986. *Terrorism and the Liberal State,* 2nd. ed. New York: New York University Press.

Willemse, H.M. 1994. Developments in Dutch crime prevention. In R.V. Clarke (ed.), *Crime Prevention Studies,* vol. 2. Monsey, NY: Criminal Justice Press.

Wilson, D.J., Rivero, R. and Demings, J. 1990. *Commercial Robbery Analysis.* Orlando, FL: Orlando Police Department.

Wilson, J.Q. 1975. *Thinking about Crime.* New York: Basic.

Wilson, J.Q. and Kelling, G.L. 1982. Broken windows. *The Atlantic Monthly,* (March):29-38.

Wilson, P. 1990. Reduction of telephone vandalism: An Australian case study. *Security Journal* 1: 149-154.

Wilson, S. 1978. Vandalism and 'defensible space' on London housing estates. In R.V. Clarke (ed.), *Tackling Vandalism.* Home Office Research Study No. 47. London: H.M. Stationery Office.

Wise, J. 1982. A gentle deterrent to vandalism. *Psychology Today* 16 (September):31-38.

Wortley, R. 1986. Neutralizing moral constraint. *Australian and New Zealand Journal of Criminology* 19:251-58

Wortley, R. 1996. Guilt, shame and situational crime prevention. In R. Homel (ed.), *Crime Prevention Studies,* vol. 5. Monsey, NY: Criminal Justice Press.

Wright, R., Heilweil, M., Pelletier, P. and Dickinson, K. 1974. *The Impact of Street Lighting on Crime, Part I.* University of Michigan for the National Institute of Law Enforcement and Criminal Justice.

Wright, R.T. and Decker, S.H. 1994. *Burglars on the Job.* Boston: Northeastern University Press.

Yablonsky, L. 1962. *The Violent Gang.* New York: Macmillan.

Young, J. 1988. Radical criminology in Britain: The emergence of a competing paradigm. *British Journal of Criminology* 28:289-313.

Zaharchuk, T. and Lynch, J. 1977. *Operation Identification: A Police Prescriptive Package.* Ottawa: Ministry of Solicitor General.

Zimbardo, P.G. 1973. A field experiment in auto-shaping. In C. Ward (ed.), *Vandalism.* London: Architectural Press.

Zyartuk, T. 1994. Scott Road worst for crime. *The Surrey Now* October 12, 1994, p. 1.

Author Index

328

Subject Index

"Abusive" phone calls and court convictions 96 n.1 (see also Annoyance phone calls; Obscene phone calls)

Access control 17-18, 42, 191, 263 (see also Electronic access)
    and car crime 157-58, 165
    case study using 59-73, 98-112, 157-66, 283-99
    and entry phones 59, 68
    to long distant phone lines 98-99, 103-104, 110 n.3 111 n.7, n.9, n.12
    to long distant phone lines, data on 106-107
    to telephones 98, 102-103, 110 n.4
    and walkway demolition 59

Action research paradigm, problem-oriented policing and 9, 15
    and situational crime prevention 6, 15

Aggression 133-34, 139, 267 (see also Violence; "Weapons effect")
    reduction in 275
    retail fraudsters, use by 259
    verbal 278
    verbal, reduction in 275, 282

Aircraft hijacking 5, 20
    and displacement 28

Alarm 36 (see also Car alarm)
    burglar 18 (see also Burglars)
    burglar, and police costs 20

Car alarms, limits of 26
    personal 5
    silent 20
    silent, use of 203, 206-207, 208 n.1

Alcohol control 2, 5 (see also Assault, alcohol-related; Drunkenness; Licensed premises; Pub-closing times)
    and alcohol-related crime 25, 263-82
    access control as 25
    banning as 25
    bar practices as 25, 263-82

dispenser as 25
    project, no long-term success of 264, 267, 277-82
    rationing as 25 (see also Alcohol rationing cards)

Alcohol rationing cards 121 (see also Alcohol control)

Alcohol-related fatal crashes, reduction of 20

America (see US)

Amsterdam, petty crime on public transport in 134-40, 142 n.5, n.8

Analysis of variance (ANOVA), use of 285, 291-92

Annoyance phone calls (see also "Abusive" phone calls; Obscene phone calls)
    data on 93-95

Anti-bandit screens (see Screens)

"Anticipatory diffusion" and publicity 143 (see also Diffusion of benefits)

Apartment watch, effect of 21 (see also Neighborhood Watch)

Assault (see also Aggression; Disorder; Violence)
    alcohol-related 19 (see also Alcohol control)
    and alcohol control 25
    and CCTV 179, 181
    data on 276, 278
    in DC Metro 296-97
    in DC Metro, data on 292-94, 299 n.7
    reduction in 20, 210, 275-77, 282
    screens against, use of 17 (see also Screens)

AT&T 103-104, 106, 110 n.2, 111-12 n.14

Atlanta, subway in (MARTA) 291-92

ATM machines, CCTV use with 167

Attack dogs, proposed use of 244

Audit survey 183, 186 (see also Counting; Safety audit; Site survey)
    internal theft only, use against 188

335